Travelers G
of Utah's N.
& Recreation Areas

Published in Salt Lake City, Utah
United States of America

TRAVELERS' CHOICE GUIDE BOOK STAFF

Researcher & Editor   Carolyn Perry Fife
Production & Design Editor   Wallace Dean Fife

D & C Publishing
8671 South Alpen Circle
Salt Lake City, Utah 84121
FAX: (801) 733-0913
Tel: (801) 944-3874

Copyright   1998 by D & C Publishing, Salt Lake City, Utah. All rights are reserved. No part of this book may be reproduced in any form or by any electronic means, including information storage and retrieval systems, without permission in writing from the publisher. Permission is granted reviewers to quote brief passages in a review. Tear sheets of the review are requested by the publisher.

ISBN: 1-883475-25-2   First Edition

ACKNOWLEDGMENTS

D & C Publishing is indebted to the Utah Travel Council and to Color Country and Canyonlands Travel Councils for their well-researched data. D & C Publishing gratefully acknowledges the many fine accommodations, restaurants, and services for their participation in Travelers' Choice Guide Book. Without them and the services they render Utah's visitors, the southwestern and southeastern portion of the state, with all its majestic grandeur, would largely go unnoticed by the world. These businesses are the ones who care for our many visitors and create the desire for guests to return as soon and as often as possible. Again our thanks to all as a group for their synergism, and to each for their individual dedication to serving the needs of Utah's greatest treasure—*its very welcome visitors*. Cover photo is courtesy of Utah Travel Council.

DISCLAIMER

All businesses included in D & C Publishing's *Travelers' Choice* guide books have been personally visited by a *Travelers' Choice* researcher. Most were recommended by participants or by local residents who frequent the businesses themselves. Many of the businesses included in Travelers' Choice guide books have subscribed to the project in advance of publication. Through in depth conversations with the recommending party and with business owners, every effort has been made to make sure that information included is factual.

TABLE OF CONTENTS

UTAH	2
UTAH'S STRUGGLE FOR STATEHOOD	3
2002 OLYMPIC WINTER GAMES	5
UTAH STATE FACTS	6
UTAH STATE LIQUOR LAWS	7
UTAH'S PLAYGROUND	7
PARK SAFETY POINTERS	7
PARK PASSES & FEES	8
COMMON-SENSE RULES FOR PUBLIC LAND USE	8
PARK REGULATIONS	9
UTAH'S DIVERSE TRAVEL REGIONS	10
THE TRIP BEGINS	14
CANYONLANDS TRAVEL REGION	14
GRAND COUNTY	14
GRAND COUNTY ATTRACTIONS	15
ADDITIONAL GRAND COUNTY ATTRACTIONS	18
GREEN RIVER	20
GREEN RIVER ATTRACTIONS	21
GREEN RIVER EVENTS	22
ACCOMMODATIONS	22
RESTAURANTS	24
SPECIALTY SHOPPING	25
MOAB	26
MOAB ADVENTURES	27
MOAB ATTRACTIONS & ACTIVITIES	31
MOAB EVENTS	31
ACCOMMODATIONS	32
ADVENTURE / TOURS	33
BED & BREAKFASTS	53
BREWERY RESTAURANTS	55
CAMP GROUNDS	56
RESTAURANTS	60
CASTLE VALLEY	68
CRESCENT JUNCTION	68
THOMPSON SPRINGS	68
SAN JUAN COUNTY	69
SAN JUAN COUNTY ATTRACTIONS	69
SAN JUAN COUNTY EVENTS	73
LA SAL	73
MONTICELLO	73
MONTICELLO EVENTS	74

BLANDING 75
BLANDING ATTRACTIONS 75
BLANDING EVENTS 79
BLUFF 80
BLUFF ATTRACTIONS 81
BLUFF EVENTS 81
ANETH / MONTEZUMA CREEK 81
ANETH / MONTEZUMA CREEK ATTRACTIONS 82
FOUR CORNERS 82
MEXICAN HAT / HALCHITA 82
MEXICAN HAT / HALCHITA ATTRACTIONS 83
OLJATO 83
NAVAJO MOUNTAIN 83
CANYONLAND LINK TO PANORAMALAND & COLOR COUNTRY . 84
PANORAMALAND 85
WAYNE COUNTY 85
WAYNE COUNTY ATTRACTIONS 85
WAYNE COUNTY EVENTS 87
TORREY 87
ACCOMMODATIONS 88
RESORTS 91
SPECIALTY SHOPPING 94
BICKNELL 95
BICKNELL ATTRACTIONS 95
ACCOMMODATIONS 95
RESTAURANTS 98
TEASDALE 100
ACCOMMODATIONS 101
BED & BREAKFASTS 102
COLOR COUNTRY 103
GARFIELD COUNTY 103
GARFIELD COUNTY ATTRACTIONS 104
BOULDER 106
BOULDER ATTRACTIONS 107
ACCOMMODATIONS 108
ADVENTURE / TOURS 109
BED & BREAKFASTS 114
RESTAURANTS 116
SPECIALTY SHOPPING 119
ESCALANTE 120
ESCALANTE ATTRACTIONS 121
ACCOMMODATIONS 125
ADVENTURE / TOURS 126
BED & BREAKFASTS 128
SPECIALTY SHOPPING 129

RESTAURANTS	130
HENRIEVILLE	132
CANNONVILLE	132
ATTRACTIONS	132
ACCOMMODATIONS	133
BED & BREAKFASTS	134
TROPIC / Bryce Canyon	136
ACCOMMODATIONS	136
BED & BREAKFASTS	143
RESTAURANTS	152
SPECIALTY SHOPPING	154
BRYCE CANYON NATIONAL PARK	155
ACCOMMODATIONS	157
RESORTS	161
RESTAURANTS	164
ANTIMONY	165
ANTIMONY ATTRACTIONS	166
RESORTS	166
ATTRACTIONS	168
PANGUITCH	170
ACCOMMODATIONS	171
BED & BREAKFASTS	177
RESTAURANTS	180
SPECIALTY SHOPPING	182
PANGUITCH AREA ATTRACTIONS	183
BRIAN HEAD	184
HATCH	186
ACCOMMODATIONS	186
RESTAURANTS	189
KANE COUNTY	189
LONG VALLEY JUNCTION	190
DUCK CREEK VILLAGE	190
ACCOMMODATIONS	191
RESTAURANTS	193
SPECIALTY SHOPPING	194
LONG VALLEY	197
GLENDALE	197
ORDERVILLE	197
MT. CARMEL	197
MT. CARMEL JUNCTION	197
RESORTS	198
RESTAURANTS	201
SPECIALTY SHOPPING	203
KANAB	203
KANAB ATTRACTIONS	205

ACCOMMODATIONS ... 205
ADVENTURE / TOURS ... 212
RESTAURANTS ... 215
SPECIALTY SHOPPING ... 219
NORTHERN ARIZONA ... 223
FREDONIA, ARIZONA ... 223
RESTAURANTS ... 224
FREDONIA AREA ATTRACTIONS ... 226
JACOB LAKE, ARIZONA ... 228
PAGE, ARIZONA ... 230
NORTHERN ARIZONA ATTRACTIONS ... 230
ACCOMMODATIONS ... 231
BED & BREAKFASTS ... 234
RESORTS ... 236
RESTAURANTS ... 240
WASHINGTON COUNTY ... 245
WASHINGTON COUNTY ATTRACTIONS ... 245
SPRINGDALE ... 247
SPRINGDALE ATTRACTIONS ... 248
ADVENTURE / TOURS ... 248
RESTAURANTS ... 254
ROCKVILLE ... 256
GRAFTON ... 257
VIRGIN ... 258
VIRGIN ATTRACTIONS ... 258
KOLOB RESERVOIR BACKWAY ... 258
BED & BREAKFASTS ... 259
LA VERKIN ... 260
HURRICANE ... 261
HURRICANE ATTRACTIONS ... 262
ST. GEORGE ... 263
ST. GEORGE AREA ATTRACTIONS ... 264
ACCOMMODATIONS ... 270
BED & BREAKFASTS ... 272
RESTAURANTS ... 280
Index ... 288

Welcome to Travelers' Choice:
A Guide to the Best of Utah's
National Parks, Monuments,
& Recreation Areas

ALL ROADS LEAD TO SOUTHEASTERN & SOUTHWESTERN ***UTAH!***

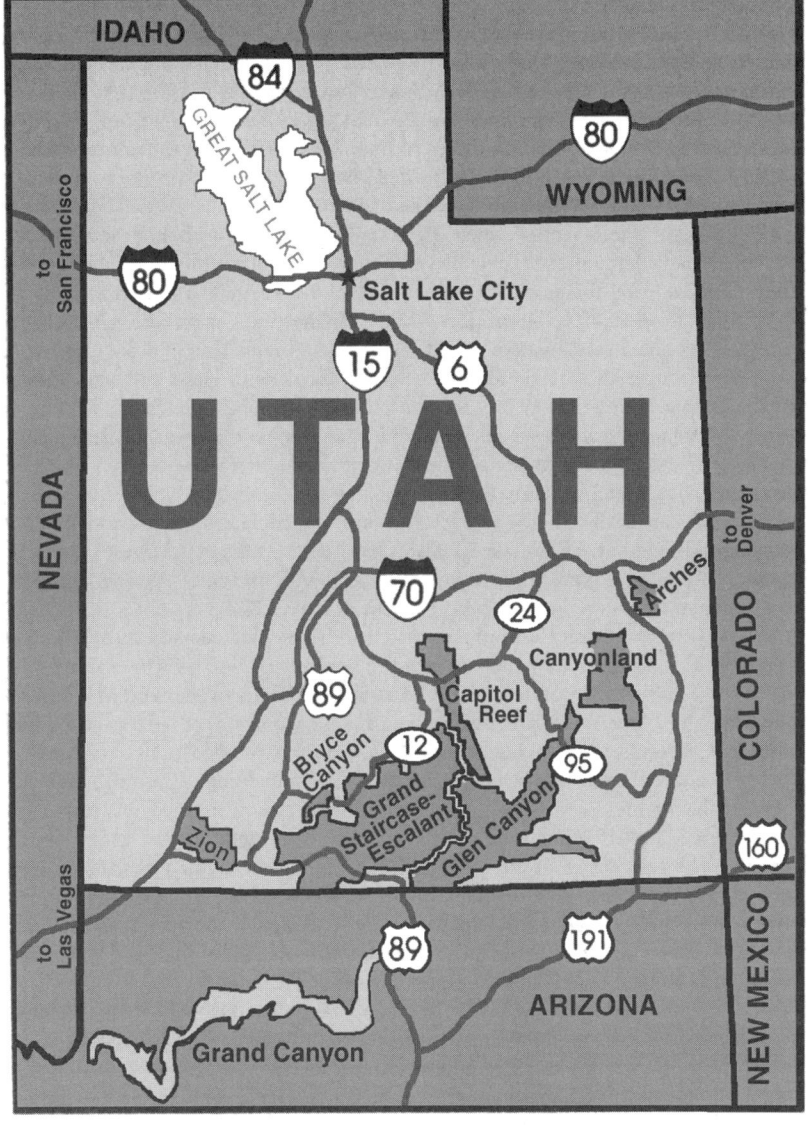

UTAH

Land of the High Mountains was the name the Ute Native Americans gave this vast mountainous terrain and desert valley. It was land that seemed largely undesirable to the white man until July 24, 1847, when Brigham Young, prophet for the Church of Jesus Christ of Latter-day Saints and legendary frontiersman, led a company of Mormon pioneers into the Salt Lake Valley. Entering the valley through what is now Emigration Canyon, the influenza-weakend Brigham raised himself out of his covered wagon bed and said, "This is the right place, drive on."

In 1778 the territory that is now Utah was explored by Spain's Fathers Dominguez and Escalante, who were looking for a navigable waterway that would make transportation from the East to the West Coast less hazardous. They never found their waterway, and though they were impressed with the bounteous game and vowed to return to claim the territory for New Spain, they never did so.

Jim Bridger, according to history books, was the first American to set eyes on this incredible land. When he discovered the Great Salt Lake, the saltiest body of water in America, he was certain that he had discovered the Pacific Ocean. It took some time for him to be convinced that he had not.

Legend tells us that when Brigham Young brought his first pioneer company into the valley, Jim Bridger called Brigham a fool for settling in what he considered the most "God-forsaken land he had ever laid eyes on." Bridger reportedly offered this so-called Mormon prophet $1,000 for the first ear of corn grown in the valley. He doubted that any crop would ever flourish in this land of desolation but he was also in hopes that he could convince the Mormons to leave and settle further West, thus preserving the territory for himself and his trapper friends.

But the Mormons stayed, set up an irrigation system, plowed the land, planted their crops, and even at that late season of the year, the rich land quickly yielded not just an ear, but bushels of corn. Bridger soon got discouraged and pushed on.

Today Utah is home to over two million people, with close to half of its population living in the Salt Lake Valley. In area, Utah is the 11th largest state in the Union. The states of New York, Massachusetts, New Hampshire, Vermont, and New Jersey could fit within the Utah borders and still have 334-square miles left over.

Once the Great Basin of Salt Lake had been irrigated and settled, Brigham Young systematically sent settlers to all of the promising valleys which surrounded the Basin. This State of Deseret, a name taken from the Book of Mormon which means 'honey bee', included all of present day Utah and large portions of Arizona, Colorado, Nevada, California, Oregon, Idaho, Wyoming, and New Mexico.

Utah's history has been shaped by people from diverse cultural, ethnic, and religious backgrounds. Most of the original Mormon pioneers had roots in Europe, having joined the church in their native land and then migrating to Utah to join the 'Saints'. The completion of the transcontinental railroad at Promontory Point, Utah on May 10, 1869, brought a diversity of Greek, Irish, Italian, Chinese, and African-American laborers, many of which stayed after completion to make Utah their new home. Discovery of silver in the hills of what is now Park City, and gold and copper booms also brought people to Utah from all parts of the country.

Though over 70 percent of Utah's population are members of the Church of Jesus Christ of Latter-day Saints, commonly called the Mormon or LDS church, nearly every one of the world's major religions are represented in the state.

Statistically, Utahns have the second-highest birthrate in the nation, the second-lowest death rate, and Utahns are rated fourth in longevity at 75.76 years. At 25.7 years, the average age of the state's population is considerably younger than the national average of 32.7. Utahns also have the largest average household size of any state.

The state's motto is the beehive, standing for industry, a motto that was never taken lightly in pioneer days and is still adhered to today. Together the values of Utah's diverse citizens make the state an industrious, clean and safe place in which to live and work.

A land of diversity, there are numerous factors that make Utah one of the fastest growing and one of the most prosperous states in the Union. A conservative state where family life is deemed of utmost importance and morality is still looked upon as being fashionable, Utah has been touted many times in national magazines as one of the best places to raise a family. *Money* magazine recently raved about the low crime rate and the abundance of jobs, and *U. S. News & World Report* lauded the hot housing market.

Because nearly 80 percent of Utah's land is in government stewardship, much of the state remains pristine. Utah is home to five breathtaking National Parks, seven National Monuments, two National Recreation Areas, one National Historic Site, and Seven National Forests. In addition Utah has 46 state parks offering camping, recreation, scenic, and heritage opportunities. Over 40 percent of Utah is BLM-administered public lands. Across the state are 774,520 acres of scenic Wilderness administered by the U.S. Forest Service. Because of Utah's diverse climate zones and terrain, wildlife abounds and varies across the state. Utah history and natural beauty can be enjoyed by taking any of the state's official scenic drives on 27 paved Byways or 58 less conventional Backways.

Throughout the state are myriad hiking, biking and backcountry adventure opportunities. There are river running, boating, and other water adventures. With hundreds of miles of backcountry trails, great four-wheel drive or ATV terrain is never far away. Utah offers adventures in golfing, historic travel, family things to do, prehistoric exploration, cultural activities, camping, and guided tours.

Most of Utah lies on a plateau above 4,000 feet in elevation. The *Wasatch* and *High Plateau* Ranges of the *Rocky Mountains* span the heart of the state for 300 miles from north to south. To the east is the *Uinta* Range, Utah's most rugged and highest mountain wilderness and one of the only large mountain ranges in North America which runs east and west. To the southeast is the *Colorado Plateau* with its famed red rock country. It is the Colorado Plateau and Southeastern and Southwestern Utah that are covered in this Travelers' Choice Guide Book.

There is always something to rave about when it comes to Utah, but those who live here and those who visit can not say enough about the grandeur and beauty that encompasses this "pretty, great state."

UTAH'S STRUGGLE FOR STATEHOOD

For early residents of the territory that would become Utah, the 45th state in the Union, achieving statehood was a monumental struggle that would last nearly 50 years. Members of the Church of Jesus Christ of Latter-day Saints had trekked across the plains, fleeing violence and persecution and seeking a place of refuge where members could live in peace and harmony, free to worship according to their faith. They wanted to be left alone, but it did not take them long to discover that they also wanted the advantages that accompanied statehood for their people.

From 1846 to 1869 approximately 70,000 Mormons traveled west from Nauvoo, Illinois, to Salt Lake City, a distance of 1,300 miles. This route, now called the Mormon Pioneer National Historic Trail, passes through Illinois, Iowa, Nebraska, Wyoming, and Utah. Departing from Nauvoo in February 1846, thousands of Mormons crossed into Iowa. They spent the winter in the Council Bluffs, Iowa, and Omaha, Nebraska areas. Early in 1847, Brigham Young led an advanced party west, generally paralleling the Oregon Trail, to Fort Bridger, Wyoming, where they then turned southwest to the Great Salt Lake Valley.

The original state of Deseret as proposed by Brigham Young covered a startling 480,000 square miles, a territory that had to be looked at with trepidation by those in the United States government, who already perceived the Mormons as growing in numbers much too rapidly. In 1850, when Utah became a territory as part of the Missouri Compromise, the size of the territory was greatly reduced. Governing powers ignored Brigham's chosen name, Deseret, and called the territory Utah, a name derived from the Ute Native Americans who also inhabited the land.

Even though the territory grew and prospered, with its population becoming a mix of Mormons and non-Mormons, many of America's leaders still looked on the territory as a province of religious fanatics with un-American beliefs. Between 1849 and 1887, Utah's territorial government would petition the United States Congress for statehood six times and each time be denied. It was obviously disheartening to watch most of the territories surrounding Utah achieve statehood, all with smaller and less settled populations.

One of the hurdles creating challenges within the Utah territory was the absence of political parties. Since Mormons were in the vast majority, they controlled all functions of government that were not controlled by the Federal Government and there seemed to be no separation of church and state. After completion of the transcontinental railroad at Promontory Point, Utah in 1869, a group of federal officers, railroad workers, miners, cattlemen, merchants, bankers, and other non-Mormon businessmen formed the Liberal Party. A People's Party, for which most Mormons voted, was also formed. Later, by 1891, both the Democratic and Republican parties were active in the Utah territory. Most of the Mormons affiliated with the Democratic party. So few church members aligned themselves with the Republican party that Mormon leaders had to petition members to join the Republican party. This was done to achieve a better political balance and present the state as being more politically favorable for statehood. Today Utah is one of the strongest Republican states in the Union.

Another impediment to statehood came as a result of territorial immigration policies. The Mormons welcomed converts to the church from all over the world, believing that these immigrants would strengthen their economy. Territorial non-Mormons believed that these immigrants were a threat to job availability and land.

The practice of polygamy among early Mormon pioneers was probably the core obstacle to Utah statehood. Within the church the practice of plural marriage was an accepted ethic. Apart from the Mormon church, polygamy was perceived as a threat to civic standards. When Federal laws were passed outlawing polygamy, those within the territory practicing polygamy were stripped of their right to vote. Later laws were passed allowing confiscation of all goods and property owned by the Mormon church. In 1890, upholding the 12th *Article of Faith* of the Mormon Church which mandates that members "believe in being subject to kings, presidents, rulers, and magistrates, and in obeying, honoring and sustaining the law," Mormon President Wilford Wooddruff issued a statement forbidding the practice of polygamy.

In May of 1894, President Grover Cleveland, satisfied that Utah had met the criteria for statehood, signed Utah's Enabling Act. During an 1895 66-day session, Mormon and non-Mormon elected delegates met to draft a state constitution. The constitution outlawed polygamy forever, was the fourth state in the Union to give women the right to vote, ensured them equal rights with men, and guaranteed separation of church and state.

The Statehood Proclamation, making Utah the 45th state in the United States of America, was signed on January 4, 1896, by President Cleveland. Statehood served as a balm of Gilead, healing the wounds that existed between Mormons and non-Mormons, and giving each the desire to work cohesively together as America's newest citizens.

Utahns across the state, Mormons and non-Mormons alike, joined to pay tribute to their pioneer heritage as they celebrated Utah Statehood Centennial in 1996. In 1997 they were joined by the world as hundreds participated in and millions watched a re-enactment of the Mormon trek West for the state's Days of '47 Sesquicentennial celebration.

Today, visitors are invited to join Utahns in a celebration of life as all, regardless of where they are from, look back to their own great heritage. Come! And enjoy the bounties that lie within the borders of this "pretty, great state."

2002 OLYMPIC WINTER GAMES

On June 16, 1995, newspapers across the state of Utah proclaimed Salt Lake's victory. After three tries and 30 years of preparation, the International Olympic Committee finally agreed that Salt Lake "is the right place" and passed the torch to Utah for the 2002 Olympic Winter Games.

In the year 2002, Salt Lake City will welcome the world when it hosts the first Olympic Winter Games of the 21st Century. Fortunately for skiers and winter sports enthusiasts from around the world, they don't have to wait that long to savor the Olympic experience and the "greatest snow on earth." Utah is ready to host the 2002 Olympic Winter Games. Most of the venues are already completed and the same slopes, ski jumps, moguls, downhill courses, and cross-country trails that will challenge the world's greatest athletes in 2002 are available for skiing—right now!

Bobsled, Luge, Ski Jumping, and Nordic Combined activities will take place at the Utah Winter Sports Park, 24 miles east of Salt Lake City and four miles north of Park City. Opened in 1992, this world-class training facility received an environmental award from the IOC for excellence in environmental planning and design. For the 2002 Olympics a 120-meter ski jump will be added to the 90, 65, 30 and 18-meter hills already in use by potential Olympians. Visitors may participate in a training program and then try out the jumps for themselves. They can also race down the bobsled runs. A splash pool makes summer training possible for freestyle skiers with the sessions rapidly becoming a warm weather favorite for visitors to the park. The 90-meter ski-jump hill is also used for summer training. Recreational ski jumping lessons are available Friday - Sunday afternoons. This state-owned 380-acre park is open to the public December - March and June - September. A snack bar, ski shop, and meeting facilities are available at the park. The Winter Sports Park can accommodate 20,000. For additional information call 649-5447.

Park City Ski Area, (649-0493) and Deer Valley Resort, (649-1000) will host the Slalom, Giant Slalom, Freestyle and Snowboard competitions. These two neighboring world-class resorts have already been the venue for the World Cup and International Alpine competitions, held successfully since 1984. Both resorts offer a host of winter and warm weather recreational activities.

Snowbasin Ski Area has been selected as the site for the men's and women's downhill and Super G competitions. Nestled in the rugged mountains of Ogden Canyon, Snowbasin has a vertical drop of 844 meters that could generate speeds of 145 miles per hour. Snowbasin is 55 miles north of Salt Lake City, and recreational skiers are welcome to test their mettle on these challenging slopes. The mountainside can accommodate some 38,000 spectators. For more information call 399-1135.

Mountain Dell Park, home of a 36-hole championship golf course in warm weather, has been selected for the Biathlon, Cross-Country, and Nordic combined skiing events. Fourteen miles east of Salt Lake City in Parley's Canyon, this popular cross-country course has been the site of World Cup cross-country competitions and other major regional races. The park is also the venue for weekly recreational competitions and is open to all those who love the sport. The area can easily accommodate 20,000 spectators for Nordic events. For more information call 582-3812.

The Ogden/Weber Ice Sheet, built in 1993, has been selected as the site for the women's ice hockey games. The facility is opened year-round to the public for skating. It will accommodate 2,000 spectators. For more information call 399-8750.

The West Valley Ice Arena, completed in the fall of 1997, is the site selected for the ice hockey and short track speed skating. Seating capacity is 10,000.

Speed skating events will take place at the Oquirrh Park Oval in Kearns, just west of Salt Lake. The oval is currently offered for public ice skating during the winter and for in-line skaters of all ability levels in warm weather. It accommodates 6,000 spectators. For more information call 966-4229.

Curling events will be held at the Cottonwood Heights Ice Arena. The facility is currently a public recreational facility with the arena accommodating 2,000 spectators. For more information call 943-6459.

Figure skating and ice hockey will be staged at the Delta Center, current home of the NBA's Utah Jazz. Over 15,000 seats will be available for these ice events. More information can be obtained by calling 325-2000.

Utahns and visitors alike have the opportunity to put themselves in the Olympic picture. Utah's state of readiness for the 2002 Olympic Winter Games translates into the ultimate winter vacation. Vacationers can skate on Olympic ice rinks, watch ski jumpers train in a year-round facility, try the jumps for themselves, and enjoy world-class skiing on the slopes that the world will be watching in 2002.

All of the sites for Utah's Olympic Winter Games are within an hour's drive of downtown Salt Lake City.

UTAH STATE FACTS

The **Area Code** for Salt Lake, Utah, Davis & Weber Counties is **801, Area Code** for all other counties in Utah is **435.**
State Capital: Salt Lake City
Statehood Day: January 4, 1896 (45th state)
State Symbol: Beehive (for industry)
State Flower: Sego Lily (The edible root was used by pioneers to stave off starvation)
State Bird: California Gull (The gulls devoured the crickets that destroyed pioneer crops.)
State Tree: Blue Spruce
State Gem: Topaz
State Grass: Indian Ricegrass

State Animal: Rocky Mountain Elk
State Fish: Rainbow Trout
State Fossil: Allosaurus
Population: Slightly over 2,000,000 (1996)
Land Area: 84,990 square miles (11th in size among the states)
Highest Point: King's Peak in Ashley National Forest, 13,528 feet.
Lowest Point: Beaver Wash Dam on Utah-Arizona border, 2,200 feet.
Salt Lake City Elevation: 4,330 feet.

UTAH STATE LIQUOR LAWS

Liquor and wine may be purchased in Utah cities at State-owned liquor stores and at package agencies, which are located in most resort centers, lodges, and major hotels. These stores are open most days, with varying hours, but are all closed Sundays and holidays. Beer containing 3.2% alcohol may be purchased seven days a week in grocery and convenience stores throughout the state. Stronger beer is sold in state liquor stores, package agencies, restaurants and private clubs.

Nearly all fine restaurants in Utah have liquor licenses. Patrons may purchase mixed drinks, wine and beer at licensed restaurants, but liquor and wine lists will not be offered unless requested by the patron. If in doubt, ask your server about the availability of wine and liquor. Patrons are allowed to bring cork-finished wine into licensed restaurants and private clubs.

Utah's non-exclusive private clubs offer "over the bar" drinks. Visitors may purchase a two-week membership to most private clubs for $5. Visitors with a two-week membership may host up to five guests.

Lounges and taverns sell only 3.2% alcohol content beer and do not offer wine service or mixed drink set-ups. Liquor, wine and beer can not be brought into such establishments.

UTAH'S PLAYGROUND

Nearly 80 percent of this "pretty, great, state" has been set aside as public land administered by federal and state agencies. Utah is replete with National Forests but, when it comes to the state's abundance of National Parks, Monuments and Recreation Areas, most are in Southeastern and Southwestern Utah. Utah has five national parks--Arches, Canyonlands, Capitol Reef, Bryce, and Zion--all of which are in Southern Utah, as is the best access route to the North Rim of Grand Canyon. Utah has seven national monuments. Of these, five--Cedar Breaks, Grand Staircase-Escalante, Hovenweep, Natural Bridges, and Rainbow Bridge--are in Southeastern and Southwestern Utah. Of her two national recreation areas, one--Glen Canyon with spectacular Lake Powell--is in Southern Utah. It is this area of the state, Utah's Canyonlands and Color Country Travel Regions, that is covered in this guide book.

PARK SAFETY POINTERS

The following precautionary measures will help make a park visit safer and more enjoyable.

1. Do not hike alone. The majority of hiker fatalities occur to those who are hiking solo.

2. When hiking, biking, backpacking, ATVing, or horseback riding, make sure to take an adequate water supply. And do not drink from water sources in the backcountry unless the water is treated or filtered. The water could be contaminated with Giardia lamblia, a parasite that will cause severe sickness.

3. Stay on designated trails. Hiking off designated trails can destroy fragile cryptobiotic soil, but the canyon's steep slopes and cliff edges can also be extremely dangerous.

4. Be aware of personal limitations. People with heart or respiratory problems should be especially cautious about overexertion in high elevations and desert heat.

5. Wear appropriate clothing. During summer months, Utah's parks experience dry, desert heat. However, in the canyons when camping overnight, the evenings can get cool.

6. Proper footwear is especially important. Hiking boots with good ankle support and rubber soles and quality outdoor socks are recommended.

7. If accompanied by children, watch them carefully. Make sure they do not wander off.

8. Cloud bursts and flash floods are a high desert phenomenon. They can be extremely hazardous. Pay attention to weather changes.

9. Each park is unique and offers special concerns. Be aware.

10. The parks are our national treasures and the responsibility for preserving them and their resources belongs to everyone. Please be a concerned and proactive user.

PARK PASSES & FEES

The following were accurate at press time, however all park fees are subject to change. Please contact the parks for current information.

The **Golden Eagle Passport**, valid for 12 months at all federal parks and recreation areas, is available for $50 at all park entrances.

The **Golden Access Passport** provides free entrance to physically impaired U.S. citizens and residents.

The **Golden Age Passport**, available to U.S. citizens or residents 62 years of age or older, has a one-time fee of $25.

For those without passes, **Arches** and **Canyonland** entrance fees are $4 per car and $2 per pedestrian or bicyclist. Park fees at **Capitol Reef** is $4 per car, per family on bikes, or individual pedestrian or bicyclist. **Bryce Canyon** and **Zion** entrance fees are $5 per car and $3 per pedestrian or bicyclist. At the North Rim of the Grand Canyon, fees are $10 per car and $4 per pedestrian. Fees at all parks, though subject to change, are good for seven days.

COMMON-SENSE RULES FOR PUBLIC LAND USE

Regardless of whether one is visiting the national or state parks, national monuments or recreation areas, or any of the national forests or BLM land, it is important that all visitors work together to preserve Utah's wide, open spaces. Nearly 80 percent of this "pretty, great state" is in parcels of land that are administered for public use by federal and state agencies.

Those of us utilizing Utah as a recreational playground have the responsibility to engage minimum impact practices while enjoying her forests and deserts.

Some valuable guidelines include the following:

1. Whether walking, hiking, biking, or driving, please tread lightly. A well-

acknowledged parameter is "leave only footprints." When camping, leave no trace of the camping area.

2. Help keep the forests and canyon country clean. Pick up and pack out trash and dispose of human waste properly.

3. To help protect and conserve high desert water sources and forest watershed areas, carry water for drinking and washing purposes.

4. If traveling with pets, keep them under control. Always allow space for wildlife. Maintain a distance, keep quiet, and do not chase or pick up wild animals.

5. When visiting the many historic sites, ancient ruins, and rock art sites, admire them from a distance. Remnants of the past need to be left as they are found and untouched for the future. Please report willful violations.

Many types of tours and activities are available in the state's public lands, including guided bicycle treks, horsepacking, ATV tours, backcountry hiking, river rafting, rock climbing, hunting and fishing. These guided adventures are led by seasoned professional outfitters and enhance the visitor's Utah wilderness experience.

Each of the national parks included in this book—Canyonlands, Arches, Capitol Reef, Bryce Canyon, Zion, and the North Rim of the Grand Canyon—are open year-round and have at least one visitor center staffed with National Park Service rangers. Most, but not all national monuments, which includes Grand Staircase-Escalante, Cedar Breaks, and Hovenweep, also have visitor centers. Glen Canyon Recreation Area has several marinas to service the needs of visitors as well as a visitor center at Bullfrog and Wahweap. Most visitor centers not only answer questions, but provide guided nature walks, offer evening programs and night walks, and expound on the area's geology. Hours vary at the parks and some are closed on major holidays such as Thanksgiving and Christmas.

PARK REGULATIONS

1. Bicycles are allowed only on paved or designated routes.

2. The removal of any park resources, including but not limited to rocks, plants, fossils, and artifacts, is strictly prohibited.

3. The disturbance of wildlife, including the feeding of wild animals is prohibited.

4. Pets must be kept on a leash at all times and are not allowed in the backcountry or on trails.

5. Handicap areas are strictly enforced. It is not advisable to park in these areas unless authorized to do so.

6. Camp only within the boundaries of designated camp sites. Flash floods make camping in arroyos and washes extremely dangerous.

7. What is taken in to the parks and backcountry must be taken out or deposited in proper receptacles. This includes cigarette butts.

8. The collecting of firewood is prohibited unless otherwise specified.

9. Backcountry use permits are required for backcountry overnight camping at all Utah national parks. Except for Canyonlands and the North Rim of the Grand Canyon, these permits may be obtained at each park's visitor center upon arrival. Canyonlands and the North Rim require advance reservations. For Canyonlands reservations, write: Backcountry Reservations Office, Canyonlands, National Park, 2282 South West Resource Boulevard, Moab, Utah 84532. The address for North Rim reservations is: Backcountry Reservations Office, P.O. Box 129, Grand Canyon, Arizona 86023.

UTAH'S DIVERSE TRAVEL REGIONS

No state in the Union offers its visitors more diversity than does Utah. Because of the contrasts in Utah's unique geographic terrain—from its world class ski slopes to its lush recreation areas and its red rock canyons and desert valleys—Utah counties have joined together to create nine Travel Regions. Geology and climates differ as one travels from one region of the state to another.

At the top northwest corner of the state is the **Golden Spike Empire**. The Golden Spike Empire got its name because it was in this region that a golden spike was driven at Promontory Point on May 10, 1869, to join the nation together via the transcontinental railroad. The region is home to three ski resorts, Antelope Island, Bear River Migratory Bird Refuge, and Lagoon, Utah's premiere amusement park. (801-627-8288 or 800-255-8824.)

The northeast region is called **Bridgerland**, a great name for country that was once Jim Bridger's stomping ground. It was on the shores of Bear Lake, now a water recreation paradise, that Bridger and his fellow trappers and mountain men gathered together for a yearly rendezvous. The land is still pristine, with herds of Elk wandering at Hardware Ranch. The region is home to the Festival of the American West with its World Championship Dutch Oven Cook-off. (435-752-2161 or 800-882-4433)

South of Golden Spike Empire is **Great Salt Lake Country**, home to the Great Salt Lake, the saltiest body of water in the world. This was the mountain and the desert land that challenged Mormon pioneers when they first arrived in the valley on July 24, 1847. The city is headquarters for the Church of Jesus Christ of Latter-day Saints and its famous Mormon Tabernacle Square. It is a city of industry, culture, the arts, shopping, and is home to four world class ski resorts. Included in its terrain are the Great Salt Lake Desert and the Bonneville Salt Flats. (801-521-2822)

East of Great Salt Lake Country is **Mountain Land**, an area that will truly be discovered by the world in 2002, when Salt Lake City and the Wasatch Mountains that front it are host to the Olympic Winter Games. The mountains of Park City are home to the U.S. Ski Team, three world class ski resorts, and Robert Redford's Sundance Film Festival. Over the ridge are Timpanogos Cave National Monument, Sundance Ski Resort, and Heber Valley with its historic Heber Valley Railroad. (435-377-2262.)

East of Mountain Land is **Dinosaurland**. Fossil remnants populate the quarry at Dinosaur National Monument and have been recreated in the landscape of Vernal's Dinosaur Gardens. But Jurassic period dinosaur bones are not all that's extinct in Dinosaurland. This portion of the state once served as the badlands and the hideouts for infamous outlaws such as Butch Cassidy and his Wild Bunch. An annual Outlaw Trail Festival celebrates their exploits. At the top of the travel region and sharing its beauty with Wyoming is Flaming Gorge National Recreation Area, a water-world paradise. (435-789-6932 or 800-477-5558.)

Panoramaland, the State's largest travel region, takes up three-quarters of the central part of the state. It is home to the state's first territorial capitol, Fillmore, with its Territorial Statehouse. The region is diverse with mountains, mining towns, deserts, sparkling lakes, and a preponderance of pioneer settlements. In its southeastern terminus is **Capitol Reef National Park** with its soaring cliffs and reefs and its remnants of an ancient Fremont Culture. Although the Travel Region is not covered in this guide, Capitol Reef National Park is. (435-623-5203 or 800-748-4361.)

To the East of Panoramaland is **Castle Country**, a land that is uncrowded and

UTAH
TRAVEL REGIONS

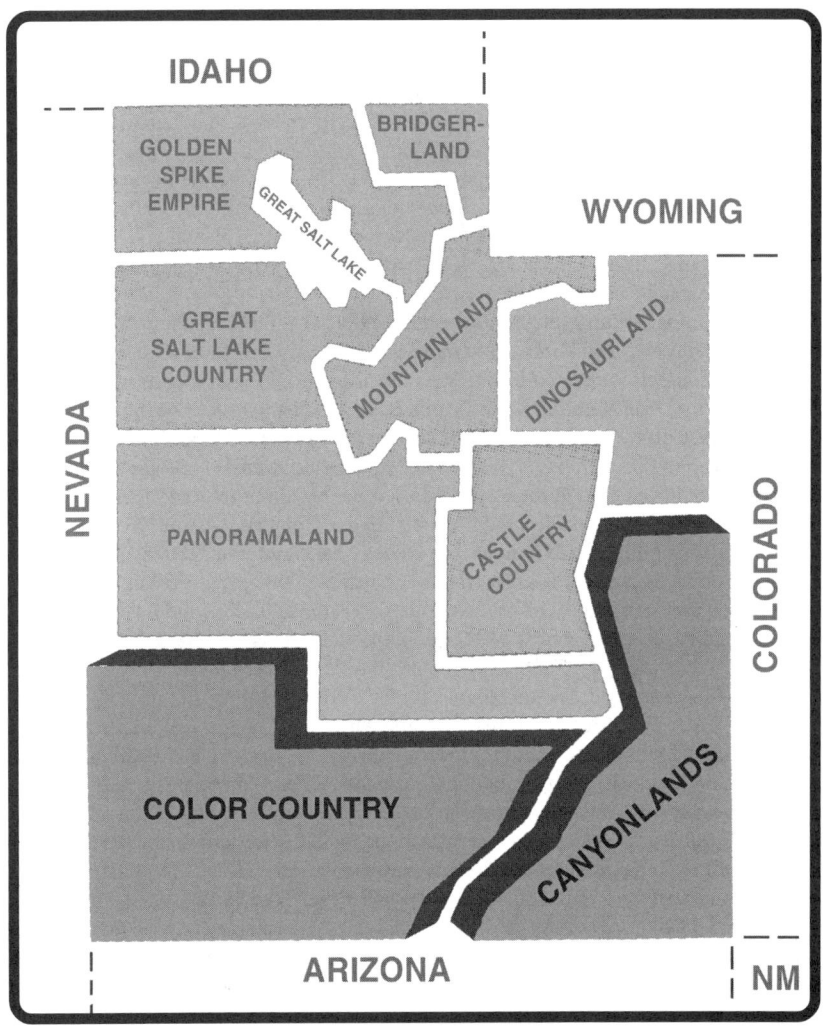

Travelers' Choice: A Guide to the Best Of Utah's National Parks, Monuments, & Recreation Areas, takes our "*pretty, great state*" visitors to the Canyonlands and Color Country Travel Regions. Here visitors may not enjoy Utah's "Greatest Snow on Earth," but they are sure to enjoy the "Greatest Earth on Show."

replete with rivers, mountain lakes, and deserts for visitors to enjoy. It is also a region profusely blessed with reminders of the past. There is the Cleveland-Lloyd Dinosaur Quarry to remind visitors of the reality of dinosaurs. The remnants of rock art and dwellings of ancient Fremont Indians remind us of previous civilizations. The **San Rafael Swell**, caused by a monumental upheaval, reminds us of the incredible forces of nature. Another jewel in the crown of Castle Country is the incongruous beauty of **Goblin Valley**. The San Rafael Swell and Goblin Valley are covered in this book, although the region is not. (435-637-3009 or 800-842-0789.)

Each of the seven travel regions mentioned above are overflowing with state parks, national forests, parks, monuments, or recreation areas, scenic byways and backways, and ghost towns. All of them afford the traveler with diverse opportunities for outdoor recreation that includes downhill and cross country skiing, snowmobiling, boating, fishing, hiking, backpacking, rock climbing, cycling, and four-wheel driving. All of Utah's travel regions are exceptional destination vacations regardless of the season. But, except for a small segment of Castle Country and the lower middle portion of Panoramaland, it is the state's two southern travel regions, **Canyonlands** and **Color Country**, on which this guide is concentrated. We have also included **Page, Arizona**, a vacation destination for visitors to Wahweap Marina at Lake Powell in Glen Canyon National Recreation Area.

Color Country, the Southwestern region of the state, is home to **Zion** and **Bryce Canyon National Parks**, and **Grand Staircase-Escalante** and **Cedar Breaks National Monument**. Operated by the state are **Coral Pink Sand Dunes, Quail Creek, Snow Canyon, Iron Mission, Kodachrome Basin, Escalante**, and **Anasazi Indian Ruin State Parks**. Color County is also the Gateway to **Wahweap Marina** and **Lake Powell** in the Arizona side of **Glen Canyon National Recreation Area**. Where else but in Southern Utah could one play a round of golf on a winter's morning and then hit the ski slopes of **Brian Head** during the afternoon? Color Country is home to the arts with Cedar City becoming world famous for its **Utah Shakespearean Festival**. Also gaining world wide recognition is **Utah!** an outdoor musical drama performed in the Tuacahn natural red rock amphitheater. Washington, Kane, Garfield, Iron, and Beaver Counties comprise the Color Country Travel Region. (435-628-4171 or 800-233-8824.)

Occupying the Southeastern portion of Utah is **Canyonlands**. Canyonlands is home to **Arches** and **Canyonlands National Parks**, and the Utah marinas of **Lake Powell—Hite, Bullfrog**, and **Halls Crossing**—in **Glen Canyon National Recreation Area**. National Monuments include **Hovenweep, Natural Bridges**, and **Rainbow Bridge**. Canyonlands is quarters to Utah's tiny segment of **Four Corners**, the only place in America where the boundaries of four states come together, and to the **Monument Valley Tribal Park**. State parks and attractions include **Goosenecks of the San Juan, Valley of the Gods, Edge of the Cedars, Newspaper Rock, Dead Horse Point, Green River State Park** and the **John Wesley Powell River History Museum**. Three great rivers—The **Colorado, Green**, and **San Juan**—flow through the canyons that make up the convoluted terrain of Canyonlands Travel Region. Along with the **Manti LaSal Mountains**, the rivers offer a most exhilarating way to beat the heat of this hot desert climate. For a real touch of class, there is **Canyonlands by Night**, a magnificent display of light and music that takes place on the Colorado River and the canyons that surround it. San Juan and Grand Counties comprise the Canyonlands Travel Region. (435-259-8825 or 800-635-6622.)

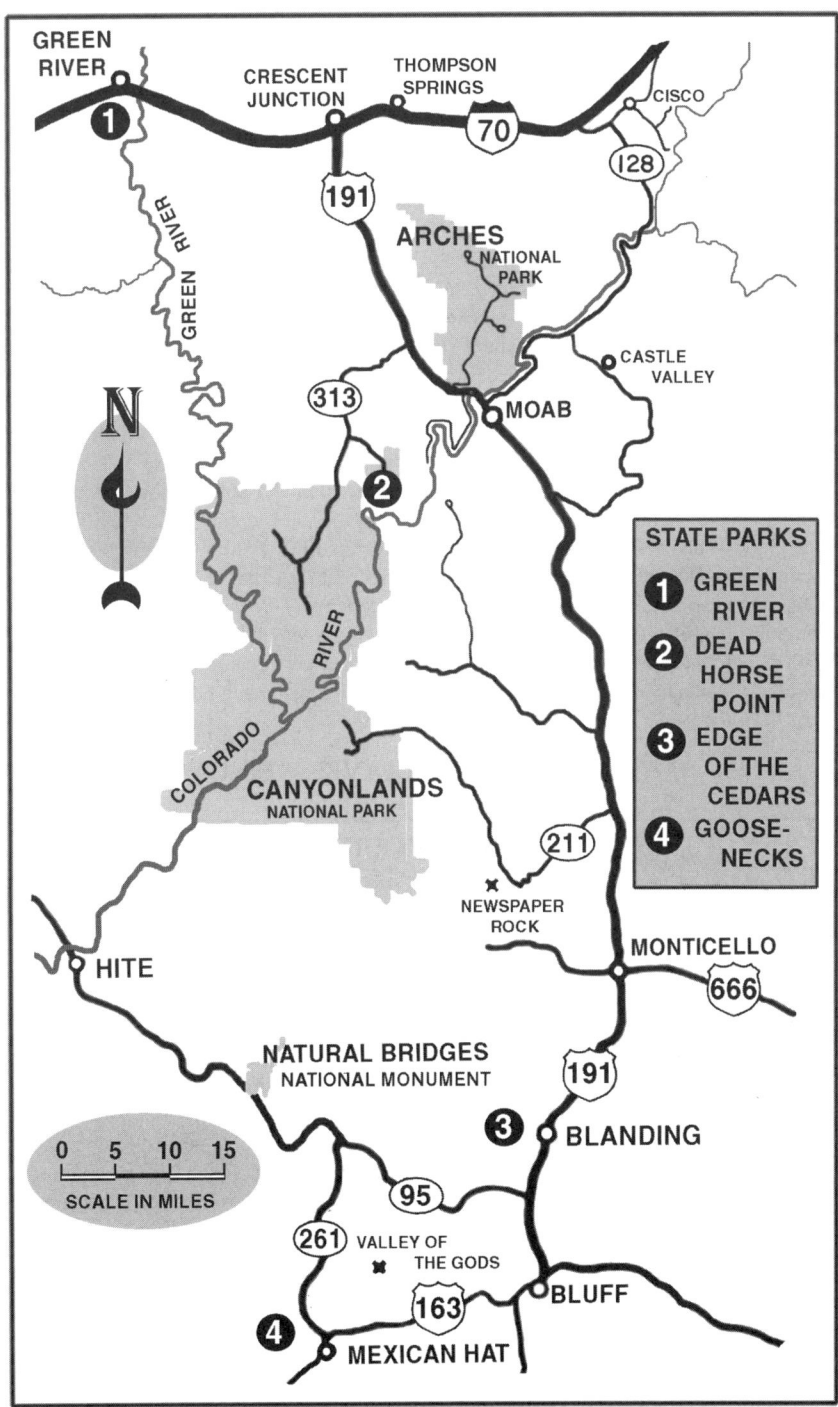

THE TRIP BEGINS

One of the best routes to Arches and Canyonlands National Parks, when coming from Southwestern Utah, is north on the I-15 to the I-70 Eastbound. About mid-way through Emery County on this route, one approaches the **San Rafael Swell**. The San Rafael Swell was created during a tremendous geologic upheaval that occurred centuries ago when a giant dome, nearly sixty miles in diameter, collapsed into a wild, broken array of multicolored sandstone. The elements worked this jumble of rock over the intervening millennia into the incredible formations, buttes, canyons, pinnacles, and mesas one sees today.

The San Rafael Swell reaches heights of 8,000 feet or more and provides sights that cannot be found anywhere else in the world. Some sections of this unique geologic region are covered with rolling pasture land that is populated with pronghorn antelope. Then, just around the bend, the terrain becomes wild and broken with rivers cutting through narrow canyons. A relatively "undiscovered" natural wonder of the American Southwest, the nearly indescribable beauty of the San Rafael Swell can be enjoyed at one's leisure, without the hustle and commercialism of the nation's national parks.

When it comes to visual impact, there is little that can compare with the spectacular **Wedge Overlook**. Known as *"Utah's Little Grand Canyon,"* the drop at the edge is so sudden it tends to take one's breath away. From The Wedge is a panoramic view of the San Rafael River as it winds its way through a maze of multicolored cliffs that open onto a vast expanse of rugged yet bewitching country. Be sure to take advantage of the many viewpoints along the rim, as each view is totally different from the last.

CANYONLANDS TRAVEL REGION

GRAND COUNTY

Grand County is a remarkable portion of the state where the grandeur and adventure go hand in hand. Grandeur reigns supreme in the beauty of Arches National Monument and Dead Horse State Park. Island in the Sky, a section of Canyonland National Park, though in San Juan County, is accessible only from Highway 313, just outside Moab. Year-round adventures include such daring activities as river running, hiking, and mountain biking. More sedate adventures include jeeping the backroads, visiting the parks, golfing, and in winter, back country skiing.

A region of incredible diversity and beauty, Grand County is a land of wild water and wide open deserts. It is a land where pinion pines and gnarled junipers add a splash of green to the red sandstone of its forbidding terrain. When spring conditions are just right, the seemingly barren landscape explodes with a profusion of wildflowers.

A sparsely populated county where tourism and ranching provide the main income, Grand County is bordered by the Green River to the west and the Colorado state line to the east. Slicing through the middle of Grand County is the magnificent Colorado River. A large portion of the county's northwestern corner is occupied by the Uintah and Ouray Indian Reservation.

Over 90 percent of Grand County is public land that is administered by the Bureau of Land Management (BLM), the USDA Forest Service, the National Park

Service, the State of Utah, and State Parks. Various recreational activities, including hiking, biking, river running, horseback riding, and off-highway vehicle exploring are permitted in many of these areas, depending upon which government agency administers the land. Keep in mind, however, that the canyons have a particularly delicate ecosystem that can easily be irreparably damaged. Learn and follow the rules that apply to the area being visited and do everything possible to help keep the land safe and clean for others to enjoy.

Grand County is a photographer's paradise, a region where magnificent sculptured rock formations provide an unforgettable experience for the amateur and professional alike. Grand County is the wild west, where Butch Cassidy and his gang roamed at will. Grand County is one of Utah's most extraordinary treasures.

GRAND COUNTY ATTRACTIONS

ARCHES NATIONAL PARK

As with all the majestic parks of Southern Utah, Arches National Park, with its graceful stone arches, towering spires, sheer cliffs, and balanced rocks, seems hardy and unchanging. Yet it is constantly evolving and continually being reshaped by water, wind, and time—the natural elements of erosion that have formed this majestic wonderland one grain at a time over millions of years.

Periodically though, the landscape can change dramatically overnight. Two examples are **Skyline Arch**, near the park campground, and **Balanced Rock**, near the Windows Section of the park. Until 1940, a giant boulder had blocked nearly half of Skyline Arch's aperture. Then, without warning but because of year's of slow erosion, the boulder dislodged itself from its footings and tumbled down the mountain. Skyline Arch, overnight, almost doubled in size. Balanced Rock, until recently, was even more of an attraction because of a small associate formation, **Chip-Off-the-Old-Block,** which imaged the larger structure. During the winter of 1975 - 76, Chip-Off-the-Old-Block toppled to the ground, lost forever as a miniature clone.

With so much that can be seen from the car, Arches National Park is a great family park. But if one truly wants to experience the aura of time, get out of the car and walk. Many foot trails lead to each of the park's diverse sections.

Located five miles north of Moab, Arches National Park features the greatest concentration of natural stone arches in the world. Over 1,800 vertical, horizontal and pothole arches, from the most minute to one of the largest natural arches in the world, **Landscape Arch,** grace the park.

Arches National Park is also known for its dramatic rock formations, massive sandstone buttes, colorful rock walls, petrified dunes, meandering canyons, and balanced rocks. Twenty-one miles of paved roads that are open year-round take visitors to the many points of interest within the park's boundaries.

Two miles from the visitor center at the park entrance is **Courthouse Towers.** It features a system of broken cliffs, ledges and freestanding formations that delight the eye. **Park Avenue,** a rocky path whose walls resemble a row of giant buildings, is the principal feature of this section of the park. Other sandstone formations easily recognizable because of their names, are **The Organ, Tower of Babel, Sheep Rock,** and the **Three Gossips.** Along the main road, going to the second section of the park, are the **Petrified Dunes Viewpoint**, and **Rock Pinnacles.**

Farther down the road is a section of eroded ruddy Entrada sandstone known as **The Windows.** These arches were so named because of the patches of blue sky that can be clearly seen through the area's North and South Windows, also called **The Spectacles.** Other features of this section are **Balanced Rock, Turret Arch, Parade of the Elephants, Double Arch, Cove of Caves, Ribbon Arch, Cove Arch, Garden of Eden, Elephant Butte, Ham Rock** and **Pothole Arch.**

Fourteen miles from the visitor center, **Delicate Arch,** while only one of 1,800 arches in the park, is probably the most popular attraction for returning visitors. Rising from a slight depression among brilliant vermilion mounds, this crimson arch—33-feet wide and 45-feet high, is one of America's most photographed, and is arguably the most famous arch in the world. In 1995 a handicap accessible viewpoint was completed. Park visitors may also hike along a well-marked trail to the arch. It is a three-mile round trip hike with an elevation gain of 480-feet. The trail is over slick rock, there is no shade, and hikers are advised to take at least one quart of water per person.

Fiery Furnace, a labyrinth of great buttresses and pinnacles separated by narrow slots, is an area of extremely broken terrain. During summer months, guided tours are available. Persons wishing to enter this maze unaccompanied by a guide should consult with park personnel before attempting the feat.

The majority of the park's arches are to be found in the **Devils Garden.** Eighteen miles from the visitor center, this is the largest and most complex section of the park. It extends along a continuous ridge of multicolored sandstone and features a seemingly never-ending array of upright fins and pinnacles, huge, interconnected amphitheaters, and massive wind-sculpted monoliths. Among spans to be visited in this area are **Sand Dune Arch, Broken Arch, Skyline Arch, Tunnel Arch, Pine Tree Arch, Landscape Arch, Partition Arch, Navajo Arch, Wall Arch, Double O Arch, Private Arch** and **Dark Angel.**

Also in the Devils Garden area is the **Devils Garden Campground** with its 52 tent and trailer sites. All are available on a first-come, first-served basis, with no reservations. Two other areas are available to tenters and may be reserved for eleven or more people. Campfire programs are offered in season at the amphitheater. (435-259-8161.)

Klondike Bluffs, the most remote and least visited section of the park, is a singular area of salmon-hued sandstone sculpted by the elements into an endless variation of shapes. This area contains the beautifully symmetrical **Tower Arch,** one of the most striking rock formations in the world.

ARCHES HISTORY

Arches National Park has an interesting history, one that is imbedded in the dreams and wishes of the "Father of the Arches," Dr. J. W. Williams, Grand County's first doctor.

By the time he had arrived in Moab from Ordway, Colorado in November of 1896, Dr. Williams had already been a cowboy, chuckwagon cook, druggist, justice of the peace, county assessor, postmaster, and county judge of Lincoln, County, Colorado.

As the only doctor in a vast frontier, Dr. Williams spent a good portion of his time on horseback with house calls often requiring days of traveling. On horseback and on foot, Dr. Williams came to know the country that is now Arches National Park with the same intimacy afforded the cowboys, rustlers, sheepmen, and outlaws who then claimed the land.

In 1919, at age 66, Dr. Williams retired as a physician and began a lifelong pursuit to introduce the world to the scenic marvels that lay just a short distance from Moab. For as long as anyone could remember, every important person who ever came to Moab was told to see Dr. Williams. Dr. Williams in turn told visitors about or took them to Arches country. It was no surprise that when Dr. Larry Gould came to Moab in 1921 to do a reconnaissance survey of the geology of the LaSal Mountains, he ended up being escorted to "The Windows" area of the park. In 1924, Gould returned to spend a summer in Moab. The following winter Gould wrote a letter to Senator Reed Smoot of Utah, encouraging a movement to make the area a National Monument. Smoot, in turn wrote to Stephen Mather, director of the National Park Service.

By that time the National Park Service, based on recommendations from the Denver and Rio Grande Western Railroad, had already begun a preliminary survey of the area. They were looking for a place that Moab prospector, Alexander Ringhoffer, had called Devil's Garden (The place that Ringhoffer described was actually Klondike Bluffs), but instead they found Dr. William's Windows. A second survey was conducted in 1925. This time they thought they were exploring Klondike Bluffs, the area Ringhoffer called Devil's Garden, and named it so. Mather was intrigued by the "extraordinary specimens of natural sculpture and architecture found north of Moab." He pushed that it become a national monument. In 1929, President Herbert Hoover, by executive order, created Arches National Monument, an area of 4,520 acres that included the Devil's Garden and The Windows. Ironically, Klondike Bluffs, the original Devil's Garden and the area for which the D & RGW Railroad was searching, were not a part of the new monument.

Though it fell far short of Dr. William's dream, newspapers credited the untiring efforts of Dr. Williams, Dr. Gould, and Senator Smoot for Utah's newest National Monument.

Shortly after the monument's formation, Utah joined the rest of the nation in the Great Depression. When the Civilian Conservation Corps was formed, it created a light of hope for Dr. Williams and Moab, who looked to the CCC for improvements to Arches National Monument. The Moab Lions Club, of which Dr. Williams was a member, lobbied for CCC support and won. In December 1933, the first of CCC crews, called the Arches Scientific Expedition, arrived in Moab and was assigned to survey boundaries, lay out roads, trails, and evaluate potential campground areas in Arches. They were also to document archaeological sites and scenic features.

It was a blessing that Frank Beckwith, editor of the weekly newspaper in Delta, Utah, was appointed survey leader. Beckwith shared Dr. Williams enthusiasm and recounted the survey's findings in spirited detail in his newspaper articles. Dr. Williams told Beckwith where he should go and which areas should have road and trail developments. By the end of his survey, Dr. William's dream of the area to be included in the park was fulfilled. In 1938, President Franklin D. Roosevelt sent a letter to Dr. Williams asking him for one of his pens. Since Dr. Williams only had an old-style dip pen, Dr. William's son, Mitch, offered his fountain pen. In November, Roosevelt signed a proclamation that enlarged Arches National Monument from about seven square miles to almost 53-square miles, a total of 33,930 acres that included Courthouse Towers, The Palisades (now Klondike Bluffs), and Schoolmarm's Bloomers, which today is known as Delicate Arch.

Roads were begun in 1941, but by the end of the year World War II had changed the course of history and dimmed the dream of Arches' expansion. It would be in 1956, when Dr. Williams was approaching his 102nd birthday, that Arches road construction would finally get under way. Dr. Williams insisted on driving the entire route and back over less than a blasted horse trail to make sure that the roads were going in the right places. Dr. Williams died 10 days after his 103rd birthday. Two years later, in honor of her husband's influence, Dr. Williams' widow, Alvina, cut the ribbon to open the new entrance road.

Before the monument would finally become Arches National Park, signed into law in 1971 by President Richard M. Nixon, the monument would be slightly diminished in size by Dwight D. Eisenhower, and then doubled in size by Lyndon B. Johnson. Today it is a park of 114 square miles for all to enjoy, and Dr. Williams' dream to share the beauties of Arches with the world has been fulfilled.

Visitors are encouraged to stop at the visitor center. Whether one is staying an hour, a day, or a week, there are questions that can be answered, geology and history exhibits to explore, and a color slide program. A self-guiding booklet is available along with many other publications and maps. In season there is a naturalist-led Fiery Furnace walk and other ranger guided programs. There is no food or lodging in the park, but nearby Moab provides all types of visitor services.

DEAD HORSE POINT STATE PARK

Dead Horse Point State Park, enroute to Canyonlands National Park on Utah State Highway 313, is 18 miles off Highway 191 between Green River and Moab.

A nearly isolated mesa, Dead Horse Point is perched on top of the Orange Cliffs escarpment. In early western history cowboys used the point's natural corral to keep wild horses. The site earned its unusual name when a group of cowboys inadvertently left a band of horses trapped for so long that they died of thirst.

Dead Horse Point, one of the state's most popular and scenic parks, offers spectacular views of the La Sal Mountains, Canyonlands National Park, and the Colorado River some 2,000 feet below. A visitor center, interpretive museum, large overlook shelter, and twenty-one unit campground, complete with modern restrooms, sewage disposal station, group camping area, and pavilion are located in the park. For more information write P. O. Box 609, Moab, Utah 84532-0609, or call (435) 259-2614.

ADDITIONAL GRAND COUNTY ATTRACTIONS

Forming a natural backdrop to Canyonland and Arches National Parks is the **LaSal Mountains,** located southeast of Moab. The **LaSal Mountain Loop** offers visitors a superb combination of alpine scenery and panoramic vistas of the corrugated red Canyonlands stretching below. A 60-mile loop that can be accessed southeast of Moab or from just north of Moab on 128, the LaSal Mountain Loop offers a spectrum of sightseeing opportunities. The LaSal Mountain Loop passes through the **Manti La Sal National Forest.**

As one rises to the national park level, they will also notice a change in vegetation. The pinion and juniper trees of the lower elevations give way to the oak, pine, and aspens of the middle ground. The highest areas are covered with spruce and fir.

Reached from side roads of the LaSal Mountain Loop, **Warner** and **Oowah Lakes** offer excellent fishing and water recreation. The lakes include well-maintained campgrounds that are complete with drinking water, modern restrooms, picnic tables and fire pits. Also located along the trail is **Geyser Pass**. At an altitude of 10,600-feet, the pass winds between **Haystack Mountain** and **Mount Mellenthin**. The road leads toward State Highway 46 and the town of Paradox, Colorado. It is suggested that motorists take precautions, such as filling fuel tanks before starting this scenic backway trip. Since potable water is not always available, motorists are advised to carry ample drinking water when touring this or any other back road.

Capped with snow most of the year, the *LaSals* offer a perfect place for beating the summer heat. The LaSals are the second highest range in Utah and offer plenty of hiking, camping, cycling and mountain climbing opportunities. Bicycles, motorcycles, and all-terrain vehicles may be used on specially approved roads. During winter there are dozens of miles of cross-country ski trails as well as hut-to-hut ski systems. (435-259-7155.)

Twenty-three miles north of Moab on a dirt road going East of U. S. 191 is the **Sauropod Dinosaur Track Site,** discovered in 1989. This is the location of the first five-toed herbivore tracks ever reported in Utah. There are also four theropods of various sizes. The dinosaurs walked in several directions across a ripple marked sand deposit that had accumulated in an ancient river channel. An interesting thing about the tracks is the pronounced turn to the right. Such obvious changes in direction are extremely rare in fossil trackways and suggest that there may have been a combative encounter.

There are many fossil and dinosaur track sites near Moab; most of which are on BLM administered public lands. Another such site is at **Mill Canyon Dinosaur Trail**, where fossils and petrified wood have been left in their natural settings. The trailhead is on a dirt road west of U. S. 191, 13 miles north of Moab. Another site is reached via Potash Scenic Byway 279, which parallels the Colorado River. Three-toed Allosaurus tracks can be seen about 4. 5 miles from the Byway's origin on U. S. 191.

Petroglyphs and Pictographs are abundant in Grand County. Petroglyphs are graphics pecked into the cliffs, Pictographs have been painted on the rocks in one or more colors made from plant dyes or mineral pigments.

The **Courthouse Wash site**, located within Arches National Park, is a half mile hike from a parking lot off U. S. 191, just north of the Colorado River bridge. The panel is almost 19 feet high and 52 feet long and has both pictographs and petroglyphs with figures resembling humans, bighorn sheep, shields, scorpions, and abstract forms.

Near the Moab Golf Course is the **Golf Course Rock Art** site. Approximately 30 by 90 feet, the panel is covered with human and animal figures. Along Kane Creek Boulevard there are panels showing bighorn sheep, snakes, bear paws, and several abstract graphics as well as human figures, some of which have headdresses.

Though many rock art sites are in remote areas, plenty are accessible to passenger vehicles. A rock art auto tour brochure is available at the Moab Information Center in Moab and at the John Wesley Powell River History Museum in Green River.

There are two ghost towns in Canyon Country, Sego, at the base of the Book Cliff Mountains, and Cisco**,** located along the Colorado River Scenic Byway, Highway 128.

Sego was a coal mining town established in 1893. It was named for the Utah state flower, the Sego Lily. The very first coal washer west of the Mississippi was constructed here. If the road is wet, a four-wheel vehicle may be required.

Cisco was a supply center and railroad town for sixty years and was the nearest shipping point in southeast Utah. Cattle ranching and mining kept the town alive during the early 1900's, but since the town depended on the pump house and the railroad for water, it has now declined to abandoned buildings and corrals.

Colorado River Scenic Byway not only offers spectacular scenery but also serves as a connecting road for those going to or from Moab and its nearby National Parks. Forty-four miles long, the byway begins two miles north of Moab from Highway 191 and passes by several points of interest. First is **Negro Bill Canyon**, named for William Granstaff, an Afro-American cattleman during the late 1800's. From the Canyon a two-mile long hiking trip leads to **Morning Glory Natural Bridge**. (This side trip takes approximately four hours.) Back on the byway it is three miles to the base of **Big Bend Picnic Area**, with its beautiful white sand beach. From this point the road closely parallels the Colorado River, beautiful at any time of the year, but during late spring, summer and fall, motorists can enjoy watching the rafting expeditions floating down the river from **Westwater Canyon**. As the road curves to the left there is a large picturesque ranch, **White Ranch,** that has been the location for several western movies. At the Castle Valley Junction, which leads to the **LaSal Road Scenic Backway**, the byway moves a distance from the river. A few miles past the junction is **Castle Rock**, a finger-like spire that is visible for several miles. Castle Rock has been the location for spectacular automobile commercials. Following the spires is **Fisher Towers**. A cluster of dark red spires, the Towers rise from the 2,000-foot high south wall of **Professor Valley** and provide great photographic opportunities. **Titan** is the tallest of the towers at 900 feet. A 2.2 mile hiking trail winds its way along the base of the towers and then climbs to a view point overlooking the **Onion Creek** drainage. About five miles northeast of Fisher Towers is the old and the new **Dewey Bridges**. The old one-lane suspension bridge, built in 1916 and used until 1986, has been placed on the National Historic Register. It is still open to foot traffic and bicycles. Motorists may either turn around at this point and return to Moab, or continue along the Colorado River, through desert country, and then onto I-70 at the Cisco interchange.

On Highway 191, one mile northwest of the Colorado River Scenic Byway is **Potash Scenic Byway 279**. The Byway follows the Colorado River on its southeast journey and takes motorists past two sets of petroglyph rock art, visible from the road, and one set of dinosaur tracks, visible through a sighting tube. Shortly past the dinosaur tracks is *Corona Arch Trailhead*, a three-mile round trip trail that takes hikers to *Corona* and **Bow Tie Arches**. Corona has an opening of 140 feet by 105 feet. Bow Tie is unique in that the arch has red rock directly behind it, but when one approaches the arch, they look up to beautiful blue skies through a hole in the top . Allow two to three hours for the hike. As one approaches the end of this 17-mile highway, a sign points to another arch—most appropriately named and visible from one's car—*Jug Handle Arch*. Beyond the arch, the canyon widens and the sheer cliffs of Dead Horse State Park are visible in the distance. The byway ends at the Moab Salt Plant, where potash is extracted. Motorists with high clearance vehicles can continue on past the plant on a dirt road that takes them into Canyonlands National Park.

GREEN RIVER

The site of an historic Old Spanish Trail river crossing, the town of Green River occupies not only both sides of the stream from which it gets its name, but parts of two counties as well. Green River is partially in both Grand and Emery Counties. Green River is literally an oasis in the middle of the desert. The town was settled in 1878 and served as a mail relay station between Salina, Utah and Ouray, Colorado until 1882 when the Rio Grande Western Railroad was built.

Green River's 120 year history has been one of ups and downs. Enduring as both a boom town and near ghost town, Green River has seen large cattle and sheep ranches and prosperous farms lost to bad weather. It has also seen the coming of the railroad and highway construction that brought one of the major East/West intestate highways, I-70, through its backdoor. Land development and the discovery of oil and uranium have been other major factors in the town's development. One aspect of the city's economy that has been a major plus has been Green River watermelons. First planted in 1917, Green River watermelons, which have commanded premium prices since 1927, can now be purchased across the country. They may also be obtained fresh from roadside stands in season.

In addition to being known today as the watermelon capitol of the world, Green River is gaining a reputation as a vacation destination. In recent years, the popularity of river running excursions has put Green River on the map. Still a small town with small town prices, Green River takes pride in providing motorists with all tourist services plus the benefits of proximity to Utah's southeast wonderland.

GREEN RIVER ATTRACTIONS

Located just off Interstate 70 along the west bank of the Green River, the **Green River State Park** offers fifty acres of well-developed public park for one's enjoyment. A new nine-hole golf course offers meandering fairways, lakes and traps that offer challenges and fun for all levels of golfers.

Another part of the park is a 42-unit campground with hot showers, modern rest rooms, pavilion, amphitheater for interpretive programs, and a boat launching ramp. For years the state park, originally a state recreation area, has been a favorite embarkation point for Labyrinth and Stillwater Canyons. The park is the beginning point for one of the town's most popular annual events, the 180-mile Friendship Cruise.

On or off the course, the well-manicured lawns and tall Cottonwood shade trees make the park a favorite of all who go there.

Located at 885 East Main Street, the **John Wesley Powell River History Museum** overlooks the Green River, the very waters that Powell and his 19th century group of explorers ran as the first white men to navigate the Green and Colorado Rivers. The large modern museum emphasizes the accomplishments of Powell, but it is also a River Runners' Hall of Fame, commemorating the feats of men and women who have matched their wits against the rivers. On display are fascinating replicas of the different kinds of boats used to explore the west's waterways. Included are a unique round hull boat used by the Indians, primitive rafts used by Powell, and modern hi-tech boats and equipment used by present day adventurers. The museum also contains a Visitor Information Center. (435-564-3427 & 564-3347.)

Extraordinary vacation spots such as **Arches**, **Canyonlands**, and **Capitol Reef National Parks**, as well as **Dead Horse Point** and **Goblin Valley State Parks**, **Glen Canyon National Recreation Area**, and **San Rafael Reef** and **Horse Canyon** are all within a two-hour drive of Green River.

GOBLIN VALLEY STATE PARK

Goblin Valley State Park is a photographer's paradise. Located between the towns of Green River and Hanksville on Highway 24, motorists are greeted by scores of intricately eroded rock formations resembling nearly anything one can imagine.

The unique and enchanting rock sculptures bear imaginative names. But so intriguing are the scores of chocolate colored goblins, spires, pedestals, and buttes, that it is a shame to let someone else's imagination name them. Part of the fun is becoming involved with one's own fantasy, and creating one's own characters in a world of folklore and mischief. There are hundreds of miles of dirt roads to explore and the numerous rocks and coves offer unlimited hiking opportunities.

Facilities at the 3,654-acre park include a 21-unit campground, observation outlook, culinary water, modern restrooms, hot water showers, and sanitary dump station. Each campsite has a picnic table, paved parking pad, and barbecue grill.

Goblin Valley became a state park in August of 1964.

GREEN RIVER EVENTS

January is the month for statewide Utah Winter Game activities. (800-959-8824.)

May features the city's famous Green River Friendship Cruise, an event that involves the cities of Moab and Green River. Begun in 1958, the two-day event is held over the Memorial Day weekend and embarks from Green River State Park. The Friendship Cruise involves as many as 400 power boats with boaters taken through a spectacular series of high, red-rocked canyons extending 120 miles down the Green River to the confluence of the Colorado, then sixty-five miles up the Colorado River to Moab. An exhilarating adventure through an enchanting wilderness area, the Friendship Cruise, if one is in the area, is not to be missed. (435-564-8448.)

July in Utah is the month for dual statewide celebrations—the traditional Independence Day festivities and Utah Pioneer Day activities, held July 24, a state holiday.

September is looked forward to as Green River celebrates its annual Melon Days Celebration. (435-259-8825.)

ACCOMMODATIONS

**BUDGET HOST
BOOK CLIFF LODGE &
RESTAURANT**
395 East Main (Box 545)
Green River, Utah 84525
Tel:
Lodge   (435) 564-3406
          (800) 283-4678 (BUD-HOST)
Restaurant   (435) 564-3650
Hrs: Restaurant & Gift Shop
 Open Daily
June - September   6:00 a.m. - 10:00 p.m.
October - May   7:00 a.m. - 9:00 p.m.
FAX: (435) 564-8359
Visa, MasterCard, American Express, Diners Club, Carte Blanch
and Discover are accepted.
Reservations for the lodge are recommended.

It is not often that one comes across a bargain find that is so special that the temptation is there, either to share it with everyone or to keep it as a deep dark secret. Budget Host's Book Cliff Lodge and Restaurant is just such a find.

When Book Cliff Lodge promotes its rooms as being spacious there is definitely truth in advertising. Even the smallest Pool Unit rooms easily accommodate two double queen beds, night stands, a small table with double chairs, a dresser, and cable television that includes HBO, ESPN, and Disney channels.

Most of the Deluxe Rooms, which offer hotel-like accommodations with entrance from a well-lit hallway, offer double king or double queen beds, a semi-circular tub/ shower enclosure, large vanity with basin in the bathroom, and separate vanity in the dressing area. The front units, slightly larger than the Pool Units, offer double or single queens, desk, glass table, elegant lamps, and an exquisite armoire with concealed television.

Every room is immaculately kept and decorated with a touch of elegance. Each of the 78 rooms offer direct dial phones with local calls free, and every unit offers a mirrored vanity completely separate from the bathroom, and a tub/shower enclosure.

But rooms so large that one can almost become lost in them is just part of the extraordinary Book Cliff Lodge discovery. When it comes to vacation accommodations, location is a most important factor. Green River is literally an Oasis in the middle of the desert, with the town occupying both sides of the river from which it gets its name. Some of the most challenging river rafting in existence begins on the Green River and continues through the great rapids of the Cataract Canyon down stream. Not far from Green River are Goblin Valley State Park, the San Rafael Swell, and the Book Cliff mountains, for which the Lodge is named. Right in town are the John Wesley Powell Museum, named for the man who navigated and explored the unknown twists, turns and rapids of both the Green and Colorado Rivers; the Green River State Park, offering a 42-unit campground, hot showers, and a boat launch; and the new Green River nine-hole golf course, which is right across the street from Book Cliff Lodge.

Arches National Park, Canyonlands National Park, Capitol Reef National Park and Dead Horse Point State Park are all an easy drive, with picturesque scenery along the way.

When one returns from the adventures of the day, or when just relaxing seems in order, it is comforting to know that Book Cliff Lodge offers one of the finest heated swimming pools in the area. A large deck and an abundance of flowers and green grass provide an atmosphere of comfort.

Guests at Book Cliff Lodge will find that the Lodge restaurant of the same name serves up satisfying breakfasts, lunch and dinner. Breakfast begins at 6:00 or 7:00 a.m., according to the season, with a wide variety of omelettes, waffles and pancakes, and eggs of choice served with steak, ham, bacon or sausage, as well as a western favorite, biscuits and gravy. Lunch begins at 11:00 a.m. and continues until closing. Traditional hamburgers, B.L.T.'s, clubs, and hot and cold beef and turkey sandwiches are served, along with an assortment of vegetarian plates, including burgers, pasta, and taco salad. Dinner features a variety of steaks that run the gamut from hamburger and chicken fried steaks to choice New York and Ribeye. Chicken entrees include the classical fried chicken dinner to Heart Smart meals, Rotisserie Mesquite and Chicken Breast Filet. Two other Heart Smart dinners are the Deep Sea Halibut and the Red Creek Trout Fillet. All dinners are served with vegetables, choice of potato, choice of soup or salad, and a dinner roll. Prepared just for children are hot dogs, hamburgers, grilled cheese, chicken tenders, and fish and chips, all served with another children's favorite, French fries.

Next to the restaurant is a small but well-stocked gift shop that features Native American artifacts such as pottery, turquoise and silver jewelry, weaving, and baskets. In addition, guests will find popular items such as Green River T-shirts, mugs, caps, and other souvenirs of the area.

The Book Cliffs, first photographed by members of the John Wesley Powell Survey team, are unequaled—constituting the longest continuous escarpment in the world (250 miles). The Budget Host Book Cliff Lodge, Restaurant and Gift Shop are also unique, standing alone as Green River's best value.

RESTAURANTS

RAY'S TAVERN
25 South Broadway
Green River, Utah 84525
Tel: (435) 564-3511
FAX: (435) 564-3347
Open Daily
Dining   10:00 a.m. - 10:00 p.m.
Bar   10:00 a.m. - 1:00 a.m.
No credit cards are accepted.
Reservations are required for large parties.

On Oahu, in the historic town of Haleiwa, there is Kua Aina. In Utah, in the remote town of Green River, watermelon capital of the world, there is Ray's Tavern. Both eateries are known around the world for their succulent, inimitable hamburgers.

Giving the shirt off one's back takes on a whole new connotation at Ray's Tavern. If a customer has, or is wearing an adventure T-shirt from anywhere in the world, he or she is likely to bring the T-shirt in, or literally take the shirt off his or her back, and give it to Cathy Gardner, Ray's Tavern owner. This is the customer's way of proving that they have made it—they have personally eaten and imbibed at Ray's Tavern. Not long after the guest departs the T-shirt will find its way onto an honored place on the wall, along with the other adventure T's hailing from as far away as Alaska.

Ray's Tavern, for the simple reason that the food is terrific, is famous all over the world. One wouldn't think of running the rivers, biking slickrock, visiting the canyons, or boating in Lake Powell without enjoying a beer, the food, and the camaraderie that exists at Ray's.

The tavern was opened in 1939 by Ray Sherill. Cathy purchased Ray's in 1995 and, according to those who have been long-time customers, Ray's keeps getting better and better.

When Ray's Tavern began serving its now famous 1/2-pound hamburgers and cheeseburgers, that and a few beer choices, were all there was. But the burgers were enough to set the town on its ears and make the world sit up and take notice. No one ever asks "where's the beef?" when eating a Ray's burger. And the condiments of delicious, thick, sweet onions, tomato, lettuce and pickles, and a huge serving of home made fries are all one needs to feel gastronomically satisfied—at a price so affordable that it will "knock your socks off!"

Though the burgers are still the highlight of Ray's Tavern menu, the menu has expanded since Cathy took ownership to include Teriyaki chicken, thick "to-die for" pork chops, New York, T-Bone, and Filet Mignon steaks, and chicken salad. All are served with a choice of fries or baked potato (after 5:00 p.m.), dinner salad, and Texas toast.

Until recently Cathy had also been the owner of another local favorite dining and take-out establishment, Cathy's Pizza. Cathy has now added pizza to the menu and guests are now able to partake of her delectable pizza concoctions with a variety of topping choices. In addition, Cathy has expanded beer choices to include a wide range of domestic and imported beers as well as draft and locally brewed beers.

The Tavern is small, and many times there is standing room only, but Cathy has also added Ray's Boneyard, a slatted covered patio with summer time dining capabilities of an additional 100. Visitors to the area love the summer courtyard. Cathy has provided the patio with its own cool mist system, a device that keeps the outside terrace temperature approximately 25 degrees cooler than the outside air. Green River can get extremely warm during the summer months.

It is a given, that when visiting Southeastern Utah one doesn't forget the unforgettable—a Ray's Tavern hamburger. The shirt off one's back is not too much to give. For at Ray's, when it comes to providing service, quality food, and good times, the staff also gives the shirts off their backs.

SPECIALTY SHOPPING

MOKI TRADING POST
17 East Main Street
P. O. Box 65
Green River, Utah 84525
Tel: (435) 564-3522
Hrs: Open Daily
April 1 - October 31
8:00 a.m. - 6:00 p.m.
Closed November 1 - March 31
Visa and MasterCard are accepted.

Moki Trading Post is the fulfillment of a lifelong dream for entrepreneurs, Homer and Verdella Davis, long-time residents of Green River, Utah. Homer and Verdella not only have a great love for their home town, they also are enamored with the history of Southeastern Utah and its ancient people. The Anasazis, for which Moki is a slang term, inhabited this portion of the state nearly 1000 years ago. So, when Homer's and Verdella's dream of opening an Indian arts and crafts gift shop finally became reality, Moki Trading Post seemed a likely name.

When a business is the realization of a long-time dream, there is something very special that accompanies it. Perhaps that is why the Davis's have so many repeat customers, and why numerous first-time shoppers have been directed to stop at Moki Trading Post when they visit Green River.

Moki Trading Post is not just a gift shop, although one will never find a finer selection of genuine Native American artifacts. Moki Trading Post is like an institution of higher education, with Homer and Verdella the docents. Moki Trading Post is also comparable to a museum with Homer and Verdella as the curators.

Moki Trading Post carries a wide assortment of artifacts that includes pottery, jewelry, Kachina dolls, paintings, wood, stone, and horn carvings, and a variety of handicrafts such as rugs, moccasins, weapons, and ceremonial items.

Homer and Verdella founded Moki Trading Post in 1990. Since that time they have spent a great deal of time on the Southwest Indian Reservations with the Navajo, Hopi, Zuni, Laguna, Acoma, Papago, Ute, and Apache. They have developed a long standing relationship with these Native American tribes that is based on mutual respect and trust. To those that shop at Moki Trading Post, that relationship often means being able to purchase items they cannot find at other gift shops. It also means a more personalized understanding of the gifts being purchased.

By the time one leaves Moki Trading Post, visitors know how to tell the difference between Hopi, Zuni, and Navajo jewelry. They are fascinated with the story of why Native Americans always leave a small imperfection in their craftsmanship. Visitors to Moki Trading Post can spot the incredible beadwork doll creations of the Zunis, as compared to beadwork dolls of other tribes. They also know and understand why a Navajo rug, whatever the size or price, is an object of increasing value. They have a greater appreciation for the Fetish and the meaning of each of the animals the Native Americans use in creating them.

Those who visit Moki Trading Post know that the Hopi are noted for their exquisitely detailed silver jewelry, most of which is double layered and without stones. The Hopi are also known for their hand-carved wooden Kachina dolls. They know that the Zuni's silver inlaid jewelry, using mother of pearl, black onyx, turquoise, and coral, is without equal. In addition, Zuni needlepoint and beadwork are priceless. They also know that the Navajo receive acclaim for their silver and turquoise jewelry, their story teller dolls, and their painted pottery.

The Lagunas and the Acomas are best known for their pottery. The Utes, also touted for their pottery, are one of the few tribes who glaze their work both inside and out. The Papago are basket weavers, and the Apaches are specifically known for their ceremonial peace pipes and rattles.

There are many other gifts to be found at Moki Trading Post, including a selection of Leaning Tree cards and copies of paintings, squash blossoms, silver belt buckles, bolo ties, mini-pottery, jewel boxes, sandstone pictures, and modern-day petroglyphs. The Trading Post also carries a selection of gifts indigenous to the area that are not made by Native Americans.

When it comes to quality merchandise and incomparable service, there is only one Moki Trading Post.

MOAB

Located on U.S. Highway 191 near the entrances to Arches and Canyonlands National Parks, Moab is known as the "Gateway to Southeastern Utah." This city of slightly over 4,000 burgeons to triple its size from early spring to late fall. This town is like a magnet for outdoor enthusiasts. Whitewater rafters come to navigate the Colorado and Green Rivers; Cyclists flock here for world class mountain biking; four-wheelers arrive to conquer the rugged terrain of Canyonlands National Park and, during the winter months, Nordic skiers arrive for the back country skiing in the LaSal Mountains.

Built on the site of a Pueblo Indian Village that dated from the 11th to the 12th centuries, the town of Moab was first settled by Mormon missionaries in 1855. Originally called the Elk Mountain Mission, the settlement was abandoned three months after its founding when Ute Indians attacked and killed three of the settlers. The site was used sporadically over the next 30 years by trappers, prospectors and cattle ranchers until 1876, when a permanent settlement was established.

The town was given the name Moab in 1880 by William A. Pierce. The surrounding terrain reminded him of the Biblical land of Moab, which lies east of the River Jordan and the Dead Sea.

Moab, in its infancy, was considered by many to be the "roughest, toughest town in Utah." It's treacherous and deserted canyons offered recluse to the west's most notorious outlaws as they hid from bounty hunters and waited for their trail to cool.

Moab, the city and its people, have eked an existence as changing as the eroding desert that surrounds it. Moab has served as a fruit growing center with irrigation water pumped from the Colorado River. It was a dock for the short-lived steam-powered Colorado River paddle boats. It's mosaic country side provided the perfect setting for many western movies and, in the 1950's, it was the nation's most lucrative uranium boom town.

Many may not remember Charlie Steen, but he is a legend around Moab. In 1952 Charlie drilled in one of his mining claims, Mi Vida, and discovered the world's richest uranium deposit—worth $60 million dollars. Charlie built an enormous home on the cliff's overlooking Moab with windows across the front on three levels that faced the sunset. Visitors may dine in Charlie's mansion. Mi Vida is now a fine dining restaurant, Sunset Grill (see related story).

Today, Moab has become one of the Southwest's most popular vacation destinations. Beautifully ensconced near the banks of the Colorado River, Moab is the embarking point for recreational adventures of every kind. Moab is home to the *Dan O'Laurie* museum, the Moab Golf Course, and several guest ranches. During the summer months, Warner Lake in the Manti-LaSal Mountains is great for fishing. During winter months the Manti-LaSal National Forest is an ideal location for snowmobiling and for hut to hut Nordic skiing. Moab, with scenery as western as it gets, was discovered by John Wayne who made several of his classic movies here. More recently, "Geronimo" and "City Slickers II" were filmed here. Thelma and Louise took their final plunge into the Colorado River from the Shafer Trail under Dead Horse Point near Moab. Moab, the town that has something to offer everyone, is also becoming increasingly popular as a retirement spot.

MOAB ADVENTURES

Moab is famous for its **river running adventures**, a thought with a "thrills, spills, and chills" connotation. But both the Green and Colorado Rivers, in addition to offering the most magnificent of whitewater rafting, also offer calm water floats.

On the Green River, the float from the town of Green River to Ruby Ranch is a one or two day trip of 23 miles. The Ruby Ranch to Mineral Bottom is a two to three day trip that covers a 45-mile stretch of river through **Labyrinth Canyon**, so-named by the Powell expedition for its twisting course and massive cliffs. This stretch is particularly popular for canoeists. From Mineral Bottom one can run the river through **Stillwater Canyon** with its high rocky walls and serrated crags and pinnacles to the confluence of the Green and Colorado Rivers, a trip that takes three to four days. Many of these trips can be navigated on one's own with raft, canoe, or kayak, all of which are available for rent in Moab. Several of the trips, however, require jet boat transportation back to Moab. **To make any river rafting experience complete, commercial river trips are often the best option.**

Whitewater rafting on the Green River is at its best on the four to seven day trek through **Desolation Canyon**, Utah's deepest, and **Gray Canyon**. There are 67 rapids on this 75 to 84-mile journey, depending on the take-out point. The Green River trip for those with only one or two days begins just north of Green River City and runs from **Nefertiti Rapid** to **Swasey's Rapid** covering a series of 7 total rapids. The **Hittle Bottom** to **Take-Out Beach** section of the Colorado is 13 miles, has six rapids, and is a stretch of river that can easily be navigated by those who can only spend a day or overnight on the river.

The Colorado River offers several whitewater rafting experiences. **Westwater Canyon**, northeast of Moab, is a popular choice for one or two-day adventures. There are 11 rapids with the 17-mile stretch of river flowing through a deep inner gorge of Pre-Cambrian black rock backed by 1,000 foot high canyon walls.

Twenty-six rapids and some of the most beautiful country available greet river runners on the most popular of all Southeastern Utah river rafting experiences. This is the 112-mile trip that begins in Moab with an easy float and ends at Hite Marina on Lake Powell. This is **Cataract Canyon**.

This spectacular chasm, with its surrounding cliffs and canyons, is a part of Canyonlands National Park. Bates Wilson, who promoted the park as a national treasure in 1964, summed up the canyons when he said: "No words, nor even pictures, adequately convey the wonder and sense of mystery that gave it dimension and meaning. Harsh and fragile, stark and beautiful, you have to see it to believe it. And even then you may go away with the awesome feeling that its secrets have escaped you, and no matter where you go, its charm will forever tug on you like a magnet."

When it comes to rafting the river, white water enthusiasts agree that the Snake and the Salmon Rivers in the Northwest, the American River in California, the Rio Grande in the Southwest, and the lower Colorado all have their share of thrills and spills, but they all pale in comparison when pitted against the upper Colorado—Cataract Canyon—during the months of May and June.

The Rocky Mountains of Utah are already internationally known for their "greatest snow on earth" to skiing enthusiasts. But when the snow begins to melt, the "greatest snow on earth" becomes the means for the greatest rapids on earth in the upper Colorado. Torrents of streams cascade down the countless washes and tributaries of the Colorado River. At the Confluence, the added thousands of cubic feet of water per second from the Green River, brings the tranquil but rapidly moving river to a raging maelstrom. White-water river rafters from all over the world converge on this out-of-the-way corner of Southeast Utah during the months of May and June to experience the rafting adventure of a lifetime.

Canyonlands is a National Park, and river rafting through Cataract requires a National Park Service permit. River-running access through Cataract is limited to approximately 10,000 people per year who can make the run. Since Cataract is considered the white-water rafting experience of a lifetime, most clamor to be among those making the run in May and June.

During July, August, and September, the rapids are just big rolling fun waves, ideal for those who have not as yet mastered the thrills and spills of white-water rafting.

Temperatures in the canyons during May, June, and September are middle to high 90's during the day and high 60's to middle 70's during the night. In July and August high 90's and low 100's are common. Evenings are in the 70's and low 80's. Brief showers are very common, so those visiting the area are expressly admonished to bring their rain gear. Because Moab and its surrounding canyon lands have extremely dry climate, the heat is not hot and humid. Besides, when running the rivers, the best part about being too hot is jumping into the river to cool off.

The Canyonlands area, of which Cataract Canyon is a part, is a mystery to geologists. They can only speculate that anciently seven seas covered the terrain, then receded over the millenniums, creating the incredible rock formations they left behind. Mystery or not, Cataract is a geologist's utopia. Three hundred million years of rock history are visible in a single glance. The river has sliced through the rock over eons of time and left it totally exposed for all—expert and novice alike—to view and to marvel at.

Along the Colorado River there are numerous 700 to 1,500 year old Indian sites, including granaries tucked under ledges in the canyon walls above the river. These canyons were the home of the Anasazi and Fremont Indian cultures, whom archaeologists believe were the ancestors of the modern day Hopi, Paiute, Havasupai, and Hualapai Indians.

The Anasazi mysteriously disappeared from this area about 700 years ago. Though no one knows for sure, tree-ring readings hint that there was a 24-year dry spell which may have been responsible for the exodus of the Anasazi from this area. Hundreds of years after their disappearance, the white man came. To them the rugged terrain of these canyons created a virtual "no-man's land." But not to explorer, John Wesley Powell.

The Colorado was first successfully navigated by Powell, a one-armed Civil War hero, in 1869. Powell had paddled down the Mississippi, but he had never been on any of the whitewater rivers. Nevertheless, against great odds and with his penchant for adventure, he took on the Green and Colorado rivers all the way to the San Juan. Although there were no river-running casualties, three deserters did not fair so well. They encountered unfriendly Indians and met their demise.

In 1960, the Glen Canyon Dam was built, stopping the river where it flows into Lake Powell, and making it impossible for anyone to traverse the entire river as Powell did. But running the rapids of Cataract Canyon, with any of the qualified Green River and Moab outfitters listed in this book, gives adventurers an inkling of what it might have been like for Powell.

The terrain that took millions of years of receding water, wind, and river to create, today are little changed from the time of Powell's adventure. Rust-red limestone and sandstone walls rise majestically 2,000 feet from river bottom to wide-open, pollution-free azure skies But, since Powell and his group never contended with the stresses of city and corporate life, the topography today is perhaps even more appreciated.

Mountain Biking in Moab has become world famous. In fact there are many who would call Moab the mountain biking capitol of the world. Most famous of the many diversified trails is **Slickrock Bike Trail**. From downtown Moab, cyclists can easily pedal the four miles to the Slickrock trailhead. From the trailhead though, the 11-mile trail is nothing short of technically demanding. Located in the **Sand Flats Recreation Area**, the trail loops through a six-square mile expanse of undulating petrified sand dune-like terrain. According to cyclists, this is the most incredible natural riding experience one can encounter. To make the ride even more magnificent, the beauty that surrounds the trail is almost as exhilarating and uplifting as the ride.

Besides the Slickrock Trail, many of the world's best known fat-tire trails are also located in the Moab area. Because of its incredible fat tire trails—**White Rim, Poison Spider, Porcupine Rim, Hurrah Pass, Kokopelli,** and **Gemini Bridges**—Moab is the annual host to two spectacular mountain biking events. **Moab Rocks** is held in late March and **Canyonlands Fat Tire Festival** in late October.

Although **Arches National Park** is closed to bikers as far as the trails are concerned, cyclists are welcome off the park's roads. The paved road through the park is 17 miles of sandstone arches, petrified sand dunes, and petroglyph rock art, with the LaSal mountains forming a magnificent natural backdrop. The route is rated for advanced cyclists because of some pretty tough hills, but many of the sections are ideal for riding at all levels.

The rugged terrain of Canyonlands National Park is an irresistible challenge to mountain biking enthusiasts. The White Rim Trail tours 110 miles of the northern part, winding 1,100 to 1,500 feet below the Island in the Sky Mesa and up to 1,000 feet above the Colorado and Green Rivers. A back country permit is required for this two to four-day biking trip. Cyclists in the know recommend the back-up support of a four-wheel drive vehicle. Permits are limited and spring and fall dates fill up fast.

Four-Wheel Driving is at a premium in the Moab area, with many of the maintained and primitive roads a remnant of Grand County's prospecting and mining days. Although there are four-wheel drive roads in both Arches and Canyonlands National Parks, it is the seemingly limitless back roads of Canyonlands that draw four wheelers to Moab like a magnet. Best known trails include craggy **Elephant Hill** in Canyonlands Needles District and **White Rim Road** in Island in the Sky District, with its majestic views of Monument Basin. As its name implies, the Maze District offers infinite opportunities for exploration.

The **Moab Rim Trail,** which is rated difficult, offers a seven mile vista of Moab, the Colorado River, Spanish Valley and the LaSal Mountains. **Poison Spider Mesa**, another popular trail, cuts across a mesa north of the Colorado River and west of Moab. The trail is profuse with slickrock terrain, is rated moderate, and offers unobstructed views of the LaSal Mountains and **Behind the Rocks Wilderness Study** area.

Skirting the highway that leads to Canyonlands National Park is the 15-mile **Monitor and Merrimac Trail** loop, named after two famous Civil War maritime vessels. The loop trail traverses generously colored canyons and stretches of mesa interrupted by cliffs and towers before it reaches the buttes.

Chicken Corners Trail follows the Colorado River and Kane Creek Canyon before climbing to Hurrah Pass and descending to the benches carved by the Colorado River long ago. The 22-mile one-way trail ends high above the river almost diagonally from Dead Horse Point State Park.

The **Gemini Bridges Trail** is an access road to several other trails, but ends at the double arch for which the trail was named. The 14-mile trail is between U.S. 191 and U-313.

Hiking and backpacking in Southeastern Utah is considered by many the only way to explore this "grand" country. Indeed, the opportunities for doing so are almost limitless. A sample of these trails includes **Hunters Canyon** off **Kane Creek Canyon Road**, **Delicate Arch** in **Arches National Park**, the hike to **Morning Glory Bridge** from **Negro Bill Canyon** on **Colorado River Scenic Byway 128**, and the **Potash Overlook Trail** and **Corona** and **Bow Tie Arch** trails that take off from **Potash Scenic Byway 279**. All of these trails have been briefly outlined in the Adventures section of Grand County. Detailed maps on hiking and backpacking, mountain biking, and four-wheel driving trails, as well as information on river running may be picked up at the Moab Information Center.

Rodeos and horseback trail rides are also big news in Moab. There are several companies in town that offer trail rides as a one-hour to a full-day activity, or as part of a camping experience.

MOAB ATTRACTIONS & ACTIVITIES

Probably the most important attraction in Moab is the *Spanish Trails Arena*, an event center that hosts weekly rodeos 26 weeks of the year and a whole lot more. In June, the arena is home to the *Butch Cassidy Days PRCA Rodeo*. The arena also plays host to the *Tour of Canyonlands Mountain Bike Race*, trade shows, horse shows, concerts, festivals, and even Hollywood, who used the indoor arena for "City Slickers II." BMX bicycle races are held on this certified course as well as private parties and conventions.

The *Dan O'Laurie Museum*, located at 118 East Center Street, offers a variety of exhibits dealing with the history, geology and economy of the area. Featured exhibits include several unusual mineral and gemstone specimens, a mining display, an outstanding display of Native American artifacts, and exhibition of local art and photography. There is no fee.

Located at the corners of Main and Center Streets, the Moab Information Center offers data on recreational opportunities and visitor services throughout southeast Utah. The center, a multi-agency facility, has interpretative displays, videos and written materials featuring public lands, hotels, restaurants, tour operators, and other services valuable to travelers. Travelers can also obtain weather and road information as well as details of upcoming special events. Hours vary according to the season, but the Center is open daily except for Thanksgiving and Christmas Day.

Moab has a variety of historic homes and buildings. A walking tour of the older section of the town offers a close-up view of over twenty historic structures. Included are the first *Moab LDS Church*, constructed in 1888, and the *Tom Trout House*, built in 1900 by an early cowboy and rancher.

MOAB EVENTS

January is the statewide month for Utah Winter Games (800-959-8824).

March is the month in Moab when the Canyonlands Half Marathon, a five-mile race, is held (435-259-7814 or 259-5934).

March or April, depending on how Easter falls, is the month for the Easter Jeep Safari (435-259-7625). Also held the last part of April is the Moab Rod Benders Car Show (435-259-8942). Spring horse races and the Canyonlands Quarter Horse Show are held at the Spanish Trails Arena. The Moab Rocks Cannondale Bike Races are also held here.

May begins each year in both Moab and Green River with the Green River/Moab Friendship Cruise (435-564-3448). The Moab Arts Festival, a big event in Moab, is held during the last half of May (435-259-8431).

June is the biggest month of the year in Moab for rodeo aficionados. The city's annual Butch Cassidy Days are highlighted with a three-day PRCA rodeo (1-800-635-6622).

July is the month for statewide Independence Day celebrations and Pioneer Days Celebrations (around July 24), an event that is highlighted with a river parade called "Anything That Floats" (435-259-6666).

August features the statewide county fair, the Dead Horse Point Square Dance at Dead Horse Point State Park (435-259-5637), and the Red Rock Four-Wheelers Labor Day Campout, which extends over the Labor Day weekend (435-259-ROCK).

September features the Moab Music Festival, a highly publicized and unique event that takes place somewhere along the Colorado River (435-259-8431).

October is a month for three big events in Moab. Held in Moab now for close to 40 years is the annual Red Rock Gem and Mineral Show (435-259-5904). The Canyonlands Fat Tire Festival draws mountain bikers from all around the world. (435-259-8825.) Last but not least is the Kokopelli Trail Super Marathon. (1-800-635-6622.)

December features the Winter Sun 10K Run. (1-800-635-6622.)

ACCOMMODATIONS

RED STONE INN
535 South Main Street
Moab, Utah 84532
Tel: (435) 259-3500
       (800) 772-1972
FAX: (435) 259-2717
Web Site:
www.moabutah.com/redstoneinn/
Hrs:
Front desk: 6:30 a.m. - 11:00 p.m.
24-hour cancellation policy
Off-Season: November - mid-February

Visa, MasterCard, American Express, and Discover are accepted.
Reservations are recommended.

Built in 1993, Red Stone Inn, one of Moab's newest motels, is "Moab's Best Deal," and, when booking accommodations during the summer months, "Moab's best deal" just got better. Red Stone Inn and King World Water Park have joined forces to offer Red Stone Inn guests an exclusive water park admittance rate that is unparalleled in the area.

Right from its onset Red Stone Inn did its homework, determining customer likes and dislikes. Dislikes were discarded and the "likes" were readily adopted. Whether visiting Moab as a hiker, biker, river rafter, cowboy, or as part of the crew for a film production, Red Stone Inn gets a "thumbs up."

Each of the 50 Triple-A rated rooms features a kitchenette, cable TV with HBO, and telephone with local calls free. Red Stone Inn is one of the few accommodations where bikers are allowed to take their bikes into their rooms. Bikers must register their bikes at the front desk.

The rustic decor offers knotty pine walls and natural pine log furniture, with pine armoire in the double-bed rooms. Bedrooms with single beds offer a modified closet. Guests with pets are welcome in the four guest rooms where the beautiful Spanish ceramic tile of the hallways is carried out. Pets must be registered at the front desk.

The exterior of Red Stone Inn blends itself into the terrain, becoming a part of Moab's rustic pine wood and red rock topography. The knotty pine motel and its welcoming sign are enhanced by red rock flower beds.

On-premise amenities include a picnic patio with gas barbecue, and guest laundry facilities. Red Stone Inn's mid-town location places guests within easy walking distance to shops, theater, and tennis court. The Inn's brochure calendars major local events for the entire year.

The fact that Moab and its surrounding territory is an ideal movie location is no secret to the seasoned Moab visitor, or to Hollywood film crews. And it's no secret to registering guests that Red Stone Inn has become a favorite domicile for visiting film crews. The lobby is adorned with marquee posters from such movies as Geronimo, City Slickers II, Lightning Jack, Elephant Man II, Larger than Life, and Pontiac Moon, all of which were filmed in Moab. The film crews, of course, were accommodated at Red Stone Inn.

Moab loves its cowboys, the screen version of which brought the area fame and acclaim as Hollywood's western frontier. Today Moab is equally well-known for its modern day cowboys, many of whom compete in Moab's Old Spanish Trail indoor arena. Red Stone Inn is a major supporter of these USTRC competitions.

Red Stone Inn reminds Moab visitors that the National Parks which surround Moab—Canyonlands and Arches—are open year-around, 24-hours a day, and that hiking and biking in wintertime are absolutely incredible. In addition, the Manti LaSal mountains offer some of the state's most challenging and exhilarating cross country skiing.

Accommodations during off-season are even more affordable, with weekly and monthly rates available.

ADVENTURE / TOURS

CANYONLANDS FIELD INSTITUTE
1320 South Highway 191
P. O. Box 68
Moab, Utah 84532
Tel:	(435) 259-7750
	(800) 860-5262
FAX:	(435) 259-2335
Web site: www.canyonlandsfieldinst.org
E-Mail:	cfinfo@canyonlandsfieldinst.org.
Hrs:
Monday - Friday		8:00 a.m. - 5:00 p.m.
Visa and MasterCard are accepted.
Reservations are required.

It is one thing to run the whitewater rapids of the Colorado and Green rivers for thrills and chills, but when that same opportunity is presented along with a truly educational experience, memories linger on, and the world's natural environment is protected.

Since its inception, Canyonlands Field Institute (CFI), a non-profit organization, has been offering educational programs for children and adults. Their mission statement, carried out in their various programs, is: *To promote understanding, appreciation, and stewardship of the natural environment and cultural heritage of the Colorado Plateau.*

Among programs offered by CFI is an Outdoor Science School with trips geared to children on elementary, middle school, and high school levels. These land and river-based programs are for school groups and are offered from March through November. The trips offer hands-on activities and instructional objectives with regard to history, ecology, and geology of the Colorado Plateau. Students who participate in the Outdoor Science School program can also experience the thrills of the river. They leave their outdoor classrooms better prepared to take part in decision-making that affects the future of the Colorado Plateau and the Earth as a whole. CFI will also customize college-level outdoor science schools for land or river.

CFI offers a Multi-Day Explorer Camp for youth 13-18, from the last part of June through the last of July. The "Whitewater Academy for Teens," which includes a three-day river trip, is for ages 13-18. The camp is designed for beginning teen boaters and offers a comprehensive introduction to river-running. Teens learn how to "read" the river. They learn rowing and paddling techniques for whitewater rafting, equipment rigging, safety and rescue issues, and river and desert ecology. This hands-on course teaches the maneuvering of rafts on calm water and on small rapids. It teaches youth the techniques of tying knots and how to tie down equipment with ropes and straps. They learn framing and loading methods, self-rescue boating and swimming practices, and minimum-impact camping procedures. Maximum is 20 participants.

Open enrollment river trips are offered by CFI from March through mid-October. The one-day "Eagle Float" gives participants the opportunity to see a world rarely witnessed—wintering bald and golden eagles and flocks of waterfowl. It also gives rafters the opportunity to participate in an ongoing resource agency raptor study. The number and variety of birds counted are turned in annually to the agency.

Other trips offered are the "Women: Wild by Nature", an inflatable kayak-self-support trip on the Dolores where women are truly on their own; the "Women and Mother Earth" trip on the lower San Juan River, which focuses on ways women can deepen their relationship with Earth and care for natural places; and the "Women in the Wilderness" canoe trip on the Green River. All of the open enrollment river trips teach how to read the river, rig and paddle an inflatable kayak or canoe, and gives invaluable insights into natural, cultural and geological history of this riparian country.

Moab area day trips offered are the "Colorado River Daily" by raft or canoe; "Arches National Park" van tour; "LaSal Mountains" van or bike tour; and a van or bike tour of "Rock Art of the Moab Area."

CFI offers a series of special multi-day hiking trips and multi-day river trips, which require a minimum of three months notice and a minimum of eight participants. "Navajo Mountain/Rainbow Trail" is a five-day/four-night spring hiking trip to Rainbow Bridge. The CFI naturalist guide is accompanied by Navajo guides. Navajo culture, geology, and wildflower appreciation, as well as moderately difficult hiking, tent camping and a boat trip on Lake Powell are offered to groups of eight to 12 participants, ages 12 and older. A three-day/four-night trip offered in spring and fall to groups of eight to 12, age eight and older, is "Cedar Mesa Archaeology." This group trip offers moderately strenuous hikes, and covers Road Canyon with its fine rock art and ruin sites.

Multi-day river trips include two San Juan River excursions. The first is three-days/two-nights and travels the upper canyon from Bluff, Utah to Mexican Hat. In addition to leisurely floating, the group learns about Anasazi rock art and ruins, fossils, and desert wildlife. The second trip covers both the upper and lower canyons of the San Juan river. The lower San Juan, known as the "Goosenecks," offers side canyon hikes. Both trips are for groups of eight or more with a maximum of 25 participants, eight-years and older.

Three multi-day trips are offered on the Dolores River. The "Ponderosa Gorge" three-day/two-night trip offers challenging, rocky rapids through a steep, narrow red rock canyon that is lush with pine and fir trees. "Stateline," also three-days/two-nights, offers smaller rapids, pioneer cabins, Indian rock art, mining history and classic side canyon hikes. Both are for groups of eight or more with a maximum of 25 participants, 12-years and older. "Slickrock Canyon" is five-days/four-nights, is for a maximum of 13, age eight and older, and offers moderate rapids. In addition to the thrills of running the rapids, this trip offers sheer sandstone walls, lush side canyon hikes with pools, and Desert Archaic, Anasazi, and Ute Indian rock art. It can be combined with the upper stretch of the Dolores for a seven-day trip.

CFI, in cooperation with Utah State University, also offers a Colorado Plateau Graduate Residency in Environmental Education. This graduate study program is offered each year from September through August.

A three-day Desert Writers Workshop, held annually in early November, offers a maximum of 33 participants the opportunity to work with guest author-instructors in a contemplative setting, ideal for creative writing. The workshop is held at historic Pack Creek Ranch and offers workshops in poetry, non-fiction and fiction. Fee includes lodging, meals, instruction, and optional afternoon hikes. Two graduate-quarter credits in English are available.

Several trips are offered through Elderhostel, an international non-profit organization that offers educational adventures for older adults who are seeking expanded horizons and new challenges. CFI is the active host and its programs are for active elders. Typical programs are for five to six nights. They include meals, accommodations, guide services and academic instruction and activities. On the river trips, participants help with camp cooking and other chores.

Many of the guides on river expedition and adventure tour companies in the area received their training through CFI. Throughout the year CFI offers open enrollment Professional Guide Training Programs. Those who love the outdoors, the desert, and the river—or who are thinking of becoming a guide—should learn firsthand from the experts at CFI. In the various courses prospective guides can learn about the area's geography, geology, ecology, prehistory, history, and lands management and recommended minimum impact methods. They can learn river skills, river rescue, receive EMT certification, and certify in the American Red Cross Emergency Response program. Essentially they can learn all that is needed to become a superlative guide on land or on the river.

Experiencing Southeastern Utah as a desert or river-running adventure is exceptional under any circumstances. But Canyonlands Field Institute has the adept and highly trained personnel necessary to offer extraordinary opportunities for experiencing the land and the river in creative, educational, and venturesome ways. CFI creates the memories that in turn create aware, concerned, and actively involved citizens.

DID YOU KNOW?

---that a marker on U.S. 50, just east of Green River, pays tribute to William H. Ashley, who led the first organized fur trapping in these mountains. The group of 100 fur trappers included Jim Bridger and Etienne Provost. Called Ashley's "Mountain Men," they extensively explored the area, opened up the West, and wrote a history of the Rocky Mountains. Because of their intensive trapping and exploration in this area, they stopped the British from further pursuing their fur interests, and thus preserved this vast wonderland for the United States of America.

MOAB ADVENTURE OUTFITTERS
650 North Main Suite 'B'
Moab, Utah 84532
Tel: (435) 259-2725
        (800) 929-8078
FAX: (435) 259-2725
E-mail: KevinChase @sisna.com
Hrs:
Open Daily   9:00 a.m. - 8:00 p.m.
Closed Christmas day
Visa, MasterCard, American Express
and Discover are accepted.
Reservations are recommended.

    In all the world there is probably not a rock climbing store that is better provisioned than is Moab Adventure Outfitters, a company that has been providing climbers with gear and up-to-date beta for more than five years. But the store is not what sets Moab Adventure Outfitters apart from other rock climbing companies in the world. That which distinguishes Moab Adventure Outfitters from other such companies is the expertise that Kevin Chase and his cadre of world renown sports guides bring to the business of scaling a mountain wall.

    Moab is an area that has come into its own in the last few years as more and more individuals seek respite through wilderness experiences. Moab is one of the most magnificent places on earth to learn the basic skills of rock climbing. The beauty of the red sandstone cliffs, as well as the challenge of scaling these canyon walls, beckons climbers of all skill levels.

    For those who have only dreamed of scaling a mountain wall, Moab Adventure Outfitters offers newcomers to the sport the opportunity to climb with the best. Each guide has his or her own unique qualifications, but all teach in a fun and nonpressured atmosphere. Kevin and his 12 associate world-class guides have been climbing internationally for years. But most have made scaling the desert towers their specialty, and all have climbed some of the hardest routes in the desert.

    Desert towers offer unique experiences to climbers, as well as a great feeling of accomplishment once one has scaled them. Moab is the capital of the world in spires, offering more than anywhere else on earth, and the views from these isolated desert towers are breathtaking and exhilarating.

    Beginner classes at Moab Adventure Outfitters are tailored to each individual's need. Beginners may choose a group environment or personal instruction. Each class focuses on fun and adventure while teaching belaying, rappelling, crack techniques, face climbing, and, above all, safety.

    Intermediate and Advanced lessons are geared to climbers who wish to expand their knowledge or who feel a refresher course is in order. As with the Beginner lessons, climbs are customized to the needs of each client. Items covered during the on-site classes are top rope anchors, gear and placements, learning to lead climb, and route finding.

    In addition to these classes, Moab Adventure Outfitters offers a Rappelling class and a Canyoneering Class--a lot of hiking with rock climbing thrown in for good measure.

    Rock climbing is great in Moab, no matter what the season. During summer months, getting an early start helps climbers avoid the intense summer heat. But even when it is really warm, Moab's dry, desert weather is never hot and humid. During the winter, adventurers climb with the sun and desert temperatures can be as pleasant as 65 degrees.

Moab Adventure Outfitters offers half-day and full-day classes with one-on-one private instruction or group classes. Never will there be more than four students to a guide. Rates for tower climbs depend on the tower involved and the size of the group.

Southeastern Utah, inhabited nearly 1,000 years ago by the Anasazi Indians, is a land rich in history. While adventurers are learning to climb, Moab Adventure Outfitters' guides share stories of the land as well as geological facts.

Whether in Moab to rock climb or for some other outdoor sport, Moab Adventure Outfitters is still the shop of choice. They are the best place in town to buy shorts, sandals, shoes, T-shirts, socks, backpacks, compasses, water bottles, sunglasses, or any other general outdoor need. But when it comes to rock climbing paraphernalia, there is no other store. And even though, in Moab, that is literally the truth, the stock and the service goes far beyond having a monopoly. Moab Adventure Outfitters doesn't have to stock over 300 camming devices, but they do, and it is the largest selection in the world. Moab Adventure Outfitters not only stock every piton available on the market, but a dozen each of every size. The store stocks a full spectrum of carabiners, from a DMM Double Mamba to the Black Diamond Hotwire and everything else in between.

When it comes to their customers, Moab Adventure Outfitters has a basic rule—they don't like climbing with inferior equipment, so why would they sell it? They don't. If the device isn't quality and if it isn't safe, it won't be sold at Moab Adventure Outfitters.

That same basic rule applies to Moab Adventure Outfitters classes and climbing expeditions. As Kevin says in his book, *Wall Street*, "It is the climbers responsibility to seek qualified instruction and then to climb within their own limits." Moab Adventure Outfitters offers guides with impeccable qualifications—guides who always put safety first. For the novice and the experienced, Moab Adventure Outfitters is the right choice.

NAVTEC EXPEDITIONS
321 North Main Street
P. O. Box 1267
Moab, Utah 84532
Tel: (435) 259-7983
           (800) 833-1278
FAX: (435) 259-5823
E-Mail NAVTEC @ SISNA.COM
Hrs:
Shoulder Season: Mid March - April & Labor Day Weekend - Mid-October
Monday - Friday   8:00 a.m. - 600 p.m.
Summer   May - Labor Day Weekend
Open Daily   8:00 a.m. - 9:00 p.m.
Mid October - Mid March   Call about Baja trips
Personal Checks, Visa, MasterCard, American Express, and Discover are accepted.
Reservations are required on all multi-day trips.

NAVTEC Expeditions, owned and operated by John and Chris Williams, is the continuation and fulfillment of a dream of sharing begun back in 1896 by John's grandfather, Dr. John Washington Williams.

In 1896 Dr. Williams entered the Moab valley on horseback, his goal to determine whether or not he would become Grand County's first doctor. His route took him through the massive red rock formations now known as Arches National Park. "Doc" Williams, who lived to the age of 103, fell in love with the terrain and did indeed become Moab's first physician. He took a leading role in the establishment of Arches National Park, a role that later earned him the title of "Father of the Arches."(See related story on Arches National Park). That role was foreshadowed by a tremendous love for the country surrounding Moab, and a great desire to share it.

Doc's son Mitch and his wife Mary, John's parents, have been exploring the rivers and canyons of the Colorado Plateau by foot, jeep, raft and aircraft all their lives. John, whose family has been in the valley for over 100 years, was raised in the Canyonlands and taught to love and appreciate the beautiful country that surrounds his hometown.

Today, John and Chris continue to carry on that tradition of exploration and adventure. Through NAVTEC Expeditions they are able to help the masses enjoy the country that Doc Williams so loved.

Moab is located in the center of some of the most rugged country in the world. The Colorado River cuts deep canyons into country that is pristine and ancient—a place of wild and raw-boned beauty that deserves to be seen from the inside out. With their vast landscape of sandstone and rock, Canyonlands and the canyons of the Colorado Plateau are national treasures.

It is to this national treasure that NAVTEC Expeditions takes its guests. Unlike the exploratory trips of Captain John Wesley Powell, toady's trips down the Green and Colorado rivers are pleasurable vacations where guests can absorb, enjoy, and explore the natural world. These are places where there are no phones and where a ride through the rapids and an extraordinary sunset are the exhilarating events of the day.

NAVTEC Expeditions, through its affiliate company, Williams Whitewater Marine, has developed the first whitewater river version of the RIB (rigid inflatable boat). The RIB is the clear choice of the U. S. Coast Guard, the U. S. Navy, and many other rescue organizations around the world. The RIB is virtually unsinkable, extremely buoyant and stable, allowing navigation in rough weather with confidence. The motorized Whitewater RIBs are more fun to ride in, they travel faster on calm water sections of the river and Lake Powell, and carry only four or five passengers per boat, as compared to the 10 or more per boat carried by the larger boats of other companies. Fewer passengers means more personalized attention. The Whitewater RIB is the most maneuverable craft on the Colorado River. Its responsiveness and smaller design also make for a much more exciting ride in the rapids. NAVTEC's state-of-the-art Whitewater RIB is used on many of their one, two, and three-day Cataract Canyon trips.

NAVTEC trips are suitable for all ages and abilities, and are diversified enough to suit every taste and budget. For those who seek the thrills of wild rapids, Cataract Canyon has some of the biggest whitewater in the United States during the spring run-off months of May and June. After July the water levels drop, producing smaller but still thrilling rapids. NAVTEC runs rapids of varying magnitude, offering guests the opportunity to experience all that the mighty Colorado has to offer.

The three days/two nights trip offers calm waters the first day so that guests can leisurely experience the dramatic canyons of Canyonlands National Park. There is time for hiking, swimming and floating quietly in the river. Guides take guests on short walks to pre-historic Anasazi Indian dwelling sites and to explore beautiful side canyons. The RIB drifts complacently between majestic Dead Horse Point and past the Confluence where the Green River merges with the Colorado. Nights are spent relaxing around a campfire, eating delicious Dutch oven meals, camping on gorgeous white sand beaches, and falling asleep to the soothing sound of the river. For those who think Dutch oven cooking is rustic and ordinary, prepare to be surprised.

Succeeding days of the Cataract Canyon trip are spent navigating the rapids of such historic whitewater names as Hell to Pay, Mile Long and the three Big Drops. Days are also spent relishing the spray of the Colorado River in one's face, and surfing a wave and playing about in the currents and eddies. Following the canyon rapids the RIB enters the quiet upper waters of Lake Powell. A short and relaxing cruise across the lake to Hite Marina brings guests to the end of their river expedition, but not necessarily to the end of their Canyon experience. Included in the price of the Cataract Canyon package is a scenic Redtail Aviation flight over the river and Canyonlands, returning adventurers to Moab. But guests are also invited at this point to combine their river vacation with a two-nights jeep trip into the spectacular San Rafael Swell country.

In addition to the RIB Whitewater Cataract Canyon Trip, NAVTEC also offers a five-days/four nights oar-powered Cataract Canyon expedition. The first 50 miles are on calm water through a geologic display of sedimentary rock, where rafters study the geologic history of the rock layers, take hikes to examine the fossil record of marine organisms, and view ancient petrified wood. They also explore ancient Native American ruins, observe the wildlife, and examine desert flora. Nights are spent under the stars, listening to the howl of coyotes in the distance and feeling the mastery of nature as one looks up at towering cliffs and hears the peaceful sound of the river. As with all Cataract Canyon trips, the river is most challenging during May and June. Adventurers forge the same rapids as mentioned above. Although hikes are optional, hiking into the remote stream-filled canyons of Indian Creek and Dark Canyon and visiting Doll House, a fairyland of pinnacles, are highlights of the expedition. The trip concludes from Hite Marina with the scenic flight back to Moab, or with the two-night jeep trip mentioned above.

Another oar and paddle raft trip is the two days/one night trip through Westwater Canyon. While the guide does the rowing and handling of the raft, adventurers take in the sights and sounds of the canyon. The steep, narrow gorges are flanked with polished walls of granite and gneiss. Within the canyon are the remains of pioneer gold mining claims and a cave used by desperadoes on the outlaw trail. Great Blue Heron fish swim along the shore and sightings of Bald Eagles are a frequent occurrence. But stunning scenery is not all that one enjoys in Westwater Canyon. The highly resistant black metamorphic rock of the canyon constricts the river channel, creating superb rapids such as Funnel Falls, Marble Canyon, and the infamous Skull Rapid, so hang on tight! Along the way are broad beaches with beautiful campsites and intriguing side canyons. The Westwater Canyon trip begins and ends either in Grand Junction, Colorado or Moab at the NAVTEC Expedition office.

NAVTEC offers full and half day Colorado River trips that are great for the whole family. Each trip features oar-powered rafts where the boatman does the rowing, as well as free inflatable kayaks for those who desire more active participation. Between rapids there is time for picture taking and relaxation as the raft lazily drifts down a river surrounded by soaring canyon walls. NAVTEC's skilled, friendly guides are well-versed in the human and natural history of the Colorado River. They are quick to point out attractions that are constant as well as point out the Great Blue Herons, Peregrine Falcons, Mule Deer and Golden and Bald Eagles that frequent the area. At noon a hearty buffet-style picnic lunch is served on a beautiful white sand beach. Later in the afternoon guests enjoy a "watermelon bust," a refreshing end to a perfect day.

Two exclusives with NAVTEC are the Whitewater Action Adventure and the One-Day Cataract Canyon Tour in Canyonlands. Both offer adventurers the opportunity to experience NAVTEC's motorized RIB. In the Whitewater Action Adventure, those on the expedition run the rapids of the mighty Colorado River, going upstream as well as down. The RIB makes it possible for river adventurers to take in a 100-mile stretch of the Colorado River in one day on the One-Day Cataract Canyon Tour in Canyonlands. Among the rapids experienced are the Big Drops, a series of three rapids considered to be among the 10 most dramatic falls in America. The experience concludes with a 30-mile cruise across the quiet waters of Lake Powell and includes a return trip to Moab via van. Guests may choose, at extra cost, to take the scenic Redtail Aviation flight or to have their private vehicles shuttled to Hite Marina.

For those who would love to experience the grandeur of the Colorado River but are a little apprehensive about rapids, NAVTEC offers its Scenic Calm Water Colorado River Tour. The boat encounters no rapids but floats beneath the towering Wingate cliffs of Dead Horse Point. Here the group stops to see petrified wood. There are several other outstanding photographic opportunities on the tour.

In addition to its river tours, NAVTEC offers full and half day jeep tours, and a one-day land and river combination tour, as well as making 4-wheel drive jeep charters available to most locations around Moab and throughout Southern Utah. Because of their expertise, NAVTEC's drivers can take visitors to the real hidden treasures of canyon country. The land and river combination tour takes visitors from the river bottom to the mesa top, truly giving the adventurer the chance to see the beauty of the canyon from every perspective.

For those participating in a NAVTEC experience, there is a time to work and a time to play. For NAVTEC the work never ends, but the work is a labor of love. So, if the months of March through October do not fit into vacation plans, give NAVTEC a call anyway. They will be happy to arrange a winter adventure with them at Baja and the Sea of Cortez. It's O.K. NAVTEC doesn't mind the work!

For more information with regards to deposit, payment and cancellation policies, in addition to what NAVTEC does and does not provide on its expeditions, please call 1-800 833-1278.

DID YOU KNOW?

The marker on U.S. 191, just north of Moab, pays tribute to the one-armed Civil War hero and explorer, John Wesley Powell, who, along with a group of nine men, started out at Green River, Wyoming on May 24 1869 to navigate and explore the Colorado River. He was told by mountain men and Indians that he would never return alive. Only six completed the journey on August 29, 1869, but none were killed in the endeavor. These valiant men journeyed over 900 miles, battling the elements and charting and navigating a treacherous river. Their boat of food was wrecked in northeastern Utah, making the journey even more of a hardship. Their journey is deemed one of the most outstanding river expeditions in the history of exploration.

REDTAIL AVIATION, INC.
Canyonlands Field
P. O. Box 515
Moab, Utah 84532
Tel: (435) 259-7421
(800) 842-9251
FAX: (435) 259-4032
After Hours (435) 564-3412
Web Site
www.Utah.com/redtail/aviation.html
Hrs: April - October
Daily 8:00 a.m. - 5:30 p.m.
November - April
Monday - Friday 8:00 a.m. - 5:00 p.m.

Green River Airport
P. O. Box 606
Green River, Utah 84525
Tel: (435) 564-3412
FAX: (435) 564-8157
Hrs: Same as above.
Visa, MasterCard, and Discover are accepted.
Charter Flights available on demand. Reservations are required.

When visiting Southeastern Utah and the National Parks, one would be doing themselves a great disservice if they did not book a Redtail Aviation scenic air tour. The canyons are exhilarating by raft, enlightening by jeep or foot, invigorating by bike, but beyond compare when seen through the eyes of the master of the sky—an eagle.

Before Orville and Wilbur conquered the skies, it was the dream of mankind to be able to fly like a bird, to soar like a Redtail hawk, and to see the world from an airborne perspective. In all the world there is little that can compare with the grandeur of Utah's canyons. Redtail Aviation puts the spectacle into that which is already spectacular.

Redtail Aviation has been specializing in scenic flight tours since 1978, when Glenn Baxter joined Redtail Aviation. He started with one plane and a dream to share two loves—flying and Southeastern Utah. Today Redtail is owned and operated by Bonnie Lindgren, Baxter's daughter, and is the largest and most experienced air taxi in the area. Redtail pilots are all FAA approved, and Redtail can boast that their planes have been safely flying passengers since inception. With their ten single engine Cessnas and two twin engine planes, one a Cessna 402 and the other a Piper Seneca, Redtail can cater to as many as six people in one plane and to groups of up to 50 when given sufficient notice.

Redtail Aviation pilots are not just experienced pilots, they are specially trained and adept in canyon flying, and they are extremely knowledgeable about the area. Before any flight, passengers gather around a large relief map. Here they take note of the varied terrain they will be flying over so that they will know where and what to look for and will not miss a thing on the trip.

But having a good experience with Redtail Aviation is initiated long before the trip begins. When reservations are made, a staff of friendly, helpful personnel is there to offer courteous suggestions and to make sure the flight chosen suits every need. When guests check in for the flight, that same group does all that it takes to ensure a memorable experience.

Once in flight, Redtail Aviation provides every passenger with individual headphones. Competent and knowledgeable pilots interpret the view below and, since Redtail's planes are high-wing Cessnas, everyone gets a window seat. This ensures every passenger with a fantastic view of the canyons, meandering rivers, and rugged terrain. The headphones also provide a great reduction in engine noise.

Scenic tours offered by Redtail Aviation include the Grand Tour, Canyons of the Escalante Tour, Canyonlands Air Tour, and Monument Valley Tour. Prospective passengers are amazed when they learn how affordable these trips are. In addition to scheduled tours, Redtail Aviation is available for charters to Salt Lake, Las Vegas, and numerous other locations.

Canyonlands Air Tour, Redtail's one hour flight for those with minimal time on their hands, may be short on time but is certainly not short on extravaganzas. From the minute the plane leaves the airport the views begin. The flight enters Canyonlands National Park over Island in the Sky, giving a peerless view of Upheaval Dome. Passengers view a deep chasm, believed to have been created 1000's of years ago by a meteor. When flying over the Maze it is immediately understood how it got its name. Even so, with its vivid colors, gigantic shapes, and varying textures, one might speculate that the Maze should be called the "amaze" district. When visiting Canyonlands, a term that is heard frequently is "the confluence," the exact spot where the Colorado and Green rivers come together. But only by air is the blending of colors of the two rivers discernible. Tour groups also experience dramatic views of the Needles district and of Dead Horse Point. Canyonlands National Park offers a vista of deep gorges, arroyos, and majestic pinnacles, all of which can only be truly appreciated through the eyes of a hawk and through the informative descriptions given by Redtail pilots.

The Grand Tour is a two hour flight that takes guests over the same Canyonlands terrain, but also includes such fascinations as Robber's Roost, Butch Cassidy's hangout; and Capitol Reef National Park. The flight follows Waterpocket Fold—an incredible ecological upthrust—to Lake Powell, the spectacular body of water created by Glen Canyon Dam at Page, Arizona. It is then that the flight returns to the airport via Canyonlands National Park.

Monument Valley is known as the "Land of Long Shadows." The two and one half hour Monument Valley tour views the unrivaled pinnacles of Monument Valley, Lake Powell, and much of Glen Canyon Recreation Area. There may be a shopping stop at Goulding's Lodge and Trading Post before taking to the air again. Passengers then view the Goosenecks of the San Juan River, Dark Canyon, and the Abajo Mountains. The flight continues back over the same area as viewed in the Canyonlands Air Tour before returning to home base.

Newest star on the horizon in Utah is the nation's newest national monument, Grand Staircase-Escalante. The Canyons of the Escalante Tour is three hours and includes the Canyonlands Air Tour and the Rainbow Bridge area of Lake Powell. Guests depart the lake area along the Escalante Drainage, adjacent to the famous Kaiparowits Plateau. They then cross near Circle Cliffs and traverse above Waterpocket Fold, an incredible geologic formation in Capital Reef National Park. During the final minutes, the flight passes over the San Rafael Desert, at 6,000 feet the highest desert in the United States. Then it is back to the Moab airport.

One of the most frequently asked questions from people not of the area who are coming to Moab, is, "how do we get there." Redtail Aviation has a viable solution. They provide air transportation services from Salt lake City, Denver, Phoenix, Grand Junction, and Las Vegas. One of the major benefits is that Redtail can quote the air fare price then and there, without having to put the prospective customer on hold while checking numerous commuter airlines to see who services the area.

The object of Travelers Choice guide books is to direct tourists in specific areas to attractions, businesses and services that locals themselves choose. Redtail Aviation has been selected by local river rafting companies such as Sherri Griffith, Tag-A-Long, and NAVTEC Expeditions, to bring their guests back to Moab after the river adventure. Max Bertola, in *Best of Southern Utah*, stated: "I saw more in an hour flying over Canyonlands with Redtail Aviation than I had seen in three years of driving around it." Friendship Tours vice president, Steve Langley, said, "I was sure the flight would be nice, but I didn't have any idea how incredible it really was."

When visitors come to southeastern Utah, they expect the extraordinary. Visiting Canyonlands National Park, or any of nature's wonders, would be anti-climatic without a Redtail Aviation Tour.

SHERI GRIFFITH EXPEDITIONS INC.
P. O. Box 1324
Moab, Utah 84532
Tel: (435) 259-8229
         (800) 332-2439
FAX: (435) 259-2226
Web Site:http://www.GriffithExp.com
E-mail: classriver@aol.com
Hrs: May 1 - September 30
Monday - Saturday 8:00 a.m. - 6:00 p.m.
Reservations are required.
Visa, MasterCard, and American Express are accepted.

No other expedition company in America has earned more national acclaim than has Sheri Griffith Expeditions, Inc. It is not just because she is a woman, although she is one of very few women to own and operate her own expedition company, it is because of who Sheri Griffith is.

Sheri Griffith is a pioneer of pioneering stock. Her grandparents homesteaded Colorado at the turn of the century, having traveled across the country by covered wagon. Sheri, in turn, grew up exploring the backcountry of the Rocky Mountains by horseback and camping under the stars when ever occasion permitted. The outdoors was Sheri's life.

It was not coincidence, in view of Sheri's devotion to the outdoors, that when it became necessary to find summer work to help put herself through college, Sheri suggested to her brothers that they buy a military surplus raft and earn money taking people down the river. That was in 1971 and since then, the river has become Sheri's passion.

But the passion extends far beyond taking adventurous souls down the world's most spectacular rivers. From the onset Sheri has known that if running the rivers was all one was interested in, the rivers would soon become as environmentally endangered as are many animal species. So one of the company goals is in protecting our natural resources through "sustainability practices" with special emphasis on rivers. Over the years Sheri's dedication has earned her awards and accolades including *U. S. Conservation Service Award, Department of the Interior Conservationist of the Year (1989), American Rivers Conservation Colleague Award, Outstanding Business Leader of the Year, Moab Woman of the Year, and a Certificate of Appreciation* from the Bureau of Land Management for contribution towards Wild and Scenic River Protection.

Back in 1981, rafting the river with an expedition company owned and operated by a woman was anything but fashionable or macho. Yet Sheri had the courage to not only purchase her own river expedition company, but to make sure that everyone would know that it was owned and operated by a woman—Sheri Griffith Expeditions, Inc. Since that time more than 100,000 passengers have experienced river running "with a touch of class." Sheri has served as president of Utah Guides and Outfitters and is the immediate past president of Western River Guides Association. She is the Association's first woman president and is the only president to have been re-elected to office. Western River Guides is an association of more than 1,000 outfits on 200 rivers.

But there is no female chauvinism here. Sheri gives no thought as to whether her guides are male or female. Her only concern when hiring individuals to take care of her customers is that the guides are fully trained and have the expertise necessary to navigate the rivers and to bestow new-found awareness, appreciation, and knowledge of the river and its terrain, to her guests.

While other river expeditions follow the sun during the winter months, Sheri turns politician in the form of a concerned citizen. Because of her business acumen and political savvy and sensitivity, Sheri has gained the respect of local, national and political arenas. Her skills are equal when it comes to navigating Cataract Canyon, considered to be one of the most challenging river runs, or testifying at a hearing for the Department of the Interior, and fighting for a just cause. Sheri's credentials expand to include that of past Commissioner for the Utah Travel Council, American Red Cross Instructor, and past Commissioner on the Governor's Commission for Women and Families. Sheri is now Commisioner for Utah Department of Transportation. She is also constantly lobbying to secure rivers for the Wild and Scenic River System. Utah's Westwater Canyon, a nine-mile gorge through pre-Columbian granite, is currently proposed for the system.

Probably more than any other river expedition company, Sheri Griffith Expeditions, Inc. offers variety. The spectrum includes family oriented trips that are tame enough for kids from five to 85, to Sheri's Expeditions in Luxury, which is four-days and three-nights of pampering the Sybarite that exists in each of us.

All of Sheri Griffith Expedition Trips are multiple-day trips, for the simple reason that Sheri believes that part of running the rivers is offering guests the opportunity to get in touch with themselves in a broader perspective. That, she believes, requires more time away from civilization. Every expedition offers restaurant-style dining, running the gamut of deluxe game hens to specialized cuisine. And every successful whitewater run dictates the popping of the cork on a bottle of champagne, Sheri's way of toasting rafters' success and offering her respects to the majesty of the mighty rivers she runs.

The Seventh Wonder of the World, the Canyons of the Colorado River become even more wonderful when seen through the eyes of Sheri Griffith's Cataract Canyon of the Colorado River experience. The 96-mile trip is prefaced with one to three days of serene, leisurely drifting, and then comes a "ride on the wild side" when rafters encounter the confluence of the Colorado and Green Rivers. Here the river doubles in size and the rapids begin. First encountered are Mile Long Rapid, a series of big waves and exploding whitewater. Almost without break, rafters encounter the really big waves, affectionately named the "Big Drops." Among these are Little Niagara and Satan's Gut, both of which leave a lasting impression on rafters, no matter what the experience level. Along the way the trip is punctuated with hikes and canyon climbing, picture taking, historical information, ecological equilibrium, rustic river bank campsites, uniquely western meals, and the exclamation point to it all, a flight over the terrain just explored. The three-day/two-night and the four-day/three night trips use motorized J-rig rafts, while the five-day/four-night trips use more leisurely oar-powered smaller rafts.

Sheri's Majestic Canyons of the Green River expedition proves that river running is more than whitewater. Majestic Canyons offers more than 50 wonderful rolling rapids and the opportunity for rafters to grab a paddle and feel the current pull, as all in the raft negotiate the river with a guide navigating from the back. So exciting and fun is this rafting experience that, in order to get more people to experience the thrills of rapids, Sheri offers special discounted rates to children between the ages of five and 16 and kids (senior citizens) between 60 and 85. Once they have experienced the excitement of the river and the back country they will be hooked for life. The expedition travels through Desolation and Gray Canyons and offers more western history than any other expedition. Desolation is the only river canyon that is a Registered National Historic Landmark.The Green River rapids are full of big rolling waves, not technically difficult but exciting and fun to navigate. Each day the rapids increase in size and excitement. This is a river of contrast, from the towering red sandstone wind-sculpted castles to the pearl-white sandy beaches on the riverbank. The scenery is unsurpassed with exquisite sunsets and a variety of wildlife. Majestic Canyons is offered in four-day/three-night and five-day/four-night trips. The adventure begins with a scenic charter air flight above the Green River, giving rafters a spectacular view of what lies ahead.

Westwater Canyon on the Colorado River commands special respect among veteran river runners and is considered the best short whitewater trip available in the west. The red sandstone cliffs change to shiny black walls as the river narrows considerably, plunging the raging water into a dramatically narrowed black granite gorge. The constriction of the river results in Funnel Falls, The Steps, Sock-It-To-Me, Little Hummer, Last Chance Rapid, and the most infamous of all, Skull Rapid. There is one day of fast and exciting rapids through a black granite gorge. The rest of the trip is slower moving with smaller, fun rapids, giving adventurers time to absorb the beautiful scenery, unwind, and enjoy each other's company. National Geographic selected Sheri Griffith's company to escort them down the river for their *Wild and Scenic Rivers* publication. This segment of the Colorado is currently a "Proposed Wild and Scenic River" site. The adventure is offered in two-day/one-night and three-day/two-night trips; is rated moderate, and is for ages 10 and above. The trip begins in Grand Junction, Colorado.

When it comes to whitewater, Labyrinth Canyon is virtually the opposite of

Cataract Canyon. The trip offers beautiful scenery, great fun, but no roaring rapids. A leisurely float, it is an adventure that begins where civilization ends, in the stark desert area near the town of Green River, Utah. Labyrinth Canyon begins the longest stretch of undammed flat water in the Southwest. This 60-mile float on the Green River runs through ever-deepening canyons of whites and grays and yellows and browns that are accented by red buttes and mesas rising 1,500 feet above the river. Ken Devore, a retired river guide, recently interviewed for a travel expose on Labyrinth Canyon, said: "Rapids get in the way of a perfectly good river trip. Labyrinth is the epitome of a great river trip." In addition to offering lazy days on the river, Labyrinth, a five-day/four-night trip, offers some of the most exciting off-water exploration available. The trip is ideal for children, seniors, families, three-generation groups, and for people of varying physical abilities.

The Dolores River, only runnable from mid-April to early June, is a snow-melt river offering spectacular scenery, constant whitewater, and technical pin-ball maneuvering. Sheri considers the Dolores to be the secret gem of the Great Southwest. As Sheri explains it, "The Dolores is an exciting challenge for river runners. If in an oar boat, you'll be busy crashing through the rapids and holding on. If in a paddleboat or kayak, you've definitely met your match." The trip begins at Moab, is a three-day/two-night trip, and is available to ages 10 and over. Five-day trips are available by request.

"Coyote Run," a float trip on the Colorado for two days and one night, is an introduction to family camping that offers everyone, ages four and up, the opportunity to step back in time for a glimpse of life at the turn of the century. Picture camping in an authentic Sioux Indian tipi and visiting an Old West homestead, restored to a living museum. Imagine making ice cream the old-fashioned way, by turning the handle on the wooden bucket. Learn how to make root beer, build bird feeders and bat houses, play horseshoes or dominoes, and strengthen the parent/child and child/child relationships. In addition to these activities there is the thrill of story telling around the campfire, roasting marshmallows, and making s'mores. The river is calm enough that children can slide off the raft and leisurely float along with just their life vests. When beached, either for lunch or for camp, there are sand castles to be built and water toys for playing. And one of the nicest parts of the Coyote Run is, that when parents want time for themselves, the guides are there to take the children on structured outings that are educational as well as lots of fun.

Families who involve themselves in Coyote Run likely return the next year for Sheri's "The Family Goes to Camp—Expedition Style." This trip was designed especially for parents who have sent their children off to camp and wish that they could go to. With Sheri, they can. Excepting for the tipi campsite and the river being run, activities are pretty much the same and are developed to engender family togetherness. The trip is five-days/four nights and covers the same terrain as the Majestic Canyons of the Green River expedition. The trip offers over 50 rolling rapids, is with paddleboats and oar rafts, plus inflatable kayaks, and is for kids from five to 85.

The "Women at Play" trips can be four-days/three-nights or five-days/four-nights on the Colorado River through Cataract Canyon, or six-days/five-nights through Majestic Canyons on the Green River. These trips are best described by Carole Jacobs of *Shape* Magazine, who joined a group of women and wrote: "Women-only adventure travel is more than a girl's night out. There is no better place to find yourself than on top of a mountain; no better time than when you're clinging to a cliff to discover that your better half is not the one you left behind, but the one you found within."

Sheri's women-only trips are fun, exhilarating sojourns into nature, offering a variety of experiences.

Expeditions in Luxury is a four-day/three-night adventure into Cataract Canyon on the Colorado River where *everything is provided*. This is a trip for those who want to be pampered. During the 94 miles no one lifts an oar except the guides, unless they want to. After floating the river or subduing the rapids, when it is time to head for shore, attendants have already gone ahead to make preparations for a gourmet continental dinner. When guests arrive at each night's camp, their tents, sleeping bags, and deluxe pads are all set up. In addition, beach chairs are ready and the cocktail lounge is open. All tables in this river-front dining room allow diners an exquisite view that stretches in every direction. Dinner, a five-course meal that is prefaced with a glass of chilled wine and hors d'oeuvres, is served by waiters. Cuisine of different countries is featured each night. Most of the guests, as well as the waiters and waitresses, dress for dinner. Breakfasts on this expedition are out of the ordinary. Expect fresh-ground imported coffees and freshly squeezed juices to be delivered to each tent. Then join the group for Mexican Huevos with authentic salsas or other specialties from a secret recipe collection. Lunch is served riverside with an array of meats, cheese, homemade breads, and, depending on the day, pasta salads, taco salads, seafood salads, fresh fruit, and fine sweets.

In addition to scheduled trips, Sheri Griffith Expeditions will customize trips for any occasion. They also offer a five-day/four-night Adventure by Mountain Bike and Raft trip in the Cataract Canyon on the Colorado River. This trip is in cooperation with Kaibab Mountain/Desert Bike Tours. (Any of Sheri's two to five day rafting trips may be combined with a biking trip).

In addition to Sheri Griffith Expeditions, Inc., Sheri is a partner of Griffith Production Services. Started in 1985, this service coordinates productions on location for feature films, documentaries, commercials, etc. A primary goal of the company is to maintain an ecological equilibrium between man and nature, preserving public lands and making sure that the canyons and the rivers remain primitive. Sheri's belief is: "We take only pictures and leave only footprints."

Griffith Production Services has worked with the crews of *Indiana Jones and the Last Crusade, Thelma and Louise, City Slickers II*, and *Larger Than Life*, to name just a few movies. Those trucks balancing precariously on buttes, cars careening down Switchbacks cut through red sandstone walls or framed by spectacular natural arches have all been coordinated by Griffith Production Services. In addition, they put Bon Jovi up on Castle Rock for his *Blaze of Glory* music video that won Best Video of the Year. They have hosted *National Geographic* on the river several times. In early June, 1997, *Good Morning, America* chose Sheri Griffith Expeditions to profile a western family vacation. They joined her for a two-day family trip with live satelite segments.

Sheri and partner, Gene Boyle, own Slickrock Air Guides, a company that gives visitors the opportunity to view the grandeur of Canyonlands National Park from on top. In addition to giving guests the chance for a bird's eye view of terrain they covered in Sheri's Cataract Canyon of the Colorado River expedition, Slickrock also offers a two-hour flight over Canyonlands National Park, Natural Bridges National Monument, and Monument Valley Tribal Park. Slickrock Air Guides grand tour is three and one-half hours and explores by air Canyonlands National Park and Dead Horse Point, as well as Lake Powell and Glen Canyon Dam, Rainbow Bridge National Monument, the Edge of the Grand Canyon, and Capitol Reef National Park.

When Sheri Griffith Expeditions, Inc. adds the footnote, "River Journeys With a Touch of Class," there is no mistaking that the "touch" will be internalized for the rest of one's life, and the "class" is exceptional excellence in the face of adventure and life preservation.

TAG-A-LONG EXPEDITIONS
452 South Main Street
Moab, Utah 84532
Tel: (435) 259-8946
          (800) 453-3292
FAX: (435) 259-8990
Web Site:http//www.tagalong.com
E-Mail   tagalong @tagalong.com
Hrs: Office
Shoulder Seasons:
Mid-April -Mid-May & Labor Day-October
Open Daily   8:00 a. m. - 6:00 p.m.
Peak Season: Mid-May - Labor-Day Weekend
Open Daily   7:00 a.m. - 9:00 p.m.
Winter Season: November - Mid-April
Monday - Friday   8:00 a.m. - 6:00 p.m.
Visa, MasterCard, and American Express are accepted.
Reservations are required on all multi-day trips.

There is so much to learn and to love about Utah's canyon country, and there is no better way to do it than by "tagging along" with Tag-a-Long Expeditions. Whether the expedition is downstream through the rugged waters of the Colorado River or in a 4 X 4 vehicle that descends 2,000 feet from mesa top to canyon bottom, Tag-A-Long is committed to literally giving their guests the sun, the stars, and the moon.

Tag-A-Long has been sharing its love and excitement for southeastern Utah for 33 years and yet the magic of the trails they blaze and the rapids they shoot still charm and captivate them after all these years.

Bob Jones and Paul Niskanan, owners of Tag-A-Long, believe that there is so much more to a canyon country adventure than just shooting the rapids. They are not blind to the fact that there are several companies who can do that. Right from its onset the philosophy of Tag-A-Long has been to give the customer everything that they paid for and then some. That is why they promise the sun, the stars, and the moon. They are aware that their expedition guests are investing precious time and resources because of a desire to escape the norm for an experience of a lifetime. For this reason Tag-Along is committed to providing the best service, the best guides, the best meals, and the best formulated tours.

Both Bob and Paul have backgrounds that include the hotel and restaurant business, transportation and bus tours and visitor service. Recently, when more than 40 guides and narrators from other tourist related services took one of Tag-A-Long's multiple-day expeditions, they said that they could not believe it was possible to cook the way Tag-A-Long's guides cooked and still stay on schedule. Tag-A-Long's guests enjoy gourmet dining that includes appetizers, salads, a main dish such as chicken cordon bleu, vegetables, rice or potato, and elegant dessert such as flaming cherry or peach cheese cake jubilee. And how often can one find a dining room that is tucked into a little explored canyon where dusk is illuminated with a warm violet glow and where a nearby river provides mood music?

Bob's and Paul's business experiences have intensified their desire of establishing interpersonal relationships with their guests. They deliver the kind of relationships that give their guests only that which is needed to show them the path and then let them walk it by themselves. When adventurers return to their humdrum life, Bob and Paul want them to be able to close their eyes and visualize an incredible journey while at the same time echoing to themselves a resounding, "I did it!"

Tag-A-Long's professional guide staff shares the wilderness with their guests, not as a job, but as a life choice. These men and women are licensed and certified in Red Cross First Aid, Wilderness Medicine, CPR, and river rescue. They have studied the rivers and canyons for years and have learned to read the wild with keen eyes and to react with skilled response. They are as comfortable in their boats or vehicles as they are in their homes. Tag-A-Long prides itself that its guides can blow the experts out of the water with their sophisticated interpretation of the terrain and the area. Confronted with questions from geologists, anthropologists, paleontologists, or any of the many experts, Tag-A-Long guides can respond with incredible ease and accuracy. They know the terrain, the fauna, flora, and the history that has been eked out by wind, water, and the Anasazis, the Native Americans who inhabited this land nearly a thousand years ago. Tag-A-Long guides serve their guests equally well as teacher, medic, ecologist, chef, social director and friend.

The word "expedition" invokes images of rugged backcountry and a call to adventure. Since 1964, Tag-A-Long has been the primary outfitter for Canyonlands National Park and its surrounding areas. Year after year they continue to develop and refine their expeditions by listening to the concerns and comments of their guests and by continually studying and exploring the canyons and rivers that comprise their backyard. Whether it is the intricate canyons of the Maze, the smooth sandstone walls of the Escalante wilderness, or the slot canyons of the San Rafael Swell, Tag-A-Long listens to their customers and delivers the trip that will make this "the best gift you have ever given yourself."

Tag-A-Long offers year-round adventure. From the end of April into mid-May the Colorado River begins to swell, providing good rapid runs. Weather at this time of the year is ideal for hiking, rafting, and 4 X 4 exploring. What a wonderful time to also enjoy the wildflowers that begin to pop out of the rocks and sand.

Mid-May through late June is known in the area as "peak season." This is the time of year that offers rafting guests maximum whitewater experiences on the Colorado River, especially through Cataract Canyon and on the Green River. It is still a season ideal for hiking, backcountry explorations and enjoying a desert where wildflowers and cacti bloom profusely.

Mid-summer still offers exciting whitewater. It is also a perfect time for guests to enjoy leisurely swims in the refreshing waters of the Colorado. July and August are perfect for children. The river offers bathwater temperature and the sand bars are perfect for picnics, beach and volley balls, and camping. It is also an ideal time for individuals to become their own raft. Simply don a life jacket and float leisurely down a more gentle Colorado River. Also, during July, August and September, the waters of Westwater Canyon offer some of the most exciting whitewater rapids on the Colorado River.

Fall takes on a completely different atmosphere. The crowds are gone and the canyons become tranquil and reflective. It is a perfect time for that last ride down the river or for a cool, refreshing backcountry exploration by jeep.

Winter is a perfect time to visit canyon country. River trips have ceased, but land expeditions into Canyonlands National Park are wonderful. Tag-A-Long also offers a very special treat—Hut-to-Hut Nordic skiing in the LaSal Mountains, Utah's second highest mountain range. Tag-A-Long offers a system of huts positioned approximately five miles apart with huts available as a tour package or individual rental. The tours include instruction, meals, complete guided tours, and shuttles.

In its multi-day tours, Tag-A-Long offers three days/two nights, four days/three nights, and six days/five nights trips down the Colorado River through Cataract Canyon. John Wesley Powell, first explorer of the Colorado and Green Rivers, named the canyon and wrote, "...the scenery is grand, with rapids and falls below and walls above, beset with crags and pinnacles of a most magnificent nature."

Late on the second day the action begins. The sound of the river—the roar of the big water—hits one first. This is the Colorado River, home to the world-class whitewater rapids that every river runner wants to shoot. Covering 100 miles, this exhilarating exploration begins quietly on calm water flowing through a 1,500-foot deep red rock canyon in the heart of Canyonlands National Park. After a day and a half of peaceful calm, river rafters experience the first of 25 rapids with names such as Little Niagara, Satan's Gut, and the three Big Drops. Adventurers scream like a child on a roller coaster, but along the way they will also sleep under the milky way, walk the same paths that the ancient Anasazi walked, splash and cavort in streams and waterfalls, and come away with an enhanced appreciation of the river and canyons. Whether it is the new found admiration for the emerald green collared lizard, a remnant of prehistoric days; a new found respect for the power of water; or gratitude for the tenacity of wildflowers, so hearty that they can still thrive in a hostile, rugged environment; guests of a Tag-A-Long river expedition will never be the same.

The six-day Cataract Canyon—Long and Lingering trip gives guests the chance to slow down the pace, explore more side canyons, and walk longer in the desert. The three-day Cataract Canyon Express trip offers the same great adventure but in a condensed program for guests with limited vacation time.

For those who really have limited vacation time and want a lot of action, nothing can replace the Westwater Canyon trips. On the two days/two night trip, adventurers face 12 spectacular rapids. The trip begins from Grand Junction, Colorado, with guests arriving deep in the wilderness of Westwater Canyon by evening. On the second day adventurers will be shooting rapids that were, until just a few years ago, considered "unrunnable". The spectacular black schist canyon squeezes the river into narrow gorges that force the water to erupt into breath-taking rapids that surface year-round. But between the rapids there is plenty of calm for swimming, showering under a waterfall and hiking. This exceptional trip is offered twice a week from early May through the end of September.

Adventurers with more time can also avail themselves of the Rapids, Rapids, Rapids trip, a six-days/five nights tour that combines the excitement of Westwater and Cataract Canyons into one never-to-be-forgotten expedition that forges 36 rapids. It is a wilderness experience unmatched anywhere in North America. Thrill seekers shoot Westwater Canyon in an oar-powered raft. After two days, rafters stop and explore Arches National Park and relax for a night in Moab. Then they switch to the J-rig for whitewater experience in Cataract. With its peaceful stretches of calm water and turbulent rides on the rapids, this trip has it all. And one last thrill, the Redtail Aviation return flight over Lake Powell and Canyonlands National Park, gives a hawk-eye view of the canyons just rafted.

Tag-A-Long is one of the few expedition companies to offer Green River excursions. While the Colorado River offers tumultuous bursts of wild waters, the Green River offers more whitewater rapids than any other trip. This five day adventure will provide 50 rapids in all. While Tag-A-Long Guides accompany the group down the river in the big raft, this is the trip that is uniquely individual and is a great family trip. Adventurers can run the rapids in a single or double person kayak. Teenagers have the opportunity of powering their own boat through the rapids while smaller children safely settle down in the raft where they can spot mule deer, eagles, coyotes, bighorn sheep and heron. Even those without river experience feel the thrill of paddling their own boat, and the raft is always there if they need a rest from paddling. The Green River trip runs through Desolation and Gray Canyons, which are abundant with wildlife and steeped in exploration, outlaw and Indian history. Day hikes include visits to ancient Indian ruins and petroglyphs.

Tag-A-Long's Wilderness Adventure offers six days and five nights of rafting, trekking and 4-wheel driving. This expedition couples the exhilaration of rafting the mighty Colorado with the wildly beautiful park lands of the Needles District of Canyonlands National Park. The Needles pinnacles are a primitive, untamed land with ancient Indian writings and rock formations and arches that few get to see. It's an unforgettable safari into the wilderness of Canyonlands. For those who prefer to by-pass the Colorado River rafting, there is the three-day Wilderness Safari into Canyonlands.

Distinctive journeys into a remote land are offered by Tag-A-Long in its Wilderness Accent Expeditions. Finding the Primitive Woman Within uses the San Juan River as its pathway for the small intimate group who visit cliff dwellings and rock art sites of the ancient Anasazi. Using traditional materials, the tour creates crafts similar to those created by Anasazi women centuries ago. They also participate in rituals handed down from Anasazi ancestors to contemporary Native American women. After rafting the San Juan River, the group takes out the boat at Mexican Hat and goes by 4-wheel drive into Johns Canyon for three days of hikes, ceremonials, rituals, and crafts.

The five days/four nights Narrow Canyons of the Escalante trip travels to the San Rafael Swell's deep rock canyon, where adventurers view petroglyphs and walk several "slot" canyons during the first two days. On the third day the expedition travels to Capitol Reef National Park, visits the visitor center, hikes along the creek at Calf Creek Canyon, and follows Hole in the Rock Trail to an overnight campsite near Spooky Canyon. Spooky, Peak-a-boo, and Brimstone Canyons are several that the group will visit and squeeze through on day four. The fifth day is spent in Escalante Canyon enjoying the riparian habitat. Conclusion to the expedition is a marvelous Redtail Aviation flight back to Moab, giving an eagle's view of the area just traveled.

Tag-A-Long's Indianland Expedition Awaken Your Spirit, a six days/five nights adventure, visits three groups of Indians—the Ute, Navajo, and Hopi. Native American guides share stories, history, and ceremonies of their tribes. The canyons, cliffs, and the land visited are rich in traditions and history.

Walking Softly in Dark Canyon Primitive Area is five days and four nights. Adventurers backpack into the upper reaches of Dark Canyon Primitive Area, where they learn about geology, ecology, and Anasazi history. Colorful canyons, emerald pools, and astonishing rock formations await the expedition. This trip includes backpacking and hiking from a base camp on a daily basis.

Custom expeditions can be arranged for as few as three people into such areas as the Escalante Wilderness, the Maze District of Canyonlands National Park, the San Rafael Swell, Beef Basin, and Nine-Mile Canyon. With just a few more people the custom excursion can include river expeditions on the San Juan, Colorado, or Green rivers.

Tag-A-Long offers one and half day mini expeditions designed to give guests a big taste of backcountry in a short period of time and on a small budget. These trips include four-wheeling to Angel Arch, the largest natural arch in Canyonlands National Park; a one-day trip in Westwater Canyon with whitewater so challenging that it will feel more like a week-long tour; a jetboat and 4 X 4 adventure, exclusive from Tag-A-Long, which skims along the flatwater of the Colorado River for the first half of the day and then explores the backcountry of Canyonlands' natural bridges and steep trails the second half; a one-day rafting adventure on the Colorado; and the Island in the Sky 4 X 4 Expedition that ventures up old Indian trails cut into the side of a mesa and offers some of the best panoramic views in Southeastern Utah.

During the winter months, what could be more exhilarating or exciting to the skier than Tag-A-Long's Hut to Hut Adventure in the central massif of the LaSal Mountain Range. With three huts placed approximately five miles apart, the system offers great Nordic and virgin powder skiing that encompasses beginner slopes to the steepest terrain. The huts offer comfort, have separate sleeping and cooking rooms as well as a south facing sundeck, propane heating and stoves, lighting, and sanitary facilities. They are also supplied with all necessary cooking utensils. All guests need to bring are their own paper plates, eating utensils, and food. The huts are offered as guided tour experiences or on a per night per person basis. Guided trips are recommended as the package includes transportation, guide services, meals and hut accommodations.

In all of Canyon Country there is no equal to Tag-A-Long Expeditions. Whether looking up or looking down, excursions are planned around the most majestic of scenery and the most enlightening ancient history. And to cap it all off, every September a music festival is offered on the banks of the Colorado in the center of Canyonlands. Whether it's opera or chamber music, there is nothing quite like the acoustics of a Baldwin grand piano resonating off the canyon walls.

The service and the amenities that Tag-A-Long offers prove that, when one is setting the standards for the industry as Tag-A-Long does, reaching for the stars just isn't enough. Tag-A-Long presents the world and the universe as it has never before been seen.

DID YOU KNOW?

The monument at 805 North Main Street in Moab is in honor of the city's earliest Mormon pioneer settlers. Called on a mission in April of 1855 by Brigham Young, the company arrived at the Grand River (later renamed the Colorado) in June. Their calling was to establish a mission among the Indians in the Elk Mountain area. They selected a site and built a fort 64 feet square with walls 12 feet high. The site of the original fort is about 800 feet from the monument. Three of these early pioneers were buried within the fort.

BED & BREAKFASTS

SUNFLOWER HILL BED & BREAKFAST INN
185 North 300 East
Moab, Utah 84532
Tel: (435) 259-2974
FAX: (435) 259-3065
Web Site:www.sunflowerhill.com
E Mail   Innkeeper@Sunflowerhill.com
Rates:
Winter   November 1 - February 28, excluding holidays
Summer   March 1 - October 31
Visa, MasterCard, American Express and Discover
are accepted.
Reservations are requested.

Ensconced in a park-like setting with red sandstone block pathways meandering throughout, Sunflower Hill Bed & Breakfast Inn is a compilation of antiquity and renaissance. Its two luxury edifices, the Garden Cottage and the Farm House, offer respite in magnificent solitude.

Sunflower Hill is a mere three blocks from the heart of Moab's downtown, yet its pastoral setting renders the feeling of being a million miles from nowhere.

The grounds are profuse with flowers, marvelous shade trees, lawn furniture, and garden swings. Scattered throughout, they render a perfect setting for casual conversation and relaxation. In the midst of the garden setting, offering ultimate placidity, is a large outdoor hot tub with red wood decking. The wrap-around porch on the Garden Cottage enhances opportunities for repose with its single and double rocking chairs, potted plants and rattan furniture.

Beautiful Pine wood floors, an antique desk, and a marvelous golden heartwood pine stairway leading to the second floor of Sunflower Hill's Garden Cottage are first impressions at check-in. Beyond the entrance is Sunflower Hill's Great Room, comfortably arranged for congenial conversation or for being off to one's self. Coffee, tea, and hot chocolate are available around the clock and a lending library, which includes a selection of books on where to go and what to do, is available to guests. A massive rock fireplace offers emblematic warmth during summer and a glowing hearth in the winter.

Each of the 11 guest bedrooms at Sunflower Hill has its own theme name. All guest rooms have private bath, color cable TV with ESPN and movie channels, air conditioning, ceiling fans, and beautifully adorned antique beds. The decor of many of the rooms is enhanced by an exquisite hand-made quilt. All rooms have plush cotton logo robes, French-milled chamomile soap and shampoo. An amenity basket is filled with an assortment of cookies, cheeses, salsa, dips, pretzels, and Utah's famous Wind River jerky, all of which may be purchased .

Innkeeper, Gregg Stucki, believes that one of the most important items a bed and breakfast can offer its guests is a unique bed. At Sunflower Hill all exquisite antique beds are over-stuffed and elegantly adorned with luxurious quilts that complement room themes.

Deluxe Rooms offer luxurious jetted tub, private balcony or garden patio, and TV concealed in an elegant armoire as additional amenities.

The Garden Cottage offers six guest rooms. The "Garden Suite" was once a small cottage and is the original Garden Cottage, an elegant Cape Cod-style lodge. The Garden Suite has its own private entrance and overlooks a splendid garden setting.

On the main floor of the Garden Cottage, down the hall from the entry, are the "Bowery" and "Ivy." Ivy is arrayed with antique brass bed, green and white bedspread, and white lace curtains embellished with ivy. At the top of the ornate pine staircase are "The Loft" and "French Bedroom," the latter of which is the Inn's luxury suite and a favorite of the Innkeepers as well as honeymooning guests and their anniversary counterparts. The French Bedroom offers an exquisite jetted tub with a vintage candelabra. Dancing shadows of the eight candles inspire romantic reflection. Decor includes an elaborate 9-foot mirrored armoire with matching bedroom set, vaulted ceiling, circular stained glass window, double sink vanity, and garden views framed by white lace curtains. "Apple Cellar," downstairs, lives up to its theme name as a unique, antique-filled hideaway.

Across the garden and over a rock bridge, is the Farmhouse. The original sunporch becomes an antique-filled entrance to the Bed & Breakfast dining room. Handwoven blue rag rugs adorn the beautiful wood plank floor. At the far end is a large fireplace. Tables are arrayed with blue and white checkered table cloths. The rest of the room is cleverly decorated with antique buffet and a mirrored umbrella coat stand. A menu on the wall outlines the week's breakfast offerings. Breakfasts include fresh baked breads and pastries, fresh seasonal fruits, and a range of entree dishes such as whole wheat pancakes with toasted pecans, bananas, and maple syrup, and breakfast burritos with garden fresh salsa. Outside is a marvelous screen-covered patio offering additional dining in an area surrounded by flowers of every color and variety.

Across the hall from the dining room is a small gift shop where logo T-shirts, robes, and other paraphernalia are sold. Perhaps the most popular gift items are children's books illustrated by renown artist, Robyn Stucki Officer. Robyn, one of the inn's owners, has an on-site studio, and is responsible for much of the beautiful room artwork and gardens at Sunflower Hill.

A pantry down the hall from the gift shop offers late night snackers an honors refrigerator stocked with a bounty of cold juices and soft drinks as well as gourmet ice cream.

Behind the Inn's guest parking lot is the garden where Sunflower Hill grows its own zucchini, eggplant, corn, herbs, chile peppers, onions, and a variety of tomatoes for their homemade breakfasts. Appropriately the fenced-in garden is lined with a row of tall, healthy sunflowers. Peach, apple, and plum trees grace the grounds and offer seasonal, straight-from-the-orchard freshness to Sunflower Hills guests. The Stucki's also have their own greenhouse where plants are started.

A much-appreciated guest amenity, especially to those who come to bike the Slickrock Trail, is the locked bike storage offered at Sunflower Hill.

Main floor rooms in the Farmhouse include the "Rose Room" and "Granny's." Granny's Room is ideal for guests traveling alone but will adequately accommodate a couple as well. Granny's is decorated with a peach, white, and green quilt, tiny end tables, antique sewing machine and rocking chair, and a skirted wash basin. Entering from the back of the house with its own private entrance is "Morning Glory." Upstairs is "Garret Suite," a two-bedroom guest quarters that is beautifully decorated with apple red, forest green, and white. A private door opens to the backyard. Another favorite room in the Farmhouse, located downstairs, is "Sunporch." The room extends out into what was originally the farmhouse sunporch, where wicker chairs and a stenciled fence intersperse with painted sunflowers. The room is flooded with sunlight and overlooks the garden.

Besides the many room and guest amenities offered, the Innkeeper and staff does everything within their power to accommodate guest needs. They are well informed on area attractions and local activities and are knowledgeable about quality dining establishments. They are happy to assist in directions and reservations for any endeavor.

From the impeccably maintained garden grounds and the scrupulously clean and well cared for luxurious rooms to the sensitive, hospitable staff, Sunflower Hill Bed & Breakfast Inn offers a demeanor of caring that is hard to find. In every sense of the word, they are a Travelers' Choice.

BREWERY RESTAURANTS

EDDIE MCSTIFF'S
Family Restaurant & Microbrewery
59 South Main Street
Moab, Utah 84532
Tel: (435) 259-BEER (2337)
FAX (435) 259-3022
Hrs: Summer
Open Daily 3:00 p.m. - 12:30 a.m.
Winter
Open Daily 3:00 p.m. - 10:00 p.m.
Closed Mid-December and January
Visa, MasterCard, and Discover are accepted.

One does not have to venture to Moab to partake of the 1996 Rocky Mountain Brew Fest's "Best Beer." Eddie McStiff's fine ales and beers are found in numerous fine dining establishments across the country. One may not have to come to Moab to imbibe, but when visiting Moab, for those who know and appreciate fine hand-crafted beer and fine dining, Eddie McStiffs is the place.

The Handcrafted Beer menu at Eddie McStiff's boasts a selection of 12 beers that range from wheat beer, McStiff's lightest in flavor, to ESB, Extra-Special Bitter. The Stout is fully hopped yet smooth and is a favorite with Europeans. A specialty is the Spruce Beer, featuring root, bark, and needle flavors of the tree, and for the hearty there is Jalapeno, where the nose of the pepper comes through with only a hint of the heat.

Non-imbibers at Eddie McStiff's are not left out. Sure to be enjoyed as refreshing drinks are the Raspberry Lemonade and the Home-made Root Beer.

When it comes to cuisine, Eddie McStiff's offers gourmet dining but with larger than usual proportions. For starters, try the House Cured Gravlox plate, a serving of basil and molasses cured salmon with crostine, capers, herbed goat cheese, slices of fresh cucumbers, and crumbled eggs. On the side is a mustard sauce made with dill and McStiff's Cisco Stout Beer.

Salad lovers cannot go wrong when ordering Salad Nicoise. Large cubes of fresh tuna filet are smoked, grilled, chilled, and served on a bed of spring mixed greens along with an assortment of haricot verts string beans, red potato, hard boiled egg, imported French olives, and herb vinaigrette. Another great salad is Insalata Caprese, which offers garden ripe tomatoes and fresh buffalo mozzarella served on a bed of mixed greens with an extra virgin olive oil basil vinaigrette.

Pasta devotees who enjoy the full-bodied flavor of Greek cuisine will love the Puttanesca. It features a spicy blend of olive oil, roma tomato, imported calamata olives, capers, and white wine, served with or without a 6-ounce smoked tuna filet over penne.

Meat fanciers who relish steak with a hearty flavor must try McStiff's filet mignon. The filet is wrapped in bacon and served with a cognac green peppercorn cream sauce, summer or winter vegetables, and scalloped potatoes. Root vegetables are normally served in winter and summer squashes during the warmer months. Scalloped potatoes are the standard at McStiff's.

McStiff's also offers "pizza that rules," a large selection of burgers, sandwiches, BBQ Ribs, grilled steaks, a Southwestern selection of enchiladas, fajitas, and burritos, and vegetarian dishes.

Whatever the choice, those who have dined at McStiff's know the importance of saving room for one of the restaurant's delectable desserts. A house favorite is the fruit cobbler, served with a seasonal choice of fruits that includes apple, peach and blueberry. A to-die-for choice is the Chocolate Fudge Cake. When one tries it, it is hard to believe, but the cake is actually low fat, low cholesterol, has no eggs and no butter, yet is incredibly rich and chocolatey.

To make sure that the Eddie McStiff experience lingers on, when leaving make sure to take a piece of McStiff's memorabilia home too. Offered are T-shirts, billed caps, water bottles and beer glasses. Also available is bottled beer, available at the front door.

CAMP GROUNDS

ARCH VIEW RESORT RV CAMP PARK
P. O. Box 1406
Moab, Utah 84532
(Located 10 minutes North of Moab)
Tel: (801) 259-7854
           (800) 813-MOAB (6622)
FAX: (801) 259-6706
Web Site:
moab-utah.com/Archview/Archview.HTmL
Hrs: February - November
Daily   7:00 a.m. - 10:00 p.m.
Reservations are recommended; drop-bys are welcome.
Visa, MasterCard, American Express, and Discover are accepted.

Arch View Resort RV Camp Park, ideally ensconced in the shadows of Canyonlands National Park on the southeast and Arches National Park on the southwest with the LaSal Mountains as a backdrop, is the epitome of what one looks for in a camping experience.

Mitch and Robyn White, on-site owners of Arch View, have created a 23-acre wonderland where history is unfolded and comes alive in the eyes of the beholder.

When traveling highway 191, the first thing that catches one's attention is a replica covered wagon, suspended on a post in mid air. As one enters the park there is a teepee, a chapel with belfry, and a knotty pine country store with hitching posts, typical of what one would have found in an old frontier town. It is not hard to visualize cowboys and Indians and to be transported back to the days of the Old West. Other artifacts along the trail, leading to check-in at the country store, are an old wagon, antique hay rake, and wagon wheels.

But once one steps into the rustic-looking general store, antiquity becomes antiquated—swallowed up in the conveniences of modern-day supplies. Whatever one might need in the form of sundries and groceries are to be found. In addition, the well-stocked mini-market offers a selection of souvenir mugs, post cards, caps, key chains, T-shirts, Indian artifacts and jewelry, area books, and magazines. Cappuccino is as easy as pushing a button; a variety of prepared sandwiches fill the deli; and the best of the best—Haagen-Dazs and Ben and Jerry's—are at one's disposal.

Behind the general store, entered from the outside, are guest laundry facilities and exceptionally clean men's and women's rest rooms, complete with double sink vanities, double showers, and an ample supply of electrical outlets.

There's no need to venture far for fuel as the on-site Texaco station offers a full line of gasoline as well as diesel and propane.

Tranquillity prevails as guests are directed to their RV or tent site. Arch View offers 50 pull-throughs with full hook-ups, 28 large grass tent areas, and several AC cabins, each of which will accommodate up to five guests. Every RV and tent space has its own picnic table and mature trees for respite from a blazing sun.

For the enjoyment of its camping guests, Arch View provides regular barbecues as well as a covered patio with barbecue and large fire pit. Very few campgrounds are allowed to offer wood-burning fires on the premise. But at Arch View roasting marshmallows, wieners, and singing around the fire pit, as well as soaking in the pool, are ideal amenities for becoming acquainted with fellow campers from around the world.

Children at Arch View adore the playground. It too is a step back in time, offering a teeter-totter and a playhouse fort with climbing ropes, bars and rings, as well as the more traditional swings and slides.

When Mitch and Robyn took ownership of Arch View, they fell in love with an old chapel in the Needles area of Canyonlands. The chapel had been used on the set of the Zane Grey film, "Riders of the Purple Sage." The chapel, relocated by Mitch and Robyn, adds to the western charm of the campground but offers much more than just appearance. Not only is the chapel ideal for weddings and receptions, but for family reunions and other group activities as well.

For those who wish to become literally 'riders of the purple sage,' Arch View offers an on-premise corral with trail rides. The stables can accommodate up to eight guests with hourly, half-day, and full day rides. Overnight rides, with camping on the outskirts of Arches National Park, are available when booked in advance.

Two other services Arch View offers are RV storage and monthly rentals in a small area of the Camp Park where 50-amp service is available.

With breathtaking views of North and South Window Arches, Castle Rock, and the LaSal Mountains, as well as the red rock sandstone bluffs of Canyonlands, it is little wonder that Arch View's entry way was selected as the entrance to the fort for the movie, "*Geronimo.*" Scenes from the movie, "*Breakdown*" with Kurt Russell was also filmed at Arch View Resort RV Camp Park.

Moab and its surrounding terrain is the wonderland that for years has provided the setting for cowboy and Indian movies of the past. It has always offered the grandeur of Arches and Canyonlands National Parks, Dead Horse Point State Parks, and the magnificence of the Manti-LaSal National Forest. Today, Moab is synonymous with slickrock and mountain biking. It is a region renown for whitewater rafting on the Colorado and Green Rivers, nature hiking, rock climbing, and for becoming a part of history. The spectrum of things to see and do in the outdoors surrounding Moab is limited only by one's imagination. In addition, Moab offers quality dining, camping, night-time river tours, scenic air tours, and Dutch oven cookouts.

Arch View Resort RV Camp Park is the perfect setting for taking in all that the region has to offer. It is an opportunity to experience the area as it has never been viewed before—from the windows and tent doors of one's home away from home. Arch View is an experience long to be remembered!

CANYONLANDS CAMPGROUND
A Good Sampark
555 South Main Street
Moab, Utah 84552
Tel: (801) 259-6848
        (800) 522-6848
FAX   (801) 259-6848
Hrs:
Convenience Store 6:00 a.m. - 10:00 p.m.
Campground Office   8:00 a.m. - 10:00 p.m.
Visa, MasterCard, American Express, and Discover are accepted.
Reservations are recommended.

Canyonlands Campground is one of those rare exceptions to the rule, a campground that proves that pre-conceived notions can be deceptive.

For those who think that camping out has to be rustic and without amenities, welcome to the world of Canyonlands Campground.

Located right in the heart of Moab, Canyonlands puts this wonderful rural city right at one's doorstep. But if all one wanted to do was enjoy a park-like setting with all the comforts of home, they could do that too—and never leave the campground. Canyonland amenities include an immaculate heated swimming pool with lots of decking, and a great playground for children.

Canyonlands Campground, a Good Sampark with Triple A and Woodall's ratings, offers 108 well-maintained RV spaces with water, sewer and electric hook-ups.

Over the bridge and across the creek is a separate tent area where barbecue facilities are available. Both RV and tent areas are flanked and surrounded with marvelous shade trees. Meandering through the campground are walking paths where one might be joined by wild pheasants and peacocks. Picnic tables are offered at every cement slab and volley ball court set-ups are available. In addition, the campbround offers a large, covered, open-air pavillion that will seat approximately 70. It is ideal for family gatherings, caravans, or for simply joining other Canyonlands guests for fun and camaraderie.

Paul and Aggie Evans, on-site owners, lived in and owned a campground in Grand Junction, Colorado, and were on the verge of retiring from the business. But when Canyonlands Campground became available, Paul and Aggie checked it out, fell in love with the area, and moved to Moab. That love for Moab and Paul's and Aggie's desire to make visitors' stay a wonderful experience is evident throughout the campground. Aggie loves nature and does all that she can to embellish what the environment has already provided. Flowers, some in very unusual planters, flourish throughout the grounds.

It would almost be impossible to find cleaner rest rooms and showers than those in the center of the campground and behind the convenience store-gift shop. The same applies to the campground itself, where campers respect the availability of trash receptacles by using them. Campers also adhere to rules that mandate owners keep their pets on a leash at all times, and they use the pet potty area, cleaning up after their own pets. Paul and Aggie, whose greatest desire is to provide a perfect campground for everyone, appreciate the high regard that campers seem to have for their efforts.

The Canyonlands convenience store is well-stocked with whatever one might have forgotten in the way of sundries, RV supplies, and groceries. Snacks available include nachos, hot dogs, cappuccino, and world-famous Haagen Dazs ice cream.

Campers needn't go too far for Moab souvenirs. The store offers a quality assortment of mugs, books, maps, rocks, Native American artifacts, silver jewelry, beads, wind chimes, caps, T-shirts, and magnets—all of which will be a pleasant reminder of the great time experienced from the Canyonlands campground. And when gas is needed an Amoco gas station is right in front of the convenience store.

Vacation opportunities in and around the Moab area are sundry. And whatever the vacationer's interest, Paul and Aggie are there to assist with arrangements. When booking a stay, let them know what the interest is. Whether it's a river trip, jeep excursion, horseback or bike trail ride, or anything else available in the area, Paul and Aggie will be happy to book the tour.

Paul and Aggie have made Canyonlands Campground a place to be enjoyed by all. They have also made Canyonlands Campground the perfect spot to stay for enjoying all that Moab has to offer.

<u>DID YOU KNOW?</u>

---That May 11 has been set aside as Migratory Bird and Wetlands Day at the Nature Conservancy's Matheson Preserve in Moab. Residents and visitors are invited to join in naturalist walks that begin at 8:00 a.m. and continue every hour until noon. Less than two percent of Utah's total land area is made up of riparian areas (a lush vegetational type of habitat found in wetlands and marshlands and occurring as swaths of greenery along rivers and canyon bottoms). The Matheson Preserve is an exceptional riparian area and is an excellent location for spotting herons, grebes, coots, blackbirds, sparrows, and robins. There are also swallows, peregrine falcons, yellowthroats, white-throated swifts, Lazuli buntings, blackbirds, long-eared owls, hummingbirds, and turkey vultures, to name just a few of birds to be spotted.

RESTAURANTS

BUCK'S GRILL HOUSE
1393 North Highway 191
Moab, Utah 84532
Tel: (801) 529-5201
Web Site:
Http://www.moabhomepage.com
Hrs:
May - October
5:30 p.m. - 10:00 p.m.
Off-season
5:00 p.m. - 9:00 p.m.
Closed   Mid-December - Mid February
Reservations required for parties of six or more
Visa, MasterCard and Discover are accepted.

When visiting an area as rich in history as is Moab, there is something about nostalgia that piques the imagination. Buck's Grill House restaurant is such a place.

The restaurant, originally named Fort Moab, was built in 1967 by D. Eccles Johnson. It was named after the original Fort Moab, built near this site by pioneers who settled the valley in 1855. Built of native pine logs to resemble a fort, Buck's Grill House, with look-out on top, evokes a feeling of history.

Tim Buckingham, born and raised in Moab, has always felt a feeling of pride in Moab's rich history and a sense of belonging and longing—knowing that Moab was where he eventually wanted to re-establish his roots. In 1991 Chef Tim Buckingham returned home to establish Moab's Center Cafe. In 1996 he and his brother, Robert, opened Buck's Grill House.

To further his desire of becoming a chef, Tim embarked on a journey in life that took him to California. Here he completed the Culinary Arts Program at Santa Barbara City College and trained under renown chefs at California resorts--the San Ysidro Ranch, and the Four Seasons Biltmore. While serving as Executive Chef at the Wine Cask in Santa Barbara, the *Food and Wine Companion* praised Tim as being one of the 10 "New American Star Chefs." They noted that "his dishes are delicately prepared, yet the flavors are robust."

From succulent starters to decadent desserts, the moderately priced menu offers tantalizing dishes to satisfy every palate. The home-made Buffalo Chorizo Quesadillas, made with aged jack cheese and topped with corn salsa, and the Smoked Trout Cake, topped with chili sauce and cilantro creams, are more than just tasty appetizers, they are a gourmet treat. Another appetizer not to be missed is the Sweet Potato Tamale, stuffed with sweet potato and goat cheese with roasted tomato sauce. Salads change frequently but the luscious Grilled Shrimp Salad is tossed with a spicy pumpkin seed dressing and topped with corn salsa.

Sandwiches at Bucks are an epicurean delight. Diners most likely never dreamed that they would be eating, let alone raving about, a Grilled Eggplant sandwich. It is stacked with eggplant, grilled red onion, jack cheese, and carrot pesto—and it is delicious. The grilled Buffalo Meat Loaf with roasted garlic mayonnaise is also a gourmet treat.

Not to be slighted at Buck's are the vegetarians. Two pastas of choice are the Linguine Tomato Pesto, the pesto of which is made with sun dried tomatoes, pine nuts, garlic and olive oil; and the Grilled Vegetable Linguine, featuring vegetables tossed with cilantro pesto. Seafood and pasta lovers will appreciate the Shrimp Linguine, tossed with roasted carrot pesto and goat cheese.

Nothing short of exceptional is the Grilled Salmon. It is spice rubbed and topped with citrus butter and chili rice. Straight out of the old west is the Buffalo Meat Loaf, served with a blackened onion sauce and mashed potatoes.

All of Buck's choice steaks are from naturally raised cattle with no hormones added. The selection includes Grilled Sirloin, New York, and T-Bone Steaks, all of which come with a choice of mashed potatoes, chili rice, or French fries, and all of which can be topped with blackened onion sauce upon request.

Buck's Grill House offers small, regular, and large cut Prime Rib, as well as Sirloin, Strip, T-Bone, and Ribeye Steaks. Specialties of the House are the Cowboy Style Steaks. These succulent cuts are rubbed with a special blend of spices, grilled, and topped with BBQ butter that adds a true smoke house flavor.

Food presentation at Buck's is colorful with well-filled plates. All entrees are served with a house specialty slaw and home made sour dough bread.

It is to be hoped that diners at Buck's have saved room for one of the restaurant's delicious desserts. Chocolate lovers will relish the great combination of flavors in the chocolate pistachio cake.

Ambiance at Buck's Grill House is western with each of the dining rooms serving as an art gallery for local artist, Pete Plastow. All of the work on display is for sale.

Hard wood floors, rough hewn open beam ceilings, and hurricane lamps add to the ambiance and set the mood for an American Western Food experience not to be forgotten.

CATTLEMAN'S RESTAURANT & LOUNGE
1991 South Highway 191
Moab, Utah 84532
Tel: (801) 259-6585
Hrs:
Sunday - Thursday 6:00 a.m. - 10:00 p.m.
Friday & Saturday Open 24 hours
Visa, MasterCard, American Express and Discover are accepted.

Those who are regular visitors to Moab know that Moab is a cosmopolitan town that seems to have something for everyone. With its coffee shop, formal dining area, and lounge, Cattleman's Restaurant is a place the locals love. It is also a restaurant that truckers love, not just because it is adjacent to Dar-C Truck Plaza, but because Cattleman's is a restaurant that provides quality food and he-man proportions.

Whether it is pancakes or eggs, Cattleman's offers a menu sure to please the heartiest breakfast appetite. Eggs any style are served with traditional ham, bacon or sausage, but also with Chicken Fried or Ground Sirloin Steak. Omelettes include cheese, ham and cheese, ham, cheese and green chili, mushroom, chili, and Spanish and Western. Biscuits and gravy have always been popular in the West, and Cattleman's serves the best.

For those who love hamburgers, the Burger Corral, with its selection of 11 varieties plus a combination plate, is hard to beat. In addition to the burgers, Cattleman's offers a nice selection of hot and cold sandwiches and sandwich platters.

Every entree on the dinner menu is served with a choice of soup or salad, vegetables, dinner roll, and a choice of potato. Steak lovers find a selection of eight-ounce and 12-ounce cuts of Top Sirloin, 12-ounce cuts of New York and Rib Eye, and six-ounce cuts of Bacon-wrapped Fillet. Seafood aficionados find the Rainbow Trout, Grilled Halibut and Grilled Salmon Steaks, and the Deep Fried Breaded Shrimp, with or without a Top Sirloin Steak, to their liking. On Fridays and Saturdays, choice cuts of Prime Rib, with or without Jumbo Shrimp, are offered. Other entrees include Ground Sirloin, Chicken Fried Steak, Roast Beef, Breaded Veal Cutlets, and Fried Chicken.

It is hard to do, based on the proportions served at Cattleman's, but diners will really miss out if they do not save room for a piece of Homemade Pie. Add a la mode for a matchless treat.

Cattleman's Restaurant & Lounge truly comes alive on Fridays and Saturdays when a live band, featuring Western and old-time rock and roll, appears in the lounge. It is easy to see why those in the know love Cattleman's. It is a restaurant that seeks to please.

CENTER CAFE
92 East Center Street
Moab, Utah 84532
Tel: (801) 259-4295
E-Mail   chefmcc@aol.com
Hrs:
Open Daily   5:30 p.m. - 10:00 p.m.
Visa, MasterCard, and Discover are accepted.
Reservations are recommended.

Travelers' Choice is a guide book that seeks to introduce travelers to the restaurants, services, and accommodations that local residents themselves would choose if it were they who were making the visit. Center Cafe, a small unpretentious restaurant in an equally unobtrusive building in the center of town, is Moab's gemstone. It is Moabites' restaurant of choice when they want an evening on the town, and Center Cafe is the restaurant local residents recommend to guests visiting them in their home.

Local residents are not the only ones who have discovered and recommend Center Cafe. The 1997 Zagat Survey rates Center Cafe as one of the top 30 restaurants in Utah. It is the only dining establishment in Moab to receive such an accolade.

Paul and Zee McCarroll, chefs and owners of Center Cafe, are constantly collaborating to develop the many specials that augment each day's traditional menu. Once they have received their diners' stamp of approval, those specials frequently find a place on their ever-changing menu. As one diner put it, "Center Cafe is a restaurant where cuisine only gets better year after year."

A diner from New York City comments that he and his wife have flown to the state for no other reason than to eat again at Center Cafe. Another diner from Connecticut orders the Ginger Chicken Pot Stickers with Cucumber Salad and Blood Orange Ponzu. Upon completion he confesses that he has a favorite restaurant in Bocca Raton, Florida, whose appetizers have for years been the criteria for judging other cuisine. The Ginger Chicken Pot Stickers have just become his new criteria.

At Center Cafe, each appetizer is an epicurean delight. One can only savor the flavor of the Roasted Eggplant Pizza with Sundried Tomato, Basil Oil, Aged Provolone, and Parmigiano Reggiano. Incredibly delicious is the House Cured Salmon on Crisp Potato Chive Latkes with Creme Fraiche and Sevruga caviar.

Soups at Center Cafe are anything but traditional. Summer diners find the chilled cucumber soup with mint, dill and cracked pepper seasoning, or the chilled carrot ginger soup refreshing taste tempters. From the selection of salads, the Grilled Asparagus wrapped with Applewood Smoked Bacon, Baby Greens, and Roasted Red Pepper Vinaigrette is a palate pleaser.

A special of the night, the Fresh Alaskan Halibut, is encrusted with bread crumbs and horseradish and is served with Thai sesame and peanut sauce and fresh vegetable salad with spicy orange vinaigrette. The sauce and seasonings are so subtle that it is the fresh, succulent flavor of the halibut that is dominant. One entree that has retained its spot on the menu since day-one is the Roasted Eggplant Lasagna with layers of Rosemary Polenta, Feta Cheese, and Moroccan Olive Marinara. Beef lovers relish the robust flavor of the Grilled Black Angus Beef Tenderloin with Caramelized Shallot Sauce and Roasted Garlic Mashed Potato.

Though desserts are not listed on the menu, the Chocolate Molten, which takes 15 minutes to prepare, is an absolute must-have. Baked individually, it is a dense chocolate soufflé turned upside down and served with a raspberry and white chocolate sauce, fresh raspberries, and a sprig of mint.

One of the most pleasant memories of a Center Cafe dining experience is the relaxed, casual atmosphere and knowing that one is not just a number. Chef/owner Paul McCarroll mingles with his dining guests and waiters and waitresses uninhibitedly share stories, creating an incredible informality between diner and server. Yet there seems to be an intuitive sensitivity for those who are seeking an intimate dining experience. Center Cafe offers an unharried atmosphere where diners are expected to take their time and enjoy the cuisine. As the menu states, "the preparation of quality food from fresh ingredients takes time. Please relax and enjoy your evening."

With a seating capacity of only 38, Center Cafe may be small, but what it lacks in size it makes up for in creative and succulent cuisine. Center Cafe Cuisine is so memorable that the memory lingers on and brings the diner back time and again to relive the experience.

DID YOU KNOW?

---That in addition to being heralded for its world-class river running and mountain biking, Moab is also gaining a reputation for its dedication to the arts. Each Memorial Day Weekend, the Canyonlands Arts Council sponsors the Moab Arts Festival. They invite all, to enjoy the festivities.

GRAND OLD RANCH HOUSE

1266 North Highway 191
Moab, Utah 84532
Tel: (435) 259-5753
         (888) 259-5759
FAX: (435) 259-6026
Hrs:
Open Daily
5:00 p.m. - 10:00 p.m.
Visa, MasterCard,
American Express,
Diners Club, Carte Blanch,
and Discover are accepted.
Reservations are recommended.

In 1996, when Utah celebrated its statehood centennial, the Grand Old Ranch House, although not always a restaurant, also celebrated its centennial. The Grand Old Ranch House restaurant is one of few buildings in Grand County to be listed on both the National and Utah Registers of Historic Places.

Spotting the Grand Old Ranch House is an exercise in enchantment. A magnificent 100-year old poplar tree still survives in the front yard along with majestic mulberry trees. Granny and Grandpa mannequins talk and wave to arriving diners from their antique carriage. There are wagon wheels, hand carts, red sandstone waterfalls, a gazebo, a flagstone patio with wrought iron railing, and miniature lights in the trees, creating an ethereal, romantic setting. During summer months guests enjoy dining on the patio and on the upstairs veranda.

Glenn and Katie Victor, owners of The Grand Old Ranch House, purchased the home in April of 1979. The purchase was much more than an acquisition, it was a love affair with history and a desire on the part of the Victors to retain and restore the romance and nostalgia of a bygone era.

An aura of sentimental yearning hangs over the 100-year old dining rooms. Each of the three main floor and three second floor dining rooms have been lovingly decorated with era furnishings. Window dressings are lace with burgundy velvet swag drapes. Dark wood wainscot, window trim and crown molding have been painstakingly restored to elegant luster. White Victorian wallpaper adorns the walls and hanging plants grace the windows. Transom doors have exquisite stained glass windows. In one room there is a French pot belly stove, in another an ornate buffet, and in another, a massive armoire. In every room there are 100-year old pictures of the ranch and of old Moab as they once were.

Candlelight dining at the Grand Old Ranch House is made just that much more enjoyable and romantic by fresh cut flowers on each table. The dinner menu is ala carte and begins with sumptuous appetizers such as the German Potato Cakes, served with smoked trout and black hackle back caviar sauce. The large Gulf Shrimp Cocktail, served with Grand Old Ranch House homemade tangy cocktail sauce, is ideal for seafood lovers. At the Ranch House, fresh seafood is flown in almost daily, meat servings are individually cut on premise, and fresh herbs are procured from the garden.

Appetizers can be followed with a choice of house salads or soups. The Traditional Spinach Salad, prepared table side with bacon, mushrooms, and onion, and topped with orange marmalade dressing, is a favorite. Those who relish creamed soups should not pass up the Potato and Leek soup with red pepper puree. It is exceptional.

Filet Mignon should always be a safe choice at restaurants, but at Grand Old Ranch House, the filet is gourmet. The thick fresh cut of Black Angus beef is wrapped in bacon, seasoned, grilled, and then finished to perfection with Bernaise and Bordelaise sauces. It is served with the Ranch House's gourmet potatoes. A house favorite is "Da other Duck." The slow-roasted Muscovy duck has a lemon thyme crust and is served with a bing cherry sauce and red potato strudel. Other entrees include Lamb Chops, Delmonico Steak, Trio Kabob, Prime Rib, Wiener schnitzel, Yager schnitzel, Santa Fe Chicken, Linguini Suzanne, Pork Tenderloin, Shrimp Scampi, Snake River Trout, Grilled Swordfish, Seared Salmon a la Glenn, Alaskan King Crab Legs, and African Lobster Tail. Each is prepared to order using the finest ingredients.

Anyone who has dined at Grand Old Ranch House knows it is wise to save room for dessert. Favorites include Almond Almaretto Cheese Cake, Chocolate Chocolate Mousse Pie, a variety of Berry Flambes, and the Berry Plate. The latter features fresh berries in season, such as blueberries, strawberries, blackberries, and raspberries, on a lattice work of whipped cream and berry sauce, and served with a caramel tulle shell.

A very special dining area at Grand Old Ranch House is the root cellar turned wine cellar. Looking very much like a setting for *Les Miserables*, the rock wall cellar has heavy wood tables, old fashioned candle holders with tallow dripping down them, and oak wine barrels with spigots. The cellar is always available for private parties and wine tastings.

Grand Old Ranch House is a State liquor licensee and offers a full assortment of alcoholic beverages along with a nice selection of white and red wines, chardonays, Chianti, cabernets, ports, cognacs, and dessert wines.

The romance and nostalgia of Grand Old Ranch House is heightened when one knows the property's history.

Built along the main wagon road leading from Moab to the Colorado River ferryboat crossing, the original home was a popular stopover for all types of travelers, from well-known lawmen and politicians to notorious outlaws. Arthur Taylor, who built the house for his family, was a rancher for a large number of sheep, cattle and horses. Members of Butch Cassidy's Wild Bunch frequented the area and once traded their tired horses for Taylor's fresh mounts.

The homestead's second owners, the John E. Brown family, added their own blend of intrigue and mystery to the house. John Brown had a son-in-law he despised and they were always at odds with each other. On one evening they met at a dance and became involved in a heated argument. The son-in-law left the dance and uprooted a picket from a nearby fence. He returned to the dance hall and challenged his father-in-law with the picket. Angered beyond rationality, Brown went home, got his gun, and waited in the darkness for his daughter and son-in-law's buggy to return home from the dance. When encountered, Brown fired the weapon at his son-in-law but his daughter stepped in front of her husband and the bullet killed them both. Brown was horrified at the outcome and fled back to his home where he holed up on the second floor for several days. From his vantage point he had a clear view of anyone approaching, and he could keep the lawmen at bay. Local newspaper publisher, L. L. "Bish" Taylor, who coincidentally was the son of Arthur Taylor and who was born in the home, talked Brown into surrendering. Attorney fees and other costs related to the shooting forced Brown into financial ruin and the sale of his home.

The Grand Old Ranch House had a succession of other owners, the most colorful of which was millionaire George Skakel's Great Lakes Carbon Corporation. George's brother, Jim, an uncle of Ethel Kennedy, moved into the home to farm the thousand acres of land across the highway. Robert and Ethel Kennedy reportedly visited the Homestead on their honeymoon.

Since Glenn and Katie purchased the home in 1979, restoration at the Grand Old Ranch House has been an on-going function. The Victors ultimate goal is not only to restore the house but also the grounds.

Because of the Victors' love and dedication, the Grand Old Ranch House has resumed its integrity in the life of Moab, and is a welcoming site to visitors in this scenic and historic corner of Utah.

LA HACIENDA
574 North Main Street
Moab, Utah 84532
Tel: (435) 259-6319
Hrs:
March - October
Daily   11:00 a.m. - 10:00 p.m.
November - February
Daily   11:00 a.m. - 9:00 p.m.
Visa, MasterCard, American Express, and Discover are accepted.

Jeffrey and Lauren Davis, owners of La Hacienda, have been doing more than just "spicing your life since 1981," they have been actively involved in every aspect of their burgeoning business. As owners of La Hacienda, one of Moab's finest dining establishments, Jeff and Lauren know that it is more than just luck that, when asked where one should dine, native Moabites heartily recommend La Hacienda.

To Lauren it seems that she and Jeff have always been in the restaurant business, and they both love every minute of it. Lauren counts on carpenter husband, Jeff, to help her provide the decor for their eating establishment. The Southwestern design chairs and other furnishings were created by Jeff, whose furniture has been featured in both Sundance and Ballard Design Catalogs.

The stuccoed walls of La Hacienda are adorned with mock shuttered windows and diverse paintings that feature such scenes as Native Americans on horseback, a portrait of Sitting Bull, and window scene murals. Foliage, pottery, curio cabinets, ceramics, and other artifacts abound throughout the restaurant, and an eclectic collection of baskets hang from the room divider.

. Jeff and Lauren pride themselves on their cuisine, serving up a menu from ingredients that are always the freshest and the best, and preparing them so that there is never a greasy taste. Flavor is accomplished with a delectable blend of spices and seasonings.

The menu offered at La Hacienda is as diverse as the restaurant decor. Breakfast choices include Pigs in a Pancho, an offering of two flour tortillas stuffed with sausage, sour cream, cheese, and La Hacienda's secret salsa with two eggs any style. Another breakfast favorite is the Breakfast Burrito, which features a flour tortilla filled with two scrambled eggs and ham and smothered in salsa and cheese.

The Monte Cisco, truly a house specialty, features two chimichangas stuffed with chicken and ham, and covered with green chili, two cheeses, and sour cream. It is served with Spanish rice and refried beans. Other Mexican Specialties include Carnitas, a southern California favorite that offers seasoned pork served with sour cream, guacamole, vegies, tortillas, beans and rice and a choice of soup or salad. Seafood lovers relish both the Camarones A La Vera Cruzana and the Crab Enchiladas. The first is a blend of shrimp lightly sautéed with a delicious assortment of spiced vegetables served over rice, and accompanied by tortillas. The enchiladas are stuffed with crab, topped with sour cream and guacamole, and served with rice and beans. Both seafood dishes also offer a choice of soup or salad.

Whatever one does, it is important to save room for Lauren's home made desserts. Truly world famous is her triple-layer Carrot Cake. Another house favorite is the Adobe Pie, a chewy, chocolate brownie with ice cream and pecan-studded chocolate sauce. Flan De Queso Crema, a creamy egg custard, is also delicious.

In addition to superb cuisine, La Hacienda, a state liquor licensee, offers domestic and imported beers, wine, and a full spectrum of cocktails.

The Gringo has not been forgotten at La Hacienda, where American classics such as Rib Eye Steak, Fish 'N Chips, and Boneless Pork Steak are also offered. La Hacienda's "little amigos" will find a selection of American and Mexican dishes.

Dining out should always be one of those experiences where atmosphere and quality of cuisine blend harmoniously, affording guests a dining experience that is equal to the occasion. At La Hacienda, that is always the way it is.

SUNSET GRILL
900 North Highway 191
Moab, Utah 84532
Tel: (435) 259-7146
FAX: (435) 259-7626
Hrs:
Open Daily
5:00 p.m. - 10:00 p.m.
Closed January - Mid-February
Visa, MasterCard, and American Express are accepted.
Reservations are requested.

Sunset Grill is a restaurant with a magnificent, colorful history and an extraordinary, picturesque view, both of which defy description.

Many may not remember Charlie Steen, but he is a legend around Moab. In 1952 Charlie drilled in one of his mining claims, Mi Vida, and discovered the world's richest uranium deposit, worth over $60 million dollars. Charlie built an enormous home on the cliffs overlooking Moab with windows across the front on three levels facing the sunset. Every night at 5:00 p.m. Charlie opened his home, and his guests would begin to arrive.

In the tradition of Charlie Steen, John and Laurie Clayton, chef-owners and managers of Sunset Grill, formerly Mi Vida, open their doors and invite their guests to enjoy the sunset, a panoramic view of the city against a backdrop of red sandstone cliffs, and an exceptional dinner by candlelight. Tables are set with fine white linen tablecloths, teal blue napkins, a peach cactus blossom, and, when the sun goes down, the candles are lit.

The entire restaurant offers a Southwestern decor with peach and teal blue accents throughout. Whether dining on the main floor, the upstairs, either of the two downstairs rooms, or on the patio, the view and the cuisine are the same—incredible.

Appetizers are varied, ranging from Norwegian Smoked Salmon to Caesar Salad for Two. The Norwegian Smoked Salmon features Norway's finest smoked salmon medallions served with Dijon mustard, capers, lemon, and diced red onions. A second exceptional choice is the Pacific Crab Cakes, a rendering of Dungeness crab meat, fresh herbs, bread crumbs, and parmesan cheese. It is served with red pepper and shallot mayonnaise.

Presentation of all dishes—appetizers, entrees and desserts—is superb. Entrees are served with a choice of soup or salad, a loaf of fresh wheat bread, fresh vegetables, and a choice of baked potato or rice. An exceptional selection from the grill side of the menu is Colorado Lamb. Rack chops are grilled with a mint butter and served on a port wine peppercorn sauce. Also from the grill are a variety of succulent dishes that include choice, juicy steaks, pork porterhouse steaks, salmon, boneless chicken breast, and Texas-style prime rib, each with its own special seasoning, sauce, or glaze.

Specialties of the house include seafood dishes, pastas, and chicken creations. Especially delectable is the Linguini Olivia. The dish features lemon pepper linguini tossed with lobster medallions and gulf shrimp and finished with parmesan cheese.

Sunset Grill offers only the freshest ingredients with meals prepared to suit one's taste. Sunset Grill is happy to adjust any dish to meet specific dietary needs. The Grill welcomes children and offers a special menu just for them.

A full service restaurant, Sunset Grill offers alcoholic and non-alcoholic drinks from the bar.

Just as with Charlie Steen, John and Laurie pride themselves in making their guests happy and comfortable. By combining their restaurant's romantic setting with chef John's exceptional cuisine, Sunset Grill became a sure Travelers' Choice.

CASTLE VALLEY

Castle Valley, located just East of Colorado River Scenic Byway, is a small but growing ranching community. In the mid to late 1800's it was populated by miners and sheepherders, and became a supply center for the whole region. The valley is about 17 miles northeast of Moab.

CRESCENT JUNCTION

Crescent Junction is 18 miles east of Green River at the junctions of U.S. 191 I-70 and U.S. 6/50. Originally the site was nothing more than a service station in a wide spot in the road. Today, however, there are several full-time residents at this small town. The junction was named for the crescent-shaped Book Cliff Mountains that dominate the view.

THOMPSON SPRINGS

Thompson Springs, east of Crescent Junction near I-70, at one time was a primary shipping point for cattle raised in the area. Today it is nothing more than a flag stop for Amtrak.

SAN JUAN COUNTY

San Juan, Utah's largest county in area, is located in the southeastern corner of the state. Nearly half of the county's population of slightly over 13,000 are Native Americans—primarily Navajo and Ute—who reside on the great Navajo Indian Reservation. This three-state reservation covers some 25,000 square miles of harsh land and is home to over 150,000 Native Americans. Utah's portion of the reservation is less than one-tenth of the total acreage yet it comprises one-fourth of San Juan County's total area.

San Juan area was home to the Anasazi Indians until around 1,300 A. D. Their presence left fascinating ancient cliff dwellings, petroglyphs, pictographs, and other ruins that captivate visitors.

The Utes, for whom the state is named, were the last free-roaming Native Americans in the continental United States. They possibly roamed the Colorado Plateau for thousands of years and once occupied most of Utah. The Navajo came late to San Juan County, shortly after the Anasazi suddenly disappeared. They are traced to the Athabascan people from the Canadian coast. Though called Navajo, a name given them by Spanish explorers, the Navajo think of themselves as the "Dine," which means "the people." The Spanish, however, brought lasting changes to the lives of the Dine, introducing them to domestic livestock, such as sheep and horses. Livestock is still an important part of the Dine's culture.

Few counties in the state offer such diverse landscape with activities for all interests. The county is replete with back-country roads, trails, rivers and lakes that provide opportunities for jeeping, mountain biking, hiking, horseback riding, rappelling, fishing, water skiing, and boating.

San Juan County is also home to some of the state's most spectacular desert scenery. Popular tourist attractions include a portion of Lake Powell, the magnificent Canyonlands National Park, Monument Valley Navajo Tribal Park, Goblin Valley State Park, Natural Bridges National Monument, and Hovenweep National Monument. San Juan County is a land of incredible beauty and certainly one of the biggest jewels in Utah's shining crown.

For travel information write or stop in at the San Juan County Visitors Center, 117 South Main, Monticello, Utah 84535. Call (800) 574-4FUN or (435) 587-3235.

SAN JUAN COUNTY ATTRACTIONS

The **LaSal Mountains** are the second highest range in Utah and, in terms of sheer beauty, are among the most magnificent in the world. The first Spanish explorers to this area named the mountains LaSal because, when they were covered with snow, they resembled a mountain of salt. Sal means salt in Spanish.

Formed by laccolithic doming, the LaSal Mountains are roughly fifteen miles long and six miles wide with the highest peak, Mount Peale, reaching an elevation of 12,721 feet. The higher slopes of these majestic mountains are covered with forests of pine, fir and aspen, while juniper, scrub oak and buck brush grow well in the lower reaches. The majority of the range is part of the Manti-LaSal National Forest.

The **Canyon Rims Recreation Area**, located on a wide expanse of gradually rising flats south of **LaSal Junction**, offers varied recreational opportunities. Canyon

Rims is best known for **Hatch Point**, a great peninsula with a ragged edge twenty miles long and only a few miles wide. Surrounded by high cliffs, some over 2,000 feet in altitude, the point offers an extraordinary view of the beauty of the vast area. Other aerial observation points include **Needles** and **Anticline Overlooks**. The LaSal Mountains are accessed best in San Juan County from LaSal Junction, and on the **LaSal Loop** road from Grand County.

CANYONLANDS NATIONAL PARK

Preserving an immense wilderness of rock in the heart of the Colorado Plateau, Canyonlands National Park, whose prime architects were the wind and the water, is actually made up of three distinct sections—**The Island in the Sky**, **The Maze**, and **The Needles**. The park is sliced into thirds at the confluence of the Green and Colorado Rivers. Utah's largest national park, Canyonlands is world-renowned for its white water river rafting down the Colorado River and through Cataract Canyon. The rugged terrain is also well known for four-wheel driving, mountain biking, hiking, backpacking, and camping.

The Island in the Sky is the highest and northernmost section of the park. About 35 miles northwest of Moab, the entrance to this section is from State Highway 313. A high, broad mesa with an average elevation of over 6,200 feet, The Island in the Sky district of Canyonlands is aptly named. From the edge of the Island one can see an unparalleled view of epic proportions, stretching across canyon after canyon to the horizon over 100 miles away. A variety of overlooks allows the visitor to enjoy vistas of nearly incomprehensible dimensions. Wildlife, such as the collared lizard and small bands of bighorn sheep, may be observed from the many excellent trails that traverse the terrain at all levels of descent. One of the most outstanding geological features of the area is **Upheaval Dome**. Some 1,500 feet deep, the Dome is actually a huge crater, possibly created by the impact of an ancient meteor. Geologists from around the world have come to study it and debate its origin.

Even more appropriately named is **The Maze**. West of the confluence of the Colorado and Green rivers, The Maze country ranks as one of the most inaccessible regions in the nation. A perplexing jumble of canyons, often described as a "thirty-square mile sandstone puzzle," makes up The Maze itself. Further on one finds geological oddities of the **Land of Standing Rocks**, **The Doll House**, and **The Fins**. This is a land of silence and solitude, demanding self-reliance of those who challenge its inner reaches. Until the park was created in 1964, only a handful of people had ever explored these bewildering canyons. Even today, a minimal amount of people per year visit this area. But those who do venture into The Maze find a haunting beauty seen nowhere else on earth. For deep within the confines of Horseshoe Canyon, on the wall of the Great Gallery, one can still see some of the finest examples of prehistoric rock art in the country. These alluring figures, left by Native Americans over 2,000 years ago, are a reminder of the spirit of this untamed land of seductive beauty.

The Needles District, about 50 miles Northwest of Monticello, is found in the southeastern section of the park. A diverse land, The Needles section of the park is made up of prehistoric Indian ruins, fascinating pictographs, and sculpted arches, spires, and canyons. The most striking land forms are the needles themselves. These mammoth sandstone columns of brilliant rust, orange, and coral-colored rocks stand needle-straight in intricate formation. Created by wind, water, and ice, the naked rock pinnacles of The Needles offer but a taste of the huge array of arches, rock spires, gardens, canyons and potholes which color the region. From the **Devils Kitchen** and **Angel Arch**

to **Elephant Hill** and **Caterpillar Arch**, the natural glamour of this singularly bewitching landscape is filled with variety and wonder.

As home to the Anasazi Indians, the ancient ones who once roamed the land growing corn and squash and hunting deer and bighorn, the land still bears traces of their advanced culture in nearly every Needles canyon. From their remarkably well preserved stone and mud dwellings to their graceful petroglyphs and pictographs, the Anasazis have left their mark on a land that was as much a part of them as they were a part of it.

Largely untouched by modern man, Canyonlands National Park remains an untrammeled wilderness. Its few roads are mostly unpaved, its trails are primitive, and its rivers run wild and free.

Tourist Information offices are in Moab, Green River, and Monticello. Visitor centers, open daily except for Thanksgiving and Christmas, are at both the Island in the Sky and the Needles Districts. The Canyonlands National Park address is 2282 South West Resource Boulevard, Moab, Utah 84532. For more information call (435) 259-7164

Dark Canyon Primitive Area, managed by the BLM, is made up of the main gouges and side canyons of three major tributaries of Cataract Canyon. Narrow, deep canyons with unscalable walls, **Dark**, **Bowdie**, and **Gypsum** canyons have become popular destinations for wilderness backpackers.

GLEN CANYON NATIONAL RECREATION AREA & LAKE POWELL

The world's second largest manmade reservoir, **Lake Powell**, was created in 1963 with the completion of the Glen Canyon Dam. Named for Major John Wesley Powell, who led the first exploratory expeditions down the Colorado river in 1869, the lake offers a seemingly endless shoreline of 1,960 serpentine miles. That is more than ten times longer than the lake itself (186 miles) and 200 miles longer than the entire Pacific Coastline of the United States. Its meandering inlets provide intriguing side canyons that invite exploration.

Located at conveniently spaced intervals, the National Park Service has built several marinas that include Hite, Halls Crossing, Bullfrog, Dangling Rope, and Wahweap.

The **Burr Ferry**, berthed at Hall's Crossing, serves as an alternative route for those going northwest to Capitol Reef National Park or those coming south and southeast to Monument Valley, Mexican Hat, and the Four Corners area of the state. The Ferry takes about 30 minutes and travels between Hall's Crossing and Bullfrog Marinas. It gives one the opportunity to experience the lake without renting a boat, and it can save the traveler 130 miles. Open to cars, motorhomes, and buses, the ferry operates on even hours from 8:00 a.m. to 6:00 p.m. between mid-May and September 30. From October 1 through mid-May the ferry's last departure is 3:00 p.m. (435-684-7000)

Lake Powell, located within the **Glen Canyon National Recreation Area,** is a traveler's paradise. There are canyons, coves, and caves to explore; Indian ruins and pictographs to photograph; and miles and miles of hiking and backpacking trails to wander. For those who indulge in water sports, the lake offers some of the best fishing found anywhere in the state, and outstanding boating, waterskiing, houseboating, and jet skiing. (See Lake Powell story.)

RAINBOW BRIDGE NATIONAL MONUMENT

The most famous geologic wonder in the Glen Canyon National Recreation Area is Rainbow Bridge National Monument. It is accessible only by boat via Lake Powell or by a rugged overland route. The bridge became a national monument in 1910 and, until 1963 with the completion of the dam, was one of the most isolated attractions on the North American continent. It has a span of 275 feet, is 42 feet thick at the top, and is 290 feet high at the arch. In case the numbers do not register, the United States Capitol Building could be placed beneath it with plenty of room to spare. The Navajos, on whose land the bridge sits, call the bridge *Nageelid Nonnezoshi*, "the hole in the rock shaped like a rainbow."

The legend of Rainbow Bridge National Monument is intriguing. A young god had entered the Navajo Mountains to hunt, but as he entered, the game disappeared. This puzzled the young god, for he knew that he was the most stealthy of all hunters. How could they have known of his presence? But the animals were not retreating from him, they were running away from a flash flood and suddenly the young god found himself trapped by the raging water. The elder gods, looking down, took pity on the young god and sent him a rainbow on which he could climb to safety. Then, as their sign that they always look out for and protect the Navajos, the gods turned the rainbow to stone.

Another famous point of interest is **Defiance House**, an Anasazi community cliff dwelling in Forgotten Canyon. **Hole in the Rock** is a monumental man-made crevice that was made by Mormon pioneers. First they made the V-shaped crevice and then they lowered 200 people, 83 wagons, 400 horses, and more than 1,000 cattle down the precipice in order to cross the Colorado River. **Lees Ferry**, which opened up travel and settlement of the Four Corners region, and which still has the remains of a fort, post office, ranch buildings, and cemetery as well as the remains of an old steamboat, is another major attraction. Then, of course there is **Glen Canyon Dam**, the architectural wonder that made Lake Powell possible. After seven years of Herculean effort in building the 568-foot dam—1956-1963—water began to back up the waters of the Colorado, San Juan, and Escalante Rivers. It reached "full pool" in 1980. The dam fulfills the goals of water storage, meets the electrical needs of 1.5 million people daily, and has created major recreational opportunities for millions around the world. Tours are available at the dam through the **Carl Hayden Visitor Center**, two miles from Page, Arizona. For more information, call (520) 608-6404.

Only 3.2 water miles separates *Bullfrog* and *Halls Crossing*. The state operates a year-round vehicle and passenger ferry between the two that can save 130 road miles. Bullfrog is located on the north side of the river channel and Halls Crossing is on the south side. *Wahweap* is on the borders between Utah and Arizona, just three miles from Page, Arizona.

NEWSPAPER ROCK STATE HISTORICAL MONUMENT

The smooth rock face of Newspaper Rock State Historical Monument, which bears over 350 distinct Indian rock writings—many of which are superimposed over those of earlier vintage—has been a canvas for Native American artists for nearly a millennium. Covering a variety of cultural origins and time periods, the "glyphs" range from the Anasazi of over 800 years ago to the Ute era of the last 100 years. The small campground located nearby offers picnicking, sightseeing and camping.

MONUMENT VALLEY NAVAJO TRIBAL PARK

Sprawling across southeastern Utah and northern Arizona, Monument Valley presents a vast landscape of spectacular scenery that is captivating any time of the year. Made famous by the motion picture industry, Monument Valley has served as the backdrop for at least 16 major western films and scores of commercials.

Whether traveling to this indisputable desert wonderland during the blazing sun of summer or in the white cloak of winter, Monument Valley presents breathtaking photographic opportunities. Photo experts agree that the buttes, mesas, canyons, and freestanding rock formations exhibit their greatest splendor at sunrise and sunset.

Although some of the park can be seen from Highway 163, there is a graded 14-mile loop that discloses much more of what the park has to offer. Monument Valley Tribal Park is home to a large population of Navajo. They, the Dine people, ask that visitors respect their land and stay on established roads.

In depth tours are available by Navajo guides that take visitors to mud and log hogans, the traditional dwelling of the Dine. Dine culture is further enhanced with the opportunity to witness beautiful Navajo rugs being created on rope and log looms.

The Dine, as they prefer to call themselves, continue to live among the red rock buttes, eroded pillars, and spires for which the valley is famous. The Dine operate the Tribal Park and Visitor Center as well as a 100-space campground. There is also the famous Goulding's Lodge. What started out as a trading post in 1920 has expanded to include a lodge, campground, gift shop and museum.

SAN JUAN COUNTY EVENTS

November features a month-long fishing derby at Hall's Crossing Marina on Lake Powell (435-684-2261).

LA SAL

Resting at an elevation of 7,000 feet on the southern slope of the LaSal Mountains, this tiny community of 300 is an undiscovered jewel of southeastern Utah. The LaSal Mountains rise at the town's edge, sheltering the community from the north and creating an unrivaled outdoor playground. Dirt roads of varying difficulty climb into the mountains for some of the best camping in the state. The mountains also offer some of the most popular and challenging hikes with trails reaching above 12,000 feet. Mountain bikes, cross country skiing, and snowmobiling are popular area sports. Four-wheel drive and fishing tours are available.

MONTICELLO

Settled in 1888, this verdant town reminded some of the earlier settlers of the site of Thomas Jefferson's Virginia home in Monticello. That is how this pretty little mountain town, with a population of close to 2,000, got its name. During the 1950's Monticello became well known for its uranium mines. Today, Monticello, which still has its share of farming and ranching, is involved in the business of pleasing people.

Many call Monticello, which is nestled at the eastern foot of the *Blue (also* known as *Abajo*) *Mountains*, the "city of views." In three different directions one can seemingly see forever. The San Juan Range of the Rockies, 100 miles away, is easily discernible to the east. The beautiful La Sal Mountains are to the north and the Sleeping Ute Mountain in Colorado is visible to the south.

Monticello, because of its cool summers, colorful fall terrain, exciting winters, and fresh spring weather, is also tabbed as a "vacation land for all seasons." Green meadows, wildflowers, mountain lakes, and sandstone canyons are breathtaking in spring. Moderate daytime and cool evening temperatures in Monticello create an ideal summer getaway, especially when one knows that mountain lakes for picnicking, fishing, and non-motorized boating are a short drive away. During fall the mountain backroads are resplendent with autumn colors. In winter the mountainsides are packed with fresh snow and the backroads are ideal for cross-country skiing and snowmobiling.

View pipes in **Pioneer City Park** allow visitors to identify **Horsehead Peak** in the Blue Mountains where the vegetation has grown into the shape of a blaze-faced horse overlooking Monticello. Pioneer Park also has picnic areas and an example of a pioneer cabin.

For those who like organized recreation, there is a challenging nine-hole golf course, racquetball and tennis courts, public swimming, a movie theater, museum, and three city parks for gatherings and picnicking.

For those with high clearance vehicles, there are several Scenic Backways that offer days of adventure. Scenic Backway forest Road 79, a 35-mile trip over the mountains to Blanding, takes two hours and offers picture postcard views. Whatever direction one travels will make an exciting day's trip. Enjoy the pleasures of touring before returning to Monticello for dining and accommodations.

MONTICELLO EVENTS

March is the month when outdoor sports enthusiasts gather to participate in the Blue Mountain to Canyonlands Triathlon. The event draws skiers, bikers and runners from all parts of the world to participate in an event that takes participants from high alpine country to Southeastern Utah's acclaimed deserts. Prizes are awarded and lunch served (435-587-2029).

May is the month for the Blue Mountain Open Horseshoe Tournament, held at the Lion's Horseshoe Park (435-587-2533 or 1-800-574-4FUN).

July features the Blue Mountain Bike Chase, an event that takes place on a 25-mile loop course of gravel, native surface road, and trail (435-587-2029). On July 24, the state celebrates Pioneer Days, also known as Days of '47. The celebration is in honor of the Mormon Pioneers who first entered the Salt lake Valley on July 24, 1847. In Monticello there is a parade, contests, softball tournament, and concessions at the Monticello City Park. All in the area on that day are invited to attend.

August is a big month in Monticello. Events include the San Juan Open Horseshoe Tournament, held at the Monticello Lion's Horseshoe Park (435-587-2533 or 1-800-574-4FUN); the San Juan County Fair and Rodeo (435-587-3225); the Hillman Triathlon (435-678-3224); and the San Juan Amateur Golf Tournament and Cookout, held at the Blue Mountain Meadows Golf Course (435 587-2468).

October is deer hunting month throughout the state. The Monticello Lion's Club hosts a Deer Hunter's Ball two days before hunting season opens.

BLANDING

The largest city in San Juan County, Blanding, at an elevation of 6,000 feet, has a population of 3,800. Blanding was settled in 1905 by Albert R. Lyman and his wife, Gladys, as the result of a dream. Called "Old Settler," Lyman established the town when his uncle Walter related a dream he'd had about a large city on White Mesa. Lyman was a noted educator and writer of local history. He and his wife dedicated their educational talents to the Native American youth. As a result of Lyman's many talents and interest in the Native Americans, Blanding today is the cultural and educational center for the Utah portion of the nearby Navajo Reservation.

Blanding was originally known as Grayson. In 1915, an easterner, Thomas W. Bicknell, offered a library to any Utah town that would take his name. Grayson and the nearby town of Thurber accepted the offer. A compromise was soon arranged—Thurber became Bicknell and Grayson became Blanding after Mrs. Bicknell's maiden name. The library was divided between the two towns.

For nearly 50 years Blanding remained an agricultural town of sheep and cattle and grain farming. Then, in the mid-1950's, the discovery of uranium, oil, and natural gas in several locations throughout the Four Corners area brought a sudden wealth that radically changed the area. Today, in spite of its prosperity, Blanding is a quiet, orderly community of modest homes and family-oriented businesses.

Blanding is a town that is proud of its past and looking forward to its future. Today it is best known for being the gateway to the Trail of the Ancients.

Blanding is a destination vacation town with its many fine accommodations, restaurants, gift shops, city parks, and campgrounds.

BLANDING ATTRACTIONS

Trail of the Ancients is a roughly defined loop that begins at Blanding and travels to some of the West's most picturesque sites, all of which are within a short distance from a paved road.

First stop is to **EDGE OF THE CEDARS STATE PARK AND MUSEUM**, located at 660 West 400 North, in Blanding.

Edge of the Cedars State Park houses a museum of Native American Culture with a strong focus on the ancestral Pueblo or Anasazi culture. An Anasazi ruin, dating from A. D. 850 - 1220, is located just behind the museum building. Six habitation and ceremonial complexes have been identified, but only one has been excavated. It includes a roofed Kiva (ceremonial room), and guests are welcome to descend the ladder through the smoke hole into the Kiva just as the Anasazi did centuries ago.

The museum at Edge of the Cedars is known for its outstanding collection of Anasazi pottery. The ***Spirit Windows Exhibit*** displays replicated ancient rock art. A rare macaw feather sash, fine basketry and an Anasazi loom are displayed in the ***Fragile Heritage Exhibit***. A Special Exhibits room displays temporary exhibits. The museum also has an auditorium where a 20-minute video on the Anasazi is shown. A gift shop provides fine books, T-shirts, and reproductions of Anasazi art. The museum is also the regional repository for archaeological materials excavated from public lands in southeastern Utah. Edge of the Cedars Indian Ruin was listed on the Utah State Register of Historic Places in 1970 and on the National Register of Historic Places in 1971 (435-678-2238).

The trail travels south to highway 95, winding its way across several washes and over slick rock before reaching an overlook of a small cliff dwelling, **Butler Wash Indian Ruins**. Round trip hiking distance to the site is one mile with traveling time approximately one-half hour. The hike is moderately easy. There is ample parking and interpretive signing at the overlook.

Continuing west on 95, the trail takes visitors to **Comb Ridge**, an eroded monocline that has historically been a serious barrier to east-west travel in the southern end of the county. The monocline, a bending of the earth's crust in only one direction, begins near Elk Ridge in the north and extends approximately eighty miles to Kayenta, Arizona. Appearing as a pink upheaval across the landscape, it is easy to see why it presented a barrier to travel for the early pioneers and forced them east to the San Juan River. Between mileposts 105 and 107 is **Comb Wash**, which is filled with a forest of cottonwood trees.

Right at the head of Mule Canyon are seven ancient Puebloan towers, three of which are easily visible at the site. Called **Cave Towers**, these ruins are over 900 years old, are extremely fragile, and precariously sit on the high canyon rim. Access to Cave Towers is by high clearance vehicles on a one-half mile native surface road just south of 95. The road does not go all the way to the Towers and a short hike is necessary. Since the site is not signed, look for mile post 103. A word of caution. One careless act could destroy a nine-century ruin. Please refrain from touching, climbing or entering the ruins and please make sure to close the gate when entering and leaving. Livestock roam the range.

A well-signed ruin and rest stop along 95 is **Mule Canyon Ruin**. These are well-preserved surface ruins of the Pueblo Indians. They include a Kiva and tower that have been excavated and stabilized, and a block of rooms. Interpretive signing, handicap accessibility, and vault toilets are provided.

Continuing west on 95 the traveler comes to **Salvation Knoll** (between mile posts 98 and 97.) In the winter of 1879 a scouting party for the main Hole in the Rock pioneer company became disoriented and feared they were completely lost. In desperation they climbed this knoll and could see the Blue (Abajo) Mountains to the north. They were able to get their bearings and continue on their search for a passage to the east. The knoll's vantage point had saved them. The Hole in the Rock company was a group of Mormon pioneers who set out from southwestern Utah to settle the Four Corners section of the state. A journey that was to have taken six weeks took six months and even then the pioneers were so wearied that they fell short of their destination. When they came to the bluffs above the Colorado River (easily seen from Lake Powell), they embarked upon a monumental task of creating a man-made "V" crevice. They then lowered 200 people, 83 wagons, 400 horses, and more than 1,000 cattle down the precipice in order to cross the Colorado River. When descending from the knoll, imagine if you can, being a part of this intrepid wagon expedition with no roads and no directional signs.

Continuing West on 95 the Trail of the Ancients Road Tour takes travelers to State Highway 275 for a visit to **NATURAL BRIDGES NATIONAL MONUMENT**

The region features three immense water-carved bridges and, once inhabited by the cliff dwelling Anasazi, the remains of a number of prehistoric villages.

Visitors should first stop at the Monument's Visitor Center Museum to examine the excellent exhibits and obtain information about the bridges, Indian sites, and the many trails. The visitor center and primitive campground are open year-round. From the visitor center a nine mile loop drive takes visitors past Sipapu, Kachina, and Owachomo natural bridges. There are trails leading down to each of the bridges. The bridges may also be viewed by walking a short distance to the overlooks.

Sipapu Bridge, the largest of the stone bridges, and second only to Rainbow Bridge, also in Utah, measures 220 feet high and spans a distance of over 265 feet. Considered by many to be the most spectacular of the three, Sipapu Bridge has been described as "a structure so magnificent, so symmetrical, and beautiful in its proportions, as to suggest that nature, after completing the mighty structure of Kachina Bridge, had trained herself for a finer and nobler form of architecture." The name Sipapu was taken from a Hopi legend referring to "the gateway through which the souls of men come from the underworld and finally return to it."

Kachina Bridge, which measures 210 feet tall and has a span of 206 feet, a width of 44 feet, and a thickness of 93 feet, is the most massive of the three bridges. James Scorup, one of the discoverers of the bridges, originally named this bridge Caroline, after his wife. The name was changed in 1906 when the area was declared a national monument.

Owachomo Bridge, at a height of 106 feet and a width of 180 feet, is the smallest and most fragile of the bridges. The width of the arch is twenty-seven feet and the thickness a mere nine feet. Formed from pale salmon pink stone and vermilion streaks that are accented with orange and green lichens, Owachomo was named for a Hopi word meaning "flat rock mound."

The Natural Bridges visitor center facility is completely powered by the sun. A large solar display is accessible for viewing. There is also a small 13-site campground. (435- 692-1234).

Returning back to 95 from 275, one retraces their steps for a short distance to highway 261, traveling south to **Grand Gulch Primitive Area**. Grand Gulch Primitive Area is a natural archaeological preserve of the U. S. Bureau of Land Management and was inhabited as ancient communities for over 1,000 years. The 52-mile long gulch is rich in rock art and represents rock writings by cultures that span 1,400 years—from 100 B. C. to 1300 A. D. Representative sites from both Basketmaker and Pueblo periods are accessible. In addition to the pictographs and petroglyphs, there are remains of Puebloan dwellings, pottery, tools, and art work. Because of its remoteness and the rugged terrain of this tremendous box canyon, Grand Gulch, a wilderness almost untouched by western civilization, is accessed only by hiking or horseback. From the Kane Gulch Ranger Station it is a minimum five-hour round trip hike. The bureau strictly controls this preserve and permits are required and fees applicable. They are available through the ranger station (435-587-2141).

Muley Point Overlook offers a panoramic view of the area's geologic and scenic wonders that stretch beyond in grand proportions. Just 17 miles northwest of Mexican Hat, the Overlook is a few miles west of 261 on a gravel road. Muley Point Overlook is at the edge of a very high cliff and offers a spectacular panorama below that includes Monument Valley to the south and Navajo Mountain to the west. There are no restraints or facilities at the site. A four-mile graded native surface road leads into the site, but should at all times be avoided when it is wet.

Once one returns to 261, travelers encounter The **Moki Dugway,** a series of steep switchbacks where the road climbs the 1,000 foot high face of Cedar Mesa. An excellent highway, the Dugway provides a thrilling ride for most drivers and takes them to another gravel road, this time heading northeast to **Valley of the Gods.** Located 17 miles north of Mexican Hat, Valley of the Gods is known as Utah's miniature Monument Valley. A land of standing rocks, colorful mesas, deep canyons, and tortured earth, the valley is part of the Raplee Anticline. The 17-mile drive through Valley of the Gods is a photographer's paradise. Of the valley's many attractions, some of the most popular are **Seven Sailors, Rooster,** and **Southern Lady.** One can continue the native surface road to highway 163, going south, or return to 261.

GOOSENECKS STATE PARK

Four miles off Utah Highway 261 near Mexican Hat is Goosenecks State Park. Tourists to the area can view one of the world's most magnificent examples of an entrenched river meander. Flowing more than 1,500 feet below, the enchanting San Juan River has forged a chasm through the Pennsylvanian Hermosa Formation. The river meanders back and forth, flowing for nearly six miles while progressing only one linear mile towards the Colorado River and Lake Powell. The canyon walls are a colorful combination of sandstone, shale and limestone and are filled with land and marine fossils of nearly every description. An observation shelter, campsites, and restroom facilities are on site. For more information write P. O. Box 788, Blanding, Utah 84511 or call (435 678-2238).

Back on 261, it is but a short drive to **Mexican Hat,** a small town that was named for its inverted stone sombrero, **Hat Rock,** located just east of highway 163 and just north of town. One of the most spectacular sites at Mexican Hat is **Navajo Tapestry,** an area of wavy geometric colors in the strata behind Hat Rock that is visible from the highway.

Proceeding northeast on 163, travelers arrive at **Sand Island,** the principal boat launch for those floating the San Juan River. Sand Island is not just a launching site, it offers visitors one of the most accessible rock art panels in the state and represents an overview of the type of rock art that is found all along the San Juan River. The glyphs represented are from 800 to 2,500 years old and feature Kokopelli, the humpbacked flute player of ancient Pueblo mythology.

From Sand Island it is back to highway 191 and the historic town of **Bluff,** where numerous washes enter the San Juan river and provide interesting long or short river hikes. From **Montezuma Creek** to Bluff there are many archaeological sites located on the river. Float trips are offered down the river with guides placing great emphasis on the ancient dwellings.

HOVENWEEP NATIONAL MONUMENT

Although it is somewhat removed from the main loop, the Trail of the Ancients Road Tour would not be complete without a visit to **Hovenweep National Monument,** 39 miles southeast of Blanding (take 191 to 262 and 262 to Hovenweep). Hovenweep, which straddles the Utah-Colorado border in a remote canyon country north of the San Juan River, was established by presidential proclamation in 1923 as a way of protecting the numerous ruins of prehistoric Native American civilizations found in the area.

Hovenweep's unique towers remind many visitors of European castles. It is noteworthy that the many ruins of these ancient Pueblo Indian villages were built about the same time as the medieval fortresses of Europe.

Hovenweep is a Ute word meaning "deserted valley." Though the area once supported a large population, the ruins are in rugged land where sagebrush grows in thick stands up to five feet tall. No one seems to know what caused the disappearance of the Anasazi Indian culture from this land, but the most validated consensus is that it was famine that created Hovenweep—a deserted valley.

Ruin Canyon and its south fork, *Square Tower Canyon*, contain the most important group of ruins. Appearing without warning, this 300 to 500 foot deep sheer walled canyon is the site of *Hovenweep House*. A large semi-circular structure that once housed as many as fifty families, this unique ruin includes circular underground rooms known as chives, which were used by the tribal shamans, and a large "D" shaped tower that rose from the center of the structure.

The largest and most accessible of the six units of ruins is *Square Tower*, where several well-preserved structures are located, including *Hovenweep Castle*, the best preserved building in the monument. Built in two "L" shaped wings, the ruin contains several sleeping and living chambers, a number of towers and the underground chives. The walls of the castle are massive rock and mud mortar structures, some more than twenty feet tall. There is a system of loop trails at the Square Tower unit and ranger-guided tours are available throughout the day.

In addition to the Trail of the Ancients Road Tour, other Blanding attractions include the *Dinosaur Museum*, a gallery that offers a glimpse into the very distant past and features realistic life size dinosaur models, fossils and skeletons. There is a History Hall of Hollywood Dinosaurs and a 275-million year old tree. The gift shop offers dinosaur treasures for children of all ages. The museum is open seasonally from 9:00 a.m. to 5:00 p.m. Monday through Saturday, April 15 through October 15.

The *Nations of the Four Corners Cultural Center* is a fascinating self guided tour along a one-half mile trail that takes visitors to a Navajo hogan, a Ute tipi, a Mexican hacienda, and a pioneer log cabin complete with old wagons and farm equipment. These four home sites are typical of the area's historic cultures. A pedestrian entrance is open at all times and there is no admission fee. In addition, there is an observation tower along the trail that provides a panoramic vista of the surrounding area(435-678-2072).

Recapture Reservoir, four miles north of Blanding, is a great place for fishing and boating. Camping is also permitted along the shore.

BLANDING EVENTS

April is just one of the months in the year that the Chrysler Corporation sponsors a Jeep Jamboree. In the spring the group explores Arch Canyon, a challenging trip through the high desert (1-800-574-4FUN).

July 4 draws county residents and tourists to its Independence Day celebration. Activities include a folk festival and fireworks (435-678-2539). Also during the month, the Edge of the Seaters presents a series of melodramas (435-678-3340 or 678-2067).

September events include the White Mesa Ute Council Bear Dance with contests, games, and cook-outs at White Mesa, just south of Blanding. Sponsored by the White Mesa Ute Council, the number to call is 435-678-3397. Chrysler's Jeep Jamboree, this time to Hole in the Rock, follows the trail crossed by the Mormon pioneers in 1879. This is one of the most difficult trails on Chrysler's Jamboree schedule. Meals are provided by the Monticello Lion's Club (1-800-574-4FUN) or (916-333-4777).

BLUFF

Located just outside the Navajo Indian Reservation on U. S. Highway 191, the community of Bluff has a long history of boom and bust, poverty and riches. An oasis-like town of around 300, Bluff is set in the dramatic red rock canyon of the San Juan River at an elevation of 4,380.

Bluff was settled in 1880 by the Hole in the Rock Mormon pioneers, whose epic journey across the Colorado River and through the slickrock region to Bluff is one of the most stirring episodes of Mormon history. Eighty-three wagons were lowered 1,800 feet to the Colorado River and then moved over almost impassable terrain in order to establish the San Juan Mission here. Bluff was the first Anglo community in southeastern Utah.

When the settlers first arrived, conditions were extremely difficult and the first houses built were crude. The original fort is still standing near the Kumen Jones ruin, as are many other old rock homes. Later photos show that it did not take long for the pioneer homes to become elaborate with fancy wood moldings and ornamental hardware of the Victorian vintage. The village of Bluff was built around five artesian wells that still provide water for the community's growing shade trees and fruit orchards.

Almost since its inception, because of its location, Bluff has been the site of numerous Indian trading posts. Even today Navajos from the nearby reservation bring wool, silver works, and hand woven rugs to trade for the goods they need.

Along the San Juan river, accessible four miles west of Bluff at Sand Island, there are signs of beaver. Raccoon and ring-tailed cat tracks are to be found in the mud and near the cliffs. Snowy egret, blue heron, black-crowned night heron, and white-faced ibis frequent the shallows along the river. Summer residents also include the blue grosbeak and mountain bluebirds.

Colorado Squaw fish, an endangered minnow species that weighs up to 80 pounds, Humpbacked Sucker and catfish call the San Juan home. Along the banks, secreted by the Tamarisk Brush and cottonwood groves, are Mule deer, Ring-Neck Pheasant, quail, partridge, porcupine and wild turkey. Soaring above the river are Bald and Golden eagles, Flickers, Shrikes, Finches, and Tanagers as well as Peregrine Falcons.

On top of the sandstone cliffs that surround Bluff are cougar, bobcat, and Desert Bighorn Sheep. Tiny pools of water that have collected in sandstone depressions have become home to the Canyon Tree Frog, and the Red-spotted Toad.

The small town of Bluff is gaining a well-deserved reputation for its historic rock homes, river rafting expeditions, pre-historic Pueblo culture, and its red rock country on the border of the Navajo Reservation. Nearby is the St. Christopher Mission to the Navajo. Also close by are a swinging bridge across the San Juan River, a boat launch, campground, and panels of petroglyphs from the Anasazi Indians.

Bluff is San Juan County's living museum. Spending a day or two in Bluff is rewarding to anyone with a penchant for pioneer history, geology or archeology. The wetlands and sightings of other wildlife give thrilling adventures of the West. Bluff is a city with a colorful history where old fashioned western hospitality has never gone out of style.

Bluff is a full service destination with accommodations, gift shops, restaurants, and several expedition companies.

BLUFF ATTRACTIONS

Most famous of Bluff's attractions is *Sand Island*, a large rock art panel along the cliffs of the San Juan River. Many glyphs of Kokopelli, the humped back flute player of ancient mythology and the most famous of all petroglyph figures, are easily discernible here. It is also at Sand Island where river expedition companies launch their rafts on the *San Juan River*.

Bluff is at the beginning of Utah *Scenic Byway 163*, which runs from Bluff to *Monument Valley*. The route passes through *Comb Ridge*, the monocline that forced the Hole-in-the-Rock pioneers to the river where they settled in Bluff. (Please refer to Blanding attractionsTrail of the Ancients Road Tour for more detailed information.)

Bluff is dotted with many handsome pioneer homes and buildings, such as *St Christopher's Episcopal Mission*. Built by Father Harold B. Liebler, the "priest with the long hair," and his many volunteer helpers and contributors, the mission is an attractive tree-shaded complex that includes a school, a hogan-shaped chapel, and other facilities.

BLUFF EVENTS

May is the month for Bluff Head Start Days, a special day for Navajo children that is highlighted with a parade, concessions, and dance contests (435-672-2643).

September is highlighted by the Utah Navajo Fair. It offers a rodeo, carnival, pow-wow, mud-bog races, BBQ, parade, and Native American dance contests. (1-800-574-4FUN).

ANETH / MONTEZUMA CREEK

The area of Aneth was not included as a part of the Navajo Nation when it was first established in 1868. The southeastern portion of Utah—all of the land south of the San Juan River—was ceded to the Navajos in 1884 and an area north of the San Juan was added in 1905.

There is not a more interesting story behind a name than that of Aneth. When the first Anglo trader came to this area and tried to do business with the Navajo, his practices were so dishonest that they called him "Aneth," a word that means "Just like the devil."

Aneth is a Chapter Headquarters for the Navajo Nation. A chapter is comparable to our city governments, but without law enforcement or city utilities.

Both Aneth and Montezuma Creek are private land owned by the Navajos and should be respected as such. The land is dotted with hogans (small round structures where the door always faces the morning sun) and shade houses, a pole structure covered with leafed branches.

The Aneth Oil Field, one of the major producing fields in the western United States, is a source of employment for many area residents.

Both Aneth and Montezuma Creek provide access to Hovenweep National Monument and both are on Utah Highway 262, the best way to get to Four Corners. Neither Aneth nor Montezuma Creek has lodging, but gasoline, sundries, and food are available.

ANETH / MONTEZUMA CREEK ATTRACTIONS

Aneth and Montezuma Creek, when coming from the southeast, provide access to *Hovenweep National Monument.* The road from Aneth is paved; the route from Montezuma Creek has a two mile stretch of graded gravel. Both roads are well signed. From Hovenweep, McElmo Canyon provides an alternate route to Cortez, Colorado. The ride through the canyon is lush and green. There is a four and one-half mile section of gravel road.

Aneth and Montezuma Creek are on Utah State Highway 262, Utah's best route to *Four Corners Monument.* The road becomes Colorado 41 at the state line and then is an eight mile drive to U.S. 160. After a right hand turn it is 12 miles to the monument.

(For more detailed information of Hovenweep National Monument please refer to Blanding attractions and the Trail of the Ancients Road Tour.)

FOUR CORNERS

Four Corners Monument, easily reached by U. S. Highway 160, marks the only place in the nation where four states come together at a common point. The monument is a marker made of granite, bronze disc, and colored concrete. Inserted are metal plates of the great seals from each of the four states—Utah, Arizona, Colorado, and New Mexico. The monument stands on a tiny corner of each state, making it possible to be in four states at one time.

Since Four Corners is entirely situated on a great Navajo reservation, the Navajo Nation invites tourists to visit them at the many vender booths that surround the monument. The tribe is noted for its tapestry rug weaving, silver crafts, and basketry.

MEXICAN HAT / HALCHITA

All one has to do is see Mexican Hat Rock, an inverted stone sombrero located just north of town, to know how the town got its name. Few, however, know the story behind the rock. Legend has it that a handsome Mexican vaquero and a lovely Indian maiden fell in love near the river. Unfortunately, the maiden was already married to a wicked old medicine man. When he learned of her indiscretions, the medicine man turned her Mexican lover into the stone sombrero.

Mexican Hat, with a population of 150, is one of the most popular launch spots for river expeditions. The river has eight sets of rapids that are navigable by most small boats and rafts.

From Mexican Hat there are numerous day and multi-day side trips to ancient ruins and geologic wonders. Even the town, accessed by Scenic Byway 163, is a tapestry of starkly beautiful country with colors ranging from white sandstone to coral and wine. Mexican Hat has restaurants, trading posts, and accommodations.

Halchita is directly across the San Juan River from Mexican Hat. Situated amidst deep red sandstone rock, the community is appropriately named. Halchita is a Navajo word meaning "the red lands." Halchita was at one time very much a part of the uranium decade, with the Vanadium Corporation of America operating its mill there. The EPA has recently cleaned up the site. There are no services in Halchita.

MEXICAN HAT / HALCHITA ATTRACTIONS

Eight miles north of Mexican Hat is *Valley of the Gods*, an 18 mile loop that is accessible from Utah State highways 163 and 261. The loop is of native surface roads and road conditions should be verified before entering from either highway.

Goosenecks State Park is nine miles northwest of Mexican Hat by taking highway 163 or 261 to 316. The Goosenecks is one of the most impressive examples of an "entrenched meander" on the North American continent. One-thousand feet below, the San Juan River has carved a six-mile meandering chasm while advancing only one mile in the direction of Lake Powell.

Monument Valley, in the heart of Utah's portion of the great Navajo Nation reservation, is twenty miles south of Mexican Hat. Here incredible monoliths are 400 to 1,000 feet above the valley floor.

There are innumerable hiking and four-wheel driving experiences in this vast primitive country. Two of note are *John's Canyon* in the Glen Canyon National Recreation Area and the *Grand Gulch Primitive Area*, managed by the BLM. (For more information on all of these attractions please refer to the Blanding attractions and the Trail of the Ancients Road Trip Tour.)

OLJATO

This small Navajo (Dine) community is located 11 miles west of Monument Valley and is home to the Oljato Trading Post, a post that is on the National Register of Historic Places.

The Oljato Trading Post was built in 1921 and continues today to do that which has been prevalent among the Native Americans for centuries—trading. Located in the northwest portion of the Navajo Nation, Oljato Trading Post houses and trades modern day items such as groceries and gas as well as Navajo rugs, baskets, jewelry and pottery.

The two-lane county road, 420, though narrow, is paved and affords the visitor with panoramic views of Monument Valley while enroute to Oljato.

NAVAJO MOUNTAIN

Though only thirty-five air miles away from Monument Valley, Navajo Mountain, the most remote community in San Juan County, is a 110-mile drive. To get to Navajo Mountain from Utah one must drive into Arizona on U.S. Highway 163, then southwest on Arizona 98, and then north on Indian Highway 16. The last 25 miles are on graded gravel.

Navajo Mountain is a Chapter Headquarters. There is no lodging but a small store is located in the community.

The range, Navajo Mountain, is the most prominent geologic feature in the Lake Powell region. At its northern base is the world's largest natural bridge, *Rainbow Bridge National Monument*.

CANYONLAND LINK TO PANORAMALAND & COLOR COUNTRY

From Canyonlands there are three major means of traveling to Color Country. The route to be taken depends upon one's final destination before leaving Canyonlands for Color Country. If one is in the northwestern portion, visiting Arches and Canyonlands National Parks, the best route is to backtrack from Moab on Highway 191 to I-70 West, then exit on Highway 24 traveling south to Hanksville, and then west to Capitol Reef National Park and Torrey.

If one is in the southern portion of Canyonlands, take Utah's Bicentennial Highway 95 from the Blanding area west and then northwest across the Colorado River to Hanksville, where the road joins Highway 24 to Capitol Reef and Torrey.

If the traveler is headed to Lake Powell, or if the idea of crossing Lake Powell on a ferry is appealing, take Highway 95 west from Blanding to the junction of Highway 276 and follow it to the toll ferry at Hall's Crossing. After crossing Lake Powell, one continues north on 276 to Hanksville, and on to Capitol Reef National Park and Torrey.

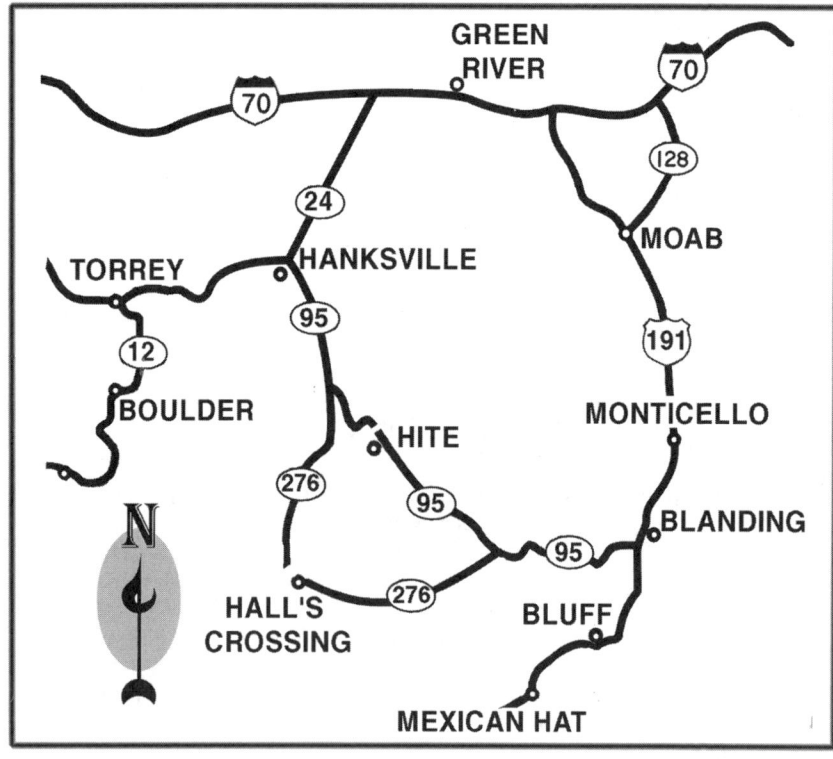

PANORAMALAND

WAYNE COUNTY

WAYNE COUNTY is a very narrow strip of land that is 23 and one-half miles wide, 112 miles long, and covers an area of 2,475 square miles. Very sparsely populated, the 1990 census listed Wayne County as having 2,177 residents.

Though the lack of roads makes them almost inaccessible from Wayne County, a large portion of Canyonlands National Park and the upper Glen Canyon National Recreation Area are in this county and Utah's Panoramaland Travel Region.

When in Wayne County, regardless of whether one is approaching from Colorado, New Mexico, or northeastern Arizona, all major roads lead to Capitol Reef National Park. Because Wayne County is home to Capitol Reef, parts of Canyonlands and Glen Canyon, as well as abundant portions of the San Rafael Swell and Dixie National Forest, more than 95 percent of Wayne County's land is owned by state and federal government agencies.

Wayne County, the lower portion of Panoramaland, was established on May 2, 1892, and named after the son of a state delegate killed by a horse in the area.

WAYNE COUNTY ATTRACTIONS

CAPITOL REEF NATIONAL PARK

Comprising nearly one-quarter of a million acres of colorful towering cliffs and eroded landscape, **Capitol Reef National Park** sprawls across the heart of Utah's slickrock country. The park combines the fantasy of Bryce and the grandeur of Zion, but with a greater variety of color than either. Larger than Bryce and Zion combined, Capitol Reef also contains many archaeological and historical resources. The Fremont Indians, who inhabited this area for nearly 600 years, called it *"**The Land of the Sleeping Rainbow.**"*

Capitol Reef is located in southeastern Utah between the towns of Torrey and Cainesville on State Highway 24, and was named for **Capitol Dome**, a white sandstone formation resembling the nation's capitol.

Thousands of years ago, the Capitol Reef area was the domain of the Fremont Indians, who carved and painted petroglyphs and pictographs on the region's cliff walls.

Mormon pioneers began to establish settlements in the area during the 1870s. In 1910, E. P. Pictol became interested in a region known as "Wayne Wonderland" as a possible site for a national park. He induced a photographer to take the first pictures of the reef. It took 27 years of work but, in 1937, Capitol Reef was set aside as a national monument by presidential proclamation. In the 1960s, following the creation of Lake Powell, a great deal of attention was re-focused on the southeastern part of the state. Capitol Reef was expanded to include the southern and northern extensions of the **Waterpocket Fold** (so named because of the 100-mile long fold in the earth's surface that holds thousands upon thousands of gallons of rainwater). In 1971 the area was enlarged once again and Capitol Reef was designated as a national park.

Capitol Reef is divided into three districts, each with its own special characteristics. Covering the original monument area, Central or **Capitol Reef District** includes the cliff-face of **Capitol Reef**, the Visitor Center Park headquarters, the site of the **Old Fruita** community, the former **Floral-Sleeping Rainbow Ranch**, and several examples of Indian rock art. This district also contains all of the park's improved hiking trails, its most renowned canyons, the only paved highway, and the **Capitol Reef Scenic Drive**. A short distance from the visitor center one can see, in addition to Capitol Dome, **Chimney Rock**, the **Goosenecks**, and the **Egyptian Temple**. **Hickman Bridge**, the **Golden Throne**, and **Capitol Gorge** are the rewards of moderate hikes. More strenuous hikes include those along the **Cohab Canyon, Rim Overlook, Frying Pan**, and **Cassidy Arch Trails**.

The North District, or **Cathedral Valley**, is an extensive area east of the Waterpocket Fold and consists of miles of beautifully sculpted dark red Entrada cliffs and hard gray Curtis that form the cathedral spires and monoliths in the valley. There are several dirt roads for high-clearance vehicles that lead into this remote wilderness area.

A long, narrow spine of the Waterpocket Fold south of Capitol Reef is the **South District**. A wilderness area of uncommon natural beauty, this district offers naked rock painted in shades of red and white, many of which rise more than 2,000 feet above its eastern base. The area, located in Garfield County, a part of Utah's Color Country Travel Region, is accessible by **Burr Trail**, a fair weather-graded dirt road that parallels the eastern base of the fold between State Highway 24 on the north and Bullfrog Marina on Lake Powell to the south. **Muley Twist Canyon** and **Brimhall Bridge** are on the southern end of the park.

There are no commercial facilities in the park, but three campgrounds are located within the park boundaries. Open year-round, the sites are available on a first-come, first-served basis. The main campground has 70 sites, each with a picnic table and grill. Rest rooms, drinking water, and a dump station are available, but no hookups. The park has a group camping area near the main campground that must be reserved in advance. The **Cedar Mesa Campground** is in the southern part of the park and the **Cathedral Valley Campground** is in the north. Each has five sites, a picnic table and a grill. There is no water at either of these two sites, which are only accessible via dirt roads. During inclement weather they can become impassable. Camping at these sites is free (435-425-3791).

Offering exquisite contrast to the red rock monoliths of Capitol Reef National Park is the 11,000 foot summit of **Aquarius Plateau**, often referred to as **Boulder Mountain**. The grandest of Utah's high plateaus, Aquarius is no longer the totally remote wilderness it once was, but is today crossed by dirt roads supplemented by a network of foot trails. A portion of Highway 12, at that juncture known as the **Olem Church Memorial Highway**, slices through one of the most picturesque parts of the Dixie National Forest and Boulder Mountain, linking the town of Boulder with the community of Torrey.

A rolling tableland of some fifty square miles, **Boulder Top** is the plateau's remarkable summit. Formed of dark lava and rimmed by steep cliffs, the majority of Boulder Top exceeds 10,000 feet with **Bluebell Knoll** the highest point at 11,328 feet. Dark lava boulders are scattered wherever one might look. Much of the summit is cloaked in stands of Engelmann spruce and fir, with deep green meadows and numerous small lakes and ponds interspersed throughout the plateau.

Scenic Byway 24 cuts through Wayne County, beginning at the town of Loa and ending at Hanksville. The Byway hugs the banks of the Fremont River as it flows past orchards at the pioneer town of **Fruita**, and the gorges and red rock formations of Capitol Reef. It ends 37 miles east of Capitol reef after winding through the stark beauty of Mancos shale hills and abandoned early Mormon pioneer settlements.

The **J. Perry Egan Fish Hatchery** is a state wildlife facility that has been in operation since the early 1970s. Serving as an important producer of fish eggs, the hatchery annually ships more than 20 million trout eggs to other fish producing stations around the state. The hatchery also produces a large number of fish for stocking the lakes and streams of the region.

WAYNE COUNTY EVENTS

September is usually the month when Wayne County holds its annual Harvest Homecoming Days, an event that provides demonstrations of traditional farming skills and crafts as well as lectures and performances of local music. There is no charge for this event, held at Capitol Reef National Park. (435-425-3791).

TORREY

Torrey, a quiet little town on Scenic Byway 24 at the northern junction of Scenic Byway 12, has, over the last 25 years, slowly developed a reputation as the "gateway to Capitol Reef National Park." In 1973 Capitol Reef National Park was host to an annual pilgrimage of 60,000 people. During 1997 the park was host to approximately 800,000 people. Torrey, with a burgeoning summer population of close to 300 and an off-season population of slightly over 150, is less than five miles from the visitor center at Capitol Reef. Its elevation of 6,800 makes it a year-round vacation destination.

Torrey is a town with a history that smacks more of folklore than of verity. Legend has it that Butch Cassidy and the Sundance Kid used to come to this central Utah community, not as outlaws, but to trip the light fantastic at the town dance hall, the "Big Apple," until the wee hours of the night. Then afterwards they would "hobnob" with the law. Reality or fiction, the area's protective red cliffs were the perfect hideout and some in the area claim to know where the hideout is, but not where the rumored treasure is buried.

The Big Apple is still a major draw to Wayne County residents and visitors alike who are drawn to the dance hall's open-air venue. A reality is that Torrey, with its penchant for dancing, has also cultivated proclivity towards the other arts. As small as Torrey is, with its one-mile stretch of town, Torrey is refined enough to recognize the importance of an art gallery. In fact, if there was a name Torrey residents would give themselves, it would be the unofficial title of being an "arts colony." Several Utah artists call Torrey home and the Torrey Gallery features sculptures, photographs, and paintings by Utah artists. Art and photography workshops are held in nearby Teasdale, art shows and displays are regularly displayed in local restaurants, and Torrey is home to the annual Bluegrass Festival. The neighboring town of Bicknell is host to the annual Bicknell International Film Festival, which, in its two year history, has had a Bugs Bunny and a UFO theme.

Torrey is the essence of what one visualizes when they think of a mecca in the middle of a desert. Located at the southern end of the Aquarius Plateau, with red rock monoliths, pinnacles, and bluffs in every direction, the verdant, tree-lined streets of Torrey are a welcome sight.

Torrey, until just a few short years ago, was indeed a sleepy little community.

Today it has awakened to the realities of growth, but also to a commitment that growth need not undermine heritage. Torrey, just like the rumored cache of Butch Cassidy and the Sundance Kid, is a hidden treasure—a treasure about to be discovered.

ACCOMMODATIONS

CHUCK WAGON LODGE
12 West Main P.O. Box 750080
Torrey/Capitol Reef, Utah 84775
Tel: (435) 425-3335
FAX: (435) 425-3434
Season: March 1 - October 31
Visa, MasterCard, and American Express are accepted.
Reservations are recommended.

Having owned the Chuck Wagon Lodge since its inception in 1972, Randy Austin, owner, is used to hearing comments such as: "It's so nice to see green again," or, "Seems like all we've seen in the last few days is red and coral sandstone, it's great to see the trees."

The comments are not downplaying Utah's beautiful Color Country with its red and coral sandstone cliffs, pinnacles and hoodoos. What they are saying is that the Chuck Wagon Lodge feels to them like an oasis in the middle of Utah's desert. The lodge is located in the "heart of the trees of Torrey."

There are three types of accommodations at Chuck Wagon Lodge, all of which are kept immaculately clean, and all of which have access to the lodge's beautiful new pool and spa. Guest rooms include a three-bedroom suite with kitchen, budget units, and the lodge's new luxury units.

Each of the three bedrooms in the apartment is furnished with a queen bed. This spacious suite has a living room with large color TV, sofa, coffee table, two easy chairs, dining room table, and a breakfast nook. The adjoining kitchen has a full range, refrigerator, toaster, coffee maker, microwave, and cooking and eating utensils. Walls throughout are of knotty pine and the carpet is rust and brown. The bathroom has a tub with hand-held shower.

The budget guest rooms at Chuck Wagon Lodge are immaculately maintained and sure to be regarded as a "good bang for one's buck." All have beautiful pine wood ceilings with fans, new light burgundy carpets, queen bed with bedding accents of mauve and teal, color TV, and wake-up clocks. Bathrooms have tubs with showers and a separate vanity.

Each of the lodge's newer luxury units is furnished with two queen beds, satellite remote control color TV, direct dial telephone, a table and two chairs, and individually controlled heating and air conditioning. The color scheme is wine with forest green accents. Bathrooms have tubs with showers and separate vanity basins. Each night at 8:00 p.m., management selects a movie from its video store for guest enjoyment.

One of the luxury units has been customized for physically challenged guests. The large and spacious room has been arranged for increased mobility. The bathroom has an additional phone and a tub with shower and approved safety bars.

The pool at Chuck Wagon Lodge is the largest private pool in the county and includes a beautiful spa that will accommodate six to eight guests. The large deck abounds with lounge chairs and tables with umbrellas. A coke machine is nearby.

In addition to lodge accommodations, The Chuck Wagon offers a small RV park with public showers that are also available to anyone traveling through the area. On the same property, below the three-bedroom suite and the budget rooms, is the Chuck Wagon General Store (see related story). The store, as its name implies, has a full selection of groceries, great produce, and an in-house bakery. Also available are sporting goods, RV supplies, videos, and a snack bar.

In the middle of the property is Sheri's Hair Design, a full service salon for both hair and nails.

Capitol Reef National Park is a five minute drive from Chuck Wagon Lodge. A short distance away is the genteel beauty of Dixie National Forest. The Grand Staircase-Escalante National Monument, Anasazi State Park, and Escalante Petrified Forest State Park are all within a one-hour drive. Kodachrome Basin State Park and Bryce Canyon National Park are approximately two hours to the Southwest.

Whether coming from one of the area's magnificent natural wonders or enroute to them, Chuck Wagon Lodge, in the heart of the trees, is an ideal home away from home.

TORREY CAPITOL REEF SUPER 8 MOTEL
600 East Highway 24 (Junctions of Highways 24 & 12)
Torrey/Capitol Reef, Utah 84775
Tel: (435) 425-3684 - 3688
FAX: (435) 425-3689
Visa, MasterCard, American Express
 and Discover are accepted.
Reservations are recommended.

There was a time when several of the national chains were perceived as economy accommodations with somewhat inferior amenities. That certainly is not true at the 35-unit Torrey Capitol Reef Super 8. Though economy still applies, inferior amenities do not.

Torrey-Capitol Reef Super 8 Motel offers its guests luxury amenities such as a year-around covered pool and Jacuzzi, guest laundry facilities, and conference facilities. The motel also offers a complimentary continental breakfast.

The lobby of the Torrey-Capitol Reef Super 8 is impressive with its high cathedral ceilings and polished brass ceiling fans. A beautiful black leather sofa and two mauve, black, and gray side chairs have been appropriately arranged to facilitate casual conversation among old and new-found friends. At the top of the stairway, which leads to an open balcony and second floor rooms, are an oak bookcase, lamp table, and two chairs.

When the motel was opened in late fall of 1997, over 800 tulip bulbs were planted. The grounds are lush with tulips, wildflowers, daisies, and a variety of seasonal flowers that have been planted in the midst of red sandstone rocks.

Torrey-Capitol Reef Super 8 offers its guests a room choice of single queen, single king, or double queen beds. Other choices are a luxury suite and rooms for the physically impaired. All rooms have remote control Prime Star Satellite TV with all the popular channels, direct dial phone with local and credit card calls free, and individually controlled heating and air conditioning systems.

There is no such thing as bare walls at the Torrey-Capitol Reef Super 8. The mauve and light gray wallpaper is decorated with wall hangings of area prints.

Rooms with double queen beds have a single nightstand, dresser, brass wall lamps above the beds, and a round table with two chairs. The color scheme of mauve and teal green is carried out in the bedding. Bathrooms have tubs with showers and separate basins with marble vanities. The single king and single queen rooms have a night stand on each side of the bed.

Whether one is on their honeymoon, celebrating an anniversary, or is just someone who loves to be pampered, the Torrey-Capitol Reef Super 8 luxury suite is ideal. The room offers guests a king bed, queen sofa sleeper, and bar with sink, microwave and mini refrigerator. The bathroom has a tub with shower, marble vanity basin, and a Jacuzzi tub that can be entered from the bedroom or the bathroom.

Each of the two rooms for the physically impaired have one queen bed and a door that adjoins a regular room for the convenience of accompanying guests. Bathrooms have tubs with showers and regulation handrails. All room amenities have been adjusted to accommodate wheelchair-bound guests.

The motel conference room, with a rich burgundy ambiance, can facilitate 50 theatre style and 40 for sit-down banquets. Amenities include TV, VCR, white board, and an overhead projector. Walls of the conference room are decorated with selected scenes of Capitol Reef National Park.

A continental breakfast, served in the conference room, includes toast, sweet rolls, juices, fruit, and coffee that is available around the clock. Another amenity offered at Torrey-Capitol Reef Super 8 Motel is its large parking lot with ample space for bus and RV parking.

Torrey, because of its incredible proximity to Capitol Reef National Park, Dixie National Forest, Boulder Mountain, and the nation's newest national monument, Grand Staircase-Escalante, is a town that has come into its own as a Utah travel destination. Capitol Reef is only five miles to the Northeast; Dixie National Forest is 10 miles to the West, and Grand Staircase-Escalante is approximately 50 miles to the West. The drives between each of these scenic wonders are along Scenic Byways and are breathtakingly beautiful and diverse.

Guest rates at Torrey-Capitol Reef Super 8 Motel are the best to be found anywhere. The service is personal and friendly, and the amenities are second to none. With all that it has to offer, why would anyone choose to stay anywhere else?

DID YOU KNOW?

---that Capitol Reef received its name as a result of the perceptions of early and more modern day explorers. Early explorers found Waterpocket Fold to be a barrier to travel and likened it to a reef blocking passage on the ocean. More modern explorers determined that the sandstone hills of the area looked like the Capitol dome in Washington, D.C. Hence, the name, Capitol Reef National Park. Capitol Reef is a compilation of the most spectacular cliffs and rock formations of the great Waterpocket Fold, which extends from Thousand Lake Mountain to Lake Powell in the south. Waterpocket Fold was so named because of the many small pools of water that would be trapped by the tilted strata. As with much of Utah's southeastern and southwestern canyon terrain, the arroyos lent themselves beautifully to a colorful past. Anasazi and Fremont Indians inhabited the land, leaving remnants of their history. Not so generous with leaving their traces behind were such legendary outlaws as Butch Cassidy and other members of the "Wild Bunch" who hid out in these remote canyons in the 1890s.

RESORTS

WONDERLAND INN RESORT

Junctions of Scenic
Highways 12 & 24
Torrey/Capitol Reef, Utah 84775
Tel: (435) 425-3775
              (800) 458-0216
FAX: (435) 425-3212
Open Year-Round
Peak Season   April 1 - October 31
Visa, MasterCard, American Express,
Diners Club, Carte Blanche, and Discover
are accepted.
Reservations are recommended.

Ensconced on a mesa overlooking spectacular views of Thousand Lake Mountain, Boulder Mountain, and Capitol Reef National Park, The Wonderland Inn does indeed offer a wonderland vista of deserts, canyons, mountains and rocks.

The Wonderland Inn, located at the junction of two Scenic Byways—12 and 24—is owned and operated by Ray and Diane Potter and their family. The Inn is the continuing dream of the Potters, life long Torrey residents who, as a family, have spent their lives working and playing together.

In 1990 the Inn and restaurant were opened with 30 spacious rooms. By 1992, an ever-increasing clientele resulted in the addition of 20 more rooms and a convention center. Two years later, garnering resort status, the Inn expanded to include a gift shop, and Texaco station with convenience store. The 1998 season will open with the addition of a campground for trailers, motor homes, and tent campers.

The location of Wonderland Inn makes it a superb accommodation for guests visiting Capitol Reef National Park, Bryce Canyon National Park, and the nation's newest national monument, Grand Staircase-Escalante. Wonderland Inn is a mere three miles from Capitol Reef. Scenic Byway 12, the road to Grand Staircase-Escalante and Bryce Canyon, has been acclaimed as one of the top 10 scenic drives in America. It is a drive that guests will want to take again and again.

Leaving Wonderland Inn and traveling South on Scenic Byway 12, visitors pass over Boulder Mountain and through the pine and aspen forests of Dixie National Forest before coming to the magnificence of Grand Staircase- Escalante. It is an approximate one-hour drive. The terrain between the gateway of the Grand Staircase and Bryce National Park is convoluted and could be driven in another hour's time—but don't. The spectacle of Scenic Byway 12 is too incredible to be driven in any other way but leisurely.

Inn amenities, in addition to the restaurant, gift shop, convention center, and panoramic view offered by the Inn's majestic perch, include a marvelous year-round pool with Jacuzzi spa. As one enters the indoor pool room, there is a Persian rug. The beautiful deck is of red and coral sandstone. There are potted plants, piped in music, ceiling fans, and a tanning room off to the side. Sliding glass doors open to a red rock enclosed patio with tables, chairs, and lounge chairs. Beyond the patio is a redwood deck with tables and umbrellas.

It is obvious to guests that the grounds are lovingly cared for by Ray. Well-manicured lawn and lighted rock gardens surround the pool. Flowers and trees give variety and color to the landscape. During the Christmas season, the grounds are flooded with the brilliance of lights for the holidays.

A Country Styles Beauty Salon is operated from April 1 through October 31 by one of the Potter's daughters, Nycole, who also serves as the Inn's assistant manager.

Wonderland Inn offers guests a choice of smoking and non smoking rooms with king or double queen beds. All rooms are decorated in a modern color scheme of mauve, teal and lavender, and all rooms have remote control cable TV with HBO, ESPN and many other popular channels. They also have clock radios, direct dial phones, and hair dryers in the bathroom. The spacious bathrooms have a tub with shower and separate vanity basin. Rooms with a king bed are furnished with two night stands, table with two Danish upholstered chairs, an easy chair, and a chandelier and wall lights. Rooms with two queen beds have a single night stand, ceiling lamps, dresser, and table with two chairs.

The Wonderland Inn is one of few accommodations in the area to offer its guests honeymoon suites. The two elegant suites are decorated in colors of teal blue and light and dark mauve. They have a beautiful chandelier, teal blue rocking chair, a king bed, and a step-up Jacuzzi spa that can be entered from the bedroom or bathroom. The bathroom also has a separate shower. Both suites have private decks with panoramic views of Thousand Lake Mountain, Boulder Mountain, and the Cock's Comb.

The Wonderland Inn Gift Shop, adjacent to the lobby, is in itself a wonderland. Guests have no problem finding mementos of a special vacation and cherished keepsake treasures. Souvenir gifts include T-shirts and sweatshirts of Scenic Byway 12, Capitol Reef and other scenic attractions. There are logo mugs, magnets, thimbles, caps, and key chains. It isn't hard to recapture the memories when one takes home scenic post cards, calendars, books and video tapes of the area's parks. The West will come back to life with the purchase of a hand-carved wooden stage coach or covered wagon. Equally reminiscent of the Southwest are the Lazer cutouts, wooden flutes, petroglyph rock art, sand paintings, Mandellas, dream catchers, and western boleros and hats. True treasures of the Southwest are found in the gift shop's selection of Native American jewelry. The selection includes rings, bracelets, necklaces, combs and barrettes, bolo ties, belt buckles, and watch bands. These sterling treasures are intricately carved and embellished with semi precious turquoise, mother of pearl, coral, lapis, and other stones. Gift shop and lobby hours are from 7:00 a.m. until 10:00 p.m.

A spectacular panoramic view of the surrounding countryside and equally magnificent sunsets can be viewed from the dining room of Wonderland Inn Restaurant. The restaurant, which is just off the Inn's lobby, is masterfully decorated. The decor combines a feminine touch with the family's love of fishing. Tables are covered with mauve or egg-shell blue table linens, and centered with a vase of mauve and burgundy silk flowers. There is also an abundance of hanging plants throughout the restaurant. On the walls are trophy fish that include Blue Marlin, Mahi Mahi, and other denizens of the sea. There are also elk mounts and oils of the national parks painted by local artists.

Breakfast is served from 7:00 to 11:00 a.m. during peak season and from 7:00 to 9:00 a.m. November through March. One breakfast favorite is the Wonderland Haystack, a serving of two eggs any style, diced ham, bell peppers, onions, and melted cheese piled high on a stack of hash brown potatoes and served with choice of toast. Another favorite is the Hungry-Man Breakfast. It offers one's choice of bacon, sausage, or ham, and two pancakes, two eggs, and hash brown potatoes. Omelettes are always a favorite in the West. Choices include ham and cheese, Western, and Spanish, served with toast and hash browns. The Wonderland Inn also offers an all-one-can-eat breakfast buffet.

Lunch is served from 11:00 a.m. to 5:00 p.m. but only during peak season. The Wonderland Burger is always a guest favorite. It consists of two beef patties on a bun with cheese, French fries, and a dinner salad. Sandwiches are numerous and include all of the traditionals as well as sandwiches such as the Rueben, Pastrami Burger, and Malibu Chicken. Hot luncheon delights include beef, hamburger, and ham, all served with real mashed potatoes, and French Dip and Fish and Chips, served with French fries.

Dinner is served from 5:00 to 9:00 p.m. during peak season and from 5:00 to 7:00 p.m. November through March. Dinners at Wonderland Inn Restaurant are elegant, beautifully presented, and quite continental. Two appetizer favorites are the Shrimp Cocktail with house sauce and the Spicy Barbecue Chicken Wings with ranch dressing. Those who relish Cajun cooking love the Inn's Cajun Chicken Salad. Tossed greens are topped with tomatoes, black olives, pineapple chunks, the Inn's special Cajun grilled chicken, and one's choice of dressing. A favorite country steak is the marinated Top Sirloin. Tender, juicy, and broiled to perfection, it is seasoned with a blend of herbs and garlic. Guests at the Wonderland are right in the heart of trout country. It would be ludicrous if one did not try the Inn's wonderful fresh filet of Mountain Rainbow Trout. It is steamed with a light lemon pepper seasoning. A local favorite is the Cowboy's Delight, a specially seasoned ground top sirloin steak that is smothered with sautéed onions and mushrooms.

The Wonderland Inn Restaurant takes pride in offering its guests the freshest garden vegetables. In season summer vegetables, straight from local gardens, include peas, beans, zucchini, spaghetti and crook neck squash, tomatoes, and green beans. Only the choicest cuts of meat, fish, and poultry are served. Soups and sauces are prepared from scratch.

The Texaco service station with mini mart is down the hill from Wonderland Inn. The Texaco station provides gas, diesel, propane, and oil products to its customers while the mini mart offers grocery and snack items as well as notions, hunting and fishing supplies, and various sundry items. There is also a guest Laundromat at the complex.

Guests have referred to the new Wonderland Inn Resort as the "Hill-Top Hilton," "Oasis in the Desert," or the "Desert and Mountain Retreat." Whatever one chooses to call the Wonderland Inn, there is no mistaking that one's sense of serenity while staying at the Inn is a direct result of the grandeur and majesty that surrounds and envelops this place called "Wonderland Inn Resort."

DID YOU KNOW?

---that about 70 million years ago, gigantic forces within the earth began to uplift, squeeze, and fold more than a dozen rock formations into the central feature of Capitol Reef National Monument, Waterpocket Fold. This uplifting and twisting of the land continues today. Nearly all layers at Capitol Reef National Park date back to the Mesozoic Era (65 to 230 million years ago), when dinosaurs ruled the earth. The exposed rocks reveal windswept deserts, rivers, mudflats, and inland seas of long ago. Erosion has since carved the spires, graceful curves, canyons and arches.

SPECIALTY SHOPPING

CHUCK WAGON GENERAL STORE

12 West Main P.O. Box 750080
Torrey/Capitol Reef, Utah 84775
Tel: (435) 425-3288
FAX: (435) 425-3434
Season: March 1 - October 31
Visa, MasterCard, and American Express are accepted.

Located on the premises of Chuck Wagon Lodge (see related story), the Chuck Wagon General Store has been serving the people of Torrey, those who stay at the lodge, and the many who pass through on their way to and from Capitol Reef National Park, since 1972.

Although the store satisfies nearly every daily need, Chuck Wagon General Store has become best known for its quality variety of home baked goods. The bakery daily bakes breads that include white, sourdough, rye, pumpernickel, cracked wheat, honey wheat, cinnamon raisin, eight-grain natural wheat bread, and squaw bread. In addition the bakery produces cinnamon and onion rolls, and a nice selection of doughnuts. At the snack bar are hot dogs, corn dogs, chili dogs, and a great selection of deli sandwiches.

If one is an outdoorsman, there is fishing and camping gear, sleeping bags, back packs, stoves, and almost anything one might need. Film and batteries? Ice? Housewares? Medical supplies? One is sure to find them at Chuck Wagon General Store.

When it comes to grocery items, one of the things appreciated most by travelers is the size. As Randy Austin, owner, knows, tourists do not like groceries in the giant, economy size. The store has a wonderful selection of milk, cheese, fresh smoked trout, and fruits and vegetables, many of which come from local suppliers.

A unique feature of the store is videos. Anyone who has tried to rent a video while on the road, knows that it is not always easy. At Chuck Wagon General Store, if one has a valid driver's license, a credit card, and if they are staying in the area, they can rent a video. In addition to first runs, classics, and top-rated Westerns, the store also has a selection of videos on the area's natural wonders—Capitol Reef National Park, Grand Staircase-Escalante National Monument, and many more.

Chuck Wagon General Store provides tourists with a great selection of souvenir items that includes caps, mugs, thimbles, magnets, post cards, calendars, and photo books. Randy knows that there is nothing more disappointing than buying a logo T-shirt or sweatshirt while on vacation and having it shrink the first time it is washed. At Chuck Wagon General Store all Tee and sweatshirts are of the highest quality. If it is a souvenir toy or games to keep the children happy while on the road, Chuck Wagon General Store has those too.

When traveling Utah's Scenic Byway, Highway 24, whether staying at Chuck Wagon Lodge or not, be sure to stop at Chuck Wagon General Store for all traveling needs.

BICKNELL

Situated at the base of Thousand Lake Mountain, the small farming town of Bicknell overlooks the Fremont River and its valley below. Bicknell, a community of slightly over 400, is a town where residents take pride in their surroundings.

Bicknell was settled in the 1870s and was originally named Thurber after a pioneer leader. In 1916, Thomas Bicknell, an eastern philanthropist, offered to build a library for any Utah town that would take his name. Thurber, in Wayne County, and Grayson in San Juan County, both accepted the offer. Bicknell arranged a compromise whereby Thurber received half of the library and became Bicknell, and Grayson got the other half of the library and became Blanding after the maiden name of Mrs. Bicknell. Today Bicknell has a diversified economy based on tourism (to nearby Capitol Reef National Park), agriculture, lumbering, and government employment.

BICKNELL ATTRACTIONS

Sunglow Recreation Area, one mile south of Bicknell, offers first rate camping and picnicking in a secluded circular amphitheater formed by high red cliffs. This is a popular area for those with an interest in geology. A region of broken and deformed rocks, situated on the Thousand Lake Fault, the area is marked by abrupt transitions between surface rocks of the high plateau and Canyonlands.

ACCOMMODATIONS

THE LODGE AT RED RIVER RANCH
P. O. Box 280
Bicknell, Utah 84715
Tel: (435) 425-3322
         (800) 20 LODGE (205-6343)
FAX: (435) 425-3329
Web Site: www.redriverranch.com
Email: thelodge@redriverranch.com
Visa, MasterCard, American Express, and Discover are accepted.
Reservations are recommended.

The Lodge at Red River Ranch, ensconced against a backdrop of red sandstone cliffs, and secreted by a queue of ancient elm and cottonwood trees, is grandiose in every sense of the word.

The Lodge is located on a private road, 300 yards off Scenic Byway 24, midway between Bicknell and Torrey. And even the private road, which traverses the Fremont River bottom, is enchanting and surreptitious. One can sense the drama and romance of yesteryear as they approach this magnificent lodge, nestled on the site of an old stagecoach rest stop. Where the stagecoach rest stop offered a brief hiatus from a long and tiring journey, The Lodge at Red River Ranch, a blend of primitive past and modern conveniences, offers repose to travelers in stately surroundings.

This imposing, rustic log edifice, constructed after the manner of grand lodges of the past, is encompassed by lush green lawn, rock gardens, and a red sandstone patio with wrought iron tables and chairs.

As one enters the Great Room, they are overcome with a feeling of awe. The magnificent cathedral ceiling has open beams, wagon wheel chandeliers, and a floor to ceiling red sandstone fireplace. The entire room is embellished with exquisite Victorian antiques that include leather and velvet divans and a cherished piano with a marvelous brass candelabra. Treasures of the West include an exquisite sand painting, Navajo rugs, a Wells Fargo trunk, and a chess table. Showcased at one end of the room is Frederic Remington's 1895 monument-sized bronze statue, The Bronco Buster, which stands about four feet tall.

Furnishings in the Great Room have been arranged to encourage the kind of casual conversation that turns strangers into friends. When reflective meditation is more appropriate, a mezzanine at the top of the stairs has been set aside for reading and pondering. At the base of the stairs is a game nook, with an assortment of challenging games and puzzles.

The Lodge at Red River Ranch has 15 guest rooms, each distinctively different in color, decor and ambiance, but each having one thing in common—unprecedented appeal. Each room has its own private bath, balcony or deck with view of the cliffs and countryside, stone fireplace, and piped in music at the turn of a switch. All also have

beautiful Douglas fir floors, ceiling fans and individually controlled central heating.

On the main floor, down the hall from the Great Room, are Rodeo, Saratoga, Chaparral, and Anasazi. All have patios and tubs with showers, and all but Anasazi have queen beds. Hallway walls are hung with Harper Magazine etchings, circa the late 1800's.

Rodeo, decorated with bold colors of reds and blue, features a heavy wood bed, Western artifacts, and a wood plank Douglas fir floor.

Saratoga opens the door to another era, a time when chivalry reigned supreme, women were placed on pedestals, and men donned hunting jackets and followed their hounds as together they tracked their prey. Saratoga is decorated with a brass bed with wedding ring quilt, elegant green chair, and beautiful rugs.

Chaparral is reflective of the Southwest. Furnishings are of smooth-hewn logs. Hand made accessories includes a bird wall hanging. Native American accents also adorn the room.

Anasazi offers its guests two twin beds with a color decor of burgundy and forest green. The Anasazis were the ancient Native Americans who inhabited this land over 1000 years ago. A bow and arrow and exquisite Native American rugs add charm to the room.

As one ascends the stairway to the second floor, where there are seven guest rooms, attention is riveted to the large and unique 1929 Navajo rug with a sand-painting pattern.

Second floor rooms are Autumn, Cornflower, Willow, Marco Polo, Safari, Arbor, and Cimarron. Each has a stone fireplace, private balcony, and tub with shower.

Autumn is ablaze with the colors of fall—orange, gold and brown—and offers a queen bed.

Cornflower features an antique king bed with a wooden canopy. Other decor includes cornflower blue Victorian chairs and corn-gold swag lamp.

A rich, antique dresser, green easy chairs, and a queen bed with willow bedspread decorate the very prim and proper English room, *Willow*.

Marco Polo conjures the feeling that one has sailed the Seven Seas. Bedding for the one queen and two twin beds is a deep teal blue. While the decor is Oriental, the furnishings are mostly Victorian and include an exquisite desk, dresser, and ornate full-length mirror. The room also has two Victorian chairs.

Safari, on the other hand, creates the feeling that one is in the wilds of Africa. Hung on the walls are the mounted heads of Greater Kudu, Impala, and Wildebeast. A chandelier hangs from the high pitched ceiling that has stripped bark support beams of Ponderosa pine. The room offers a king and a double bed, has bamboo furnishings, and an incredible view of the sun as it sets behind red sandstone cliffs.

Like a garden hideaway, *Arbor* brings back childhood memories of sitting in a garden surrounded by lush flora. The room offers a king bed with rattan head board, Victorian love seat, and covered church bench.

Native American artifacts abound in *Cimarron*, a room embellished with light red and coral, the colors of the surrounding landscape. The white-washed four-poster king bed and the brass twin bed have floral printed bedspreads. An antique lamp hangs above the bed.

Ascending the stairs to the loft, one is impressed with the series of Wide Ruins Navajo rugs.

Third floor rooms include Vintage, Wildflower, Provence, and Tyrolean. All have stone fireplaces, private balconies, high beamed ceilings, and tubs with showers.

Vintage is the perfect name for this very Victorian room with blue and mauve wall paper. In front of the coral sandstone fireplace, is an elegant love seat. The king bed has rattan head board, beautiful traditional 1800's log cabin pattern quilt and shams that match the wallpaper. Other adornments include a Victorian lamp and desk.

Wildflower has a red sandstone fireplace, high beamed ceiling, Victorian antiques, and hand made quilts with matching shams on the king bed and two single beds. One wall is log, another is beautifully papered. Paintings of wild flowers adorn this room, where the window looks out over the Fremont river and massive red cliffs. The room is split into two halves with the bathroom in the center. This elegant bathroom has a wildflower motif.

Provence offers guests a queen bed and an alcove with twin bed. Furnishings are very French and include a matching chair and love seat, barn wood bookcase, and a green chandelier.

A beam up the center, a full pitch ceiling, and dormer windows create a European flair in *Tyrolean*, a room that offers two queen beds with Swiss headboards to its guests.

There are no phones and no televisions in the rooms, but a game room, accessed from outside the lodge, offers a surround sound, large screen projection TV with satellite dish. Also in the game room are a ping pong table, foos ball game, lots of parlour games, and stair stepper and weight machine. A public telephone and cold drink machines are also in the room..

Adjacent to the Great Room is the Ranch's dining room, where guests can choose a continental breakfast, included with their stay, or an express or full breakfast for a slight additional cost. Continental breakfast includes a choice of bread or pastry, juice, and hot drink. With an express breakfast the guest can add a choice of fruit plate, homemade granola, and hot or cold cereal. Those who desire a full breakfast can add a choice of eggs, bacon or sausage, and pancakes or waffles. Breakfasts are served between 7:30 and 9:30 a.m. The dining room will seat approximately 40 guests.

The Lodge at Red River Ranch is owned and operated by the John Alexander family, who purchased the cattle ranch in 1978. John saw in the land a rustic beauty he felt should be shared with others. Almost immediately he began drawing up plans for a lodge that would not only be a respite for visitors from around the world, but a haven for his own family as well.

During the next 15 years, John continued making sketches while he and his wife, Linda, acquired furniture for the lodge. By 1993, when groundbreaking took place, the entire family was involved in the lodge project. Members contributed in the planning, construction, and decorating of The Lodge at Red River Ranch. Today, one of those sons, Matthew, is the Ranch host.

Capitol Reef National Park, just a half-hour drive from The Lodge at Red River Ranch, offers petroglyph-etched canyons, immense chasms that stretch beyond the scope of one's eyes, and picturesque red sandstone columns that separate azure sky from green valleys where mule deer graze in grassy orchards.

All the beauty and grandeur of the park, plus a five-mile meandering stretch of the Fremont River and a two-acre spring-fed reservoir, are also found at The Lodge at Red River Ranch.

Wander the fields, hike the red rock cliffs, fish the sparkling streams and reservoirs, or simply relax and enjoy bird watching, the sunset, or a good book. Whatever the choice, an experience at The Lodge at Red River Ranch is so unforgettable, it will be a vacation to cherish forever.

RESTAURANTS

RABBIT VALLEY BAKERY & CAFE

P. O. Box 320
374 South 300 East
Bicknell, Utah 84715
Tel: (435) 425-3953
FAX: (435) 425-3952
Hrs:
Summer Season   May 1 - November 1
Open Daily   7:30 a.m. - 9:00 p.m.
            Winter Season
Tuesday - Thursday & Sunday   11:00 a.m. - 7:00 p.m.
Friday and Saturday   11:00 a.m. - 9:00 p.m.
Closed January 1 - mid-March
Visa, MasterCard, and American Express are accepted.

Debra Walker and Graydon Briggs, DDS, married in September 1991 and moved the following spring to Wayne County. They spent two winters in a two-room mouse trap, which Debra immediately named "Spider Heaven," and commuted back and forth to work in Salt Lake City.

It was not exactly the picture of serene, country life that they had anticipated. They began looking for a place to live permanently and a place to work that was closer than three hours from home. Initially they pictured a cute three-bedroom bungalow in the country, but ended up with a brown and mustard yellow two-story, 12,000 square-foot cinderblock warehouse on Highway 24. "Could this really be home sweet home?" they wondered. "Well, maybe." After three years of remodeling, the building now houses Graydon's dental practice, a homey apartment to live in, and the Rabbit Valley Bakery and Cafe.

Rabbit Valley, to those passing through, may seem like a strange name to give a bakery and cafe. But it was the name given to this entire alluvial lowland by Charles Dutton, an assistant to John Wesley Powell.

Breakfast, lunch, and dinner menus at Rabbit Valley Cafe change daily and are printed on the blackboard above the bakery. Emphasis is always placed on quality and food preparation, not on the quantity of menu items offered. Debra secures as many of her ingredients and fresh fruits and vegetables as possible from local sources. All of the cheeses come from the cheese factory in Loa. Organic summer produce, such as peppers, tomatoes, green beans, leaf lettuce, spinach, and beets, come from an organic farm near Capitol Reef. Cherries, apricots, peaches, apples and pears come from the Pioneer orchards in Fruita.

Rabbit Valley Bakery & Cafe serves an assortment of imported Italian coffee as well as great locally roasted coffees from Salt Lake City. The Cafe offers an Espresso bar with cappuccinos, caffe lattes, flavored coffee drinks, and decadent hot chocolate.

With a coffee house atmosphere, the menu at Rabbit Valley includes cranberry, apricot, and almond scones; homemade sticky buns, cinnamon rolls, and homemade granola. There is also an assortment of vegetable quiches and omelettes such as Spinach and Asago or Green Chili and Pepperjack. Smoked trout and Feta cheese are always on the menu.

All sandwich breads and rolls on the menu are homemade. Favorites include pastrami on rye and Debra's curried chicken salad sandwich on green onion and dill bread. The chicken is roasted in garlic and lemon juice, added to a blend of mayonnaise, onions, celery, curry and other spices, and served with leaf lettuce.

House specialties include Spinach Lasagna and Baked Chili Releno. Dinner entrees include Pork Roast with garlic mashed potatoes and gravy; Ground Lamb Meatloaf, and Chicken and Rosemary Ravioli in garlic cream sauce. French Onion, Cream of Potato, and Homemade Chicken Noodle are a sampling of available soup choices. When fresh tomatoes are in season, the Tomato Basil soup is a country favorite. All sauces, stocks, and dressings are made fresh nightly from scratch.

In addition to its dining on premise business, Rabbit Valley Cafe prepares sumptuous box lunches and picnic baskets that include local trout, cheeses, fruits, and fresh breads or sandwiches. Whether traveling individually or with tour groups, the lunches to go are great on the road or when visiting the parks. The Cafe also caters banquets, special occasion parties, and family reunions.

Regardless of what time of day it is and which meal one is enjoying, the aroma of fresh baked goods comes wafting through the air. Is it any wonder that one can rarely leave the restaurant without taking home an offering from the oven?

Fresh rolls and breads include rye, green onion and dill, and honey whole wheat with sunflower seeds. But the favorites continue to be Debra's sundried tomato and garlic bread and her honey whole wheat bread with dried carrots, cranberries, pinenuts, and sunflower seeds. Cheesecake is serious business at the Rabbit Valley Bakery. The most popular choices include Espresso Spice, Pumpkin Hazel Nut, Peanut Butter, and Chocolate Mint. Other favorite desserts include homemade pecan, apple, and pumbkin pies, and bread pudding in bourbon sauce.

Rabbit Valley Bakery & Cafe has a relaxed though eclectic architectural design which the owners have laughingly named, "Southwestern Prairie French." It combines huge hand-cut timbers with whole trees framing the main entrance. Walls are heavily textured Spanish-style with ragged-on paint. The French windows face the magnificent vista of Thousand Lakes and Boulder Mountains. Handmake wooden tables, antique furniture and pottery and mismatched wooden cafe chairs complete the interior decor.

An outside patio is surrounded by a garden wall of lichen-covered basalt rock. The patio offers dining "alfresco" and entertainment during warm summer months.

Because of the owner's interest in music, Rabbit Valley Bakery & Cafe hosts music festivals, and concerts. They sponsor a weekly "open mic" for local musicians and poetry readings.

Rabbit Valley Bakery & Cafe, in the short time it has been opened, has already developed a dining and bakery clientele that comes from miles around. Many, however, who stop at Rabbit Valley Bakery & Cafe, will be passing through Bicknell on their way to or coming from Capitol Reef National Park. They will be from all parts of the country and from around the world. But they will all have one thing in common. When they think of succulent foods and delectable breads and pastries, they will remember the quality experience they had and how much they enjoyed dining at Rabbit Valley Bakery & Cafe.

TEASDALE

Teasdale, at the junction of Bullberry Creek and the Fremont River, was originally settled in 1879 as a farming, ranching, and sheepherding community. Named after an early Mormon pioneer and church apostle, George Teasdale, the town, until recently, has been an obscure village about one mile off Scenic Byway 24. There are still few services in Teasdale, but this sleepy rural town, just a short drive from Capitol Reef National Park and the Dixie National Forest, is an ideal respite for the weary traveler. Among quality accommodations are the Cactus Hill Motel and Pine Shadows Cabins. (See related stories.)

The Teasdale Ranger Station of the Dixie National Forest has information about hiking, horseback riding, and road conditions in the northern and eastern parts of Boulder Mountain and the Aquarius Plateau. Their office is two miles west of Torrey on U-24, then 1.5 miles south. For more information wrtite Box 99, Teasdale, Utah 84775 or call 435-425-3519.

DID YOU KNOW?

---that magnificent Boulder Mountain, which sits to the southeast of Teasdale, has over 100 lakes and some of the finest fishing in Utah. Offering cool, high mountain vistas, Boulder Mountain has over 192 miles of trails.The views from the rim are nothing short of spectacular and among the most breathtaking vistas in Utah. Thousand Lake Mountain, directly north, also offers panoramic mountain views.

ACCOMMODATIONS

CACTUS HILL MOTEL
P. O. Box 36
Teasdale, Utah 84773
Tel: (435) 425-3578
        (800) 50 RANCH (507-2624)
FAX: (435) 425-3578
Visa, MasterCard, and Discover are accepted.
Reservations are recommended.

Cactus Hill Motel, just outside the small rural town of Teasdale, offers guests the best of the west in cleanliness, charm, hospitality, affordability, and quiet seclusion. Guest book comments at Cactus Hill call the motel "a place to dream," 'an experience of the *real* West," and "a great place for a get-away."

Cactus Hill Motel, secluded as it is, is a short 13-mile drive to Capitol Reef National Park, and just eight miles to the splendor of Dixie National Forest. One of the state's most famous ATV trails, Great Western, is just a mile away. An unusual sandstone formation called the Cockscomb is an easy two mile hike.

Cactus Hill Motel was built in 1994 by owner hosts, Linda and George Coombs. The motel, on a 100-acre working sheep ranch, occupies a regal spot with majestic views of Capitol Reef and the Boulder and Henry Mountains. The ranch, with all of its red and white sandstone hills and pasture, is open to guests. They are free to roam at will, hike and bike the many trails, and even help with the chores.

Through local area outfitters, Cactus Hill personnel can arrange evening, half, full, or multiple day mountain bike tours or short to multiple day horseback and jeep tours of the area for their guests.

With so much to do and see in and around the Cactus Hill Motel, it is no wonder that guests who had planned a one-day stay end up staying much longer.

Accommodations at Cactus Hill include five modern motel guest rooms and, everyone's favorite, a country cabin. All rooms are decorated in modern colors of teal blue and coral. Four of the rooms offer two queen beds, remote control color TV, phone with local calls free, and individually controlled heating and air conditioning. Petroglyph wall hangings add a Southwestern ambiance to the rooms. These same four units have a spacious bathroom with large vanity basin, double mirrors, and bathtub with shower. One smaller room is available with one queen bed and bath with shower only.

Ensconced against a white ledge of the Boulder Mountain foothills, the Cactus Hill Ranch Cabin offers total isolation. It is a favorite retreat for honeymooners, writers, artists, and anyone who wants to get in touch with themselves and with nature. The two-bedroom log cabin has a beautiful oak floor, except in the bedrooms where it is carpeted. The modern kitchen has a stove, refrigerator, microwave, coffee maker, dining room table, and cooking and eating utensils. Interior walls are log and add to the rustic charm of the cabin. In the living room there is a wood burning stove that is ideal for taking the chill off spring and fall mornings, or for cozying up to in the evening. The cabin has a TV, but no phone. A queen bed is in one bedroom and two single twins are in the other. The queen bed is topped with a quilt, handmade by George's mother, Phyllis, who has won county and state fair grand prizes for her quilts.

Linda and George encourage travelers to stay at Cactus Hill Motel, not just

BED & BREAKFASTS

during the summer months but all year round. In the spring, as the snow begins to melt, there is nothing more spectacular than red rock blazing through crystallized snow. Fall offers the splendor of brilliant gold Aspens intermingled with red and white sandstone cliffs and Ponderosa Pines.

Cactus Hill Motel is also at the doorstep of Dixie National Forest and Boulder Mountain, where dozens of lakes and open meadows create spring wild flowers that are almost beyond belief. In the fall, Scenic Byway 12, only six and one-half miles Southeast of Cactus Hill, is ablaze with the colors of Autumn. There is nothing so breathtaking as the gold coin-like leaves that hang from the Aspen forests along this route.

Though secluded, Cactus Hill Motel is very easy to find. When traveling southeast along Scenic Byway 24, take the Teasdale exit and travel three and one-half miles to the ranch. When traveling north on Scenic Byway 12, take the Teasdale exit and continue northwest for five miles to the motel. Coming from either direction there are signs along the way.

As one guest wrote: "Cactus Hill Motel is beautiful, quiet and secluded, a real treasure. Thanks for the warm hospitality. We'll be back soon!"

PINE SHADOWS CABINS
P. O. Box 25; 125 South
Teasdale, Utah 84773
Tel: (435) 425-3939
         (800) 708-1223
FAX: (435) 425-3940
Web Site: color-country.net/~cabins
Email: cabins@colorcountry.net
Visa and MasterCard are accepted.
Reservations are recommended.

in Teasdale, Utah

Located in a Pinion Pine forest and ensconced against the shadows of coral Navajo sandstone bluffs, Pine Shadows Cabins offers an ideal solitary retreat to travelers visiting Capitol Reef National Park and other nearby treasures.

Each of Pine Shadows' spacious chalet-style cabins is fully equipped for the long stay and is perfectly suited to those planning family gatherings, business retreats, or small executive training meetings. The cabins are extra large, 16 by 28 feet, and have high beam ceilings and a ceiling fan.

Color decor is teal blue with burgundy and forest green. The spacious cabins have two queen beds and a television with VCR. Guests are invited, at no extra charge, to select from Pine Shadows' limited selection of videos. Bathrooms have bathtub with shower, a vanity basin, and a separate dressing table.

A kitchen affords each guest with the option of cooking in or eating out. The kitchen includes sink, range, toaster, coffee maker, microwave, small refrigerator, glass table with chairs, and cooking and eating utensils

. Every cabin has a front and back entrance and a covered porch for viewing the Cockscomb ridge, cedars, and pinion pines. The sandstone bluffs and rock formations a short distance to the south are especially enchanting. As the early morning sun changes its position in the sky, one can sit and watch these sandstone mountains turn bright orange, then coral, and finally, almost a pure white.

From the veranda or the cabin windows, guests are likely to see chipmunks frolicking in the trees, rabbits scurrying by, bluejays fluttering in the azure sky, and mule deer bounding in the distance.

There is an outdoor gathering area with a fire pit and picnic tables. Guests are welcome to bring their own charcoal and broil steaks or do Dutch oven cooking, a favorite of the West. Teasdale's temperature is moderate and there is almost always a slight afternoon breeze.

It is difficult to portray the beauty that surrounds Pine Shadows Cabins. It is a 15-minute drive to Capitol Reef National Park and its sheer-walled canyons, sandstone domes, and its red rock cliffs. It is a 10-mile drive to the entrance of Dixie National Forest and the Boulder Mountain Range with their sparkling mountain lakes and pine and aspen groves.

But spectacular as these better known attractions are, the treasures that exist within walking distance of Pine Shadows Cabins are equally inspiring. It was the untouched beauty of the land that brought Wayne and Sherrie Shumway, owners of Pine Shadows, to Teasdale.

A 40-minute hike from Pine Shadows Cabins takes guests to red rock formations that include arches, small caves, Goblin Valley-type pinnacles, and pinion pines and junipers. From the crest one can see nearly a hundred miles in almost every direction.

No more than a few hundred yards away from Pine Shadows is one of several entrances to the Great Western Trail for ATV's. It is also the start of an annual endurance ride—168 miles—for horseback riding.

Though one knows it is not pristine, the land that surrounds Pine Shadows is blissfully peaceful and unsullied. In its bucolic habitat, Pine Shadows Cabins offers an idyllic setting for rediscovering one's self and the beauties of nature.

COLOR COUNTRY

GARFIELD COUNTY

Covering nearly 3 million acres in size, Garfield County ranks as the fifth largest county in the state. Yet with all its acreage only four percent is privately owned. Garfield County has the distinction of having over 95% of its land owned by the Federal Government through its national forests, monuments and parks.

Garfield County, with an approximate population of 4,000, may have started and existed for most of its life as a livestock-ranching and timber-cutting section of the state, but today the county is securely entrenched in tourism.

Garfield County is home to Bryce Canyon, Grand Staircase-Escalante National Monument, the lower half of Capitol Reef National Monument, and a major portion of Glen Canyon National Recreation Area. It is little wonder that the county is deemed a land of spectacular beauty.

The county is also unique in that it has only two primary river drainage systems. On the west side of the county, the two forks of the Sevier River drain the Great Basin. On the east side, the Colorado River forms the county's eastern boundary.

Another singular feature is the Henry Mountains, located in the eastern section of the county. These mountains are considered to be the youngest range in the world—truly a geologist's paradise.

From the thickly forested areas of the Boulder and Escalante Mountains to the fantastic, unbelievable creations of desert sandstone, the scenic splendor of the area's natural resources has helped Garfield County become a popular Southwestern vacation spot.

Garfield and Wayne Counties share a border and Scenic Byway 12 leads the tourist from Wayne County to Garfield County and a major portion of the grandeur that is Color Country.

GARFIELD COUNTY ATTRACTIONS

SCENIC BYWAY 12

Regardless of whether one embarks on Scenic Byway 12 from Torrey or from Highway 89, just south of Panguitch, the trip is magical and sure to be a highlight of any Southern Utah vacation. Scenic Byway 12, named as one of the nation's top ten scenic byways, is 122 miles long and takes approximately four hours. It is one Utah highway that should be "pondered," not accomplished through "speed reading."

Beginning in one of the state's hottest new vacation towns, Torrey, just west of Capitol Reef National Park, the highway climbs through the **Boulder Mountains** and **Dixie National Forest**. It matters not what time of year, for the glories of nature abound during all seasons. Autumn, however, finds the mountain ablaze with the golden aspen intertwined with pines. Along the route are view areas where one is captivated by panoramas of **Capitol Reef**, the **Henry Mountains**, and **Circle Cliffs**.

Just over the Boulder summit is the town of **Boulder**, at one time considered to be one of the country's most remote towns. Here visitors can be taken back a thousand years as they visit the remains of a prehistoric Indian Village and a museum at **Anasazi State Park**.

Boulder sits on one of the northern-most points of the nation's newest national monument, **Grand Staircase-Escalante**, and as one leaves the town of Boulder they embark on a 68-mile drive through the monument. From Boulder the highway ascends to one of the most spectacular roads to be found anywhere. Called the **Hogback Road** because of the narrowness of the two-lane highway and the sheer drop on either side, the vastness of the panorama that unfolds is indescribable. Beyond are oceans of slickrock and scenic canyons cut by the **Escalante River**.

A short distance farther is **Calf Creek Campground**. Devotees of beauty will delight in taking the five-mile round-trip nature trail to **Lower Calf Creek Falls**. It is here that tributaries of the Escalante River plunge 126 feet over **Navajo Sandstone**.

Continuing down the road and across the **Escalante Natural Bridge**, one comes to **Hole-in-the-Rock Backway**, an unimproved road suitable only to 4-wheel drive vehicles. The popular 50-mile backway follows a trail made by a company of early Mormon Pioneers.

Almost at mid-point is the town of **Escalante**. One mile west of town is **Escalante Petrified Forest State Park**. From Escalante it is approximately 30 miles to the first of three towns—**Henrieville**, **Cannonville** and **Tropic**—each of which is seeped in a rich pioneer heritage. From Cannonville it is an eight mile drive to one of Utah's most colorful state parks, **Kodachrome Basin**.

Where Scenic Byway 12 passes through Tropic, the road comes to one of the western boundaries of **Grand Staircase-Escalante** and to the northeastern boundary of **Bryce Canyon National Park**. Tropic is the closest community to Bryce. Byway 12 then

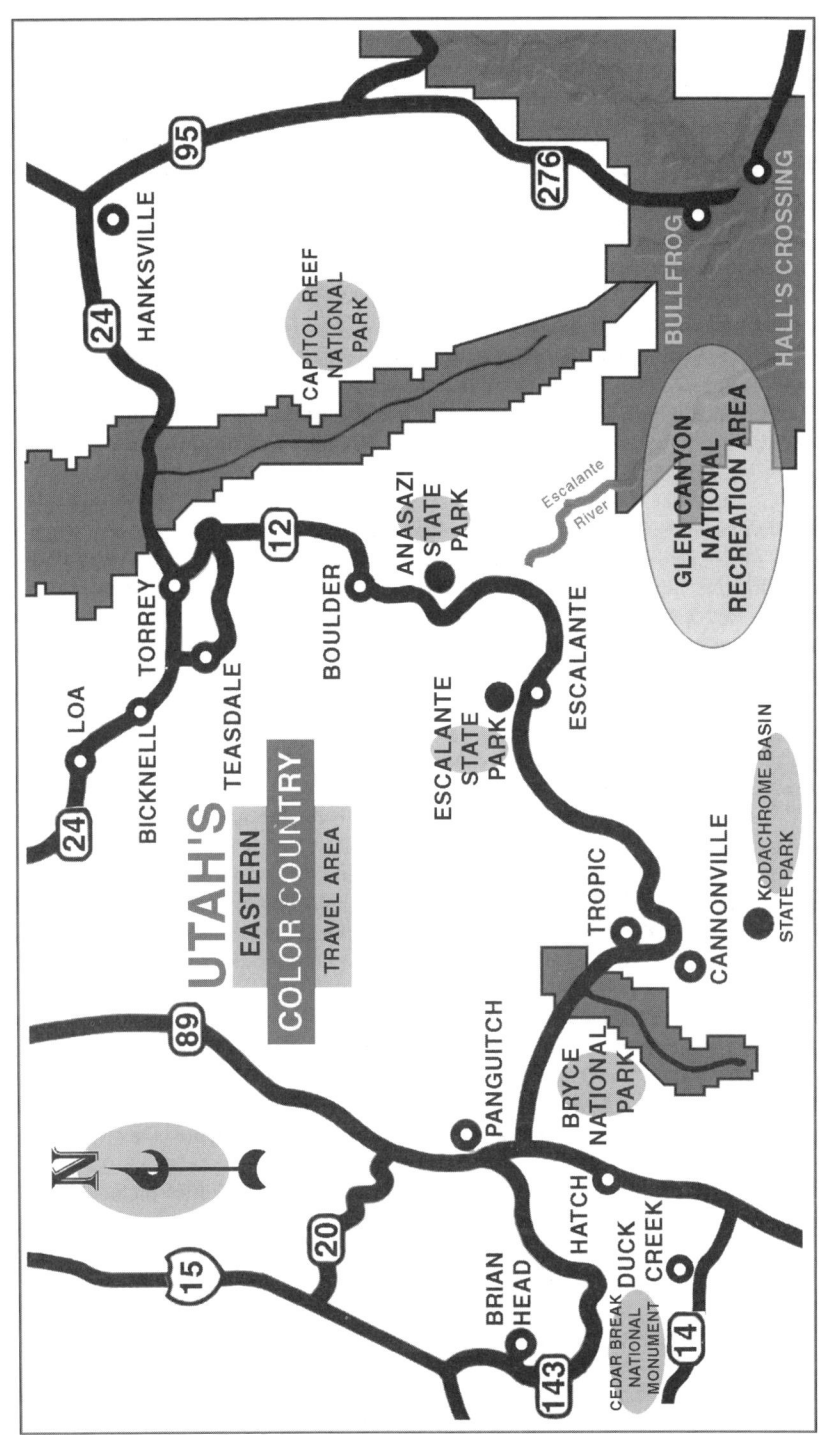

passes through the northern portion of Bryce on its way to the junction of U-63, an 18-mile road that winds its way through Bryce, a park that is known for its red rock, hoodoo-filled amphitheaters and for its lush forests and cool meadows.

From Bryce, U-12 descends through the **Dixie National Forest** and **Red Canyon**, a stretch of road so brilliant and picturesque, that those who have never been to Bryce often think they have just driven through it. Scenic Byway 12 ends at US 89, a road that, when traveling south, is another Scenic Byway.

BOULDER

First settled by two ranchers from nearby Richfield, who in 1789 brought 500 head of cattle into the region, the remote town of Boulder became an important cattle and dairy center during the decades that followed. It has been estimated that during the years between 1890 and 1900, more than 12,000 head of cattle grazed in the area. A few more families soon moved into Boulder and a school was begun in 1896.

Boulder is a town with an ancestral heritage and many of the families who live here today bear the names of those first pioneer settlers.

Nestled on the sloping base of Boulder Mountain along Scenic Byway 12, the small town of Boulder was, as recently as 1942, so isolated from the outside world that its only source of supplies was by pack mule from Escalante, 35 miles away. Boulder was the last town in the United States to receive its mail by mule, and was also the last incorporated town in Utah to have a paved main street.

According to a 1941 edition of the *Utah Writer's Project*, Boulder was so isolated that one man mule-packed a dissected pick-up truck into Boulder. He then reassembled it and ran it for eight years without a license on gasoline that he imported on pack mules at a cost of 75 cents a gallon.

A road from Escalante to Boulder was constructed as part of the CCC project that followed the Great Depression. The road is part of Utah's Scenic Byway 12, voted one of the top ten Scenic Byways in the country, and forms the link between the coral hoodoos of Bryce Canyon, the vermicular topography of Grand Staircase-Escalante, and the convoluted geography of Capitol Reef National Park. One section of the road, known as "The Hogsback," offers sheer drops on both sides and a view as spectacular as one could possibly imagine.

One would not want to miss traveling Scenic Byway 12 from Highway 89 to its end at Scenic Byway 24 and the town of Torrey. Having once traveled this Byway, visitors to the area might be inclined to traverse the route that the pack mules took prior to 1942 between Escalante and Boulder. The road, known as "Hell's Backbone," is graded gravel and its name says it all. It is a road for those who love beauty and the thrill of exploration.

While still a remote town, Boulder's fine visitor facilities include several motels, restaurants, adventure tours, a state park, gasoline, and groceries.

Modern roads and an appreciation for the magnificent and unusual scenery of Boulder country are attracting visitors from around the world. Utah's best kept secret of a few years ago has come into its own. In addition to being a gateway to Grand Staircase-Escalante, the Dixie National Forest, Capitol Reef National Park, and Lake Powell at Glen Canyon National Recreation Area via the Burr Trail, Boulder Mountain is without equal when it comes to hiking, mountain biking, horse back riding, and hunting and fishing.

Proud of its heritage, Independence Day and Days of '47 celebrations in Boulder are second to none, celebrated with parades, barbecues, rodeos and dancing.

BOULDER ATTRACTIONS

ANASAZI INDIAN VILLAGE STATE PARK

A partially excavated Indian Village, the Anasazi Indian Village State Park, located on Scenic Byway 12 in the town of Boulder, Utah, offers a glimpse into the life of the Native Americans who inhabited this area nearly 800 years ago.

Anasazi is a Navajo word meaning "ancient ones." Anasazi is used to describe the Basketmaker-Pueblo culture that existed in the Four Corners plateau region of Utah, Colorado, New Mexico, and Arizona from about A.D. 1 to 1300.

The Anasazi who inhabited this village, according to tree rings and pottery found, indicate that the people lived here from A.D. 1050 to 1200. Their ties were with the Anasazi who occupied the Kayenta region of Northeastern Arizona. Here the Anasazi raised corn, beans and squash. In the surrounding mountains and canyons the villagers hunted deer, desert bighorn sheep and small game. They also gathered wild berries, nuts, and seeds.

Research has not yet found the answers as to why the ancient ones left the village, but leave they did in about A.D. 1200 and they never returned. The village was burned, possibly by the inhabitants, shortly before it was abandoned. It is thought that the villagers then migrated back to the Kayenta region where they re-established themselves.

Exploratory excavations have indicated that the village was one of the largest ancient communities west of the Colorado River. The Anasazi Indian Village was excavated in the late 1950s with 87 rooms uncovered. The rooms were, however, re-covered with plastic and dirt until 1978 when re-excavation and stabilization were begun. A self-guided trail leads through the site. A life-size six-room replica of an Anasazi dwelling has been constructed to give visitors a better idea of what life was like in the village nearly 800 years ago.

The park's visitor center museum contains several interesting historical and cultural displays, including a diorama of the original village. Exhibits include information about pottery and stone tools, and replicas of a storage granary and a petroglyph panel. Most of the museum artifacts were found on the site. A picnic area adjoins the site but no camping facilities are available.

The village and museum are administered by the Utah Division of Parks and Recreations. The Park is open daily, 8:00 a.m. - 6:00 p.m., from mid-May - mid-September, and from 9:00 a.m. - 5:00 p.m. during the remainder of the year (435-335-7308).

BURR TRAIL

Covering 66 miles of some of the most rugged and scenic country in the American Southwest, the Burr Trail begins at the rural town of Boulder and Scenic Byway 12 and ends at **Bullfrog Marina** on beautiful **Lake Powell** in the **Glen Canyon National Recreation Area**.

Less than a mile from the trail's beginning, the road enters the nation's newest national monument, **Grand Staircase-Escalante**. The trail covers 66 miles of the most rugged and scenic country in the American Southwest and includes several vantage points. One such overlook is **Long Canyon**, with its view of unbroken red cliffs contrasting with the delightful blue of the **Henry Mountains**. **Capitol Reef Overlook** has a magnificent view of the great **Waterpocket Fold**. **Lake Powell Overlook** offers an outstanding view of deep blue Lake Powell set against the contrasting red of its surrounding sandstone canyons.

At one point the Burr Trail drops more than 800 feet in little more than a mile as this tight combination of switchbacks crosses the steep face of the Waterpocket Fold in **Capitol Reef National Park**. The view from this narrow, winding road is extraordinary. Canyons, buttes, mesas, plateaus, and mountains may be seen in the brilliant, multi-colored landscape below.

The trail is much better than it was in pioneer days and is paved nearly two-thirds of the way to Bullfrog. Nevertheless, stretches of road that remain unpaved make Burr Trail impassable to low clearance vehicles during inclement weather.

OTHER BOULDER AREA ATTRACTIONS

An alpine region of numerous small lakes, **Boulder Top**, located north of the town of Boulder, is a volcanic table mountain 11,000 feet high. It is the site of one of the nation's highest evergreen forests.

To the east of town, a ring of sandstone cliffs form a natural amphitheater known as **Circle Cliffs** or **Wolverine Petrified Wood Area**. Within the amphitheater there are several scenic points around the multi-colored Chinle slopes where petrified wood, often in the form of giant logs, may be seen.

ACCOMMODATIONS

POLE'S PLACE
465 North Highway 12
P. O. Box 1342
Boulder Utah 84716
Tel: (435) 335-7422
        (800) 730-7422
Visa, MasterCard, American Express, and Discover are accepted.
Reservations are recommended.

If one did not stop to spend the night at Pole's Place in Boulder, Utah when visiting the Southwest, they would have made a grievous mistake. Boulder, a small, friendly, affable community, is on Utah's famous Scenic Byway 12, one of the nation's top 10 byways. This little town serves as the Northern border to the nation's newest national monument, Grand Staircase-Escalante. Boulder is also surrounded by the beauty of Dixie National Forest.

Pole's Place, owned and operated by the Eugene Napoleon Griffin family, has a special western ambiance that helps guests to enjoy country living at its best. A bubbling brook running behind the small motel creates the sounds and the feel of being in the mountains. The motel is rustic with a frontier town facade, hitching posts, and a wood plank deck. Camille, one of the owners, has a green thumb and a penchant for flowers. During warmer months the property is profuse with the colors of the season. In addition to the twelve-room motel, Pole's Place offers a small gift shop and a quaint little eatery (see related stories).

The lobby, though small, is warm, inviting and lush with plants. The love seat and couch are forest green and burgundy.

Each of the spacious, modern rooms is attractively decorated in a color scheme that combines teal blue, mauve, and forest green. Rooms are furnished with queen bed, table and two easy chairs, a rocking chair, dresser, end table, and remote control color TV. Rooms are decorated with area art by Spike Ress, a local artist and friend of the family. Each room also has an alarm clock, direct dial phone with local calls free and, when one checks in, mints on the pillows. Bathrooms have tubs with showers and separate vanity basins.

One of the best things about Pole's Place is the rates. Nominally priced, the cost per unit is the same throughout the year and everyone pays the same. For the convenience and health of their guests, Pole's is a non-smoking facility and does not allow pets.

Boulder has a history that is as colorful and interesting as the diverse sandstone ledges that surround it. So isolated was the community that, until as late as the 1940's, mail and other supplies were still delivered by pack mules on trails that were nothing short of harrowing.

The Roundys, the Griffins, the Kings, all relatives of the Griffin family, were among the first ranchers and farmers who settled Boulder in 1889. Kings' Bench, Griffin Top, and King's Pasture are just three of the several scenic wonders around Grand Staircase-Escalante National Monument that have been named for the Griffin's pioneer ancestors.

Eugene Napoleon Griffin, affectionately known as "Pole," established the eatery in 1987. Nothing brought him more joy than being able to extend hospitality to Boulder visitors. In remembrance of Pole, Camille, Karen, and Gaden and their families take great pride in welcoming guests to Pole's Place, where hospitality is at its country best.

ADVENTURE / TOURS

BOULDER MOUNTAIN RANCH

P. O. Box 1375
Boulder Utah, 84716
Tel: (435) 335-7480
FAX: (435) 335-7480
Website:
www.boulderutah.com/bmr
Email: bmr@boulderutah.com

One-third deposit required via personal check, money transfer, or Travelers Cheques. Reservations are recommended.

Ensconced in a verdant valley against rolling hills of pinion pines, junipers, and red cedar, Boulder Mountain Ranch is a working cattle ranch that fulfills every Western fantasy of riding the range as a real live cowboy or cowgirl.

Rugged outdoorsmen and city slickers alike love Boulder Mountain Ranch, as there is truly something for everyone to do. If it is adventure one is looking for, the ranch offers numerous trail rides that explore the rugged beauty of the West. If it is peaceful solitude one hungers for, Boulder Mountain offers incomparable surroundings for serenity. If it is sharing habitat with coyotes, eagles, blue herons, elk, deer, and mountain lions, Boulder Mountain Ranch can satisfy that need as well. And when it comes to a good night's rest, guests have a choice of camping on the trail and sleeping under the stars, or enjoying the comforts of a lodge.

Everything about Boulder Mountain Ranch bespeaks the lure and grandeur of the West. Located in Southwestern Utah, Boulder Mountain Ranch is reached by traveling along Utah's Scenic Byway 12, one of the nation's top ten byways, and Hell's Backbone road, one of Utah's most popular Scenic Backways. The ranch, situated in tranquil Salt Gulch, is three and one-half miles off Scenic Byway 12, and is set back in a secluded valley about one-half mile off Hell's Backbone road.

Secluded as it might be, Boulder Mountain Ranch is seven miles from the town of Boulder with its Anasazi Indian State Park; is on the northern border of the nation's newest national monument, Grand Staircase-Escalante, and is within an easy drive of Bryce Canyon and Capitol Reef National parks. It is also just a few miles from Burr Trail, another Scenic Backway leading to Lake Powell.

Boulder Mountain Ranch offers ecology-oriented cattle drives, multi-day scenic horseback trips, and shorter daily rides through many natural splendors. These are not trail rides where riders do nothing more than walk a horse on a trail. Though riders stay together, the trips, depending on the riders, go from trots to full gallops, and from sagebrush and chaparral to sequestered rides beneath pines and towering red rock cliffs. Following the day's activities, guests return to the ranch for great western dining that includes fresh from the garden produce and meats cooked to perfection.

The Bryce Canyon to Salt Gulch five-day ride travels the Great Western Trail from Bryce Canyon to Boulder Mountain Ranch. This incredible journey traverses some of the most rugged and wild country in the Southwest, yet is suitable for all riding abilities. Guests experience five to seven hours of riding per day, a magnificent new campsite each night, great Dutch oven breakfasts and dinners at campsite, as well as hearty lunches while on the trail and a cozy bedroll.

For experienced riders only, Boulder Mountain Ranch offers its Long in the Saddle five or six nights horseback riding adventures that offer guests the chance to participate in a real live cattle roundup and drive. Different rides leave each day and feature scenic slickrock adventures or lush, shady mountain trail rides. The Cattle drives are purposeful and not just there for the enjoyment of Boulder Mountain Ranch guests. Bob and Sioux Cochran, owners of the ranch, have discovered that by moving the cattle daily at Boulder Mountain they become better land stewards. Frequent moving of the cattle prevents overgrazing, fertilizes the land, and aerates the soil.

The Boulder Mountain Ranch Short in the Saddle two-night stay is ideal for guests whose saddle is a little tender. One need not ride to enjoy the experience at Boulder Mountain Ranch, but for those who wish to enjoy the backcountry, Short in the Saddle is an ideal adventure. The trips are tailored to the group's ability level, from beginner to experienced, and travel through diverse terrain including slick rock, red rock canyon bottoms, and thick stands of aspen forest on the Aquarius Plateau. Short in the Saddle refers only to time spent riding, and not to decreased adventure.

In addition to the multi-day trips, Boulder Mountain Ranch offers Daily Trail Rides, a great way to introduce one's self to the adventures of horse riding. Daily trips include Scenic Loop, Half Day, Full Day, and No Pansy. All but the Scenic Loop ride include a hearty lunch on the trail.

In addition to horseback riding activities, Boulder Mountain Ranch offers hiking and a creek that is stocked with trout for great fishing. A weight room is also available.

Boulder Mountain Ranch, sequestered as it is, offers an average of 350 days per year of sun and clear, blue skies. The area's dry humidity creates ideal weather conditions for enjoying the winter months. Great winter activities in the area include Nordic skiing, snowmobiling, snowshoeing, and horseback riding. Boulder Mountain Ranch offers a two-nights, one-day package and three-nights, two-days package. Packages include food, lodging, horses, guides, snowshoes, a weight training gym, conference room, and all taxes.

One doesn't have to be a cowboy or cowgirl to enjoy life at Boulder Mountain Ranch. Sleeping facilities at Boulder Mountain include rooms at the Lodge, private log cabins, and private and group camping for tent campers and mini-vans.

The Lodge is rustic and offers a common room with high open beam ceiling, massive rock fireplace, plank floor, rustic furnishings, and a magnificent view to the South from floor to ceiling windows. A marvelous rustic deck surrounds the lodge and offers quiet serenity to indulge one's self in the beauties of nature. See deer and elk grazing at the doorstep, eagles soaring through the sky, a star-studded sky, and extraordinary sunsets. Whatever the time of day or the season, Boulder Mountain Lodge has a million-dollar view.

Five rooms are offered at the lodge. The two on the main floor have private baths with showers. One room offers two singles or a king bed. The second room has a queen bed. The three rooms upstairs are similar to a hostel, offering two shared baths and rooms with double bunk beds or a bunk and full-sized bed.

Two of the three cabins have one room and offer a choice of one queen and a set of bunk beds or one king or four single beds. The third cabin has a loft and will sleep six. All cabins have small bathrooms with showers and an outside deck for enjoying one's surroundings.

For those planning family reunions, the Boulder Mountain Ranch Lodge and cabins can accommodate groups of 25 to 30. Boulder Mountain offers a small conference room that is ideal for businesses planning management seminars.

Camp sites for tent and mini-van campers are also available and feature a fire barbecue pit, large pavilion, hot showers, picnic tables and outhouse facilities.

Bob is not only a cowboy at heart, but a cowboy from birth. Born on a ranch in Montana, he has spent much of his life seeing the West by shoeing horses as he traveled. Sioux is a city slicker who was born in Wisconsin and became Bob's mail order bride. She met Bob while on vacation in San Francisco. For the next two years they never saw each other but continued to write. Once the question was popped, Bob and Sioux moved to Northern California where they built a business offering trail rides. In 1989 they heard about the ranch near Boulder, Utah,, fell in love with the area, and became Boulder Mountain ranchers for life.

Boulder Mountain Ranch—guests fall in love with it too!

DID YOU KNOW?

---that the Anasazi State Park was excavated in 1858 - 1859 by University of Utah archaeology students. It was originally called Coombs Site. History tells us that the Anasazi did not remain here long, probably 50 - 75 years. The reason they left is still a mystery, although drought and the lack of food are most probable. It is also believed that they burned the village before abandoning it.

ESCALANTE CANYON OUTFITTERS
P. O. Box 1330
Boulder, Utah 84716
Tel: (435) 335-7311
 (888) Eco-hike (326-4453)
FAX: (435) 335-7499
Web Site: www.gorp.com/escalante
Email ecohike@color-country.net
Season March 15 - November 15
Personal checks are accepted.
Reservations are required.

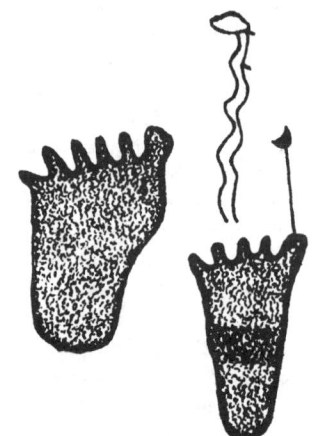

Millions of years ago on the Colorado Plateau, all of the elements of nature began combining forces to create deep Navajo and Wingate sandstone canyons in what is now the country's newest national monument, Grand Staircase-Escalante. The meandering Escalante River has carved its path deep in the colorful red sandstone canyon and left the canyon floor lush and green.

This beautiful, remote and seemingly untouched sanctuary is the wilderness home of Escalante Canyon Outfitters. Their motto and logo, leaving only footprints behind, ensure the world that, at least where Escalante Canyon Outfitters is involved, Grand Staircase-Escalante will remain a primitive respite for those who seek seclusion.

Grant Johnson and Sue Fearon have been operating Escalante Canyon Outfitters out of their home near Boulder since 1991. They took a campfire idea and turned it into a business that now offers full-service guided trips into Escalante Canyons.

The serenity and beauty of the nine different itineraries offered by Grant and Sue is difficult to fathom. These are pack horse supported walking trips that leave hikers unencumbered to enjoy the beauty and solitude of the canyons and to explore ancient trails, narrow canyons, and deep gorges without being burdened by a heavy pack.

The locations of Escalante Canyon Outfitters trips and activities change with the seasons. Spring (during April and May) is the ideal time to explore the dramatic narrow canyons of the Escalante. Walls of the Wingate sandstone canyons are so narrow in some places that one can touch both sides at the same time. Looking up, the sky is a slit of deep blue, so narrow that it appears as a meandering river. In other places the canyon walls open to form a cathedral-like room with the ceiling displaying arches carved by water and reflected in a pool below. By following ancient trails, with pecked hand and foot holds created by the Anasazi Indians who inhabited this area for more than 1200 years, hikers can ascend above the canyons. Here in the spring, explorers are treated to spectacular pockets of wildflowers and Indian Ricegrass surrounded by orange slickrock. Above the canyons, guests stand in awe as they view the breathtaking panorama of the Escalante.

During late spring and early summer (May through July), the itinerary of Escalante Canyon Outfitters takes exploring guests to Deer Creek, in the heart of slickrock country. Deep swimming holes offer refreshment during the course of each day's activities. From the camps, guests venture out of the canyon to explore the domes and pinnacles of colorful Navajo sandstone. Groves of Aspen trees and Ponderosa pines are a welcome sight on these hot, sunny days. Camp sites are near creeks and surrounded by beautifully streaked canyon walls where seeping water has created hanging gardens of Maidenhair fern and wild flowers.

Late summer and early fall (August through October) are considered by many to be the most comfortable times of the year for exploring canyon country. Escalante Canyon Outfitters takes hikers down a spectacular winding red gorge to the Escalante River. The winding river has created towering canyon walls and giant alcoves that provide perfect settings for the base camps. From the camp hikers wade along the river, dive into the deeper pools that form at the base of the canyon, and explore intriguing side canyons and amphitheaters. Cascading waterfalls, created by brief summer showers, are a spectacle to behold as tiny rivulets plunge down the sandstone cliffs. Cooler fall weather also creates an ideal time for exploring the intricate terrain above the River.

Late fall and early spring (November or March) are the best times of the year for exploring the very unusual and rugged sections of the lower Escalante, where the river empties into Lake Powell. Here the canyons are the deepest and the ridges are a maze of highly eroded slickrock. The least explored region, this remote area offers adventurers the opportunity to hike to high vantage points and view a jumbled horizon of half-domes, bubbly slickrock, and distant mountains. Far below, nestled between cottonwood and oak groves, is the Escalante Canyon Outfitters base camp, ensconced along a stream. Five and seven day trips are offered at two different locations, depending on the season.

Every hike offered brings new and exciting discoveries. Perhaps that accounts for the fact that 40% of Escalante Canyon Outfitters' business is made up of returning guests. *National Geographic* camera crews are among those returning guests. They found Escalante Canyon Outfitters to be indispensable as they gathered information and photographed Grand Staircase-Escalante National Monument. Look for *National Geographic's* full-color story, to be released in the fall of 1998.

Commodious base camps set up by Grant and Sue offer adventurers a beautiful place to gather for delicious meals, hot showers, and to discuss activities of the day. Grant has explored the region extensively, both on foot and on horseback, and has studied in depth the area's geology, prehistory and ecology. When Sue came to Southern Utah in 1985 it was with a degree in Outdoor Recreation. She has worked as a park ranger, is an organic farmer, and has taught environmental programs to groups of all ages. Both are well qualified to answer questions about the forces that shaped the land and about the prehistoric Anasazi Indians who anciently inhabited the land.

There are no age limits for participants in Escalante Canyon Outfitters adventure hikes. Grant and Sue have discovered that attitude and altitude are things to be considered most when joining their adventure hikes. For the most part the walking is easy and fairly level, but steep areas are encountered when entering and leaving the canyons. Altitude in the canyons is approximately 5, 000 feet and can require an elevation adjustment.

Since the base camps are supplied by horses, guests are only required to carry a day pack for water, lunch, camera, and whatever else one might need or want during the day's activities.

Since supplies are carried into the canyon by horses, Escalante Canyon Outfitters is able to provide hikers with the finest quality of foods available, including many organically grown fruits and fresh vegetables. Grant and Sue invite guests to bring them their favorite recipes so they can add it to their menu of great outdoor meals.

The season of the trip being taken influences the hiker's daily needs. All one basically needs is to dress appropriately for the season and to bring a sleeping bag. A list can be provided if requested.

Grand Staircase-Escalante National Monument and the small town of Boulder, Utah are approximately 250 miles southeast of Salt Lake City. The shortest and most picturesque route is to follow I-15 South to Nephi and exit on Highway 28. Take Highway 28 to Scenic Byway 24, traveling south to Scenic Byway 12. Boulder is approximately 35 miles Southeast on Scenic Byway 12.

Escalante Canyon Outfitters is the longest running full-service private business in the Escalante. They are a Permittee of the National Park Service and Bureau of Land Management.

Discover slickrock country above the canyons, swim in crystal clear pools of water, carefully explore petroglyphs and the remains of ancient Anasazi Indian camps, and exhilarate in the joy of life. Then return home, satisfied and deeply moved by the beauty and peacefulness of the land, with a commitment to return as soon as possible. Time, space, and the enjoyment of nature are the essence of Escalante Canyon Outfitters.

BED & BREAKFASTS

EAGLESTAR RANCH
BED & BREAKFAST
330 East Boulder Pines Road
P. O. Box 1456
 (1.2 miles southeast on Burr Trail Road)
Boulder, Utah 84716
Tel: (435) 335-7438
FAX: (435) 335-7463
E-Mail: belnap@color-country.net
Visa and MasterCard are accepted.
Reservations are recommended.

EagleStar Ranch Bed & Breakfast, ensconced on a small hill that overlooks the lush 350-acre EagleStar Ranch Wildlife Preserve is, as its guests pronounce, "Not just a piece of heaven, but heaven itself."

Even though EagleStar Ranch Bed & Breakfast, owned by D. Jan Belnap and hosted by Jan and her service dog, Jake, has only been open for business since the summer of 1997, rave reviews continue to fill the guest book.

EagleStar, nestled among native pine and cedar trees, overlooks a crystal clear holding reservoir that is used to feed the rich pasture lands and alfalfa fields of the full production ranch. The preserve is cradled between dramatic white sandstone mountains and red rock mesas. On a clear day, a 100-mile corridor view extends all the way to Navajo Mountain.

EagleStar was named after the prevalence of Eagles that soar above the ranch during the day; and the star-studded night skies.

Inside and outside the ambiance is restful, with time moving to the rhythm of the seasons and weather.

Upon entering EagleStar, one steps into the Great Room with beautiful oak floor, high ceiling, and a double gray rock fireplace that extends through the rafters. Furnishings are refined Southwestern, enhanced with authentic wool Navajo rugs. A large telescope at one end of the Great Room is used by guests to enjoy the brilliance of the stars at night, the variety of birds that inhabit the area, and the inn's magnificent panorama. French doors with transom windows are the exit to a lovely deck that affords these same scenic vistas.

Adjacent to the main floor Great Room is a spacious kitchen and bright, cheery dining room. It is here that guests enjoy a hearty continental breakfast of fresh breads, an assortment of juices, cold cereals, granola, fresh fruits and coffee, teas, and hot chocolate. A special treat of fresh honey is afforded by Jan, "the bee charmer," and her hives.

At the bottom of a wide stairway is the Group Room, a sunny room with a contemporary look and access to a covered patio. On the patio one can hear the babbling creek that runs through the back yard on its way to the nearby reservoir.

In this area of the home are nestled the four guest rooms. The View Room, with large windows that bring the world inside, is very spacious and offers guests a queen bed, leather chair, and an antique dresser. Color scheme is an elegant burgundy and forest green. The private bath has tub with shower and vanity basin.

The Ranch Room, though not as capacious, displays authentic worn cowboy gear acquired from the surrounding ranches and the EagleStar ranch. The decor provides guests with a real taste of the West from one of the last authentic ranching communities in the West, Boulder.

The Southwest Room offers a queen bed with comforter of purple, teal and mauve. Native American rugs and an exquisite pottery lamp add to the Southwestern decor. In this room one is submerged in the smells, sights and sounds of the Southwest. The bathroom, in colors of forest and burgundy, has a pedestal basin and a shower.

The Romantic is a large room with queen bed and fanciful colors of mauve and black. A pottery lamp, spacious love seat, and Native American rugs on the walls and draped on the divan add to the Southwestern decor. Bath facilities include a tub with shower and separate vanity with antique chair.

As a special amenity, complimentary wine is available in the evening to EagleStar Ranch Bed & Breakfast guests.

Not too far from EagleStar's main house is an authentic tipi under four large cottonwood trees. It is 18-feet in diameter, well insulated, has a firepit in the middle, and a cook stove. The tipi is furnished with a twin bed and genuine hides from the local game of beaver, antelope, rabbit, coyote and deer. In the summer and fall season, Jan, who has multiple sclerosis, lives in the tipi. She has discovered the healing benefits of dwelling close to mother earth.

Jan has had so many inquiries flavored with enthusiasm regarding her tipi, that she is planning additional guest tipis for the 1999 season. There is the possibility that some of the tipis will be in place for the 1998 season. Each will be privately fenced in to protect guests from the 80 head of cattle and the five horses that roam the surrounding pasture land.

On the opposite side of the ranch from the tipis one finds the campground, nestled among Pinion pines. Twenty tent sites are scheduled to open this season with shower and toilet facilities.

The 1998 season also features, when previously arranged, Dutch oven cookouts. Guests gather around a bonfire and dine on traditional Dutch oven dishes made even more succulent because of Jan's wonderful garden. Fresh spinach, kale, onions, snow peas, lettuce, carrots, and tomatoes, as well as fresh juicy raspberries thrive under Jan's watchful eye. Also with prior arrangement, the Belgium work horses can be harnessed to a wagon to take guests to their cookout or farther down the Burr Trail.

Boulder, home of EagleStar Ranch Bed & Breakfast, is within an easy drive of Capitol Reef and Bryce Canyon National Parks. The Anasazi Indian Village State Park, with its museum and partially exposed ruins, are in Boulder. Escalante Petrified Forest and Kodachrome Basin State Parks are respectively less than one and two hours drive from Boulder. Hell's Backbone, so-named because of the sheer drops on both sides of the road, is an adventure in itself, and is only fifteen miles away. Burr Trail Road, which begins almost at EagleStar Ranch's front door, is a 66 mile drive through some of Utah's most spectacular wilderness, including Long Canyon, a colorful gorge that resembles Zion Canyon.

Opportunities for sightseeing, hiking, biking, fishing, backpacking, and horseback riding in this scenic wilderness are endless. EagleStar Ranch Bed & Breakfast is ideally located as a center for enjoying Utah's beautiful Color Country. All who come here are moved by the magic and spirit of this unique and special place.

RESTAURANTS

BURR TRAIL CAFE
P. O. Box 1391
Junction of Scenic Byway 12 & Burr Trail Highway
Boulder, Utah 84716
Tel: (435) 335-7432
Hrs:
Breakfast 7:00 a.m. - 12:00 noon
Lunch   12:00 noon - 5:00 p.m.
Dinner   5:00 p.m. - 9:00 p.m.
Visa and MasterCard are accepted.

When Billie Jones, a construction worker from Salt Lake City, Utah discovered the quaint little town of Boulder in 1984 it was love at first sight. Fortunately, things came together the way they should. Billie bought the Burr Trail Cafe and Trading Post and she has never looked back since. The Trading Post (see related story) is across the driveway from the Burr Trail Cafe.

Billie, along with her Boulder company of friends and helpers, welcomes travelers to a cafe that is every bit as quaint and western as the town itself. The building, built in 1939 as a small motel and cafe, has a western town exterior. Inside there are hand-carved rustic stools at the bar and local cattle ranchers' brands blazed into the counter. An old pot bellied stove separates the counter bar room from a small dining room that seats 15. An outside terrace is the most popular dining spot from May through September.

Breakfasts at Burr Trail Cafe are delicious, different, and strictly country. The homemade scones with butter and honey and the muffins and sweet rolls are hard to pass up. For more hardy appetites there is Huevos Rancheros, consisting of flour tortillas, eggs, refried beans, green chili, tomatoes, onions, cheese, and homemade salsa. No one should visit the West without trying biscuits with sausage milk gravy, and at Burr Trail Cafe, where everything is homemade, they are the best. Pancakes or waffles with blueberry or strawberry topping is another breakfast favorite. All breakfasts at Burrs are served with a generous portion of in-season fresh fruit, homemade hash browns, white or wheat toast from homemade bread, or Burr's homemade scones.

The sandwich selection at Burr Trail Cafe is almost endless. The menu includes ham, turkey, roast beef, French dip, bacon, lettuce and tomato, pastrami, club, and grilled cheese as traditional choices, as well as egg and tuna salad sandwiches. Other choices include patty melt, fishburger, chicken burger, and chicken cordon bleu. A veggie sandwich, incredibly delicious, is loaded with sprouts, guacamole, tomato, onions, lettuce, and mushrooms. Burr Trail Cafe is known for its Canyonland Burger Heaven. Burgers, in one-fourth and one-half pound sizes, are made with lean ground chuck and served on a sesame bun. Burger fixings include Swiss and American cheese, pastrami, bacon, and mushrooms. Burr Trail recommends trying their homemade ranch dressing on the burgers. All sandwiches are served with a generous portion of fresh fruit, tossed green salad and French fries. Bread choices include homemade white, wheat, rye, or bagels.

Butch Cassidy and Calamity Jane are names given Burr Trail's 12-ounce and 10-ounce thick, juicy and lean top sirloin steaks. Other menu items with names that reflect Burr Trail's 'real country cookin'' include the Rancher, a ground chuck steak; and Cowboy, a one-pound hamburger steak that has a pepper jack cheese filling, is lightly breaded, and grilled to perfection. Sundance Kid is a ham steak with pineapple and raisin sauce; Country Pal is chicken fried steak, served with country gravy. Cajun Strips are spicy and delicious top sirloin strips; Fisherman is a rendering of lightly breaded fillet of Haddock; Outlaw is homestyle meatloaf, and Country Boy is an offering of two center cut loin pork chops with homemade applesauce. A real western favorite, straight from the cold Utah mountain streams, is Mountain Man rainbow trout, grilled to perfection. All dinners are served with salad, baked potato, French fries or mashed potatoes, and homemade scones.

Desserts are not to be missed at Burr Trail Cafe. Made fresh daily favorites include the warm and delicious bread pudding with lemon sauce, a selection of fruit pies, and a variety of cakes.

When Utah's "million-dollar road" was built during the great depression between Escalante and Boulder, it formed the connecting link between delicate Bryce Canyon National Park and the massive convoluted geography of Capitol Reef National Park. The Burr Trail, after which the cafe is named, connects Boulder with Bullfrog on beautiful Lake Powell. In 1996 the nation's newest national monument, Grand Staircase-Escalante was announced. Boulder is situated on the Northern boundary.

Even with all of these natural wonders that exist along Utah's famous Scenic Byway 12, Boulder continues to be one of Utah's best kept secrets. It should not be so. The Anasazi Indian Village and Museum State Park, located in Boulder on excavated ruins of an ancient Indian village, is open year round. Calf Creek Recreation area is a short 12 miles from Boulder and several other reservoirs offer incomparable fishing. With all that there is to do and see in the surrounding area, Boulder should be a hot spot of the nation. Billie invites travelers to stay a little longer in Boulder so they can see and do it all.

The stay in Boulder is made even more enjoyable by the hospitality of Billie and her company of friends and helpers at Burr Trail Cafe. They are eager to help guests in whatever way they can. Burr Trail Cafe—where travel information is free, the service is wonderful, and the food is great and worth every penny one spends on it.

POLE'S PLACE EATERY
465 North Scenic Byway 12
P. O. Box 1342
Boulder Utah 84716
Tel: (435) 335-7422
          (800) 730-7422
Hrs:
Open Daily   9:00 a.m. - 6:00 p.m.
Visa, MasterCard, American Express, and Discover are accepted.

Eugene Napoleon Griffin Family

Directly across the street from Anasazi State Park on Scenic Byway 12 is Pole's Place Motel, Gift Shop (see related stories), and Eatery. Pole's Place Eatery has been serving hamburgers that taste like a burger should taste, and thick, eat-them-with-a-spoon milk shakes since Eugene Napoleon Griffin, "Pole" first opened his doors in 1987.

Pole's Place Eatery is small but cozy and has an eclectic ambiance. Gabby, a bearded pioneer mannequin, sits at the main entrance. Though he doesn't say much himself, Gabby is a favorite topic of conversation. He also finds his way into many a souvenir photograph as guests of Pole's Place Eatery stop to have their pictures taken.

In addition to the inside dining room, which will seat 15, Pole's Place Eatery offers an outside deck that will seat 20, picnic tables on the grounds, and a pass-through window for take-outs.

Pole's Place Eatery has a breakfast menu that includes pancakes, homemade cinnamon rolls, special muffins, and a breakfast sandwich of egg, cheese, bacon, or ham. Also offered are coffee, hot chocolate, milk, and fruit juices.

Pole's Place Eatery serves a full line of the best hamburgers and cheeseburgers ever; all served with special sauce, lettuce, pickles and onions. Specialties of the house are the double cheeseburger with bacon, and the Boulder Burger, two quarter-pound patties with Swiss cheese.

Specialty shakes include Oreo, Butterfinger, Chocolate Chip Cookie Dough, Snickers, Banana, Reese's Peanut Butter, and Grasshopper. Traditionals, such as chocolate, strawberry, blackberry, raspberry, pineapple, and caramel are also available. In addition to their famous shakes, Pole's Place Eatery offers root beer floats, sundaes, and cones.

Pole's Place Eatery serves an assortment of sandwiches, chicken strips, hot dogs, corn dogs, and pizza. Mexican dishes include Taquitos, burritos, and nachos. From the salad menu are chef, taco and garden salads served with a choice of dressings. Fish and chips and chicken strip dinners are served with salad, roll and French fries.

Although foods are served promptly, Pole's Place Eatery is not a fast food restaurant. Food tastes as it used to taste, back when people cared. That's because, at Pole's Place Eatery, they still do.

SPECIALTY SHOPPING

BURR TRAIL TRADING POST

P. O. Box 1391
Junction of Scenic Byway 12
 & Burr Trail Highway
Boulder, Utah 84716
Tel: (435) 335-7432
Hrs: Open Daily
   7:00 a.m. - 9:00 p.m.
Visa and MasterCard are accepted.

    Burr Trail Trading Post, built originally as a small motel in 1939, is more than a gift shop to passers-by, it is a place to hang out and enjoy the camaraderie that only a small town can offer. With a year-round population of under 200 people, everyone knows everyone. And in all the world there is not a group of more friendly, amiable, and helpful people than those that reside in Boulder. The Trading Post and the Burr Trail Cafe across the parking lot (see related story), are owned and operated by one of those amicable people, Billie Jones.

    During the winter of 1996 Burr Trail Trading Post underwent a major renovation. Now, in addition to its genial gift shop, the Trading Post has a classic Coffee Shop, delectable Deli, and aromatic Bakery, where guests are welcome to browse and shop to their heart's content.

    The Trading Post ambiance has been kept Western eclectic. An old wood plank porch with Ponderosa pine posts runs the full length of the store front. A cowpoke mannequin sits at the store entrance, and antique pop machines as well as other collectibles are to be found along the porch. The store is wheelchair accessible via a wooden ramp.

    The gift shop is filled to the brim with Native American artifacts from the Zuni, Hopi, and Navajo tribes. Gift items include a stunning collection of pottery in all sizes, shapes, colors and designs. Another popular gift item is a piece of sterling silver jewelry. These treasures include rings, bracelets, earrings, necklaces, hair pieces, watch bands, belt buckles, and bolo ties. They are hand-crafted of the finest sterling, with many embellishments of turquoise, mother of pearl, coral, and blue lapis semi precious stones, to name a few. The Native Americans are famous for their fine hand woven baskets, rugs, and blankets, all of which are available at the Trading Post. Shoppers will also find Kachina and Story Teller dolls, dream makers, Mandellas, and sand paintings. Those looking for logo mementos will find a great selection of T-shirts, caps, mugs, thimbles, and magnets as well as colorful books, postcards, videos, calendars, and note cards on the parks.

    Grab a great cup of espresso, cappuccino or caffe latte at the Coffee Shop and browse through a book collection that features authors from and stories about the area. An example is the classic, *Desert Solitaire*, the story of Everett Ruess by Edward Abbey. Everett was an artist, prolific writer, and vagabond for beauty, who suddenly disappeared in the Escalante Canyons. The book draws from his journal, which was found along with his mules, but Everett, just 20 at the time, has never been heard from since his uncanny disappearance. Great area cookbooks are also featured as well as slick rock art prints by Kip Green and other area photographers.

    The Deli offers soups, sandwiches to go, and potato, taco, and salad bars. An assortment of great cheeses and slicing meats is also available.

Pumpernickel, rye, bagels, rolls, and many hard to find breads, as well as cakes, brownies, and cookies are always available at the Trading Post's fresh-daily Bakery. Regardless of whether one is a resident of Boulder or just passing through, if there is a craving for baked goods, one is likely to find it here.

An 1800's definition for trading post might read: "the place where friends and neighbors gather to chat, share news of the day, and to trade their wares." Today that definition still holds true, as locals and passers-by gather to unite in friendship at the Burr Trail Trading Post.

POLE'S PLACE GIFT SHOP
465 North Scenic Byway 12
P. O. Box 1342
Boulder Utah 84716
Tel: (435) 335-7422
       (800) 730-7422
Hrs:
Open Daily   9:00 a.m. - 6:00 p.m.
Visa, MasterCard, American Express, and Discover are accepted.

Eugene Napoleon Griffin Family

Located at Pole's Place (see related story), a small motel with a western frontier ambiance, Pole's Place Gift Shop offers a quality assortment of keepsake gifts, souvenir items, and country hospitality.

Cherished gifts for a lifetime include Navajo and Zapatec rugs, Anasazi Indian pottery and Native American jewelry. This fine selection of silver craftsmanship includes rings, bracelets, earrings, necklaces, hair pieces, belt buckles, bolo ties, and watch bands. Most are embellished with semi-precious stones such as turquoise, mother of pearl, coral, black onyx, and lapis.

There are exquisite hand woven baskets, porcelain figurines, quality copper jewelry, dream catchers, Mandellas, and the most popular petroglyph figure of all, Kokopelli..

Mementos of a trip to Southwestern Utah include T-shirts of Boulder, the Burr Trail, Hole in the Rock, and Grand Staircase-Escalante National Monument. There is also a nice selection of post and note cards, area magnets, mugs, and thimbles. Colorful calendars and books of the parks are also available. Youngsters enjoy the variety of pioneer games.

Whether staying at Pole's Place or just traveling through, Pole's Place Gift Shop is the place in Boulder to stop and shop.

ESCALANTE

Surrounded by millions of acres of land that includes enchanting green forests and over twenty-two natural stone arches and bridges, the town of Escalante is the center of one of the state's most outstanding scenic areas. Until recent years the town was almost isolated because of poor roads. While no longer a "one-horse town," Escalante still retains an atmosphere of frontier isolation and the rugged look of the Old West.

Escalante is one of few Southern Utah towns that was not settled as a result of Brigham Young's direction for settlement expansion. In 1874 a vanguard of pioneers from Panguitch was exploring the area on its own, looking for a warmer climate. They encountered two John Wesley Powell topographers who had already named the valley and its river, Escalante, in honor of Francisco Silvestre Velez de Escalante, a Spanish Catholic priest who explored sections of Utah in 1776. A curiosity is that the Spanish Dominguez-Escalante expedition never came closer than 65 miles to the town that now bears its name.

One year later, in 1875, encouraged by the amount of cultivatable land, water, timber, and grazing land there was in the Escalante, half a dozen men brought two wagons over the pass between the Table Cliffs and the Aquarius Plateau to begin building a settlement. The following year several families moved in and land was divided, canals were dug, and irrigation and farming begun. On July 4, 1876, though they did not have a proper flag, the handful of Escalante residents raised a striped Navajo blanket and, amid shouting and fanfare, officially named their community, Escalante. Those first settlers lived in dugouts or their wagons. Water was transported to homes by a barrel placed on a wooden sled they called a "lizzard." Until the canal or "big ditch" was constructed, the water came from the Escalante River. Most of the first homes were log, as the settlers took advantage of the abundant lumber. Later three kilns were constructed near where the race track is today. Coal was soon discovered, providing fuel for the settlement and jobs for early Escalante residents..

The first recorded visit of white man to the site that is now Escalante was in 1866. Captain James Andrus and a party of militiamen, enroute from St. George to Green River on a matter related to the Indian Uprising of 1866, camped in Escalante and cooked and ate wild potatoes that were found growing in the valley. They recorded the site and named the area Potato Valley.

Escalante residents for years relied on farming, ranching and lumbering for their livelihoods but today the town of close to 900 enjoys a broad economic base. Although at this printing it had not been finalized, Escalante is expected to be home to a visitor center for Grand Staircase-Escalante National Monument.

Escalante, smack-dab in the middle of Scenic Byway 12, one of the Nation's Top Ten Scenic Byways, is an ideal vacation destination and offers restaurants, motels, bed & breakfasts, and other tourist amenities.

ESCALANTE ATTRACTIONS

ESCALANTE PETRIFIED FOREST STATE PARK

In addition to the convoluted terrain of Grand Staircase National Monument, nature has created a very different wonder. Rivers of 140 million years ago carried trees to the site of present-day Escalante and then burried them in her backyard. The burial preserved the wood and prevented decay. Over the millenia, wood cells gradually gave way to silicone dioxide crystals. These crystals and mineral impurities worked their magic, embellishing these trees-turned-to-stone with glorious rainbow colors. Much of the wood, again over the milenia, has gradually been exposed by weather, and can be seen at Escalante Petrified Forest State Park, 1.5 miles west of Escalante. The park was established to protect and preserve the fossilized remains of an ancient tree forest.

In additon to the colorful deposits of mineralized wood, there are also dinosaur bones that were deposited in muddy flats millions of years ago. They were entombed and preserved from decay by sand and gravel of the Morrison Formation. An interpretive nature trail winds through this forest of rainbow-hued petrified rock.

In additon to the Bailey Wash, Wide Hollow and Rainbow Loop Trails, which are in the park, there is a three-quarter mile round trip nature trail that crosses the dry wash, climbs a small hill, and loops through the colorful petrified wood.

Facilities at the park include a visitor center, 22-unit campground, modern rest rooms with showers, and sanitary disposal station. Bordering the park is the 130-acre **Wide Hollow Reservoir**, which adds water recreation and fishing to the park's amenities (435-826-4466).

GRAND STAIRCASE-ESCALANTE NATIONAL MONUMENT

Grand Staircase-Escalante, the nation's newest national monument, was created by a presidential decree in the fall of 1996. The Monument encompasses 1.7 million acres of Utah's public land.

Because the Grand Staircase-Escalante has for over a century been the backyard of the communities that border it, Grand Staircase-Escalante is the only national monument to be managed by the Bureau of Land Management. The BLM will preserve this relationship between the communities and the monument and continue traditional uses of the land such as hunting, fishing, grazing, and various forms of recreation.

Grand Staircase-Escalante is divided into three regions—Escalante Canyons, Kalparowits Plateau, and the Grand Staircase.

The **Escalante Canyons** region is a 1,000 mile maze that has been carved by the sinuous Escalante River. This region borders the Waterpocket Fold of Capitol Reef National Park to the east and abuts the Glen Canyon National Recreation Area. Scenic Byway 12 slices through the northern tip of this section and Hole-in-theRock Road Scenic Backway, a trail forged by a company of Mormon pioneers, separates the Escalante Canyons from the Kalparowits Plateau.

The **Kaiparowits Plateau** anciently was the dwelling place for prehistoric Anasazi and Fremont cultures. It is in this region of the Escalante-Grand Staircase that one finds petroglyphs, pictographs, campsites, granaries, and other ruins left behind from a civilization that vanished more than 600 years ago. The Kalparowits also serves as a refuge for wildlife and is home to extremely rare forms of vegetation.

The **Grand Staircase** region is a geological gold mine with its pastel Navajo sandstone cliffs covering five periods of history that range from the Sonoran desert to the coniferous forests.

Scattered throughout the three spectacular regions are bridges, fossils, petrified wood, and stone arches. The size, geology, and scientific value of the land set it apart from other national monuments. Grand Staircase-Escalante is living documentation of the archeology, geology, paleontology, and biology of this hemisphere from prehistoric days to the present.

There are only two paved roads providing access to the Monument—Scenic Byway 12 along the northern tip, and Highway 89 along the southern boundary. Five secondary roads of varying grades intersect the Monument from north to south.

Scenic Byway 12 has been nationally acclaimed as one of the country's top 10 byways. A paved two-lane highway, the road through Grand Staircase-Escalante, from Tropic to Boulder, is 68 miles long. Panoramas include vast oceans of slickrock and scenic canyons carved by the Escalante River. Along its route there are numerous overlooks. The Monument borders on several small towns that are rich in pioneer history and that are also along the Scenic Byway. In addition U-12 gives access to

Escalante Petrified Forest State Park, Calf Creek Recreation Area, the Escalante River, and Anasazi State Park.

Most of the 57-mile **Hole-in-the-Rock Road** is graded dirt and gravel and passenger cars with clearance are normally adequate. The last six miles, however, are rough and may require 4-wheel drive. The road follows the historic route taken by Mormon settlers in 1879-80 on their journey across the Colorado River. The road also gives access to **Devil's Garden**, **Escalante Canyon** trailheads, **Dance Hall Rock**, and vistas of Lake Powell from Hole-in-the-Rock.

Burr Trail is paved for the first 31 miles between Boulder and Capitol Reef National Park. The rest is dirt and gravel surface with some rocky and sandy stretches. High-clearance vehicles are recommended if exploring off the Burr Trail. The road gives access to **Deer Creek**, **The Gulch**, **Long Canyon**, **Wolverine Petrified Wood Area**, and **Circle Cliffs** region.

Along its southern route, **Highway 89**, also a paved two-lane highway, it is 72 miles from Kanab to Page, Arizona. The road offers views of the **Vermilion Cliffs** and the Kaiparowits Plateau. It also gives access to the Grand Staircase region, the **Pahreah movie set**, and the **Paria Canyon-Vermilion Cliffs Wilderness** area.

The Paria River Valley, Johnson Canyon Skutumpah, Cottonwood Canyon, and Smoky Mountain roads all junction with Highway 89. The **Paria River Valley Road** is five miles of dirt and gravel and is only accessible during dry weather. The road was built to access Pahreah, a movie set town ensconced against the Paria River Valley and its Technicolor badlands. The town is still a tourist attraction during clement weather.

Johnson Canyon Skutumpah Road is 46 miles of paved and graded dirt road with the upper 22 miles becoming impassable when wet. The road traverses the Grand Staircase steps and gives views to **Pink Cliffs**. It gives access to **Grand Staircase Cliff and Terrace Steps** and **Bull Valley Gorge**.

Cottonwood Canyon Road becomes extremely slick and treacherous when wet. This 46-mile graded dirt and gravel road follows the **Cockscomb**, a major flexure of the earth's crust that divides the Grand Staircase and the Kaiparowits Plateau regions. Paralleling the axis of the east Kaibab Monocline, Cottonwood Canyon offers the traveler one of the most stimulating drives in the state. The road also gives access to **Round Valley**, **Cottonwood Narrows**, **Grosvenor Arch**, and **Kodachrome Basin State Park**.

Smoky Mountain Road is 78 miles of graded dirt and gravel, but there are also several sections that require high clearance vehicles, even when weather is good. This road gives access to the remote Kaiparowits Plateau back country and provides magnificent vistas of **Lake Powell**. Drivers must navigate with care, especially at intersections, to stay on this plateau-top road. All who travel Smoky Mountain Road must come prepared. Vehicles must be in good working condition and properly supplied for emergencies. Good maps and plenty of water are also requisite.

Above all else, visitors to Grand Staircase-Escalante National Monument are vehemently cautioned that this is a **fierce and dangerous land** and nearly all roads leading into the Monument are primitive and remote. The best way to see the Monument is with seasoned professional outfitters, such as Escalante Canyon Outfitters and Rainbow Country Tours (see related stories). They can arrange tours and activities such as back-country hiking trips. Other guided tours which include hunting, fishing, bicycle treks, and vehicle tours are available.

At present there is no visitor center. For more information call Garfield County Travel Council, 800-444-6689.

HOLE-IN-THE-ROCK ROAD

Five miles east of Escalante, beginning from Scenic Byway 12, is Hole-in-the-Rock Road, the route used by an 1879-80 company of Mormon pioneers as the quickest way to cross the Colorado River. The road is about 57 miles and, although traveling the route one way takes about two hours, with exploration and photo stops it should be considered an all-day trip.

The route runs between the **Straight Cliffs** and **Fifty-Mile Mountain** on the southwest and the **Escalante Canyons** on the northeast. The route is of gravel and graded dirt and is suitable for passenger vehicles for most of the trip. The last four to six miles of slickrock near the actual Hole-in-the-Rock are considered best for 4-wheel drive vehicles.

Attractions along the way include the Straight Cliffs escarpment, which is in view the entire trip, and **Dance Hall Rock**, **Soda Cabin**, and **Devils Garden**. Highlight of the route is Hole-in-the-Rock, a slot in the wall of Glen Canyon that was chipped and blasted out by the company of Mormon pioneers in order to lower their wagons, livestock, and their company to the river floor. Once lowered they were able to cross the Colorado River and continue their journey to the southeastern Utah colony of Bluff. From Hole-in-the-Rock, there is an exceptional vista of **Lake Powell**.

POSEY LAKE & HELL'S BACKBONE

An alternative route from Escalante to Boulder is on the Posey Lake and Hell's Backbone Roads, the route used for decades as the only link between Boulder and the outside world. As recently as 1942, mules and these roads were used to deliver mail to this very rural town.

Posey Lake Road begins in Escalante and ends 40 miles to the North in Bicknell. However, 13 miles from Escalante the road forks to the right and becomes Hell's Backbone Road. When one stays to the left on the backway route, they come to **Posey Lake**. Posey Lake offers camping, fishing, and trail access to other mountain lakes. The right fork in the road, Hell's Backbone Road, skirts **Box Death Hollow Wilderness Area**, a series of quiet canyons carved by the Escalante River and its many tributaries. The wilderness area, managed by the BLM, can only be entered by foot, but offers unlimited hiking possibilites. Nearby is the **Blue Spruce Campground**.

SMOKY MOUNTAIN ROAD

Almost running perpendicular from the Posey Lake Backway is Smoky Mountain Road, a 78-mile backway that begins at Scenic Byway 12 in Escalante and runs south to the small town of Big Water, near **Wahweap Marina** at **Lake Powell** in **Glen Canyon National Recreation Area**.

Smoky Mountain Road follows the rugged landscape of the **Kaiparowits Plateau** section of **Grand Staircase-Escalante National Monument**. Though only 78 miles in length, the drive is rugged, should be driven very carefully, and plenty of extra water should be included for the trip. High clearance vehicles are recommended as the road is rough and rutted, dusty during dry weather, yet completely impassable when wet. Suggested driving time for Posey Lake Backway is five hours.

From Byway 12 and Escalante one is given spectacular overviews of **Boulder Mountain**, the **Table Cliffs**, and **Bryce Canyon**. The rugged terrain of the Kaiparowits

Plateau dominates the drive. Descending from the plateau there are five miles of switchbacks down the 1,200-foot face of **Smoky Mountain** via the **Kelly Grade**. The **Warm Creek Badlands** in Glen Canyon Recreation Area might well be remembered as the setting for two blockbuster movies, the biblical saga, *"The Greatest Story Ever Told,"* and *"Planet of the Apes."*

ACCOMMODATIONS

PROSPECTOR INN

380 West Main
Escalante, Utah 84726
Tel: (435) 826-GOLD
       (4653)
FAX: (435) 826-4285
Hrs: Gift Shop
Open Daily   7:00 a.m. - 10:00 p.m.
Visa, MasterCard, and American Express are accepted.
Reservations are recommended.

Prospects are good that if one is prospecting for a good night's rest, quality service, and affordable rates, they will find it at Escalante's Prospector Inn.

The first thing that catches one's attention when approaching the Prospector Inn is the exterior decor. Knotted tree trunks, with a beautiful array of flowering plants growing from them, are spaced across the front of the Ponderosa pine edifice. To help guests enjoy the beauty of the surrounding area, log garden swings have been placed outside the lobby. A turn of the century carriage and an old Allis Chalmer tractor, both at the parking lot entrance, draw glances from passers by and guests alike.

Upon entering the lobby of the Prospector Inn, guests are impressed with the prompt and courteous service rendered by the Inn's staff. The lobby is fashionably decorated with blue and white furnishings. They are drawn, almost immediately, to browse through the well-stocked gift shop that is adjacent to the lobby. (See related story.)

Each of the Inn's 51 spacious rooms has been attractively decorated in a color scheme of burgundy with mauve and forest green accents. Pictures of Grand Staircase Escalante National Monument adorn the walls. Scenes in the pictures are of canyons, petroglyphs, moqui caves, and waterfalls, most of which are within 10 miles of the Inn.

Rooms are furnished with two double beds, table with two easy chairs, and wall and swag lamp lighting. Every room has remote controlled color cable TV with HBO, TNT, and ESPN as well as several other quality channels. Credit card calls, phone card calls, and local calls are all free on Prospector Inn's direct dial phones. Bathrooms have tubs with showers and separate vanity basins. Guests have a choice of smoking and non-smoking rooms. Portable cribs are available upon request.

In addition to their regular guest rooms, Prospector Inn offers a room for the physically impaired. The tub has adjustable shower head and regulation hand-grip bars. Clothes racks have been adjusted to lower levels for guest convenience.

To the rear of the West parking lot is the Inn's continental restaurant, The Ponderosa (see related story). Cuisine at The Ponderosa has been compared to dining at restaurants in cosmopolitan cities. Imri Kun, who leases the restaurant, is from Hungary and speaks several European languages fluently.

In addition to its clean, comfortable and spacious rooms and its quality restaurant, The Prospector Inn offers self-guided tours in comfortable, air-conditioned Ford Broncos. They are available by the day, multiple days, or by the week. Touring maps and additional information are available at the front desk.

Escalante is literally at the heart of Scenic Highway 12, one of the country's top ten Scenic Byways. There is so much to see—petroglyph rock art and cliff dwellings, reminders of the ancient Anasazi Indians who inhabited this area over 1000 years ago, picturesque mountains, desert canyons, panoramic lakes and streams. There is Bryce Canyon National Park and Kodachrome Basin State Park to the southwest and Capitol Reef National Park and Anasazi State Park to the northeast. They are all within comfortable drives of the Prospector Inn. And Escalante Petrified Forest State Park and the nation's newest national monument, Grand Staircase-Escalante, are right in the Prospector Inn's backyard. When booking a reservation to visit Southwestern Utah, make those reservations at the Prospector Inn and stay to see it all.

ADVENTURE / TOURS

RAINBOW COUNTRY TOURS

P. O. Box 333
Escalante, Utah 84726
Tel: (435) 826-4567
         (800) 252-UTAH (8824)
Web Site: escalante-cc.com
Email:
rainbow@color-country.net
Peak Season   April - November
Off-Season   December - March
Visa and MasterCard are accepted.
Reservations are recommended.

RAINBOW COUNTRY TOURS

Rainbow Country Tours, owned and operated by Gene Windle, offers area visitors a chance to see the nation's newest national monument, Grand Staircase-Escalante, on a grand scale basis.

For the past three years, Gene, also the owner of Rainbow Country Bed & Breakfast (see related story), has been taking his bed and breakfast guests and other area visitors to see the convoluted countryside in his backyard.

Rainbow Country Tours offers its guests air conditioned comfort in a four-wheel drive, eight- passenger Suburban. The four-wheel drive tours are augmented by guided hikes into the nooks and crannies of this spectacular playground. Rainbow Country Tour guests explore the stunning beauty of narrow canyons, slickrock hills, towering sandstone formations, ancient petrified forests, and prehistoric Indian rock art in Grand Staircase-Escalante. They also visit the serene mountain lakes in nearby Dixie National Forest.

The Escalante River Trailhead is directly across the street from Rainbow Country Bed & Breakfast, which is also headquarters for Rainbow Country Tours. During warmer months of the year, guests tour the Escalante River and its canyons, hiking and playing in the river. In 1872 the Escalante was the last river in the United

States to be mapped and explored by the John Wesley Powell party.

Another favorite tour is down Hole in the Rock Road to explore Harris Wash. The Suburban can take hikers two miles beyond the point where most vehicles must park. Once at their destination, explorers hike along a creek that meanders through an ever-deepening canyon, verdant with lush trees and plants. The canyon is home to beavers, mule deer, and many species of birds. Further down Hole in the Rock Road is Devil's Garden, where kids of all ages revel in the peculiar and extremely photographic rock formations. Even further along the road are the entrances to Peek-a-Boo, Dry Fork, and Spooky slot canyons, with cliff walls so close that one can touch both sides by extending their arms.

Gene, a most experienced guide through the Escalante, knows his backyard like the palm of his hand. He is well qualified and can take guests into little-known scenic wonderlands. In addition to regular tours, Gene will custom design a tour to fit any hiking ability, and to suit weather conditions of the day. But, if it is only directions one is after, Gene will do that too, offering suggestions on how best to enjoy the trip.

One of the most dramatic stretches of road in the country is Hells Backbone. Appropriately named because of its narrow stretches of road that are flanked by sheer drop-offs on both sides, the road offers plenty of opportunities for dramatic photo shoots.

Dixie National Forest is a densely forested area, lush with white aspen, golden oaks, and towering Ponderosa Pines. If the opportunity arises to visit the area during Autumn, don't pass it by. Nothing is more awe inspiring than seeing a mountain turn to gold. Dixie National Forest has many magnificent lakes, so crystal-clear that one can literally see the fish before they jump.

Escalante, without a doubt, is the ideal central location for touring Grand Staircase-Escalante National Monument. But more than that, Escalante is a superb location from which to visit Bryce and Capitol Reef National Parks, with Bryce to the southwest and Capitol Reef to the northeast of Escalante. Escalante Petrified Forest State Park is at the west side of town. Anasazi Indian Village State Park is a short drive to the north, and Kodachrome Basin State Park is a short drive to the southwest.

The magnitude of all that there is to see and do is nearly as overwhelming as the 1.7 million-acres of multicolored cliffs, mesas, pinnacles, plateaus, buttes, and canyons that make up the Grand Staircase-Escalante National Monument.

This is the backyard of Rainbow Country Tours and Bed & Breakfast. Gene invites all to come and stay at the bed & breakfast and play in it's great backyard.

In addition to the convoluted terrain of Grand Staircase Escalante National Monument, nature has created a very different wonder. Rivers of 140 million years ago carried trees to the site of present-day Escalante and then buried them in her back yard. The burial preserved the wood and prevented decay. Over the millenia, wood cells gradually gave way to silicon dioxide crystals. These crystals and mineral impurities worked their magic, embellishing these trees-turned-to stone with glorious rainbow colors. Much of the wood, again over the millenia, has gradually been exposed by weathering, and can be seen at Escalante Petrified Forest State Park, just west of town. In addition to the Baily Wash, Wide Hollow and Rainbow Loop trails, which are in the park, there is a three-quarter mile roundtrip nature trail that crosses the dry wash, climbs a small hill, and loops through the colorful petrified wood.

BED & BREAKFASTS

RAINBOW COUNTRY B & B & TOURS

P. O. Box 333
Escalante, Utah 84726
Tel: (435) 826-4567
    (800) 252-UTAH (8824)
Web Site: escalante-cc.com
Email: rainbow@color-country.net
Peak Season   April - November
Off-Season   December - March
Visa and MasterCard are accepted.
Reservations are recommended.

RAINBOW COUNTRY BED & BREAKFAST

    Rainbow Country Bed & Breakfast, with Gene Windle and his pals as hosts, invites guests to enjoy an atmosphere that is much more than a bed & breakfast. The invitation is to be surrounded by the nation's newest national monument, Grand Staircase-Escalante, as one relaxes and tours this magnificent country. Gene's co-host pals are Betty the cat and Ned and Jake, his poodles.

    Relaxing at Rainbow Country B & B is to relax in an establishment that offers much more than just four great guest rooms with private baths. The front and sides of the house offer a wrap-around sun deck with panoramic vistas of the surrounding mountains and desert. The Escalante River Trailhead is across the street from Rainbow Country Bed & Breakfast. On the patio behind the home is a marvelous hot tub. It is ideal for relaxing and enjoying magnificent sunsets and a myriad of stars.

    Upon entering Rainbow Country B & B one cannot help being impressed with the first Great Room. It is beautifully furnished with exquisite antiques and sofas and easy chairs that are ideally arranged for casual conversation or relaxing with a good book. At the top of the staircase is a well-stocked library.

    Descending the stairs, one enters immediately a second Great Room. Here guests can unwind with a game of billiards, relax in front of a large screen TV, or, through appropriately arranged seating, read in one's own little alcove. The room has beamed ceilings, an eclectic decor, a microwave, and an endless supply of popcorn.

    The lower level of Rainbow Country B & B houses three guest rooms. A first is light and airy, has a desk and two twin beds with brass headboards and floral bedspreads. Across the hall is a private bath with large shower and pedestal basin.

    The Sand Room offers a queen and a double bed, a large marvelous pencil sketch of Torrey Pines, elegant white and silver-edged furniture, and a color decor of sand and blue. A large private bath has a tub with shower and vanity basin.

    The Wood Room has a twin bed and a queen bed with brass headboards and beautiful antique furnishings. The color decor, using a shell motif, is pink and blue. A private bathroom has double mirrors, pedestal sink and large shower.

    The Ivy Room on the main floor has a twin and a double bed with dark wood headboards and ivy and off-white bedspread. The private bathroom across the hall has a color decor of blue and sand and offers a tub with shower and vanity basin. Robes are provided for all guests.

Breakfasts at Rainbow Country B & B are sumptuous. Two signature breakfasts are Gene's famous hotcakes or waffles with homemade maple and strawberry syrups, and his modified vegetarian omelette with mushrooms, tomatoes, onions and green peppers. Breakfast also includes an assortment of specialty coffees with decaf and regular mixed.

Gene has been opening his home to bed & breakfast guests from around the world for the past three years. Today, most of his guests are referrals from those who have stayed and played before or, they are guests who have stayed and simply could not get enough of this incredible heterogeneous topography.

Just as dear to his heart as the bed & breakfast, is Rainbow Country Tours (see related story). Gene offers half day and full day tours in an air-conditioned eight-passenger Suburban. There are many stops along the way, and guests hike into the diverse scenic terrain that surrounds Escalante.

Gene and his pals—Betty, Ned, and Jake—look forward to sharing Grand Staircase-Escalante National Monument with those who visit the area. There is no better way to see the monument than by staying at Rainbow Country Bed & Breakfast. Then, while here, view the beauties of the land with Rainbow Country Tours.

SPECIALTY SHOPPING

PROSPECTOR INN GIFT SHOP
380 West Main
Escalante, Utah 84726
Tel: (435) 826-GOLD
      (4653)
FAX: (435) 826-4285
Hrs: Gift Shop
Open Daily   7:00 a.m. - 10:00 p.m.
Visa, MasterCard, and American Express are accepted.

PROSPECTOR INN

Just off the lobby of the Prospector Inn is a unique and attractively displayed gift shop with an array of gifts to satisfy the most discriminating shopper.

Most travelers, when they visit the Southwest, long for a cherished piece of Native American jewelry. The sterling silver and precious stone jewelry at the Prospector Inn includes rings, bracelets, earrings, necklaces, hair ornaments, belt buckles, bolo ties, and watch bands. All are moderately priced.

The Prospector Inn Gift Shop showcases a nice assortment of dream catchers, Mandellas, animal pelts, wooden artifacts, and pottery magnets. Sure to be treasured are the beautiful Goldenstone paintings by noted artist, Trunnell.

For those who are looking for vacation mementos, the gift shop has a large selection of logo T-shirts, caps, magnets, puzzles, pottery toothpick holders, antique bottles, and Old West collectible cards.

Shoppers will also find a good variety of colorful postcards, books, videos, and calendars on the many national parks in Southwestern Utah.

RESTAURANTS

THE PONDEROSA RESTAURANT
400 West 50 North
Escalante, Utah 84726
Tel: (435) 826-4658
FAX: (435) 826-4285
Season April 1 - November
Hrs: Open Daily
Breakfast: 7:00 a.m. - 11:00 a.m.
Lunch: 11:00 a.m. - 2:00 p.m.
Dinner: 5:00 p.m. - 10:00 p.m.
Off-season November 1 - April 1
Hrs: Open Daily
Dinner 5:00 p.m. - 9:00 p.m.
Visa, MasterCard, and American Express are accepted.
Reservations are recommended.

    The town is Escalante, a small, rural town in the heart of Utah's Color Country. The place is The Ponderosa, a restaurant with a Ponderosa pine exterior and a rustic western motif throughout its dining rooms. There are copper and brass western figurines, bucking broncos, western napkin holders made by a local artist, and Mandellas and other Native American artifacts on the wall. A cozy rock fireplace adds to the rural ambiance.

    None of the above is surprising. That which is extraordinary, to those who dine at The Ponderosa for the first time, is the cuisine. The Ponderosa, operated by Chef Imri Kun of Hungary, is gaining a worldwide reputation for having the type of continental cuisine one expects to find in large cosmopolitan cities.

    For breakfast, diners will find such menu items as the European Cold Plate with its offering of Hungarian salami, sausage, ham, goose liver pate, cheese, and fresh bread. Another eye opener is the ham and eggs served with cucumbers with dill and fresh bread. Of course there is the more traditional fare of three egg omelettes with one's choice of filling, hotcakes, and biscuits with sausage milk gravy.

    The luncheon menu is extremely diversified, offering lunches to go, European lunches, American lunches and light lunches.

    Lunches to go include a pepperoni pizza, a Golden Horseshoe sandwich—beef, turkey, and chicken on a croissant with salad and chips; and the French Sandwich, a combination of ham, cheese, eggs, French creamed salad dressing, and French Fries.

    European lunches are served from noon to 5:00 p.m. They include Wiener Schnitzel with French fries, Chicken Paprikash with colored noodles, Stuffed Cabbage Rolls with sauerkraut, and Chicken Cordon Bleu with French fries and salad.

    American lunches may sound mundane, but when prepared by Imri, they still have a continental flare. They include hamburgers, cheeseburgers, turkey sandwiches, deep fried chicken strips, and breaded, deep-fried cheese.

    On the light side are chef salad, paloc goulash soup, European fish soup, and Golden onion soup. Items on the light side are also served on the soup and salad menu for dinner.

    Equally continental are the appetizers. Delectable tidbits include Smoked Red

Trout with lemon, onions, and olives; and Stuffed Crepes with sweet pepper sauce.

Main Course entrees on the dinner menu include traditional American steaks, such as top sirloin, T-bone, New York, and Filet Mignon, but prepared with a European touch.

Continental cuisine includes Stroganoff Fricassee, prepared French-style with rice and vegetables; Salmon Filet and Newburg Sauce with baked potato and vegetables; and Chicken Paprikash with colored noodles.

All entrees are served a la carte.

Sinful and decadent as the dessert might be, it would be a sin not to try Imri's famous crepes with chocolate, and his Strudel. Other desserts include Chestnut Puree and Ice Cup Jacque.

A children's menu includes hamburgers, cheeseburgers, fried chicken strips, grilled cheese sandwich, and breaded fried cheese, all of which are served with a choice of salad or French fries.

The Ponderosa is located on the grounds of The Prospector Inn (see related story).

With its out of this world cuisine and down to earth prices, The Ponderosa is definitely the restaurant of choice when staying at the Prospector or just traveling along Scenic Byway 12.

HENRIEVILLE

Henrieville, settled between 1877 and 1878, is truly a rural community with no designs on fame. The town was built for irrigation farming and range grazing, still the principal means of livlihood, with incomes supplemented by employment at Bryce Canyon.

The town has an elevation of 6,000 feet and a 1990 census of 163. Henrieville received its name in honor of James Henrie, a presiding church authority who lived in Panguitch.

CANNONVILLE

Cannonville, named after early Mormon church leader, George Q. Cannon, was settled in 1876 by a group of families relocating from drought-stricken Southern Utah. Because the forage was plentiful along the Paria River, the little town prospered and grew rapidly for a short period of time. Overgrazing of the semi-arid land soon destroyed much of the protective vegetation that held the desert soil and flooding resulted, carrying away valuable agricultural top soil. With a depleted range, incapable of sustaining the large number of livestock that had been introduced to the area, the cattle industry steadily dwindled.

Today Cannonville, along with other small towns along Scenic Byway 12, has turned its attention to the many tourist attractions that lie in their back yards. Cannonville is at the Gateway to Kodachrome Basin State Park, and is just a short ten miles to the junction of Bryce Canyon National Park.

ATTRACTIONS

GROSVENOR ARCH

Grosvenor Arch is approximately 20 miles southeast of Cannonville on the Kodachrome Basin road. The arch stands as a remarkable natural buttress that has been sculptured by wind and water from a cream colored cliff. The arch was named in honor of the National Geographic Society's president, Dr. Gilbert Grosvenor, by one of the Society's expeditions into the area. Grosvenor Arch, a beautiful, pastel double arch that is in a class by itself is over 150 feet tall at the crest and nearly 100 feet wide. The arch is considered one of the natural wonders of the world.

KODACHROME BASIN STATE PARK

Just nine miles southeast of Cannonville off Scenic Byway 12, Kodachrome Basin stands as a spectacle of massive sandstone chimney formations that are ever-changing from gray and white to shades of red, depending on the day's climatic mood.

The landscape of Kodachrome Basin is part of the geologic feature known as the Grand Staircase. Its numerous rocks and coves offer a unique desert beauty to be found nowhere else. Adjacent to Grand Staircase-Escalante National Monument, Kodachrome Basin offers overnight camping facilities with modern rest rooms, showers, picnic tables, fire pit, barbecue grills, electricity, and a sewage disposal station. There is also a concessionaire to provide horse rentals and camping supplies.

Kodachrome Basin State Park is ideal for group outings. (435-679-8562).

ACCOMMODATIONS

GRAND STAIRCASE INN & COUNTRY STORE

105 North Kodachrome Drive
Cannonville, Utah 84718
Tel: (435) 679-8400
        (888) 679-8401
FAX: (435) 679-8817
Gift Shop Hours
Monday - Saturday
   7:00 a.m. - 10:00 p.m.
Note: Everything, including motel check-ins, is closed on Sunday.
Visa, MasterCard, and Discover are accepted.
Reservations are recommended.

Located at the intersections of Scenic Byway 12 & Kodachrome Highway, Grand Staircase Inn and Country Store is ideally located for guests who are visiting Bryce Canyon National Park, Grand Staircase Escalante National Monument, and Kodachrome Basin State Park. The 26-room inn, Cannonville's only motel, is on the perimeter of Grand Staircase Escalante, is nine miles from Kodachrome Basin, and is 13 miles from Bryce Canyon.

Opened in late fall of 1997, the Grand Staircase Inn is Color Country's newest hotel. This uniquely different edifice can be readily recognized by its outstanding facade. Stucco for the Inn is in gold and coral, the basic colors of Grand Staircase Escalante. Mock cliffs and other rock veneers grace the building. Archways, similar to the many natural arches in the area, are over the doors.

Each room is named for a Grand Staircase Escalante formation with a plaque above the door identifying the attraction. Inside the room, as part of the decorations, is a picture of the land formation for which the room is named.

All rooms have individually controlled heating and air conditioning as well as ceiling fans. A unique closed loop system enables each room to have its own water furnace that both heats and cools the water from a well that is 250-feet underground. Room furnishings include night stands with lamps, table with two chairs, dresser, wall-mount remote control color TVs, and direct-dial phones with local calls free. VCRs, with a selection of 100's of classic and latest release videos, are available to guests upon request. Sleeping choices include rooms with single king, double king, or double queen beds. Fourteen rooms, those on the second floor, have a vaulted ceiling. Carpets and accessory decorator items vary from room to room. Color schemes include burgundy, light or dark teal, forest green, and peach with gray. Smoking and non-smoking rooms are available.

Grand Staircase Inn is one of few Southwestern Utah accommodations to offer its guests the luxury of an in-room Jacuzzi. The honeymoon suite, named Promise Rock, has a view that looks directly up into Promise Rock. The story is told of an Indian Brave who took an Indian Maiden to the rock and threatened to throw her over unless she promised to marry him. The honeymoon suite is as impressive as the story. A marvelous peach cultured marble Jacuzzi tub is in the living area with a view of the large-screen TV. The peach and gray carpet is accented with peach bedding for the king bed, and peach draperies. Other furnishings include an antique desk, hard wood chairs, and dresser. The bathroom has a shower and separate vanity basin. Honeymooners, at check-in, receive a special basket of niceties.

In addition to its honeymoon suite, Grand Staircase Inn offers an anniversary suite, Red Rock, which can also be viewed from the room. This formation is known for its strength and endurance. The room offers a single king and has an adjoining room with two queens, just in case the guests want to bring their children along for their anniversary. The suite is also ideal for families traveling together, even if it isn't their anniversary.

Two rooms for the physically impaired offer access from the parking lot. Special amenities include wheel-in showers with seat and hand-held shower head, lowered closet racks, a basin in the bathroom and separate vanity in the dressing area, and an additional phone outlet in the bathroom. Furnishings have been arranged for improved ambulation.

The lobby at Grand Staircase Inn is small but impressively appointed in a color scheme of teal blue and mauve. Adjacent to the lobby is the Country Store Gift Shop. As its name implies, the store offers a full line of groceries, sundries, over-the-counter drug items, and a special selection of quality gifts. Guests at the inn will have no problems finding a suitable logo gift of the canyons they have visited. Guests can choose from T-shirts, caps, mugs, thimbles, magnets, spoons, and other souvenir items. Also available as mementos are park picture books, videos, calendars, and post cards. Keepsake gifts include sterling silver and semi-precious stone jewelry from the Southwest's Native Americans, as well as their gifts of pottery, Kachina and story teller dolls, dream catchers, Mandellas, and exquisite loom-woven rugs.

In addition to the Country Store and Gift Shop, Grand Staircase Inn offers Sinclair gas at their pumps.

Where ever one might choose to visit in Southwestern Utah, there is no finer accommodation than Grand Staircase Inn. Much thought and effort have been employed to make sure that everything about the inn is aesthetic to the eye. But even more important to Carlon Johnson and his family, owners, is the conscientious service and hospitality they render. Grand Staircase Inn and Country Store is the place to stay in Color Country.

BED & BREAKFASTS

**FLETCHER'S
CANYON COUNTRY B & B**
95 North Red Rock Drive
Cannonville, Utah 84718
Tel: (435) 679-8570
Email: fletcher@color-country.net
Visa, MasterCard, personal checks and Traveler Cheques are accepted.
Reservations are recommended.

FLETCHER'S
CANYON COUNTRY
BED & BREAKFAST

Fletcher's Canyon Country is a small bed & breakfast in the little town of Cannonville that offers two lovely guest rooms to visitors from around the world. Those who have already enjoyed a stay with the Fletchers know that what the bed and breakfast lacks in size, it makes up for in comfort and gracious hospitality.

The Fletchers, Glenna and Larry, love the color blue and have used it creatively in their decor. Carpet in both rooms is a warm blue. One room has two queen beds with maple headboards and bedding of blue, mauve, tan, and light burgundy. A second room has one single and one queen bed with maple headboard and blue and white bedding. All beds have pillow-top mattresses that are firm, yet soft and extremely comfortable. Both rooms have large closets, built-in dresser drawers, and beautiful paneling with off-white and light gold antiquing.

Both of the guest rooms are on the second floor and enjoy a large common area and a shared bathroom between them. The common area has several easy chairs and a remote control Color TV for guest convenience. Guests are also welcome in the family room on the main floor, which offers a second color TV, VCR with selection of video movies, rock wall fireplace, and a couch and loveseat in green, mauve and burgundy. The common bath for guests has a pastel and floral decor and offers a tub with shower, and vanity with basin.

Since everything at Fletcher's Canyon Country B & B is directed at guest convenience, breakfast, as long as arranged in advance, is as early or as late as the guest desires. Their breakfast menu is directed to the premise that guests will be spending several days with them. Two favorite menu items are homemade bread for toast with honey or jelly, and Cheese Melts.

The menu also includes waffles, hotcakes, muffins, rolls, hash browns, and an assortment of hot or cold cereals with fruit on occasion. A variety of fruit juices, tomato juice and hot beverages are also included.

The Fletchers wish to be as much a part of the guest's vacation as the traveler desires. When guests prefer to be alone, the Fletchers, as the saying goes, "disappear into the woodwork."

Glenna and Larry Fletcher, hosts, are both natives of this colorful Southern Utah area. Larry was born in Cannonville, has spent much of his life there, and he knows the history and geology of this picturesque country. For those who desire a greater understanding of this convoluted topography, Larry is eager to share historical and geological insights. Both Larry and Glenna enjoy making new friends and meeting people from around the world.

Cannonville and Fletcher's Canyon Country Bed & Breakfast are right at the entrance to the nation's new Grand Staircase-Escalante National Park. The entrance to Bryce Canyon is only 12 miles west. Kodachrome Basin State Park, offering a spectacle of imposing sandstone chimneys, is just nine miles to the south. There is an abundance of other picturesque scenery within a short drive. One can spend days or even weeks exploring this vast territory without running out of new places to go and things to see.

A little farther, but still within an easy day's drive, are Capitol Reef National Park to the northeast, Cedar Breaks National Monument to the west, and Zions National Park to the southwest.

Cannonville is in the very heart of Utah's Color Country, a magnificent part of the state that is sliced through the middle by Scenic Byway 12, one of the nation's top ten scenic byways. Fletcher's Canyon Country B & B is 22 miles Southwest of Highway 89 on Scenic Byway 12, with Red Rock Drive the first street one will come to in Cannonville. If coming from Capitol Reef on Scenic Byway 12, it is the next street after the Kodachrome Basin State Park sign.

Whichever direction one is coming from, the Fletchers and Cannonville welcome visitors with a western welcome that makes guests want to return.

TROPIC / BRYCE CANYON

Pioneer residents in the Paria Valley—namely Cannonville and Henrieville—had discovered before the turn of the century that although there was good arable land in the upper valley, area streams were neither large enough nor dependable enough for irrigation purposes.

To the West of the Paria Valley lay the Paunsagunt Plateau with a bounteous stream, the East Fork of the Sevier River. An earlier attempt to divert this water for irrigation purposes had failed, but residents had not given up on its possibilities. In 1888 a stock company was formed, surveying officials elected, and a plan initiated for the digging of a ditch to secure the water. By the winter of 1890 -1891, the prospects of water in the upper Paria prompted several area residents to move into Bryce Valley. The following year a town was surveyed.

There was nothing easy about the task, but workers were resolute and in May of 1892 water was successfully brought over the rim of the basin, making it the only place where a stream of considerable size had been diverted from the Great Basin into another drainage area.

No feat in Bryce Valley has been so heralded. After triumphant rejoicing, valley residents held a meeting to choose a name for the new community. It didn't take them long to select the name, Tropic. Weather on top of the Paunsagunt Plateau, especially during winter, can be harsh and biting. The climate in the upper Paria Valley, specifically around Tropic, is moderate. Thanks to the diverted water, the town's climate is ideal for growing fruits and vegetables. Most residents have bounteous gardens and fruit trees.

Today Tropic flourishes as a vacation destination. The closest town to Bryce Canyon, Tropic has blossomed with an abundance of motels, bed & breakfasts, restaurants, gift shops, adventure tours, and other guest conveniences. Bryce Canyon is named after one of Tropic's earliest pioneers, Ebenezer Bryce, whose original log cabin can be seen at the Southeast end of town.

In addition to being only seven miles from the entrance to Bryce, Tropic is also at the doorway to the nation's newest national monument, Grand Staircase-Escalante.

ACCOMMODATIONS

BRYCE COUNTRY CABINS
320 North Highway 12
P. O. Box 141
Tropic/Bryce Canyon,
Utah 84776-0141
Tel: (435) 679-8643
FAX: (435) 679-8989
Visa and MasterCard are accepted.
Reservations are recommended.

A stay at Bryce Country Cabins is more than just "a little bit country," it is a chance to experience real country living from private log cabins that are decorated with a country western motif.

Just think of it! One of the nicest things about a fresh Christmas tree is the smell of pine that fills the house. When staying in Bryce Country Cabins, the smell of knotty pine is aromatherapy. Each individual cabin has two queen beds that are topped with handmade quilts in a color scheme of green, coral, beige and burgundy. Matching decorator pillows and cafe curtains complete the decor. Each cabin has a ceiling fan, color TV with remote control, clock radio, table and two chairs, and a dresser. Bathrooms have showers and separate vanity basins. All of the cabins have their own porch for relaxing and enjoying a view that looks up into Bryce Point. Between and behind the cabins is a yard of flowers and lawn with picnic tables and barbecue facilities in the backyard.

In addition to the rustic cabins, Bryce Country Cabins offers an authentic pioneer home that was built in 1905. Sure to raise some eyebrows and some questions, this home is really just one-half of a house. Danny and Wendy Brinkerhoff, owners, are happy to relate the story of this home's unique and intriguing historical past. This one-half house offers two rooms that are delightfully decorated with blue carpet, white curtains, and queen beds with handmade puff quilts of blue and burgundy. The rooms have ceiling fans, clock radio, TV with remote control, and a bathroom with tub and shower.

Bryce Country Cabins is ensconced on a 20-acre parcel of farm land. The farm and the cabins are surrounded by the flaming cliffs of Bryce National Park on the west, the Escalante Plateau to the east, and the nation's newest national monument, Grand Staircase-Escalante to the northeast.

A visit to Bryce Country Cabins puts guests right in the middle of some of the nation's most picturesque terrain. In addition to Bryce and Grand Staircase- Escalante, Tropic is within a magnificent drive of Capitol Reef National Park and Kodachrome, Escalante Petrified Forest, and Anasazi Indian state parks to the northeast. Cedar Breaks National Monument and Panguitch Lake are to the northwest, and Zion National Park is on the southwest. All are within an easy and awe-inspiring drive from Bryce Country Cabins.

The Brinkerhoffs welcome travelers with small children. Almost like a petting zoo, their farm offers kids of all ages the chance to see sheep, rabbits, horses, chickens, roosters and peacocks in their own habitat. In back of the farmhouse is a herd of beef cattle.

When one stays at Bryce Country Cabins, they have the opportunity to rise when the rooster crows or sleep like a baby. They can walk among the fruit trees and, in season, pick cherries, peaches and apples. Guests can feed the hens and even steal an egg or two. They can hike around the farm or to Mossy Cave and its waterfall. Since Tropic is situated right on the edge of Bryce Canyon, those with stamina can hike the three miles to Peek-a-Boo Loop. From there it is a two and one-half to three-mile hike into Sunset or Sunrise Points in Bryce Canyon.

There is so much to see and do from the hub town of Tropic. Bryce Country Cabins, with its affordable rates, its country atmosphere, and its western hospitality, makes staying and playing in the spectacular West the experience of a lifetime.

<u>*DID YOU KNOW?*</u>

---that out of the six villages settled near the upper Paria River between 1876 and 1891, three--Tropic, Cannonville, and Henrieville--are still there.

BRYCE PIONEER VILLAGE
80 North Main
(Scenic Byway 12)
P. O. Box 119
Tropic/Bryce Canyon
 Utah 84776
Tel: (435) 679-8546
          (800) 222-0381
FAX: (435) 679-8607
Web Site:
www.onpages.com/bpvillage/
Season: April 1 - November 1
Dutch Oven Cookout
May 1 - Mid-October
Hrs: Breakfast

Open Daily   7:00 a.m. - 9:00 a.m.
         Dinner
Open Daily   6:30 p.m. - 9:00 p.m.
Hrs: Gift Shop
Open Daily   6:30 a.m. - 10:30 p.m.
Visa, MasterCard, and Discover are accepted.
Reservations are recommended.

     Ever since Bryce Pioneer Village opened its doors in 1984 as the first motel in Tropic, the LeFevres have been dedicated to providing the traveler with comfort, convenience, and quality service.
     When they started their family business, the Reed LeFevre family began with two rooms. Today, out of the approximately 180 guest rooms in Tropic, Bryce Pioneer Village has 62.
     Guest rooms at Bryce Pioneer Village have come along way since the LeFevre's first opened with their two-room motel. The majority of the spacious guest rooms at Bryce Pioneer Village are decorated in a modern color scheme of teal blue and peach. Most offer a choice of two double beds or a single queen and bathrooms with tub and shower. All have color TV with remote control, telephone with local calls free, dresser, and table with two chairs. Truly a home-away-from-home is the kitchenette unit. It has a living room, dining room, and two bedrooms, each with a queen bed. Two large family units have three queen beds.
     Those who relish a western experience will love the knotty pine cabins. The cabins cater to a variety of needs, offering two family units and 16 single rooms with choices of queen bed or twin and queen. The decor is a western ambiance. Most have bathrooms with showers; two have tub and shower.
     For guest enjoyment, there are two hot tubs, one at either end of the complex. Also available for guest convenience is the Bryce Pioneer Village Gift Shop (see related story), which adjoins the motel lobby. It offers a unique selection of area gifts as well as quality Native American jewelry and artifacts.
     Progress and keeping an eye single to the needs of the traveler has always been the watchword at Bryce Pioneer Village. When Reed LeFevre realized that the area's history seemed as intriguing to tourists as it was to him, he promptly purchased and moved the Ebenezer Bryce cabin to his motel property and established the Ebenezer Bryce Museum.

Bryce Canyon National Park was named after this salty western pioneer, one of the first settlers in Tropic. At one time, when asked what he thought of these majestic coral hoodoos, Ebenezer reportedly replied: "It's a hell of a place to lose a cow!"

When the LeFevres discovered that tourists hunger for a taste of the old west, they literally fulfilled guest longings with their popular Dutch Oven Cowboy breakfasts and dinners.

A meandering creek winds its way the full length of the LeFevre's 14-acre property. A bridge crosses the creek and a pavilion, nestled among verdant trees, forms a natural amphitheater and the ideal spot for country western cooking.

The Dutch Oven Cowboy breakfast buffet includes old-fashioned baking powder biscuits, scrambled eggs and bacon, fresh fruits in season, coffee, tea, hot chocolate, and a selection of juices. For those Bryce Pioneer Village guests with light appetites or who are simply too eager to get on the road and enjoy the sights, there is a continental breakfast of coffee, hot chocolate, tea, apple cider, and Danish rolls served in the motel lobby.

Adding to the enjoyment of the Bryce Pioneer Village Dutch Oven dinner is Country Western live entertainment, performed by some of Southern Utah's most talented entertainers. Along with their repertoire of country music, guests, in a most entertaining fashion, receive historical and geological data about the area. Dinner includes New York and Sirloin steaks or tender chicken breasts grilled over an open fire. An accompanying buffet includes cole slaw, bread sticks or rolls, Dutch oven potatoes, baked beans and Dutch oven cobbler.

Again, catering to the needs and desires of Bryce Pioneer Village guests, the LeFevres this year have added a marvelous western fort to their property. It truly feels like a step back in time as guests browse and shop in turn-of-the-century stores that include a blacksmith shop, leather boutique, old-fashioned ice cream parlour, candy store, and country store.

Since progress and guest comfort and convenience are ongoing bywords at Bryce Pioneer Village, guests rest in cozy serenity, assured that the family is working overtime to fulfill their needs and desires.

WORLD HOST BRYCE VALLEY INN
199 North Main Street
Tropic/Bryce Canyon, Utah 84776
Tel: (435) 679-8811
           (800) 442-1890
FAX: (435) 679-8246
Email: bvi@color-country.net
Hrs: Lobby and Gift Shop
April 1 - November 1   7:00 a.m. - 10:00 p.m.
November 1 - April 1   8:00 a.m. - 8:00 p.m.
Visa, MasterCard, American Express, and Discover are accepted.
Reservations are recommended.

Triple A approved Bryce Valley Inn, located in the very heart of Color Country along Utah's famous Scenic Byway 12, is ideal headquarters for Bryce Canyon National Park and the nation's newest national monument, Grand Staircase-Escalante. It is also the place to stay when visiting the many other national parks, monuments, and recreation areas that dot Southwestern Utah.

With its 65 deluxe rooms, unique gift shop, and Western-American restaurant, it is no wonder that Bryce Valley Inn has been acclaimed as a World Host accommodation.

This very western two-story edifice offers guests the security of entering rooms from an interior hallway. Guest rooms are decorated in modern colors of burgundy and blue, with a touch of tan in the bedding. Each room has individually controlled heat and air conditioning, remote controlled color TV, table with two chairs, wall and table lamps, and direct dial phone with local calls free. Bathrooms have tubs with showers and separate vanity basins. Guests have a choice of two queen beds, two double beds, or one single king bed. They also can choose between smoking and non-smoking rooms.

In addition to regular guest accommodations, Bryce Valley Inn caters to the needs of the physically impaired. This room offers unique furniture arrangement for increased mobility, regulation hand bars in the bathtub, and lowered clothes racks.

Bryce Valley Inn spared no expense in making sure that their guest Laundromat would properly facilitate their guests. The laundry facility, with Maytag washers and dryers, is open 24-hours a day for guest convenience.

Children under 12 stay free at Bryce Valley Inn when accompanied by an adult. Also available to their guests are Triple A and Senior Citizen discounts.

In addition to the front desk for check-in, Bryce Valley Inn's lobby hosts a well-stocked gift shop. Guests have no problem finding national park logo T-shirts, Henleys, sweatshirts, and caps. Other clothing items include moccasins, cowboy hats, and jackets. In addition to logo apparel, guests have a large selection of souvenir spoons, thimbles, magnets, and mugs from which to choose. There are also books, tapes, videos, calendars, and post cards that reflect the beauty of Southwestern Utah.

The gift shop at Bryce Valley Inn offers a quality variety of Native American jewelry and artifacts. Sterling silver and semi-precious stone jewelry sold at the gift shop includes rings, bracelets, earrings, necklaces, watch bands, belt buckles and bolero ties. There is also a nice selection of beaded jewelry. Artifacts to be found are Kachina and story teller dolls, Mandellas, dream catchers, sand paintings, rugs, rain sticks, wind chimes, porcelain Indian dolls, exquisite pottery in all sizes, shapes, designs and colors, and intricate Yucca plant and Devil Claw woven baskets.

Across the parking lot from the lobby is The Hungry Coyote Restaurant (see related story). The restaurant features Western/American fare. It is open April through October for breakfast, lunch, and dinner. Behind the restaurant is an Ice Cream Parlour that is open June through August, and offers the perfect solution for beating the summer heat. Served is Utah's favorite, Russell's ice cream, in a variety of flavors.

From Bryce Valley Inn guests can view the peaks of Bryce Canyon and see Powell Point in the country's newest national monument, Grand Staircase-Escalante. Several national and state parks are short scenic drives from Bryce Valley Inn, making the inn ideal as an evening respite.

With its courteous service and attention to detail, it is no wonder that Bryce Valley Inn has earned a reputation as a World Host facility.

DID YOU KNOW?

---that, if one has a high clearance vehicle and likes to hike or mountain bike, Powell Point, a little known perch at the southern tip of the Table Cliff Plateau, offers one of the most spectacular vistas to be seen anywhere. With much of Southern Utah and Northern Arizona stretched out below from a height of 10,188 feet, one cannot help but feel they are standing at the top of the world.

BYBEE'S STEPPINGSTONE MOTEL

21 South Main Street
Tropic/Bryce Canyon, Utah 84776
Tel: (435) 679-8998
FAX: (435) 679-8998
Visa and MasterCard are accepted.
Reservations are recommended.

Ask area residents where they would send out of town guests if they could not accommodate them themselves, and many would quickly respond, "Bybee's Steppingstone Motel."

Bybee's Steppingstone Motel, located in the small community of Tropic, is appropriately named. Tropic is not only the closest town to the entrance of Bryce Canyon National Park, but it is the steppingstone to the nation's newest monument, Grand Staircase-Escalante. The town of Tropic is also just a stone's throw away from the back entrance, via Peek-a-Boo Loop, to both Sunset and Sunrise Points in Bryce Canyon.

The Steppingstone Motel is owned and operated by the Bybees—Rick and Renon and Aaron and Julie. They offer seven large guest rooms, three with single queen beds and four with one queen and one double bed. A room for the physically impaired has a sit-down shower with hand-held head and an adjoining room to accommodate accompanying guests.

Bybee's Steppingstone Motel, small though it might be, offers what guests are looking for—all the comforts of home. Each of the seven guest rooms is decorated with original art work of the Escalante's Aquarius Plateau and surrounding areas, painted by Renon. Renon and Julie have also included in the decor of each room, one of their rustic wood artifacts embellished with local art objects. Every room has a color TV with remote control, night stand with reading lamp, a ceiling light, and country style comforters on the beds. Bathrooms have a tub and shower combination, heat lamp, separate pedestal basin, and a peach silk floral arrangement as an added decorator touch.

Behind the small motel, the landscaped yard provides guests with a spectacular view of the Aquarius Plateau. Picnic tables and lounge chairs are there for enjoying the evening and the view.

Bybee's Steppingstone Motel is a non-smoking facility and no pets are allowed.

DID YOU KNOW?

---that Bryce Canyon National Park occupies the Paunsaugunt Plateau, and is part of the Colorado Plateau uplift which occurred approximately 16 million years ago. Uneven pressures beneath the plateau caused it to break along fault lines into a series of smaller plateaus, all at different levels, which are today known as the Grand Staircase. The intricate Pink Cliffs, on the east edge of the Paunsaugunt, make up Bryce Canyon and contain the famous erosional features known as the "***hoodoos.***" Contrary to appearances, the wind has played only a small part in creating these hoodoos, so eerily sculpted that they appear to have once been alive. For the most part the sculptors are the elements of freezing and thawing, the snowmelt, and constant rainwater that over the years have dissolved weak layers of sandstone, pried open cracks, and carved the famous hoodoo sentries. Even today the cliffs recede at the rate of about one foot every 50 to 65 years.

DOUG'S PLACE COUNTRY INN MOTEL

120 North Main, P O Box 157
Tropic, Utah 84776
Tel: (435) 679-8632
FAX: (435) 679-8605
Web Site:www.onpages.com/dougsplace
Email: dougsinn@color-country.net
Grocery & Gift Shop Hours:
    May - September
Open Seven Days   6:30 a.m. - 11:00 p.m.
    October - April
Monday - Saturday 7:30 a.m. - 9:00 p.m.
Sunday   2:00 p.m. - 6:00 p.m.

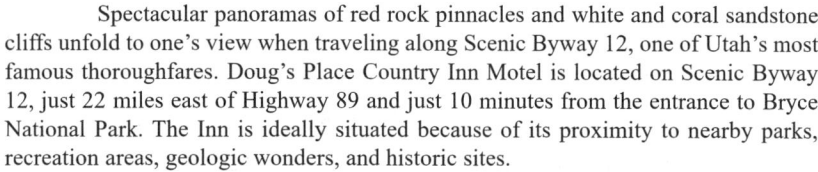

Visa, MasterCard, American Express, Diners Club, Carte Blanche, Discover, and Phillips 66 are accepted, as well as Gas Card at the pump.
Reservations are recommended.

Spectacular panoramas of red rock pinnacles and white and coral sandstone cliffs unfold to one's view when traveling along Scenic Byway 12, one of Utah's most famous thoroughfares. Doug's Place Country Inn Motel is located on Scenic Byway 12, just 22 miles east of Highway 89 and just 10 minutes from the entrance to Bryce National Park. The Inn is ideally situated because of its proximity to nearby parks, recreation areas, geologic wonders, and historic sites.

Along this 120-mile Scenic Byway are Bryce and Capitol Reef National Parks; Grand Staircase-Escalante National Monument; Kodachrome Basin and Anasazi Indian Village State Parks, the Lake Powell and Glen Canyon National Recreation Area via Burr Trail; and Calf Creek State Recreation Area.

Because of the affordable rates offered at Doug's Place guests discover that they can stay and play for an extra couple of days. They can see and enjoy all of the sights along this memorable stretch of highway. In addition to the above mentioned points of interest, Doug's Place personnel are there to assist guests with arrangements for trail rides, 4-wheeling, scenic flights, fishing, boating, water skiing, hunting, mountain biking, rock climbing, and rock hounding. The country town of Tropic still offers such western activities as rodeos, Country Western dancing, and yes, cattle drives down main street. Night time silence is punctuated by an occasional coyote's howl. The only alarm clock needed is the neighborhood rooster, welcoming guests to a bright and beautiful new day.

The comfort and convenience of their guests are not compromised by affordability at Doug's Place. Both the Country Inn motel and the Country Kitchen Restaurant (see related story) have received the Triple A rating. The 28 immaculate and spacious guest rooms offer a delightful country decor with each bed topped by an exquisite handmade quilt. All rooms have been tastefully decorated in Southwestern colors of forest green, teal, mauve and coral. Amenities include color TV, telephone with local calls free, and individual air conditioners. Guests have a choice of single queen, two double beds, or single queen with one twin bed. Smoking and non smoking rooms are available. For a small additional charge, pets are also allowed as guests at Doug's Place.

A hot tub, which comfortably seats six to eight guests, affords a relaxing means for unwinding after a busy day of sightseeing.

In addition to its accommodations and restaurant, Doug's Place offers Country Curios, a quality gift shop with fine Indian jewelry, dream catchers, Mandellas, pottery, Kachina dolls, bronze figurines, and sand paintings. Souvenirs of the area include T-shirts, caps, scarves, sweatshirts, magnets, key rings, tiles, post cards, books, and other notable gift items. Guests also are treated to an assortment of locally handcrafted items, including quilts and ceramics.

Doug's Place is home to the town's largest grocery store, an Associated Food's Bestway supermarket. In addition to a wonderful selection of fresh meats and produce, Doug's Place offers variety in health needs, camping supplies, canned food, dairy products, and deli sandwiches.

In front of the building, which houses the gift shop, restaurant, and grocery store, is a Phillips 66 gas station. Services available are unleaded and premium gasoline, diesel, oil, coolants, and auto accessories.

In one form or another, Doug's Place has been serving members of the community and travelers to the area since 1963. As a child, Doug worked at the family service station that was built and operated by his parents, Melford and Rachel Ahlstrom. In 1974 Doug and his wife, Vicki, took over the business. In 1975 they added a snack bar, convenience store, and game room. In 1984 the game room was discontinued and the Country Kitchen restaurant built. During 1993-1994 Doug's Place was expanded to include a Bestway Supermarket, quality gift shop, and the 28-room motel. Today, Doug's Place continues to be a family business with the complex run by Doug and Vicki Ahlstrom and their children.

Doug's Place is country through and through and proud of it. There was a time in the West when country folk used to gather at the local general store to share their lives. That feeling of warmth and camaraderie, called the "Cracker Barrel" philosophy, is alive and thriving at Doug's Place. All along the store front are benches just waiting to be filled with guests chatting about their day's adventures. The benches are waiting and so are the Ahlstroms. Stop by and enjoy the flavor of the West.

BED & BREAKFASTS

**BRYCE POINT
BED & BREAKFAST**
61 North 400 West
P. O. Box 96
Tropic/Bryce Canyon,
Utah 84776-0096
Tel: (435) 679-8629
FAX: (435) 679-8629
Web Site:www.bbiu:orgbrycepoint
Visa and MasterCard are accepted.
Triple A approved; Member Utah B & B Association.
Reservations are recommended.

Bryce Point Bed & Breakfast, owned and operated by LaMar and Ethel LeFevre, has been a respite for the weary traveler since 1990 when the LeFevres built a two-story modern addition onto their home to be used as a bed & breakfast.

Everything about Bryce Point is inviting and agreeable. A colorful rock and flower garden, with flagpole proudly flying the red, white and blue, graces the front of this impressive edifice. Surrounding the home are marvelous pieces of petrified wood and dinosaur bones.

When the LeFevres modified their home as a bed and breakfast, the first in Garfield County, they built it specifically for guest comfort and convenience. Guests can come and go via a separate hallway that enters from the south. The five spacious guest rooms and guest cottage are all separate from the host home and afford the privacy most guests desire. Guests are, however, always welcome in the living room to socialize with the LeFevres or other guests.

Above the LeFevre carport is a marvelous redwood deck that offers guests spectacular views of Bryce Point to the west, and Powell Point and the Grand Staircase to the east. The deck is also a great place to soak up the sun, read a good book, or simply enjoy the peace and serenity that Tropic has to offer.

Nothing is much more relaxing after a long day of sightseeing than soaking in a soothing hot tub. The spa, with redwood and glass gazebo enclosure, has sky lights that surrender the heavens to star gazing.

Each of the five guest rooms has a remote control TV and a VCR. Guests are welcome to select movies from the bed & breakfast's substantial video library, choices that include the classics and latest releases. Each of the five rooms has a ceiling lamp and fan, private bathroom with shower, large closet, and queen bed with decorator accessory items.

Since the LeFevres are the proud parents of four children and many grandchildren, it only seemed fitting that four of the rooms should bear the names of their children and their spouses, and that the fifth room should be named for their grandchildren.

Clark and Stacy has a dark green ambiance and offers guests a twin bed as well as a queen. *Susan and Jon, Les and Dela,* and *Lynn and Karen* have trundle beds along with a queen. Each room, through family pictures and other paraphernalia, tells the story of the child's life, avocation and occupation. The Grandkids room, arrayed in a color scheme of deep blue and burgundy, offers a queen bed and table with two chairs and mirrored sliding glass closet doors.

The Cottage, which has the hot tub right outside its front door, is ideal for honeymooners and for romantics of all ages. This large yet cozy knotty pine cabin offers guests a living area with TV and VCR, sofa bed, and gas fireplace for romantic moods. The separate bedroom has a king bed and second television. The bathroom is spacious, has a tub with shower, and a marvelous skylight. Because the cottage offers a full kitchen with all eating and cooking utensils and its own laundry room, the cottage is also ideal for extended stays.

The LeFevre's son, Lynn, is an accomplished furniture maker and has built many of the furnishings in the LeFevre home and in the guest rooms.

Breakfast at Bryce Point is so exceptional that the LeFevres receive many requests from their guests for recipes. A guest favorite is the 7-Up Pancakes with apple cider syrup. Breakfast also includes a selection of cereals, muffins, fresh fruits and melons in season, juice, coffee, tea, and bacon and eggs, any style.

When LaMar and Ethel, both natives of Tropic made the decision to remodel their home as a bed & breakfast, they developed a motto: "Operational friendliness and cleanliness at all times". The fact that Bryce Point has been written up in papers, magazines and guides throughout the United States, Canada, and Europe is confirmation that the LeFevres are living up to their axiom. It is also a remarkable tribute to the hosts that one-third of the guests who stay at Bryce Point are there as return visitors.

As a history buff, there is little about the parks and the surrounding terrain that LaMar does not know. LaMar and Ethel are eager to help each guest experience the best and the most of Bryce Canyon, Grand Staircase Escalante, and all that the Southwest has to offer.

THE CANYON LIVERY BED & BREAKFAST
50 South 660 West
P. O. Box 24
Tropic/Bryce Canyon,
Utah 84776-0024
Tel: (435) 679-8780
         (888) 889-8910
Web Site: www.canyonlivery.com
Email: tclbnb@color-country.net
Reservations are recommended.

When Kevin and Jeanee Shakespeare decided eight years ago that they would like to share their lives and their knowledge of the Southwest with visitors from around the globe, it was not just a spur of the moment decision. The entire family joined together to plan and design what they felt would be an ideal bed & breakfast. The planning and development took over seven years. Those who have been guests at The Canyon Livery since it opened in 1996 agree that the time and the effort expended were worth the wait.

The Canyon Livery Bed & Breakfast is an add-on to the Shakespeare's existing home, but no one would ever guess it. Drafted by their son, Kenny, the white gabled bed and breakfast ediface is a replica of the grand old mansions of yesteryear.

Each of the five spacious and elegant guest rooms has its own private outside entrance. Every room has been dedicated to a specific group of pioneers who so courageously settled this unyielding, unmerciful, yet magnificent land. All rooms are air conditioned and have ceiling fans, queen beds, private baths with tubs, showers and pedestal wash basins; and picture windows looking west to the marvelous coral cliffs of Bryce Canyon National Park.

The first room is dedicated to the ranchers and farmers, those hardy stalwarts of little fame. Furnishings are of heavy pine. The room's color scheme is enhanced by a hand-made quilt of peach and teal.

A second guest room is devoted to the memory of Jacob Hamblin. Jacob, it is said, probably did more for peacefully bringing together the Western and Native American cultures than any other man. He was so respected by the Navajo, Hopi, Paiute and Shiviwit Indians of Utah, Arizona, and New Mexico that he was given the honored title of "Father" by these tribes. The room has rough hewn furnishings of Ponderosa pine and a color scheme of navy and burgundy. This room has a larger than average bathroom and is ideal for the physically impaired.

Pioneer women of Southwestern Utah are honored by a third room. Here, femininity reigns supreme. The guest room offers a four-poster white and brass bed with white lace pillows and bedding of gray, burgundy and pastels. This room has a private balcony and a magnificent view of farmland, Bryce, and the emergence of Grand Staircase-Escalante.

So important were the pioneer women who settled this vast area that a second room is also dedicated to them. The bed frame is brass and crystal with bedding of mauve, burgundy, purple, and deep green.

The last room is dedicated to the more colorful characters of the West—the gun slingers—some with stories that are legend and some who are little known but who nevertheless played an important role in the making of the West. More rugged and masculine, the room is decorated with cowboy pictures and artifacts. An eyebrow window makes it possible for guests to lie in bed and view the stars. This room also has its own private balcony. Just as each room has a picture window looking into the west, so all rooms have a common balcony with chairs facing the east. Rugged mountain views are impressive on both sides.

Kevin and Jeanee know that most people who stay at bed & breakfasts enjoy socializing with their host and hostess but, they also appreciate their privacy. Hence, the private entrances. The Shakespeares also know that the area's sights are more enjoyable when guests learn about the area's history and the terrain they will be exploring. Kevin and Jeanee delight in sharing that information.

The Shakespeares have a great country kitchen with beautiful hardwood floors and oak cabinets. It opens to a light and roomy breakfast nook where breakfast is served. Many guests comment that an alarm clock is not necessary at The Canyon Livery. The smell of fresh breakfast breads being baked is alarm clock enough for them. Specialty breads, one or two a day, include molasses oat bran or zucchini bread, and squash, currant, and blueberry muffins served with homemade jams and jellies. The picture-perfect, all-one-can-eat breakfast buffet also includes fruit in season from the Shakespeare orchards (cherries, apricots, peaches, plums, and apples), and a table laden with an assortment of fresh melons, grapes, and berries. There is always a selection of juices, coffee, and herbal and regular tea.

In addition to sending their guests out the door, content from a sumptuous country breakfast, the Shakespeares leave a bounteous supply of home-dried fruits on the counter at all times. Guests are welcome to take a supply with them as they explore the canyons.

Both Kevin and Jeanee are inveterate outdoorsmen and feel as much at home on a horse as they do in their own back yard. One of their goals is to set up cattle drives with local ranchers that would take guests through the nation's newest national monument, Grand Staircase-Escalante. It's a monumental goal, (no pun intended) but if anyone can do it Kevin can. He is Range Management Specialist for Grand Staircase-Escalante.

Kevin and Jeanee encourage tourists to contemplate visiting them during the off-season months of October through March. Much of the terrain along Scenic Byway 12 is ablaze with the colors of autumn during October. During the winter nothing is more spectacular that coral hoodoos exposed through glistening snow of the purest white. And in early spring the valleys are exploding with wondrous wild flowers. Horseback riding at these times of the year is incredible. Sunsets and sunrises, which change with the seasons, are equally marvelous. Kevin and Jeanee also point out that, located in the high desert as they are, warmer climates, even during the winter months, are just 20 miles to the south and 40 miles to the east.

Both Kevin and Jeanee have roots that go back four generations to the settlement of Southwestern Utah. Kevin is a native of Tropic, Jeanee of nearby Parowan. Both love their pioneer ancestry and the stories that abound of the first Mormon settlers. They know and love the vastness that is their back yard and they excitedly look forward to sharing their bounty and directing their guests to less traveled paths.

COWBOY DREAMS BED & BREAKFAST

80 South 100 East
(Located just East of Scenic Byway 12)
Tropic/Bryce Canyon, Utah 84776
Tel: (435) 679-8734
Reservations are recommended.

Cowboy Dreams seemed the perfect name for the small two-room bed and breakfast developed by Raymond and Ronnie Brinkerhoff. Ronnie is an artist whose western art is inspired by her favorite author, Louis L'Amour. Raymond is a cowboy in every sense of the word.

While Ronnie takes care of the bed & breakfast and gift and video stores, Raymond's days are spent herding the cattle back and forth from winter to summer ranges, calving and doctoring his cattle, and loving them in such a way that most of his cattle have names and all of them are known to Raymond by sight. Raymond has also performed in rodeos all his life. It was Raymond's love for a cowboy's life that inspired the name, Cowboy Dreams Bed & Breakfast.

Cowboy Dreams is a split level home with guest rooms and common area all on the main floor. The Great Room is always available and Raymond and Ronnie invite their guests to use it as they would their own living room. Decorated in a quasi Spanish decor, the room features an antique rocking chair, collection of old bottles, antique table with cactus and Christmas cactus, a cozy fireplace, and a variety of flowers, vines, and other plants.

It is obvious, both inside and outside, that Raymond and Ronnie have green thumbs. Raymond's expertise is exhibited in a well-kept vegetable garden, his fields, and the family orchard where guests are invited to pick the seasonal fruits that include apricots, peaches, apples and plums.

These same fruits are offered in season for the continental breakfast served each day. In addition to the fruits, breakfast includes juice, toast with jam or jelly, coffee, tea, and a variety of cold cereals. Guests are invited to use the refrigerator and even the kitchen for light meals.

Rooms are named, most appropriately, Cowboy and Dreams. Cowboy offers a single queen bed and Southwestern decor with a color scheme of green, burgundy, and brown. When one turns out the light at night there is a pleasant surprise—the stars on the wall illuminate. Dreams has a more whimsical color scheme, using deep blue, burgundy and pastels to enhance the two double beds. The shared bathroom is decorated in burgundy and forest green and offers both tub and shower. Each room also has a remote control TV and VCR.

The VCR's come with a nice surprise. In addition to operating Cowboy Dreams Bed & Breakfast, Ronnie and Raymond own one of the town's best stocked video selections. Videos, as many as one can watch during their stay, are free of charge to Cowboy Dreams guests. The selection of nearly 700 includes classics, Westerns, and latest releases.

Cowboy Dreams has another advantage that most bed & breakfasts do not have. Attached to the Brinkerhoff home is a very special country gift shop. Most of the items are hand-crafted by local residents, Ronnie, and one of her daughters.

The gifts available are constantly changing but include country kitchen artifacts such as roosters, sheep, chicken, and pigs; silk flower arrangements, needlepoint, crocheted doilies, raffia ribbon wreaths, toll painted decor, plastic canvas stitching, afghans, table cloths, baptismal or confirmation dresses, homemade jams and jellies, acrylics, ceramics, and exquisite hand-stitched quilts, pillows and pictures.

Tropic is located on Scenic Byway 12, Utah's number one Scenic Byway (rated among the top ten in the nation). This 122 mile stretch of road begins off US 89, just south of Panguitch, and offers the state's most varied and spectacular scenery, among which is Bryce Canyon and the nation's newest national monument, Grand Staircase-Escalante. Tropic is the closest town to the main entrance of Bryce Canyon and it sits on the northwest border of Grand Staircase-Escalante.

With so much to see and do in the area, it simply makes sense to let dreams come true by staying at Cowboy Dreams.

FOX'S BRYCE TRAILS BED & BREAKFAST

P. O. Box 87
1001 West Bryce Way
Tropic/Bryce Canyon,
Utah 84776-0087
Tel: (435) 679-8700
FAX: (435) 679-8727
Web Site:
http://www.utah.com/lodging
/foxsbrycetrails
Email:
RFox633638@aol.com
Visa and MasterCard are accepted.
Reservations are recommended.

Fox's Bryce Trails Bed & Breakfast, a spectacular modern edifice with classic touches of yesteryear, is sequestered against the flaming cliffs of the east boundary of Bryce Canyon National Park. From the bed & breakfast's front door it is a short two mile hike to Peek-a-boo Loop, a trail that takes hikers into the bottom of either Sunset or Sunrise Points.

Fox's Bryce Trails was built in 1994 by owners, Richard and LuCine Fox, as a bed & breakfast. In the building process, Richard and LuCine and LuCine's sister, Elaine Haas, who is Fox's Bryce Trails hostess, took note of all the things they look for in a home away from home. Everything had to be as nice as if not nicer than that which one experiences at their own home.

In planning their bed & breakfast a great deal of emphasis was placed on location. All agreed that scenery, serenity, and proximity were most important factors, not only to them, but to their visiting guests. Fox's Bryce Trails Bed & Breakfast offers all three. Tropic is not only the closest town to Bryce Canyon National Park, just eight miles north to the entrance, but is also on the west boundary of the nation's newest national monument, Grand Staircase Escalante.

Located exactly one mile west of Scenic Byway 12 at the end of Bryce Way Drive, Fox's Bryce Trails Bed & Breakfast offers seclusion and exhilarating tranquility. What could be more tranquil or exhilarating than panormic vistas and the sights and sounds of songbirds, deer, elk, and other small wildlife creatures. And when city lights are minimal, a star-studded sky becomes a spectacle to behold.

Outside, the downstairs terrace is lush with flowers and plants. The upstairs decking is great for lounging and enjoying breath-taking panoramas.

Inside, everything is modern and immaculately cared for. In the common areas of the bed & breakfast and down the hallway the home overflows with ferns, ivy, plants of all kinds, needlepoint, oil paintings, and other art objects. Every piece of furniture, every decorator item—all are tastefully appointed.

Each evening, or any time during the day if guests choose to remain at the bed & breakfast, movies may be selected from the video collection downstairs in the Great Room. Guests may choose to watch the movie on the large TV in the Great Room, or the movie can be received in their room. A second room downstairs has been set aside as the Quiet Room. A large couch and two rocking chairs create the ideal setting for guests to relax, read a book, or converse with new friends.

All five guest rooms are located on the second floor and can be accessed from the upstairs redwood balcony or through the home. Each of the spacious guest rooms has been named for one of the Bryce Canyon National Park trails. All rooms have ceiling fans, air conditioning, color TV with remote control, and private bath with tub, shower, and vanity basin.

Queen's Garden Room features an exquisite white wrought iron trundle bed and elegant brass-framed king bed, both with beautiful rose bedspreads and decorator pillows. Floral garden pictures and silk flower arrangements adorn the walls along with other decorative artifacts.

Under the Rim offers a queen bed, floral skirted end tables, and an alcove sitting area that looks out on Bryce Point. Walls are adorned with country western art objects.

Native American art adorns the walls of *Navajo Loop*, a spacious guest room with a queen bed and beautiful green, red, blue, and gold southwestern bedding, table covers and side drapes.

The king bed in *Bristle Cone* has southwestern bedding and a raffia swag in burgundy and green. Two beautiful wing back chairs make relaxing in the room a pleasure. Beautiful hand made quilts adorn the wall and silk flowers and doilies add to the decor.

The decor of *Mossy Cave* revolves around a selection of bamboo and wicker furnishings. The furniture includes a dresser, bookshelf, and wall unit, all in simplistic elegance, and a queen bed with hunter green, floral rose, and tan accents in the bedding, table cloth and curtains.

A full breakfast is served each morning from 7:30 to 9:00 a.m. Breakfasts always include a selection of cold cereals, hot drinks, and fruits in season. In addition, the menu might include French toast, bacon or sausage; pancakes, bacon and eggs any style; and a guest favorite, Cheesy Oven Omelette Bake, a marvelous blend of eggs, cheese, mushrooms, and crumbled bacon. Also available are bran, blueberry or poppyseed muffins.

All of the creature comforts of home are offered at Fox's Bryce Trails, but they are offered in such a way that one feels like royalty. Triple A approved with a two diamond rating, Fox's Bryce Trails Bed & Breakfast will have guests purring like a kitten while they sleep like a baby.

DID YOU KNOW?

---that Bryce Canyon National Park is named after the area's first homesteader, Ebenezer Bryce, who settled Tropic in 1875. But Ebenezer Bryce apparently had to work so hard at eking out a living that he never had the chance to appreciate the park's wonders. His statement, "It's a hell of a place to lose a cow" and the fact that he left in 1880 for Arizona are sad testammonials of his lack of appreciation for the park that bears his name.

FRANCISCO'S FARM BED & BREAKFAST

51 Francisco Lane, P. O. Box 3
Tropic/Bryce Canyon, Utah 84776-0003
Tel: (435) 679-8721
     (800) 642-4136
Winter rates available November 1 - April 1.
Visa, MasterCard, and Personal Checks are accepted.
Reservations are recommended.

    Ensconced at the end of a romantic farm lane that bears their name, Francisco's Farm Bed and Breakfast is all that its name implies and much, much more.

    Awarded a triple A two-diamond rating, Francisco's Farm has found its way into the hearts of those who write about bed and breakfasts and those who stay at bed and breakfasts. Francisco's is listed in *Best Places to Stay in the Southwest*. *Country Magazine* has chosen to write about Francisco's three years in a row. Those are fulfilling kudos to bed and breakfast hosts. The accolades, however, that mean the most to Evedean and Charlie Francisco, owners, are the pictures drawn in their guest books by the children who stay there and call the Franciscos "Grandma and Grandpa".

    Evedean calls their bed and breakfast a "comfortable, quiet, no-frills estab-

lishment." But frills, it seems, are in the eye of the beholder. Evedean's evaluation is accurate if she is talking about pretense and pomposity. There is none of that here. Nevertheless, if frills refer to the special things one cannot normally do, Francisco's Farm has a lot of frills to offer.

    It is not often that one gets to lodge in a large, comfortable log home. But, say Evedean and Charlie, the logs are only functional, keeping guests cozy and warm in the winter and refreshingly comfortable during the summer.

    Outside are the farm animals—hounddogs, cat, chickens, horses, ducks, geese, goats, and strutting peacocks. Those who wake up early enough or return in time from their day of sightseeing are welcome to gather their own eggs for breakfast, and even try their hand at milking a goat. It is not often one has those kinds of opportunities.

    A true highlight of being a guest at Francisco's Farm is the genuine all-one-can-eat breakfast served in Francisco's bright and airy Garden Room. The aroma of fresh baked bread, muffins, or biscuits wafting in the air is likely to be the mornings wake-up call, unless, of course, the rooster gets up first. Breakfast is served regularly, as early as 6:00 a.m. and as late as 9:00 a.m., unless guests have pre-arranged to have breakfast earlier or later. Guest's eggs, served any style, are guaranteed fresh that day. Jams, jellies, and applesauce have all been lovingly preserved by Evedean. In addition to farm-fresh eggs and goat's milk, breakfast also includes choices of pancakes, waffles, hash browns, bacon, and sausage. There is always a selection of coffee, tea, hot chocolate, and cold cereals. Country cooking such as this is rare indeed.

Guests are always welcome to use the kitchen. Evedean and Charlie admit that some of their most memorable dinners have been prepared by guests who are tired of eating out (or of eating American food), and want to eat something that tastes more like home. Use of a bed and breakfast kitchen is highly unusual.

On a redwood deck in the backyard is the Grande spa. It will comfortably accommodate up to eight individuals and it offers guests the opportunity to hear what country feels and sounds like in the evening. The silence can be deafening, and while the brilliance of a star-studded sky may not be blinding, it certainly is awe-inspiring.

The Great Room at Francisco's Farm is spacious and unpretentious. Pictures of ancestors on both sides of the family, pioneers who helped to settle southern Utah, grace the walls. The decor is teal, mauve and blue, and seating is arranged so as to encourage congeniality among the guests.

Those who are physically impaired appreciate the spacious convenience of The Peach Room. Handicap accessible, the room offers a full tub and shower with regulation safety bars, sliding mirror doors on the closets, flowers in the window box, antique dresser, and a queen bed with hand-made quilt. There are also built-in oak cabinets with plenty of drawers.

Upstairs, the Big Blue Room is spacious enough to accommodate two queen beds. It has a private bath with shower, a separate vanity basin, love seat, antique trunk, ceiling fan, and two wonderful hand-sewn quilts. The Rose Room offers one queen bed, two roll-aways if needed, private bath with shower, ceiling fan, and hand made quilt.

In addition to all of the unpretentious frills already mentioned, Francisco's is a haven for several varieties of nesting birds and one that rarely rests, the hummingbird. They are delightful to watch from the kitchen and dining room windows or from the comfort of a soothing Jacuzzi spa.

Tropic, located 21 miles west on Scenic Byway 12, one of the nation's top ten byways, is without question a hub of the Southwest. The closest town to the entrance of Bryce Canyon (seven miles), Tropic is also situated on the north boundary of the nation's newest national monument, Grand Staircase-Escalante. Charlie was a wrangler with the Bryce Canyon horse rides and awaits the opportunity to help guests discover the majestic scenery in the area.

When it comes to the frills that really count, a down-to-earth western experience with hosts who become family, there is no better choice than Francisco's Farm Bed & Breakfast.

DID YOU KNOW?

---that Bryce became Bryce Canyon National Monument in 1923, Utah National Park in 1924, and did not revert back to the name Bryce until 1928 when it became Bryce National Park. The Union Pacific Railroad was largely responsible for the park's immense popularity. The railroad built a spectacular rustic lodge near Sunset Point and began bringing tours into the area in 1930.

RESTAURANTS

DOUG'S PLACE COUNTRY KITCHEN RESTAURANT
120 North Main, P. O. Box 157
Tropic, Utah 84776
Tel: (435) 679-8632
FAX: (435) 679-8605
Web Site: www.onpages.com/dougsplace
Email: dougsinn@color-country.net
Hrs:
    May - September
Open Seven Days 6:30 a.m. - 9:30 p.m.
    October - April
Monday - Saturday 8:00 a.m. - 8:00 p.m.
Breakfast Opening - 11:00 a.m.
Lunch   11:00 a.m. - 5:00 p.m.
Dinner   5:00 p.m. - Closing
Visa, MasterCard, American Express, Diners Club, Carte Blanche, Discover, and Phillips 66 are accepted.

    Located in the heart of Utah's Color Country on Scenic Byway 12 is Doug's Place Country Kitchen Restaurant, an eating establishment that offers more than just a little bit of country ambiance.
    The marvelous old-west decor includes wagon wheel chandeliers, exposed beams, hardwood booths, and adobe walls with bared brick. Decorating the walls are lanterns, Native American Mandellas, and antique farm and home artifacts such as harnesses, irons, and the like.
    Guests have a choice of sitting at booths or tables to enjoy the day's bill of fare. Always a country favorite, the Biscuits and Gravy breakfast includes two buttermilk biscuits smothered in homemade sausage gravy. Breakfast specials include Ham and Cheese, Denver and Spanish Omelettes, Steak N' Eggs, and Wrangler's Special, which features two pancakes, two eggs, hash browns, and a choice of bacon and sausage. The Country Kitchen also offers eggs any style with choices that include hash browns, ham, bacon, and sausage.
    Lunch specials are hearty helpings and include an all one can eat soup and salad bar, homemade cornbread, vegetable, and a choice of potato or rice. Country Fried Steak, Fresh Rainbow Trout, Broiled Chicken Breast, and Top Sirloin Steak are a sampling of the lunch specials offered. Soups are homemade, made fresh daily, and are delicious. Favorite sandwiches, all of which are served with French fries or potato chips, include the Vegetable Melt, a rendering of two kinds of cheese, onions, tomatoes, and lettuce on rye bread; and Country Kitchen's Munch Burger, one-fourth pound of extra lean beef with bacon and ham. The restaurant's varied assortment of hot and cold sandwiches is available with a cup of soup.
    Doug's Place Country Kitchen deserves the reputation it has earned for serving up the area's best steaks and seafood. All meats are cut on premises and are succulent to the taste. The House Specialty on the dinner menu is Milanesa Ala Neopolitonia. It is an Argentine Breaded Steak with specially seasoned tomato sauce, ham, and Swiss Cheese, and it is a dining experience not to be missed. Regular steaks include T-Bone, Filet Mignon, Top Sirloin, and Country Fried. Fresh Rainbow Trout, a western favorite,

tops the list of fresh fish preferences. Also popular is the restaurants famous Giant Fantail Shrimp. The Broiled chicken Breast is not only delicious but heart smart and healthy. All dinner entrees include the all-one-can-eat soup and salad bar, homemade cornbread, vegetable, and a choice of potato or rice. The all-one-can-eat salad bar and the soup and salad bar are available to lunch and dinner diners.

Country Kitchen recently introduced diners to the world of Italy. They now offer a selection of pasta dishes for both lunch and dinner.

Regardless of the lunch or dinner menu selection, those dining at Doug's Place Country Kitchen should always save room for dessert. Pies are baked daily and include apple, a variety of berry pies, cream pies, caramel pecan, and pumpkin.

Doug's Place Country Kitchen Restaurant, a part of Doug's Place Country Inn Motel, (see related story), offers diners the opportunity to savor the goodness of homemade cuisine in a relaxed country atmosphere.

THE HUNGRY COYOTE RESTAURANT
195 North Main Street
Tropic/Bryce Canyon, Utah 84776
Tel: (435) 679-8811
          (800) 442-1890
FAX: (435) 679-8846
Email: bvi@color-country.net
Hrs: April 1 - November 1
Breakfast 6:30 a.m. - 10:30 p.m.
Dinner
5:00 p.m. - 10:00 p.m.
Visa, MasterCard, American Express,
 and Discover are accepted.
Reservations are accepted.

A rustic western ambiance prevails both inside and outside The Hungry Coyote, where diners have the choice of relaxing in one of two dining rooms and being waited on by the restaurant's attentive staff or choosing their own steak and cooking it themselves on the patio barbecue.

The Hungry Coyote Restaurant, located at Bryce Valley Inn (see related story), is housed in an old western town setting with hitching posts, plank walkway, and desert landscape. Inside, walls of rough hewn knotty pine are embellished with antique western artifacts. Most of the artifacts and collectibles are for sale. Even the men's and women's bathrooms are decorated in turn of the century decor that reflects a feminine or masculine theme.

The all-one-can-eat breakfast buffet stands out as an early morning favorite. It offers diners their choice of hot cakes, French toast, scrambled eggs, bacon, sausage, fruits, cold cereal, toast, English muffins, and coffee, tea, hot chocolate and juice. Other breakfast choices include three-egg omelettes and one or two eggs, any style, served with ham, bacon, sausage, hash browns and toast or biscuit.

An all-one-can-eat salad bar with soup and a variety of salads and salad fixings is a great choice for the light eater. The Western side of the menu includes a great selection of steaks. Choose from among a 20-ounce T-bone, thick, juicy and sure to be a man-pleaser; or the 10-ounce Rib Eye and New York and the eight-ounce Filet Mignon. Pork Chops, Grilled Chicken Breasts, Trout, Short Ribs, and Roast Beef are other hearty choices. All Western dinners come with a one-time soup and salad bar, homemade bread, and rice or choice of potato. For a small additional charge, guests may choose to have three golden fried jumbo shrimps served with their meals.

One-half pound hamburgers, cheeseburgers, mushroom cheeseburgers, and bacon cheeseburgers are served all day at The Hungry Coyote. They are accompanied by all the garnishes, French fries, and a choice of American or Swiss cheese.

During the summer months from June through August, be sure to stop by the Ice Cream Parlour, located at the back of the restaurant by the patio. The Ice Cream Parlour offers an inspiring selection of ice cream choices and serves one of Utah's favorite brands, Russell's ice cream.

It's a good bet that after dining at The Hungry Coyote and reading the souvenir menu, guests will pick up the jargon and leave the restaurant muttering, "It was the best dern food I ever et!!"

SPECIALTY SHOPPING

BRYCE PIONEER VILLAGE GIFT SHOP
80 North Main Highway 12
P. O. Box 119
Tropic/Bryce Canyon
tah 84776
Tel: (435) 679-8546
      (800) 222-0381
FAX: (435) 679-8607
Web Site
www.onpages.com/bpvillage/
Hrs: April 1 - November 1
Open Daily
6:30 a.m. - 10:30 p.m.
Visa, MasterCard, and Discover are accepted.

Bryce Pioneer Village Gift Shop, located in the lobby of Bryce Pioneer Village motel (see related story), has earned a reputation for being sensitive to the needs of area visitors. The Gift Shop is organized in an orderly manner, making it easy for guests to find mementos of a treasured vacation and keepsakes to treasure.

Bryce Pioneer Village Gift Shop is located in the small Southwestern town of Tropic, Utah. Tropic is the closest town to the entrance of Bryce Canyon National Park, situated right on the borders of both Bryce and the nation's newest national monument, Grand Staircase-Escalante. It is also close to the beauty of Red Canyon in the Dixie National Forest and Kodachrome Basin and Escalante Petrified Forest state parks. Within beautiful drives are Zion National Park, Capitol Reef National Park, Cedar Breaks National Monument, and the North Rim of the Grand Canyon.

Recognizing that guests traveling through Tropic are either coming from or going to these national treasures, Bryce Pioneer Village Gift Shop has selected quality varieties of national park videos, puzzles, posters, pictorial books, calendars, and post cards. At the gift shop it is also easy to find T-shirts, caps, mugs, magnets, spoons, thimbles, and other logo souvenirs of one's trip to Tropic and the surrounding national parks.

A glass-enclosed display showcases a quality selection of Native American silver jewelry that includes rings, bracelets, hair pieces, necklaces, watch bands, bolo ties, and belt buckles. Many are embellished with semi-precious stones such as turquoise, coral, mother of pearl, and lapis. Others are simply elegant pieces of handcrafted silver.

Native American artifacts include all sizes and colors of pottery, sand paintings, dream catchers, Mandellas, Kachina and story teller dolls, fetishes, rainsticks, and blankets. Southwestern gift items include candles, copper jewelry, ceramic wall decorations, petroglyph figures, Leaning' Tree cards, pottery bells and wind chimes, aprons, canvas bags, vests, and sweatshirts.There is also a nice selection of inexpensive cowboy and Indian toy souvenirs for the children.

Discriminating shoppers love Bryce Pioneer Village Gift Shop.

BRYCE CANYON NATIONAL PARK

Bryce Canyon National Park, hollowed out of the Pink Cliffs of the Paunsaugunt Plateau, is a series of fourteen enormous amphitheaters extending over 1,000 feet down into the multi-colored limestone. A land the Paiute Indians called "Unka timpe-wa-wince-pock-ick," or "red rocks standing like men in a bowl shaped canyon," Bryce Canyon is filled with a myriad of fantastic shapes and figures of nearly every conceivable shape and in a kaleidoscope of colors.

Paiute Indians say that Bryce Canyon was built by Coyote as a city for his people, including the birds, animals, lizards, and those who walked upright on two feet. The story continues that the Coyote people began to spend all their time beautifying their city, which made Coyote angry. In a fit of rage he spilled their paints and turned the people to stone. To this day they stand there, row upon row, their faces colored with the paint Coyote threw at them in his anger.

Geologists, however, have a very different story of the creation of Bryce Canyon. Their version, simply stated, is that the multi-hued layers of sandstone were set down one on top of another over a time span of 10 million years. This continued until the sea that covered the area drained away and the plateau was raised to an altitude over a mile above modern day sea level. The wind and rain then took over to sculpt the wonders we see today.

Ebenezer Bryce, who came to the Paria Valley to live and harvest timber from the plateau in 1875, and after whom the park was named, when asked what he thought of Bryce Canyon, succinctly stated: "It's a hell of a place to lose a cow."

Established as a national park in 1928, today Bryce Canyon features several excellent methods of viewing the park, including a thirty-six mile round trip paved road that gives the visitor the chance to see the entire park. Sights such as Fairyland Point, Sunrise, Sunset, Inspiration, and Bryce Points, and Paria View may be seen within a four mile drive. The entire park, plus thirty miles of the Pink Cliffs, may be seen from Rainbow Point at the far end of the park. From the various points and overlooks there are more than 50 miles of walking trails that take hikers into close proximity with the hoodoos.

It is wise, before entering the park, to stop at the visitor center. At the center travelers can study the exhibits, browse through books, maps and other publications about the park, and watch a free slide program. Park rangers conduct walks, talks, and campfire programs during the summer months on topics ranging from geology and wildlife to air quality. The park is open year-round and closed only on Thanksgiving, Christmas, and New Year's Day. Park hours are extended from April - November.

Fairyland Point, because it is before the main park entrance and a mile off the main road, is missed by many park visitors. Don't make their mistake! Fairyland Point, highlighted by **Sinking Ship**, offers views and scenery that rival any in the park. In addition to its Fairyland Amphitheater, the panorama presents a backdrop of the Aquarius Plateau and distant Navajo Mountain. During winter months this area is used for cross country skiing and the road is not plowed.

Sunrise, Sunset, Inspiration, and Bryce Points ring the Bryce Amphitheater, the largest in the park. From ***Sunrise Point*** one can hike down the **Queen's Garden Trail**. From ***Sunset Point*** the most popular hike is to ***Thor's Hammer*** and ***Wall Street***. The best views of ***Silent City*** are from ***Inspiration Point***. ***Under-the-Rim Trail*** begins at ***Bryce Point*** and continues all the way to ***Rainbow Point*** at the southern end of the park.

At ***Paria View*** one looks out across hoodoos in an amphitheater that is carved by Yellow Creek. The Paria River valley and Table Cliffs Plateau form the backdrop. The White Cliffs, carved of Navajo Sandstone, are visible to the south.

Since all of the remaining overlooks are on the east side of the road, it is recommended that park visitors drive to the southern end of the park and then stop at the overlooks on their return. For this reason we take you to Yovimpa and Rainbow Points at the far end of the park, then point out the overlooks as we head north again.

Incredible views of southern Utah and even Arizona and New Mexico can be seen from both ***Yovimpa*** and ***Rainbow Points***. On most days one can see Navajo Mountain and the Kaibab Plateau, 90 miles away in Arizona. On the clearest of days the only thing that hampers one's view is the curvature of the earth. The most looked for hoodoo at Rainbow Point is ***The Poodle***, a natural carving that is so realistic that, when one spots it, it seems to be posing for the camera. The Pink Cliffs form a photographer's backdrop, but also make spotting The Poodle difficult. The **Bristlecone Loop Trail** takes visitors through a grove of 100s of years-old Bristlecones.

Aqua Canyon displays contrasts of light and color that are among the most satisfying in the park. It also affords visitors with good views of the vertical cliffs that typify the southerly Paunsaugunt Plateau. The hoodoo to look for at Aqua Canyon is ***The Hunter***, identifiable because of the small trees that top it.

Pine-covered foothills and the Table Cliffs Plateau to the north frame the multicolored hoodoos of ***Ponderosa Canyon***.

One of the more popular roadside sites is **Natural Bridge** with its view of ponderosa pines through the arch. Because it was formed by the combined forces of rain and frost erosion, acting from the top of the rock and not by a stream, Natural Bridge is, in reality, an arch.

Farview Point offers visitors a panoramic view that includes, to the northeast, the Kaibab Plateau of the North Rim of the Grand Canyon. It is at this elevation that ponderosa pines begin to give way to the spruce and fir trees of the higher elevations. From Fairyland Point's elevation of 7,758 feet to Rainbow Point, with its elevation of 9,115, there is a gradual climb of 1,355 feet. It is interesting to watch as one makes the drive the changes in the forest from ponderosa pine to spruce, fir, and aspen.

Camping is available within the park at North and Sunset campgrounds. Tent and RV sites are available on a first-come, first-served basis. A fee is charged and the maximum length of stay is 14 days per visit with a maximum of 30 days per year. Sites have picnic tables and fireplaces with water and restrooms nearby.

Bryce Canyon Lodge, built in 1924-25, reflects the rustic style of the period. Rooms and cabins are available from April - November. The lodge has a restaurant, gift shop, and post office. Park tours and horse rides are available from the lobby.

A small general store with shower and laundry facilities are available at the Sunrise Point parking area. Non-denominational and LDS church services are held on summer Sundays in the park. Other services are offered in neighboring communities (435 834-5322).

ACCOMMODATIONS

FOSTER'S MOTEL, BAKERY, & FAMILY STEAKHOUSE
P. O. Box 640101
Highway 12, 4 miles from Bryce Canyon.
Bryce Canyon, Utah 84764-0101
Tel: (435) 834-5227
FAX: (435) 834-5304
Web Site:
www. fosters@bryce.com
E-Mail: fosters@bryce
Visa, MasterCard, American Express, Diners Club, Carte Blanche, and Discover
are accepted.
Reservations are suggested.

That which one desires most when traveling is the ability on the part of one's host to make them feel that they are not a stranger in the land. The Foster family, with Al and Leda Mae at the helm, has developed that capability. The Fosters are owners of Foster's Motel, Foster's Supermarket and Bakery, and Foster's Family Steak House, all of which are within a short, four-mile drive of Bryce Canyon National Park.

Each guest room is attractively appointed in modern colors of peach and teal blue. Scrupulously clean, the rooms are furnished with a choice of single queen or two regular beds, remote control cable TV, direct dial phone, dresser, and table with two chairs. Single queen rooms have two night stands while the rooms with two regular beds have one. Both configurations have a large closet and dressing area, bathroom with combined tub and shower, and a separate vanity basin. One of the features most appreciated by guests is the hotel-style entry, where guests enter their rooms from an indoor hallway and not from the outside.

The lobby of Foster's Motel is also the waiting area for Foster's Family Steak House. An extremely impressive lodge-like vestibule, the steak house has a high open-beam ceiling. Although the restaurant is a single large room, a creative booth seating arrangement gives diners a feeling of privacy. The restaurant has an eclectic decor of hanging plants, lantern light fixtures, prize elk and deer head mounts, grapevine and silk floral arrangements, and paintings by one of the area's most famous residents, Lynn Griffin.

During peak season, from April 1 through October 31, the restaurant is open for breakfast, lunch and dinner with service from 7:00 a.m. to 10:00 p.m. Restaurant hours, from November 1 through March 31, are Thursday through Sunday, 3:00 p.m. to 10:00 p.m.

One factor that contributes to the success of the restaurant breakfast menu is the selection of breakfast pastries, straight from Foster's bakery. Even the toast is made from Foster's fresh home baked breads. Two farm-fresh eggs, any style, are served with a choice of bacon, sausage, or ham, and country fried potatoes and choice of toast. Diners would be hard-pressed to find lighter pancakes and waffles than those served at Foster's. The three-egg omelettes are also served with a choice of toast and country-fried potatoes.

The luncheon menu offers guests a large variety of hot and cold sandwiches, a selection of hamburgers, salads, and soup.

From the dinner menu, it is hard to beat a broiled steak that is cooked to perfection, especially when it is a bacon-wrapped filet mignon. The Prime Rib, a house specialty, is succulent, juicy, and served with au jus and a marvelous horseradish sauce. The hamburger steaks, served with sautéed onions, and the chicken-fried steak, topped with country gravy, are delicious. And while the grilled salmon and halibut filets are wonderful, the writer recommends Foster's Trout Almondine. Fresh from the crystal clear lakes and streams of Utah's mountains, the boneless trout filet is grilled and served with toasted almonds. All entrees are served with a choice of soup or salad, steamed vegetables, choice of potatoes, and a small loaf of bread from the bakery. Soup connoisseurs are sure to love the selection of made-from scratch soups—two daily—that include French onion, chicken noodle, split pea, creamed broccoli, and others. Fosters also offers an all-one-can-eat soup and salad bar.

Across the parking lot from Foster's Family Steak House are the bakery, supermarket, and gift shop. Though only open during peak season, April 1 through October 31, the all-inclusive store makes it easy for guests to find what they need in one single stop. Store hours are from 7:00 a.m. to 10:00 p.m.

Fresh baked bread includes hard to find choices such as two very different types of pumpernickel, rye, and a to-die-for secret recipe of cranberry-banana nut bread. There is also a large variety of scones, doughnuts, cinnamon rolls, and pies.

In the supermarket travelers find snack items, fresh produce, dairy products, groceries, notions, non-prescription drug items, soft drinks and cold beer, fried chicken, and a good supply of camping and fishing supplies.

The gift shop makes it easy to take home a memento and a treasured keepsake. Foster's has a quality selection of area T-shirts, sweatshirts, caps, key chains, magnets, thimbles, and spoons. If it is a scenic post card, calendar, note card, video or book on the magnificent parks of Southwestern Utah that one is looking for, Foster's has those as well.

The Southwest is known for its Native American art and artifacts. At Foster's one is sure to find the perfect treasure from among the sand paintings, petroglyph art reproductions, exquisite pottery, Navajo rugs, and sterling silver creations. Silver craftsmanship, most of which are embellished with semi-precious stones such as turquoise, coral, mother of pearl, black onyx, and blue lapis, is a well-known art of the Southwestern Native Americans. Silver treasures include bracelets, rings, necklaces, earrings, bolo ties, belt buckles and watch bands. The gift shop also carries Mandellas, dream catchers, Kachina dolls, and hand-woven baskets.

Foster's has always been known and respected for its quality accommodations at affordable prices and for its warm, Southwestern hospitality. Visitors to the area will soon be afforded an even greater choice of Foster benefits.

When it opens in late spring or early summer of 1998, **Foster's Holiday Inn Sunspree Resort** will offer 186 luxurious new rooms, a pool with Jacuzzi spa, exercise room, and conference and banquet facility. Two restaurants, Wendy's and Outback Steakhouse, are on the grounds. One year later, in June of 1999, the resort will be surrounded by an 18-hole world class golf course.

Foster's Holiday inn Sunspree Resort will offer three room choices—rooms with king bed, two regular beds, or two-room master suites. The suites will have a king bed and a queen sofa with hide-a-bed. Other features of the suites are a wet bar and a business convenience center with computer desk and computer jack.

All rooms will be beautifully appointed is a Southwestern motif using teal, mauve and coral as the color scheme. All rooms will have individually controlled heating and air conditioning, remote control color cable TV, direct dial phone, and bathrooms with combined tub and shower, and a separate vanity.

A continental breakfast will be served in the food court service area adjacent to the conference room, which will accommodate 160 theatre style.

Whether one chooses to stay in the new Holiday Inn Sunspree Resort or at Foster's Motel, there is one thing guests can always count on. When it comes to making a guest feel welcome and comfortable, the Foster family is second to none.

PINK CLIFFS VILLAGE
P. O. Box 640006
13500 East Highway 12
Bryce, Utah 84764
Tel: (435) 834-5351
          (800) 834-0043
FAX: (435) 834-5256
Visa, MasterCard, American Express, and Discover are accepted. Reservations are recommended.

Built in the 1960's as one of the area's most spacious and deluxe accommodations, Pink Cliffs Village, which was updated in the 1980's, is at the junctions of State Highways 12 and 63 and only three miles from the entrance to Bryce Canyon National Park.

Pink Cliffs Village derives its name from the rose-colored Table Cliff region of the Escalante Mountains, 10 miles east of the motel. This scenic and convenient location makes Pink Cliffs Village an ideal accommodation for guests visiting not only Bryce Canyon, but the nation's newest national monument, Grand Staircase-Escalante.

Pink Cliffs Village, with its 44 deluxe rooms, eight economy rooms, 14 rustic cabins, and its dormitory-style hostel can accommodate most guests with their traveling needs.

Pink Cliffs Village offers guest amenities that include an indoor heated swimming pool with doors leading to a patio with lawn chairs and picnic tables. Beyond the patio the well-manicured grounds offer a volleyball court and horseshoe pits. Pink Cliffs Village also has a nice selection of bikes for rent. On premises are a 24-hour guest laundry facility, gift shop and convenience store; full-service gas station with on-duty mechanic, an espresso bar, and The Cowboy Cafe (see related story).

Guests are delighted with the commodious rooms afforded at Pink Cliffs Village. Decorated in a color scheme of rust, forest green and coral, the rooms offer a dresser, desk, remote control color TV, built-in AM-FM radio, direct dial phones, and room-controlled air conditioning and radiant heat. All have spacious bathrooms with tub and shower and two vanities, one in the bathroom and one in a separate dressing area. Rooms with a single king bed have a love seat sofa and two night stands. Rooms with double queen beds are furnished with a night stand and table with two chairs. All rooms are well lit and have double mirrors.

The hip roof and Dutch hip roof cabins are rustic and were actually the very first accommodations at Bryce National Park. Built in 1934 for CCC workers, they were moved to Pink Cliffs Village in 1984. Each of the rooms has an adjoining door that connects to another small room. Furnishings are sparse, with beds being a single, a double or two twins. All have a bathroom with shower only. Four of the units have barn-wood walls. The rest have wainscot wood panels and a clothes tree that is just that—a real tree.

The hostel at Pink Cliffs Village is above the store and will accommodate 12 people in a bi-sexual dormitory style atmosphere. The hostel has two bathrooms with showers. Outside the hostel is a wrap-around deck with view.

The Country Store, gift shop, and Sinclair Gas Station provide guests with groceries, notions, non-prescription drug items, and a selection of souvenir gifts that include logo T-shirts, caps, mugs, scenic post cards, books, and calendars, key chains, and thimbles. They also have a selection of Native American jewelry and memento artifacts such as Mandellas, dream catchers, pottery in all shapes, colors, and sizes, rugs, and baskets. A part of the Country Store is a small cafe and an espresso bar that serves bagels, ice cream, various deli sandwiches, and coffee.

The cabins, hostel, Country Store, Sinclair Gas Station and Cowboy Cafe are only open to guests during peak season at the parks, April 1 through October 31.

Summer activities in the area include a nightly rodeo, fishing, horseback riding, and scenic flights from the Bryce Canyon Airport, which is located less than one-half mile from Pink Cliffs Village. During winter, Bryce Canyon is open for cross-country skiing, snowmobiling, and ice fishing. Those who have never viewed snow encrusted red and coral hoodoos are in for a magical experience.

There is so much to do and see within a one to two-hour drive of Pink Cliffs Village. It only makes sense to make Pink Cliffs ones home away from home. All within two-hour drives to the Northeast are Grand Staircase-Escalante National Monument, and Kodachrome Basin, Escalante Petrified Forest, and Anasazi Indian Village State Parks. To the South or southwest are Cedar Breaks National Monument, Zion National Park, and Pipe Spring National Monument. No more than three-hour drives to the Southeast are the North Rim of the Grand Canyon and Glen Canyon National Recreation Area, home of Lake Powell.

The location of Pink Cliffs Village is ideal and the rooms are spacious and well appointed. But most important, the friendly and dedicated staff at Pink Cliffs Village are there to make sure that every stay is a pleasant and relaxing one.

DID YOU KNOW?

---that Bryce Canyon National Park is equally desirable as a vacation destination during the winter months. Red sandstone hoodoos "peaking" out after a fresh snowstorm gives the appearance of frosting on the cake. Air between storms is crystal clear, creating a panoramic view of majestic proportions. The sky is of deepest blue and one's entire perspective is of pure exhilaration. Roads to most viewpoints are kept plowed for visitor convenience. Snowshoes are loaned out free of charge at the park's visitor center, located a short distance past the entrance on the right hand side. Cross-country skis are available for rent at Ruby's Inn, and Snowmobiling is permitted outside the park entrance at Fairyland Point. Free day-use and free backcountry permits are available at the visitor center.

RESORTS

BEST WESTERN RUBY'S INN
Entrance, Bryce Canyon National Park
P. O. Box 1
Bryce, Utah 84764
Tel: (435) 834-5341
        (800) 528-1234
FAX: (435) 834-5265
Web Site:www.rubysinn.com
E-Mail: www.bob@rubysinn.com

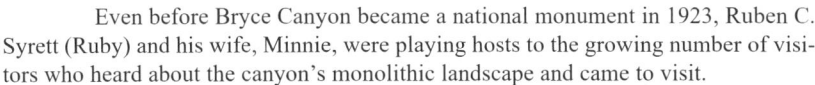

Visa, MasterCard, American Express, Diners Club, Carte Blanche, and Discover are accepted.
Reservations are recommended.

Even before Bryce Canyon became a national monument in 1923, Ruben C. Syrett (Ruby) and his wife, Minnie, were playing hosts to the growing number of visitors who heard about the canyon's monolithic landscape and came to visit.

The Syretts moved to the wilds of Southern Utah in 1916 and built a ranch very near the present site of Ruby's Inn. In 1919, before Ruby's Inn opened at its present location, the Syretts obtained permission to build a lodge, Tourist Rest, near the brink of the canyon. When Bryce became a national monument the Syretts relocated their services to their ranch and called it Ruby's Inn.

What started out as tent houses and a place to serve meals to the first Bryce Canyon tourists has expanded today to include one of the most complete tourist facilities in the state. Ruby's Inn, with all its features, has earned a reputation as vacation headquarters for Bryce Canyon. Ruby's Inn amenities include a deluxe motel, family dining & steak house, trailer park, Laundromat, post office, banquet and convention center, quality tours, several gift shops, one-hour photo finishing, full-service Chevron American Car Care Center, Texaco gas station, Bryce Canyon Country Rodeo, and a winter sports area.

Rooms at Ruby's Inn are spacious, comfortable, and well maintained. The tent houses of yesteryear have grown to include 369 rooms and suites in eight different lodges. The main lodge has three-floors of guest rooms that are located behind the lobby shops. This complex is home to the Inn's new year-round indoor swimming pool and spa. Other lodges include Columbine, Antelope, Elk, Lakeview, Deer, and Aspen, which is adjacent to a large outdoor hot tub and Laundromat, and Ponderosa Lodge, which houses the Inn's game room.The hot tub and game room are open 9:00 a.m. to 10:00 p.m. during summer season.

Room amenities at Ruby's include room controlled air conditioning and heating, double queen or single king beds, remote control color TV with Satellite movies, and direct dial phones. Ruby's also offers two-bedroom units with cooking facilities, and rooms with electric fireplaces. Suite amenities include in-room whirlpool tubs and spas.

The lobby at Ruby's Inn Main Lodge is massive and rustic. Ponderosa pine support beams, pine furnishings, and pine walls give evidence that one is in Dixie National Forest country. A massive floor to ceiling rock fireplace with pine mantel is more than a figurative welcoming gesture. Above the hearth, emblazoned into the rock, is the word, "welcome." On all sides of the lobby are vendor booths offering amenities that include scenic rim, horseback outlaw trail, and buggy rides; covered wagon rides to a chuckwagon dinner and western hoe-down, ATV rides through the Dixie National Forest and plateaus of Bryce Canyon country, van tours throughout the national park, helicopter and bi-plane flights into the heart of the hoodoos, and personal car rentals. Also located in the lobby are a Utah State Liquor store, ATM machines, Foreign Currency Exchange, pre-paid phone cards, safety deposit boxes, and FAX and photo copy machines.

To the left of the lobby is Ruby's General Store, where guests have no problem finding daily needs and tourist supplies. Open daily from 7:00 a.m. to 10:30 p.m., the store offers one of the area's finest selections of fresh produce, meats, grocery items and toiletries. If it is camping, hiking, biking, or automotive supplies one is in need of, Ruby's General Store is likely to have it. And when it comes to souvenirs and photo equipment, the General Store maintains a quality inventory that is bound to please. Ruby's Inn General Store has a wide selection of Western apparel, boots, and hats. They also feature a fine collection of Native American arts and crafts. The Bryce United States Post Office was established at the Inn in 1923, when the Inn was first opened, and still serves the area throughout the year. The post office is located in the General Store.

Behind the lobby and next to the General Store is Ruby's Western Arts Gallery. In all the state there is not a finer collection of Native American pottery, weavings, Kachina dolls, Navajo rugs, and jewelry. Ruby's Western Arts Gallery also exhibits fine art and collectibles of the American West. The gallery is an exclusive dealer of Legends Western Art Sculptures. As an extension of Western Arts Gallery, the walls of the wide hallway between the Main Lodge Lobby and the guest rooms are decorated with original oils and water colors of local artists. Other hall embellishments include sculptures and rare pieces of exquisite petrified wood.

Down the hall on the right side is the Inn's new convention and banquet center. Offering a state of the art sound system and a conscientious catering staff, the Bryce Canyon Conference Center can accommodate as many as 400 people for a sit-down banquet. Break-away folding doors make it possible for several smaller groups to meet at the same time. The Inn's new indoor swimming pool and spa are adjacent to the conference center. Across from the Conference Center are a beauty salon and the area's only one-hour photo service. A seasonal ski shop is also available to winter guests.

To the right of the lobby is Ruby's signature restaurant, Cowboy's Buffet and Steak Room. During summer the restaurant is open 6:30 a.m. to 9:30 p.m. Winter hours are 6:30 a.m. to 8:30 p.m. The Canyon Diner, which features great western fast food, is open 6:30 a.m. to 9:30 p.m., summers only. Both restaurants serve breakfast, lunch and dinner.

Across the street from Ruby's Inn Main Lodge is Old Bryce Town Shops. Built to resemble a Western Frontier Town, the unique shops offer specialized stores that include a rock and gem shop.

Next to the Old Bryce Town Shops are a free Trick Horse Show, an area where guests can pan for gold, and an admission-free petting farm. More information about these guest amenities as well as the Mountain bike rentals and shuttle service is available at the Old Bryce Town Shops.

One of the most popular attractions at Ruby's Inn is the Bryce Canyon Country Rodeo, held at 7:00 p.m., Monday through Saturday from Memorial Day through Labor Day. A mini-rodeo, the show is designed to give guests a sampling of professional rodeo events. Rodeo displays include Bareback Bronco Riding, Bull Riding, Team Roping, Barrel Racing, and Saddle Bronco Riding.

Bryce Canyon American Car Care Center is a welcome sight to area guests. Open year-round, the Center offers full service car care that includes Chevron gas and oil products as well as tune-ups and lubes. Batteries, brake service, mufflers, shocks, struts, and transmission service are also available. Name brand tires such as Michelin, BF Goodrich, Uniroyal and Pirelli are available in sizes to fit cars, trucks, RVs, and tour buses. Electrical and refrigeration experts are on hand to handle the toughest jobs. The Center offers self serve and fully automatic touchless car, bus and RV wash; propane, and a dump station for RVs. Bryce Canyon Towing is on hand to service all of south-central Utah.

Many who come to visit the Southwest bring their homes with them. A quarter of a mile down the road is Ruby's RV Park and Campground. With over 200 shaded campsites, the Park offers full RV hookups, electricity, water, hot showers, a Laundromat, dump site, Indian Tipis, and group and individual tent sites. Recreational amenities include a game room, swimming pool, hot tubs, area for outdoor cookouts, pond that is stocked with trout, and a recreation area with play ground and campfire circle. A Campers Store, open from 7:00 a.m. to 10:00 p.m., is stocked with camping and RV supplies that include bagged ice, firewood, coffee, soft drinks, and picnic supplies.

Bryce Canyon is a year-round attraction and Ruby's Inn is a year-round accommodation. Snowmobiling, cross country skiing, and snowshoeing are increasing in popularity. And where could one experience more spectacular winter vistas than at Bryce Canyon—especially since the roads are kept open inside the park along the rim for winter enjoyment.

Every Presidents' Day weekend in February, Ruby's Inn hosts the Bryce Canyon Winter Festival. This three-day event has something for everyone, including free clinics and hands-on demonstrations, contests and races. Activities include Cross Country ski clinics and races, snowshoe tours and races, photography clinics and contests, ski archery clinics and competition, snow sculpture contest, children's' races, and entertainment.

Ruby's Inn Nordic Center grooms over 30 kilometers of Cross Country ski track for classical and skating techniques. Two Piston Bully groomers keep the tracks in excellent condition. The ski trails start just outside the motel and wind through meadows and forests to the rim of Bryce Canyon National Park. Some of the trails interconnect with the ungroomed ski trails inside the national park. There is no track fee at Ruby's Inn Nordic center. Ski equipment is available for rent at the ski shop in the Main Lodge.

Snowmobiling also begins at Ruby's Inn. Twenty miles of groomed trails wind through the Dixie National Forest to overviews of Bryce Canyon and on to the East Fork/Tropic Reservoir area, a premier snowmobile destination. Snowmobiling is not permitted inside the park. Trail maps and guide service are available at Ruby's Inn.

There can be no question that Ruby's Inn is centrally located for those exploring Bryce Canyon National Park, considered by many to be the jewel of the national parks. But Ruby's Inn is also a central starting point for exploring other scenic attractions. Scenic Byway 12 is the main link to Red Canyon, Kodachrome Basin State Park, Escalante Petrified Forest State Park, Calf Creek Falls and Recreation Area, Anasazi Indian Museum and State Park in Boulder, the Boulder Mountains, Capitol Reef National Park, and the nation's newest national monument, Grand Staircase-Escalante. Southwest of Ruby's Inn and Bryce Canyon are Cedar Breaks National Monument and Zion National Park, both within an easy and exquisitely beautiful two-hour drive.

With all that the Inn has to offer in service, accommodations, and amenities, there is no doubt that a stay at Best Western Ruby's Inn will be a highlight of one's Bryce Canyon and Southwestern Utah vacation.

RESTAURANTS

THE COWBOY CAFE
P. O. Box 640006
13500 East Highway 12
Bryce, Utah 84764
Tel: (435) 834-5351
      (800) 834-0043
FAX: (435) 834-5256
Hrs: April 1 - October 31
Breakfast: 7: 00 a.m. - 11:00 a.m.
Lunch: 11:00 a.m. - 5:00 p.m.
Dinner: 5:00 p.m. - 11:00 p.m.
Visa, MasterCard, American Express, and Discover are accepted.
Reservations are recommended.

    Black silhouettes of lazy cowhands give indication of the interior ambiance of The Cowboy Cafe, located on the premise of Pink Cliffs Village (see related story). Both the Pink Cliffs and the Cowboy Cafe are at the junctions of Scenic Byway 12 and State Highway 63, less than three miles from the entrance to Bryce Canyon National Park.
    Pick up the lazy pace of the silhouettes and saunter on into The Cowboy Cafe for regional cuisine that has been described by many as the best in the West.
    Old antique western paraphernalia that includes saddles and tacks as well as sombreros and serapes decorate this casual cafe. The Cowboy Cafe offers a variety of meals for every appetite with western and Mexican cuisine a specialty.
    Breakfast menu at The Cowboy Cafe includes eggs any style with choice of bacon, eggs, hash browns, and a choice of toast or biscuits. Hotcakes and Biscuits with sausage gravy is a western favorite. No one will ever go wrong when choosing one of the cafe's famous Spanish omelettes.
    Cold sandwiches, all of which are served with a helping of potato salad, include ham, sliced turkey, ham and cheese and tuna fish salad. A pseudo cold sandwich of bacon, lettuce and tomato is served on a choice of toasted bread. Triple decker club sandwiches, served with a choice of French fries or potato salad, are ham and cheese, turkey and cheese, and turkey, bacon, and cheese. Hot sandwiches served with mashed potatoes include turkey, beef, and ground steak. Hamburgers, cheeseburgers, bacon cheeseburgers, and chili size burgers are served with or without an order of French fries or onion rings.
    Youngsters have not been overlooked at The Cowboy Cafe. Favorites, such as chicken nuggets, grilled cheese, hot dog, and fried fish fillets, are served all at the same low price. Each menu item includes a small fountain drink, French fries, and dessert.
    The Cowboy Cafe is well known in the area for its two daily specials. They are good enough that they keep guests returning, just so they won't miss out on the next day's offerings.
    Dinner selections would not be complete in the West without an offering of broiled New York, Ribeye, and T-Bone steaks. Favorites from the grill are Chicken Fried Steak, Roast Beef, Liver and Onions, and Pork Chops. A favorite fish entree comes not from the sea but from the sparkling streams and lakes of Utah mountains. No one should visit Utah without trying its Rainbow Trout. At The Cowboy Cafe the trout is grilled to perfection and second to none. Seafood favorites include Deep-fried Cat Fish Fillets

and Jumbo Shrimp. The Surf & Turf includes a six-ounce steak with three shrimp. All of the above entrees are served with fresh homemade soup or salad, choice of potatoes, and fresh hot dinner rolls.

Served from South of the border are three cheese and onion enchiladas, three beef enchiladas, or three tacos. Mexican entrees are topped with lettuce, tomatoes, and cheese and served with rice and beans.

The Cowboy Cafe is a Utah State Liquor licensee with a bar and serves domestic, imported, and draft beers, wine by the glass, liter and one-half liter, and cocktails.

Whether staying at Pink Cliffs Village or enroute to or from the many national parks and monuments that dot Southwestern Utah, The Cowboy Cafe has a relaxing atmosphere for enjoying great food at reasonable prices.

ANTIMONY

Antimony, established as a permanent settlement in 1878, carried the name Coyote until 1921, when residents voted to rename their community Antimony after the metal that has been mined in the area since 1880.

Antimony is approximately 48 miles directly north of Bryce Canyon National Park and 42 miles off Scenic Byway 12 on U-22.

The town's original name came about as the result of a peace-keeping mission with the Fish Lake Indians. Twenty-two men arrived here in 1873 to meet the Indians at Cedar Grove near Koosharem. While near the present site of Antimony, the men caught and earmarked several coyote pups. This incident led to naming the area, Coyote.

Although the meadows surrounding Antimony were used for grazing as early as 1873, the first families did not homestead the valley until 1878. When antimony, a metal used in alloys, was discovered two years later in 1880, Coyote/Antimony became a mining community as well as a ranching town.

Today Antimony, one of the last real western frontiers, has gained world-wide reputation as home to the Rockin'R Ranch, an authentic "Old West" working cattle ranch (see related story).

ANTIMONY ATTRACTIONS

OTTER CREEK STATE PARK

Four miles north of Antimony on State Route 22, Otter Creek Reservoir is one of the area's most popular fishing and boating sites. In addition to a 3,120-acre reservoir, Otter Creek State Park offers camping and picnicking units, modern rest rooms with hot showers, fish cleaning and sewage disposal stations, boat launching ramp and courtesy docks (435-624-3268).

PIUTE STATE PARK

Another popular site for boating, fishing, camping, rock hounding and waterfowl hunting in season is Piute State Park. This 3,360-acre mountain lake is approximately 12 miles northwest of Antimony. Take Route 22 west to U.S. 89 north. Although facilities are primitive, the park is open year-round for trophy fishing.

RESORTS

ROCKIN'R RANCH
Antimony, Utah
Reservation Office
10274 Eastdell Drive
Sandy, Utah 84092
Tel: (801) 733-9538
FAX: (801) 942-2680
Web Site:
www.infowest.com/rockin
Email:
rockinr@infowest.com.
Visa and MasterCard are accepted.

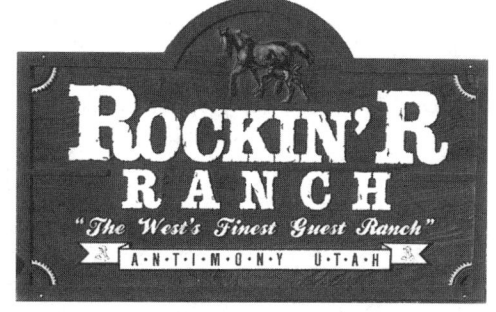

Embedded in the heart of most Americans is a deep-seated desire to saddle up, ride the range, and recapture an era that most have only dreamed about. Long before space took over as the last frontier, the West was where dreams came true.

The world renowned Rockin'R Ranch, located in the Color Country rural town of Antimony, is an authentic "Old West" working cattle ranch. Here, real live cowboys still do the work one has only conceptualized and guests have the chance to participate if they desire.

Rockin'R Ranch offers guests an impressive three-story Ponderosa Pine lodge with 37 private guest rooms. In addition there are four cabins and four new rooms above the Tack shed for a total of 45 guest rooms. All of the guest rooms have pine furniture and many have furnishings that are rough hewn aspen, cedar, and pine, very reminiscent of the old West. Nine of the rooms have one regular or one queen bed. The cabins have two queen beds and a bunkbed, sleeping facilities that accommodate six. The remainder of the guest rooms have either double or queen beds. A number of the rooms have ceiling fans. Thirty of the bathrooms have showers only; 15 have tubs with showers and separate vanity basins. Many of the rooms enter from the outside from a wrap-around deck.

While rooms are comfortably rustic, the lodge itself is nothing less than majestic. Entrance is through double doors with cut glass windows and two large round windows, one on each side. Upon entering the lobby one cannot help being impressed with the magnitude and spaciousness of the vestibule. Completely open, a marvelous rock fountain lends the feel and sound of a mountain stream. On the south side of the lobby are a combined gift shop and ice cream saloon. Beyond the fountain it is three steps up to a second antechamber, this one filled with marvelous Ponderosa pine support beams, some of which still have stub branches. In one of the branches a mountain lion lurks menacingly, crouched for the kill. Walls are bedecked with elk and deer heads. An open stairwell of rustic half logs leads to the second floor.

Rockin'R Ranch, located in the heart of Utah's Color Country, is an ideal place to stay when visiting many of Southwestern Utah's national parks, monuments, and recreation areas. Bryce Canyon National Park is 45 minutes south. Grand Staircase-Escalante National Monument, and Escalante Petrified Forest State Park are an hour's drive to the southeast. Capitol Reef National Park, Cedar Breaks National Monument, and the Anasazi Indian Village are all 90 minutes from the Ranch. Zion National Park is a two-hour drive. The North Rim of the Grand Canyon and Lake Powell in Glen Canyon National Recreation Area are within three-hour drives.

Exciting and enticing as these natural scenic wonders are, one of the features that sets the Rockin'R Ranch apart from other accommodations is that the ranch, with its many cowboy experiences, is itself a destination vacation.

Work at the Rockin'R Ranch is a choice, not a requirement. Since the ranch encompasses over 1,000 acres of meadows and fields with another 40,000 acres of high mountain land leased for grazing, the work of branding cattle and cattle roundups must go on. Guests are invited to participate in such activities as riding the fence, herd riding, and calf roping. For those who have not mastered the arts of calf roping and horseback riding there are clinics and lessons for beginners, intermediate, and advanced cowhands. Guests can also learn how to brush, feed and saddle the horses.

For those more exuberant cowhands, who relish the glamour more than the mundane, there are horse relays, barrel racing, pole bending, and rides in an authentic stage coach. In addition, guests can swim, not in the traditional motel swimming pool, but in the ranch's "ol' swimmin' hole." There are lakes and streams where the fishing is terrific. When blue azure skies give way to crimson and coral as the sun sets behind flaming sandstone ridges, campfires are lit and Western dancing and entertainment begin. Guests also appreciate the wealth of historical and cultural history imparted by extremely knowledgeable staff.

Occasionally, guests at the Rockin'R Ranch prefer to simply loaf. Since none of the ranch activities are obligatory, kicking back and doing nothing is sanctioned. To accommodate those desires, the Rockin'R Ranch has provided its guests with a marvelous hot tub, game room with billiards, a library or quiet room, a large outdoor patio for sunning, an exercise room, a gift shop, and an ice cream parlor.

One of the nicest benefits of a stay at the Rockin'R Ranch is that all of the above activities can be arranged as an all-inclusive package. That package includes hearty ranch breakfasts, lunch, and dinner served daily in the ranch restaurant. There is no minimum stay required, but a multi-day stay of at least three days is encouraged so as to be able to do all that Rockin'R Ranch has to offer.

The Rockin'R Ranch also offers Cattle Drives, Round-ups, and Multi-day Exotic Mountain Trail Rides that are great for individuals, couples and small families. To find out more about these packages, check the Rockin'R Ranch web site, listed at the top of the story, or call or write for a brochure.

Rockin'R Ranch is also an ideal facility for business conventions and seminars, family reunions, youth and young adult conferences, and club gatherings and getaways.

The Black family, owners of the Rockin'R Ranch, has been ranching this very same land since the 1870's. During those 120-plus years little has changed. The land is as urban and as "real old west" as a ranch can be. Almost 100 years after the Blacks first homesteaded the property, the family unanimously agreed that what they had should be shared with others. In the 1970's Rockin'R Ranch opened its heart and its doors to cowboy "wannabes" from around the world.

The Rockin'R Ranch, with its exceptional location and extraordinary amenities, is like no other place in the West. At the Rockin'R Ranch, *dreams do come true*.

ATTRACTIONS

From the Rockin'R Ranch, in order to continue with visiting the many natural wonders that Southern Utah has to offer, one returns back towards Bryce Canyon National Park and, if they have not yet visited Bryce, makes that their number one priority before heading West on Scenic Byway 12 to the Red Canyon in Dixie National Forest.

RED CANYON

Red Canyon, a fascinating area that is mistaken by many to be Bryce Canyon, is approximately seven miles west of Bryce on Scenic Byway 12.

Whether one's interest is photography, sightseeing, geology, or botany, Red Canyon, with its spectacular colors, beautiful formations, and plants that are unique to this area, has something for everyone.

Cassidy Trail, an 8.7-mile horse and foot trail, passes through scenic red rock country and offers adventurers the chance to discover stands of old-growth ponderosa pine. Sections of the trail are believed to have been used by Butch Cassidy, the infamous outlaw. As there are no drinking water sources on this one to two-day hiking trail, hikers are admonished to bring an ample supply of water. The trail for hikers is easy, moderate and strenuous. If on horse, the trip from the mouth of Red Canyon to Casto Canyon takes six to seven hours of steady horseback riding.

One of the most colorful trails in Red Canyon, **Tunnel Trail**, is seven-tenths of a mile and begins along the highway near one of the Canyon's two short tunnels. Allow one-half to one hour for this moderate foot trail.

Golden Wall Trail is a little over one mile up the bottom of a canyon on an easy-to-walk trail. **Castle Bridge Trail**, a little over one-half mile, offers spectacular scenery and unique red rock formations. There are sections of trail switchbacks in moderately steep terrain. **Birdseye Trail,** which offers a birdseye view of this spectacular area, begins at the visitor center and travels into the vivid pink and scarlet rock formations of Red Canyon. All of the above are for foot traffic only.

Pink Ledges Trail, also for foot traffic only, is one-half mile, begins at the visitor center, and winds through some of the most unique formations in the canyon. The one-mile **Buckhorn Trail** begins at the Red Canyon Campground and ascends to a vantage point high above the canyon.

Casto Canyon Trail begins at the mouth of Casto Canyon and connects with the **Cassidy Trail**. The 5.3-mile trail is considered the most scenic of all the large canyons in Red Canyon. The trail lies in the bottom of the canyon and is for foot, horse, and ORV travel.

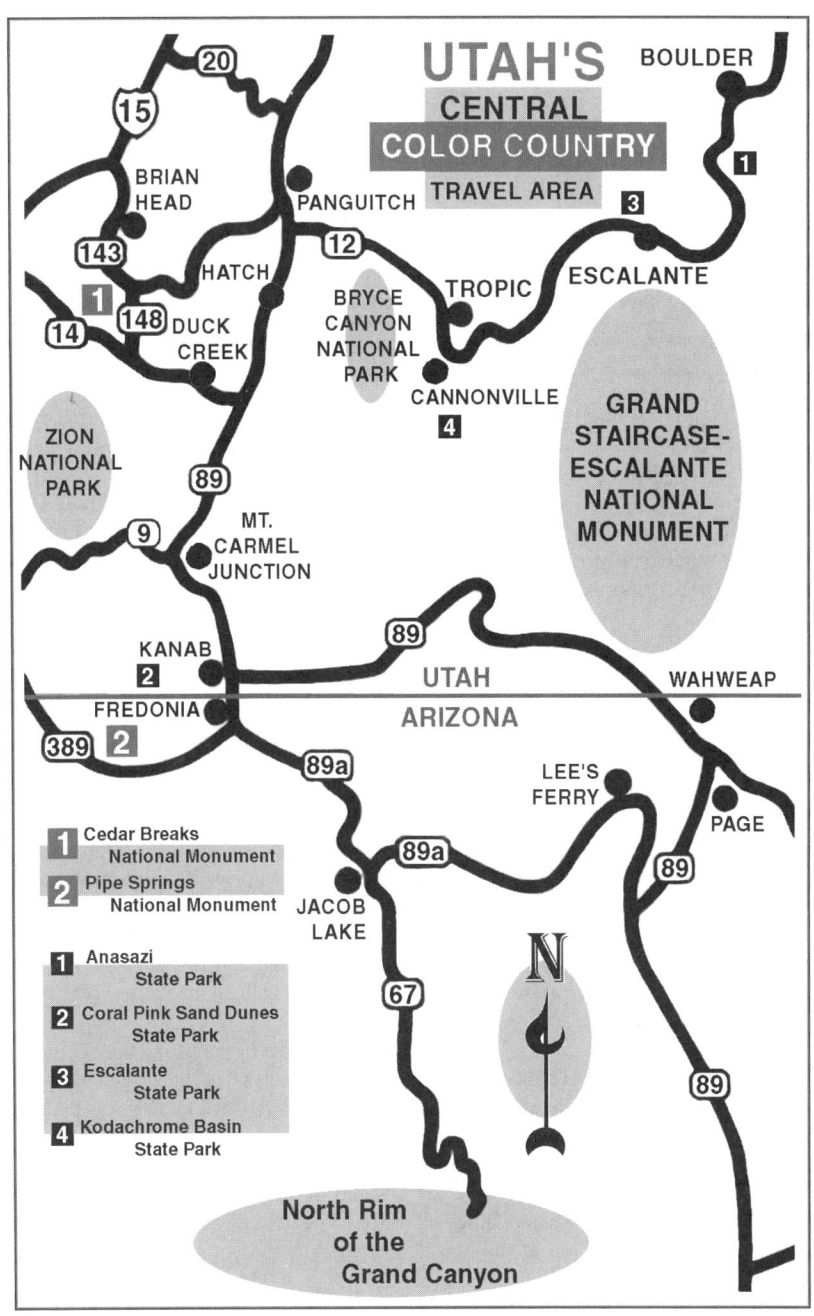

The three-mile **Losee Canyon Trail** is for horse and foot traffic and traverses the bottom of Losee Canyon. The trail connects with Cassidy Trail, allowing adventurers to go north to Casto Canyon or south to Red Canyon.

Ledge Point Trail, a short horse and foot trail, travels through old growth ponderosa pine to a ledge point that overlooks Red Canyon to the south. **Rich Trail** can be used in conjunction with the Cassidy Trail for longer or shorter hikes or rides.

Red Canyon, located within the **Dixie National Forest**, has a visitor center with restrooms, medical first aid, and general information. Tent and trailer camping facilities are available on a first-come, first served basis at the **Red Canyon Campground**. Campsites have picnic tables, fireplaces, water and restrooms. There are no hookups. Camping is limited to 14 days in any calendar year. A fee is charged.

PANGUITCH

After passing through the spectacular scenery of Red Canyon in the Dixie National Forest, one comes to the end of Scenic Byway 12 and approaches the beginning of yet another byway, Scenic Byway 89. Although the byway actually begins at the Junction of U-12 and 89, heading South to Kanab, in this book we backtrack seven miles to the Garfield County seat, Panguitch, and its rich pioneer heritage.

Strategically located in the heart of Southern Utah's famous Color Country, Panguitch was, from its raw beginnings as a small Mormon farming settlement, destined for success. Utah's state symbol is the Beehive for industry. The Mormon pioneers who settled the Panguitch area in March of 1864 were industrious, hardy, and persevering. Were it not so they would not have survived.

That first year in Panguitch was not kind to its new settlers. The crops that were planted in early spring failed. The first winter was exceptionally cold, biting, and hard. There was no food and the settlers were hungry. In an effort to save their families, seven men set out for Parowan, 40 miles to the West, to secure flour. But the snow was so deep that the men had to abandon their oxen and wagons. It seemed they were destined for failure. The hand of providence intervened and the men hit upon an idea. Unfolding the quilts they had brought with them, the men placed a quilt on the snow, walked to the end of it, placed another quilt in front of it, stepped onto it and retrieved the first quilt while they walked to the end of the second. By doing this repetitively and with perseverance they made it to Parowan, got the flour, and saved Panguitch from starvation. This Herculean accomplishment is celebrated in Panguitch as the **"Panguitch Quilt Walk."**

Panguitch residents are grateful for their pioneer heritage and they delight in telling the story of their brick homes. During the Black Hawk War Panguitch was abandoned, but it was resettled in 1871. As the settlement grew, a brick factory was built and most in the community subsidized their farming income by working at the mill. But they weren't paid in money, the workers were paid in bricks. By so doing the townspeople were able to build themselves large, beautiful brick homes, most of which are still standing today. English and Dutch as well as Victorian designs were incorporated into the architecture. Many of the homes are replete with "gingerbread," Dixie dormers, Queen Anne bay windows, and other decorative work and filigree.

In addition to the many fine homes that were built, a Social Hall, Courthouse, and Bishop's Storehouse (now a Pioneer Museum) were built of the extra thick bricks fired in the East Panguitch kiln. In 1908, Andrew Carnegie, who was donating money to communities across the country for libraries, donated money to Panguitch on the condition that once the library was built, the community would maintain it. These buildings and many more are still in use today. A walking tour pamphlet of historical Panguitch is available throughout the town.

Today Panguitch, a thriving town of close to 1,600, flourishes with tourism as its main source of income. The city boasts several fine motels, RV campgrounds, bed & breakfasts, restaurants, gift shops, and all other guest services and amenities. Regardless of the season, Panguitch is ideally situated for the enjoyment of such outdoor activities as fishing, hunting, boating, camping, biking, hiking, and sightseeing, or, during winter, cross-country skiing, snowmobiling, and skiing at nearby Brian Head Ski Resort.

ACCOMMODATIONS

BEST WESTERN NEW WESTERN MOTEL
2nd East Center Street
P. O. Box 73
Panguitch, Utah 84759
Tel: (435) 676-8876
         (800) 528-1234
FAX: (435) 676-8876, extension 165
Visa, MasterCard, American Express, Diners Club, Carte Blanche, and Discover are accepted.
Reservations are recommended.

There is nothing misleading about the name, Best Western "New Western" Motel. From its carpets to its bedding, its furnishings, and its wall decor, the Best Western New Western Motel is kept, not just immaculately clean, but fastidiously up to date. Although parts of the motel are over 30 years old, while others are seven and some only four, all rooms look modern and new in every detail.

Gary and Coleen Orton took over the 55-room motel in 1982 when Coleen's mother passed away. Since then, every effort has been made to ensure that guests, no matter what parts of the world they are from, feel comfortable and at home.

Guest amenities include a beautiful fenced in outdoor pool with spacious decks for lounging. Above the privacy wall is a quaint picket fence with lantern lights for romantic evening swims. The large tile Jacuzzi, which will comfortably seat 15 guests, is enclosed in a garden-like setting with ample chairs and tables. A sliding glass door opens to an outside deck with lounge chairs. A Laundromat is provided for guest convenience. Smoking and non-smoking rooms are available at the Best Western New Western Motel.

Because rooms are constantly being modernized and updated, there are several configurations and a variety of color schemes. But in every room a woman's caring touch is evident. All rooms have remote control color cable TV with HBO and ESPN, direct dial phones with local calls free, and scenic wall hangings of the area. Most rooms are either wall-papered or painted in light modern pastels that enhance the room's carpet and decor.

Several rooms, with a color scheme of burgundy, forest green, mauve and blue, have a king bed, two easy chairs with table, two night stands, floor and table lamps, and an elegant armoire. Mauve and blue floral wallpaper decorator trim adorns the top of the wall. The bathroom has a large shower with decorator tiles and separate wash basin vanity.

Another room configuration, with a color scheme of light mauve, teal and burgundy, also offers a king bed, desk with chair, enclosed TV, wallpaper border below the ceiling, and decorator tiles on the shower walls.

Families and groups traveling together enjoy the two-room arrangement. A first room has a lovely sofa sleeper in light teal, burgundy and tan, queen bed, and elegant walnut furniture. A second bedroom has a queen bed, large closet, walnut furnishings, and bath with tub and shower and separate vanity basin. Carpet throughout is a lush deep blue and burgundy.

Another family unit has a room with burgundy carpet, mauve chairs, queen bed, two end tables, an enclosed TV, and an alcove seating area with table and two chairs. The bathroom has a tub with shower and separate vanity. It adjoins a second room with the same decor and amenities.

Guests who plan to stay awhile appreciate "the house." One large bedroom has two queen beds, an end table, large dresser, a table with two chairs, overhead lighting and lamps. Off the bedroom is a sitting room with hide-a-bed couch, TV, table with two chairs, a closet with love seat, and a mini refrigerator. A large bathroom has a tub with shower and a commodious vanity basin. A second bedroom has a queen bed with two end tables, built in drawers, two chairs, a second TV, and a clock radio. A subsequent bathroom has tub with shower and two vanities, one with basin and one without. The house is beautifully wall-papered. The carpet throughout is a rich burgundy.

The Best Western New Western Motel is located on both sides of Center Street. Across the street from the lobby, the rooms are even more spacious. Several offer double queen beds, an armoire, desk dresser, table with two chairs, and wall, ceiling and table lamps. Bathrooms are roomy, have a tub with shower, and a large separate vanity.

Rooms with a single king bed offer two easy chairs and walnut furnishings that include a dresser, enclosed TV with drawers beneath, and two end tables. Rooms are beautifully papered with wallpaper border below the ceiling. There are two vanity basins, one in the bathroom that has a tub with shower and one in the dressing room where there is also a full length mirror.

In addition to their standard rooms, the Best Western New Western Motel offers three rooms for the physically impaired. All are especially roomy for easy movement and have lots of extra room in the bathrooms, where everything is in place for the wheel-chair bound. All have two queen beds and blonde furnishings that include a desk, table with two chairs and a night stand. Two of the rooms have tub with shower and two vanity basins, one in the bathroom and one without; the other room has a roll in shower.

Without a doubt, the Best Western New Western Motel is a traveler's choice when visiting Bryce Canyon National Park, a beautiful 24-mile drive to the southeast. Cedar Breaks National Monument is 32 miles and Zion National Park 74 miles to the southwest. The boundary of the nation's newest national monument, Grand Staircase-Escalante, along Scenic Byway 12, is only 25 miles to the southeast. Other area attractions include Dixie National Forest, Panguitch Lake, Red Canyon, and Brian Head Ski Resort.

There are so many things to see and do in Utah's Color Country, that regardless of how long one had planned to stay, the desire will be there to remain a little longer. The triple A-approved Best Western New Western Motel, with all the creature comforts of home, makes that stay even more enjoyable.

ROCKING HORSE INN

2762 North Highway 89
Panguitch, Utah 84759
Tel: (435) 676-2287
              (435) 676-2682
Season   April 1 - October 31
Reservations are recommended.

Rocking Horse Inn, located three miles north of Panguitch on Highway 89, is a small, six-unit economy inn with a variety of amenities that beckons families. Two of the six rooms have kitchenettes. A large play area provides guests with activities that include horse shoes and a nine-hole miniature golf course.

Julianne and Lee Mullenaux, manager-owners, admit that there is nothing fancy about their facility. But the Inn has an eclectic charm and unique family features that bring guests back for return visits. To those features, Julianne and Lee add personal attention to make sure that guests enjoy their stay. They also keep the rooms spotlessly clean and the yard well groomed.

The yard, without a doubt, is the Rocking Horse Inn's biggest drawing card. When something has been lovingly created for one's children and grandchildren, it has to be the best. Twenty-three years ago, when J. J. Cook and his wife, Rose Marie, purchased the property, it was a disaster. Previous to being deserted, a semi truck had crashed into the front and doors were left open for sheep to seek refuge. The Cooks gutted the entire complex and began a lengthy restoration process, preparing a place for their children and their children's children to stay when they came for visits.

The Cooks, over the years, took great pains to make sure that when the family came, there would be no boredom. Almost as much fun as the nine-hole golf course are the ten rules that accompany one's score card. A sample is rule #1 which reads: *Repair all divots by placing a $1 bill under each. It doesn't improve the grass but we can use the green!*

In addition to the backyard golf course there is a wonderful fountain and pool with redwood bridge. There are picnic tables, double shuffle board, basket ball court, horseshoe pit, swings, old fashioned teeter totters, net set-up for badminton, and games of croquet. Hammocks between the shade trees provide lazy-day relaxation. There is also a unique covered patio that houses a barbecue, lawn swing, couch, and table with chairs.

Another favorite with the Cook grandchildren, and now with Rocking Horse Inn guests, is the authentic Indian Teepee in front of the inn with Western and Indian scenes hand-painted by J. J. Cook.

Five years ago, when Julianne and Lee moved back to Utah from California with three of their children, the Cook family reunion complex was opened to the public as the Rocking Horse Inn. The Inn received its name because of the marvelous custom rocking horses that Lee makes in his spare time.

All of the individual guest rooms have a regular bed, individually controlled heat, Color TV, small closet, and bathroom with shower. Since this is the West, several of the rooms reflect a Western ambiance. Western Room #1 has pictures of wolves, horse statuettes, and a mirror with horses. Western Room #2 has a duplicate mirror with horses and bull's horns on the wall. The Spanish Room is decorated with mirrors and conquistador statues.

The first family unit has two bedrooms, one with a regular bed and two twins, the second with a king bed, two twins, and a crib. The kitchenette has a full refrigerator, sink, stove and table with chairs. There is one bathroom with a shower.

A second family unit, called the Fireplace Room, has a regular bed, sofa bed, a fold-away bed, and, best of all, a wood-burning fireplace.

From the Rocking Horse Inn it is little more than a 25-minute drive to one of Utah's most acclaimed national parks, Bryce Canyon. Other natural splendors within easy drives include the nation's newest national monument, Grand Staircase-Escalante, Cedar Breaks National Monument, the beautiful Red Canyon in the Dixie National Forest, and Zion National Park. Panguitch Lake, for boating, fishing, and water skiing, is a short, 20 minutes away from the Inn. Going to and from these scenic wonders are several other attractions and state parks.

If economy, personal care, and family fun are important factors when seeking accommodations for that next visit to Utah's Color Country, the Rocking Horse Inn, with its many family activities, is the perfect place to stay.

BRYCE CANYON'S WESTERN TOWN
Motel-Restaurant-Gift Shop-Western Movie Collection Museum

Crossroads of Highways 89 and 12
3800 South Highway 89
Panguitch, Utah 84759
Tel: (435) 676-8770
FAX   (435) 676-8771
Web Site:
wwwonpages.com/westerntown

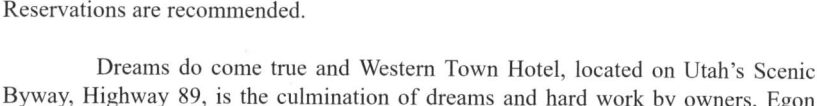

Visa, MasterCard, American Express, and Discover are accepted.
Reservations are recommended.

Dreams do come true and Western Town Hotel, located on Utah's Scenic Byway, Highway 89, is the culmination of dreams and hard work by owners, Egon Boldt, Fred Levin, and Layne Cannon.

For years Egon had been bringing people from all over the world to the Bryce Canyon area for other business reasons, but he had always envisioned an authentic western town, offering real western hospitality to visitors from around the world. Like the movie, *"Field of Dreams,"* Egon knew that if he could build it, they would come. After a separation of 30 years, good friends Egon and Fred were re-united and, to Egon's surprise, he discovered that Fred had a similar dream. The match was made and through the financial support of another friend, Layne, the dream became reality. Tony Krueletz, a retired western movie stuntman, joined the team with his collection of movie memorabilia.

Because of their dedication to making Western Town a reality, the dreams of thousands around the world, who fantasize about being a part of a real American western town, can also come true.

Egon and Fred, who both grew up in Germany, know how real the fantasy can be. To many Europeans, America is cowboys and Indians. Western Town gives everyone the chance to be a part of the American frontier. The owners, because of their heritage, speak and can greet guests in several languages. They also offer personalized service in the universal language of caring to those traveling alone or in tour groups.

In March of 1997 Western Town was nothing more than cleared and leveled ground on a section of Highway 89 that is only 15 minutes from one of Utah's natural phenomena, Bryce Canyon National Park. By the beginning of August there were seven frontier buildings, each with its own unique facade, making up the 56-unit hotel complex. Adding to the nostalgic aura of the property is the fact that Western Town is built on the first pioneer road that linked Panguitch and Kanab. The grounds are dotted with antique pioneer and farming equipment as well as a stage coach and chuck wagon from the John Wayne movie, *Red River*, the "snake oil" wagon from Lee Marvin's *Paint Your Wagon*, and props from many other western movie sets.

In addition to the modern, comfortable western rooms, the 126-acre complex offers a Cowboy Kitchen, horseback and ATV trail rides, petting farm, self-guided tours, gift shop, 12-person covered wagon Jacuzzi, and a museum.

Maybe Western Town is "just pretend." It is not likely, at least for the present, that a sheriff and his posse will come riding into town or that guests will hear the war cry as Indian warriors appear at the crest of the hill to attack. But the owners, in a quest for realism, have gone the extra mile to create the feeling of a real Western Town.

The sound of footsteps on the boardwalks and the hitching posts and overhangs on each of the seven units clearly look and feel as if one has gone back in time to the 1800's. Floors in the spacious 14 by 28 foot rooms are beautiful knotty pine. The rooms are furnished with massive-looking western furniture and decorated with an impressive old west ambiance. All rooms, except for the four for the physically impaired, offer double queen beds. Rooms have telephones with local calls free, tub/shower combinations, separate vanity wash basin, ceiling fans, and air conditioning. A highlight of a Western Town experience can be the absence of televisions in the room as guests relearn the arts of communicating, reading, or gazing at a star-filled sky. But for those few who need to be entertained, Western Town can provide a VCR, TV screen, and free videos.

Rooms for the physically impaired are furnished with one queen bed, allowing for extra mobility. Vanity basins have been thoughtfully placed with the wheelchair-bound in mind and bathtubs have hand bars and a hand-held shower for safety and convenience. Rooms have doors to an adjoining room for those traveling with the impaired.

A group of physically impaired Nephi residents are responsible for the marvelous pine benches that grace the boardwalks of each unit. These same bench-types are used as additional seating in most of the rooms.

Of special interest to guests is the Western Town Museum, which houses the Tony Krueletz Elk Horn Movie Ranch Collection. Tony was a western movie stuntman who amassed over a million dollars worth of western movie memorabilia from many of the famous western stars, including John Wayne. Krueletz has also been able to acquire saddles from real live outlaws, such as Butch Cassidy and Pancho Viva. The museum, housed in a 50 by 120-foot steel Quonset building, is truly like walking into a western town. Replicated are the facades of the authentic Colorado Leadville Bar, a blacksmith shop, bank, jail, millinery, general store, doctor's office, dentist, beauty shop and other 19th century businesses of the day. In addition to the Elk Horn Movie Ranch Collection, the museum shows era clothing, guns, farm implements, and saddles.

Until the restaurant is completed, Western Town guests and the public are invited to the Cowboy Kitchen to join in the camaraderie that only a Dutch Oven cookout can create. Under a massive canvas canopy guests can enjoy a continental breakfast of muffins and bagels, cereal, juices, milk, and coffee, tea and milk. For lunch, the Cowboy Kitchen creates a good selection of sandwiches and the best Bratwurst this side of the Atlantic. Steaks or Dutch Oven dishes of barbecued chicken or beef, baked beans, potatoes with onions and bacon, vegetable, salad bar, hot breads or rolls, coffee, soda, and dessert, make for memorable dining.

    No vacation would be complete without a souvenir memento of the trip. The gift shop is housed in what was the oldest log cabin in Panguitch until it was recently moved to Western Town. It offers a full selection of artifacts and memorabilia. The gift shop features silver jewelry creations of the Hopi, Navajo, and Zuni, who have extended their expertise to include fine craftsmanship with blue lapis, denim lapis, sugulite opal, black onyx, amalekite, and spiny oyster shell, as well as the traditional semi-precious stones of turquoise, coral, and mother of pearl. Western Town gift shop offers shoppers a tremendous selection of rings, bracelets, necklaces, barrettes, money clips, key chains, bolero tie, belt buckles, and watch bands. Western Town also stocks a good selection of liquid gold necklaces in both silver and gold, the newest sensation from Native American artisans. Pottery, created by the Hickory, Apache, and Navajo, are in every size, color and shape. Other gifts include rugs, dream catchers, Mandellas, war bonnets, story teller dolls, beadwork, Kachina dolls, sand paintings, baskets, bows and arrows, carved fetishes, hand made petroglyphs, and spear and arrow heads. Western Town is especially pleased with what shoppers are calling the "Grandparent's Corner." Here guests will find a nice selection of hand made gifts from local residents. Among the selection are full size quilts, baby quilts, candles, candies, jellies, jams, and honey. Western Town Gift Shop has one of the state's finest selections of cowboy wear, western saddles, statues, and polished rocks. In addition, the gift shop offers a full line of inexpensive logo and regional souvenir items.

    Children and adults visiting Western Town adore the burros, llamas, miniature donkeys and horses in the Petting Farm. But at Western Town the animals aren't just for petting. Western Town staff are happy to let the children ride—at no cost.

    In addition to being only 15 minutes to Bryce Canyon, Western Town is a 45 minute drive to Grand Staircase-Escalante National Monument and Zion National Park and two hours to the North Rim of the Grand Canyon, Lake Powell, and Capitol Reef National Park.

    Today there are no cowboys, posses, or Indian warriors at Western Town but, looking into the future, if the owners' dreams continue to be fulfilled, anything is possible. Western Town staff are there to do whatever they can to help guests feel a part of the western experience. After all, the best part of dreaming is being an active part of the dream and making others' dreams come true.

DID YOU KNOW?

    ---that just five and one-half miles south of Panguitch Lake is one of two hidden treasures--**Mammoth Springs.** Though the last two miles are gravel road, the trip is worth the effort. Moss and an abundance of other streamside vegetation surround this crystal clear spring. There is a foot bridge that leads across the stream to the spring. **Mammoth Cave**, the second hidden treasure, is approximately 9 miles south of the springs. The caves are the result of a lava flow and are called lava tubes. Mammoth Cave was discovered as the result of a cave-in. There are two tunnels, the lower of which goes back beyond the large entrance for one-fourth mile. To explore beyond that or to check out other sections, one has to stoop or crawl. The caves are extremely dark and it is recommended that spelunkers bring at least two reliable flashlights.

BED & BREAKFASTS

L & L BED & BREAKFAST
1026 North, 700 West
Panguitch, Utah 84759
Tel: (435) 676-2228
Web Site:
www.color-country.net/landl/index.html
Reservations are requested.

Once in a while one discovers an accommodation that is so out of the ordinary that one knows the proprietors have cared enough to give their very best. Such is the case with L & L Bed & Breakfast, owned and operated by Linda and Larry Mrkvicka.

L & L Bed & Breakfast is not a home converted into a bed and breakfast, it is a home that was built for the very purpose of being able to offer pampered guest services in a setting of tranquillity and seclusion.

Nestled in the high mountain valley overlooking the small, rural town of Panguitch, L & L Bed & Breakfast has an enviable location. Not only does the vista encompass the entire valley but the red rock sandstone cliffs beyond. When the sun sets, the eastern sky and mountain range are bathed in an explosion of red, coral, and lavender.

Another facet that makes L & L Bed & Breakfast a superb location, is its proximity to Bryce Canyon National Park. The park is a beautiful twenty mile drive to the southeast. Other parks and scenic attractions within an easy drive are Grand Staircase-Escalante National Monument, Kodachrome Basin State Park, Panguitch Lake, Cedar Breaks National Monument, and Zion National Park.

L & L Bed & Breakfast has three distinctively different rooms for specific tastes and needs. Two of the rooms, The Blue Rose Room and the Victorian Room are on the home's main floor.

The Blue Rose Room offers elegant walnut furniture and two twin poster beds with bedding in a blue rose motif. The blue rose decor is also carried out in the private bathroom, located across the hall, which has a sit-down shower.

The Victorian Room has an exquisite cherry wood four-poster queen bed, brass lamp, and rocking chair with Victorian doll. The four posters are entwined with ivy. The queen bed is topped with an elegant white lace comforter with matching shams and dust ruffle. Silk floral arrangements and Victorian family pictures and art adorn the walls.

As one leaves the main floor they step down into what can only be described as the greatest of all Great Rooms. The feeling, as one enters this lodge-like room, is one of awe. The vaulted open beam ceiling and the floor to ceiling rock fireplace add credence to the room's sheer magnitude. For one's recreational pleasure there is a large screen TV with 100's of channels from which to choose, a telescope for bird watching and gazing at the stars, a pool table, several chess sets, and a foos ball game. Two easy chairs and a sofa have been ideally arranged for casual conversation. A sofa and loveseat surround the fireplace.

From the Great Room one exits to a covered and uncovered patio where amenities include a barbecue pit and horse shoes.

Just off the Great Room is the Rustic Room. The modified canopy bed has rustic pine posters, a hand knit bed cover with outdoor scene, rustic nightstand and chair, and Western art and silk floral arrangements on the wall. This room, set off from the others, offers lights that dim for extra mood magic. It is ideal for honeymooners and those interested in keeping the love light burning. The private bath is decorated with accents of blue and has a tub with shower.

All rooms are provided with French milled soaps and other toiletries and extra pillows for the beds.

Breakfast, served from 7:00 to 9:00 a.m., includes yogurt, granola, choice of hot beverage and juice, muffins, and fresh fruit. Upon check-in, guests can specify whether or not they want a hot breakfast. When desired by guests, breakfast can include pancakes, French toast, or Linda's famous egg and cheese casserole. Breakfast is served in the Sun Room, a solarium off the kitchen that is decorated with sunflowers, a wicker table, and chairs.

Linda, a hair stylist, owns Linda's Beauty and Barber Shop which is also located on premise. Most of the time she can accommodate guests with haircuts, styles, perms and other beauty needs.

L & L Bed & Breakfast, in spite of its secluded location, is very easy to find. When coming from the north on Highway 89, look for the "Welcome to Garfield County" sign and turn right at the street just south of the blue storage buildings. When traveling from the south, stay on Highway 89, pass through the town of Panguitch, and turn left at the road just before the blue storage buildings. From either direction, L & L Bed & Breakfast is one mile off Highway 89 on a well-maintained country road.

L & L Bed & Breakfast may be a little out of the way but, just like the poem, *The Road Less Traveled By*, those who take the country road to L & L Bed & Breakfast find it is well worth the effort.

MAE MAE'S BED & BREAKFAST

501 East Center Street
(Highway 89)
Panguitch, Utah 84759
Tel: (435) 676-2388
         (800) 550-2388
Open:
April 1 - November 1
Visa and MasterCard are accepted.
Reservations are recommended.

Mae Mae is the name lovingly given to Nida Mae Jensen by younger siblings who couldn't pronounce her first name. The name seemed to ring true and today, all those who know and love Nida Mae call her Mae Mae.

Douglas and Mae Mae Jensen, owners, are host and hostess at Mae Mae's Bed & Breakfast, the first brick home to be built outside of old Fort Panguitch. Their invitation to all who visit them is "Come as a stranger, but leave as a friend."

There is no question, based on guest comments, that all who enter the doors of Mae Mae's Bed & Breakfast not only leave knowing that they want to return as soon as they can, but leave with two new friends in Douglas and Mae Mae.

Douglas and Mae Mae purchased the 100 year old home in 1958 and remodeled it for their family. In 1992, with children grown and gone, Douglas and Mae Mae opened as a bed and breakfast.

Guests at Mae Mae's Bed & Breakfast love having their own private entrance away from the family's quarters. Just off their private entrance is the Great Room. Here guests can relax and enjoy a turn-of-the-century atmosphere reflected in the elegant Victorian wallpaper, marvelous antique furniture, lamps and pictures, as well as an original wood mantel fireplace and original woodwork.

One of the telltale signs of the home's age is the steep stairwell leading to the second floor. When Douglas and Mae Mae purchased the home they discovered the banister for the stairway in the Grainery (the storage building out back). They retrieved the banister and restored it to its original purpose.

Mae Mae's offers three large, quiet, and immaculate guest rooms, each with queen beds, beautiful antiques, handmade quilts, private bathroom, and color TV with remote control. Rooms, rather than having names, carry the first initial of Douglas and Mae Mae's two children, Diane and Catherine, and of Mae Mae.

"D" offers an old-style carpet, brass queen bed with quilt made by Mae Mae, antique desk, bed tables, Victorian chair, and a quilt displayed on the wall. Both "D" and "C" have large adjoining bathrooms with tub and shower, vanity basin, and spacious dressing areas.

"C" has a southwestern decor and features knotty pine, an old trunk, antique bed tables and lamps, and armoire. Swinging cafe doors hide a closet and selection of old books and magazines.

"M" features an exquisite burgundy and gold queen bed with ornate golden head and bed boards. Other furnishings include a glass vanity, petrified wood table, gold chair, and antique bed tables, lamps and dresser. "M" guests use the home's original bathroom with its double sink vanity and small corner tub and shower. Since the bathroom is down the hall, "M" room guests are provided with bath robes.

The upstairs hall that connects with each of the three guest rooms has a beautiful collection of miniature dolls in duplicate, one for each of the Jensen's two daughters. The hall also leads to a large redwood deck, ideal for outdoor lounging.

Antiques in the dining room, where a continental breakfast of Doug's homemade sweet rolls, cereal, fruit juice and choice of hot drink is served, include an exquisite china closet, buffet, and green and pink depression glass. The original kitchen fireplace has been kept, modernized, and is combined with the fireplace in the adjacent bottle collection room. This two-room fireplace is unique.

Mae Mae's personality is reflected in the furnishings and decor throughout the house. For as long as she can remember Mae Mae has had a passion for antiques and most particularly for antique bottles. Where ever she has ventured in the West, one of the first things Mae Mae did was check to see if there were any ghost towns around. If there was, Mae Mae was off to dig in the dirt. That digging has produced one of the largest and most varied collections to be found anywhere other than a museum. Following breakfast, guests are invited to visit the family living room (called by many the bottle collection room) where every bottle has its own adventurous story.

In addition to Mae Mae's collection of antique bottles in the bottle room, Douglas, who retired as a truck driver, has a contemporary collection of whiskey bottles. While on the road Douglas learned first hand the states where each bottle would be released and either arranged to be there himself or have one of his trucking friends obtain the bottle for him. These bottles are replicas of nearly every well-known outlaw and lawman in the West. There are also bottles in the shape of cannons, guns, steamboats, fire engines, railroad cars and locomotives. Both Douglas and Mae Mae love to relate the story behind the bottle.

Mae Mae's Bed & Breakfast is an ideal respite. It offers guests a chance to peek into the past while enjoying the bounties of the Southwest. National parks and monuments within an easy drive are Bryce Canyon, 19 miles; Cedar Breaks, 30 miles; Grand Staircase Escalante, 25 miles, and Zion 75 miles. The 106-mile drive to Capitol Reef National Park traverses Scenic Byway 12, one of the nation's top 10 byways. It travels through Red Canyon, Grand Staircase-Escalante, the nation's newest monument, and across Boulder Mountain. The trip itself is worth the drive. North Rim of the Grand Canyon, also a beautiful drive, is 156 miles from Mae Mae's.

State Parks that are close by are Kodachrome Basin, 35 miles, Escalante Petrified Forest, 70 miles, and Anasazi Indian Village, 96 miles.

If fishing is a hobby, don't forget to bring the poles. Utah's greatest fishing is in this part of the state. Panguitch Lake, Panguitch Creek, the Sevier River, Otter Creek, and Piute Reservoir offer the best of the best.

Those who have not visited this part of America have a hard time visualizing the beauty that exists in Southwestern Utah. When making reservations to stay at Mae Mae's, plan to stay and play for at least a week. Guests discover that when they return for a second week's stay, there are still plenty of places to see an abundance of things to do.

RESTAURANTS

FLYING M RESTAURANT
614 North Main Street
Panguitch, Utah 84759
Tel: (435) 676-8008
FAX: (435) 676-8089
Hrs: Seasonal
April 1 - November 1
7:00 a.m. - 10:00 p.m.
November 1 - April 1
7:00 a.m. - 9:00 p.m.
Visa, MasterCard, Discover, and
Travelers Cheques are accepted.
Reservations are only required for large groups.

The Flying M Restaurant, owned and operated by Rick and Janet Oldham, is one of those rare establishments where management receives as much enjoyment out of their business as their customers do.

Rick and Janet subscribe to the philosophy "it is fun to work where it is fun to play." The town of Panguitch is perceived by many to be the Gateway to Bryce Canyon, Zion, and Capitol Reef National Parks as well as Cedar Breaks National Monument and Brian Head Ski Resort. It is fun to have a business in a place where so many of one's customers are overwhelmed with the beauty that is all around them.

It is apparent to diners at Flying M restaurant that the Oldhams enjoy satisfying the desires of their customers. Made fresh daily, are soups, pot pies, fruit pies, individual loaves of bread, and gravies.

Flying M's sweet roll, perhaps the largest in the country, brings customers from all over the world. They have heard about the sweet roll from others and are told that when they pass through Panguitch, they must stop and try one. The Sweet Roll covers a nine-inch plate and is two to two and one-half inches tall. It's taste is as rewarding as it's size.

Service throughout the restaurant is friendly and cheerful with congenial interaction between server and guests.

Breakfast at the Flying M Restaurant is served until 11:30 a.m. The breakfast menu includes eggs, any style, with choices of bacon, beef patty, smoked ham, or sausage. Omelette lovers appreciate the ham and cheese, cheese, and Spanish omelettes. All of the above are served with hash brown potatoes, toast or biscuits, and jelly.

Two customer favorites are Biscuits and Country Gravy with sausage, and Buttermilk Pancakes, served with a choice of syrups.

Both lunch and dinner begin at 11:30 and are served throughout the day until closing. Favorite lunches include the Roast Sirloin of Beef sandwich with mashed potatoes and gravy, large bowl of homemade chili, the Patty Melt with French fries, and Flying M's homemade turkey pot pie, served with a garden salad. Another favorite is the Crock Special for Two, which is the soup of the day and a choice of salad or pie.

Dinner choices at the Flying M are many and include such western favorites as Roast Beef, Grilled Pork Chops, Top Sirloin and Ribeye steak, as well as chicken, halibut, and ground sirloin. Diner favorites however at the Flying M are the Liver and Onions, Country Fried Steak, and a local special, Mountain Trout. Dinners include soup or salad, individual loaves of bread, vegetable, and a choice of potato.

From Easter through October the Flying M offers a beautiful all-one-can-eat salad bar during lunch and dinner. For a very nominal charge diners may have the salad bar included as part of their lunch or dinner entrees.

Flying M caters to children and to adults 65 or over, offering them a well-rounded menu of Roast Sirloin of Beef, Spaghetti and Meat Sauce, Fish and Chips, Deep Fried Chicken Strips, and Pattie of Beef.

Flying M has two public dining rooms. The coffee shop with counter bar and booth seating, can comfortably seat 50. The dining room, with a 40's ambiance, has a color decor of mauve and burgundy and elegant lace curtains. Seating is at tables that will accommodate two to six guests.

Flying M has a full Utah liquor license and also serves beer and wines in the bottle. A wine and liquor list are available upon request.

Ever Since Rick and Janet took over the restaurant in 1987, they have been making the kinds of changes that let customers know they care. In 1997 the Oldhams added a beautiful banquet facility that is ideal for receptions, business banquets, club meetings, and for tour buses. With a decor of mauve and burgundy, the facility has elegant furnishings, mauve and white linen, and elegant silk floral centerpieces with candles for romantic candlelight dining. The room can accommodate large groups of 80 for dinner or the room can be divided to seat 50 in one room and 30 in the other.

Also added in 1997 was a unique gift shop. Rick and Janet have worked hard to make sure that their gift shop was not like every other Southwestern store. While they do offer Native American jewelry and artifacts, most of the selection at Flying M Gifts are non-traditional (see related story).

In 1890 Elijah Moore brought one of the first herds of cattle to this area from Texas. He called his ranch The Flying M. In 1947 Elijah's son, Dewey founded the Flying M Restaurant and built a reputation for himself through hard work and his open hospitality. Today, the Flying M is still an active brand. It is the hope of the Oldhams that all who travel Highway 89 will stop to dine and enjoy a bit of old west hospitality with them.

SPECIALTY SHOPPING

FLYING M GIFTS
614 North Main Street
Panguitch, Utah 84759
Tel: (435) 676-8008
FAX: (435) 676-8089
Hrs: Seasonal
April 1 - November 1   7:00 a.m. - 10:00 p.m.
November 1 - April 1 7:00 a.m. - 9:00 p.m.
Visa, MasterCard, Discover, and Travelers Cheques are accepted.

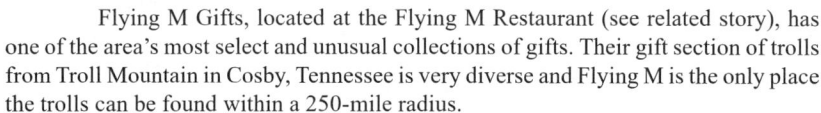

Flying M Gifts, located at the Flying M Restaurant (see related story), has one of the area's most select and unusual collections of gifts. Their gift section of trolls from Troll Mountain in Cosby, Tennessee is very diverse and Flying M is the only place the trolls can be found within a 250-mile radius.

Trolls, in five to 60-inch sizes, are cowboys, artists, nurses, and grandparents, to name just a few. Each Christmas there is also a special edition troll that can only be purchased at that time, then it is gone forever and becomes a collector's keepsake. Hard as it is to fathom, these trolls are made out of such earthy items as pine cones, nuts, cockle burrs, hemp, palm fibers, and the trunks and branches of trees. And yes, they are irresistible.

When selecting treasures for their store, Rick and Janet Oldham, owners, look for items not usually found at other gift shops. The trolls are indicative of the quality and uniqueness of gifts at Flying M.

One portion of the gift shop houses a nostalgic collection of old west photographs available as post cards or matted and framed. Available in the assortment are such famous and infamous characters as Annie Oakley, Doc Holiday, Sitting Bull, the Wild Bunch, and Butch Cassidy.

Another section of the gift shop is devoted to limited edition and one-of-a-kind porcelain dolls from Jo's, an area artist from nearby Circleville. These Victorian dolls are exquisitely dressed in elegant fashion creations of the 1800's.

Also from that same era are Victorian flue covers and beautiful Victorian prints. Aromatic candles, a carry-over from the Victorian era, can be found in the Candle Station.

Flying M Gifts has an unusual selection of ornate pottery, hand painted as one-of-a-kind treasures by one of Rick's friends. The gift shop also carries a quality assortment of Native American pottery.

Infatuated with Elvis? John F. Kennedy? The First Landing on the Moon? Flying M Gifts has an assortment of Special Edition Papers on significant people or events. If one's particular fetish doesn't happen to be in stock, the Oldhams can more than likely special order it.

Among the selection of Native American artifacts are pelts, bone art, medicine masks, dream catchers, Mandellas, suede pouches, rugs, blankets, and sterling silver jewelry that includes rings, bracelets, earrings, hairpieces, necklaces, watch bands, bolo ties, and belt buckles.

In addition to the Native American belt buckles, Flying M Gifts has a selection of Western buckles in silver, silver and gold, and bronze.

Recognizing the fact that many travelers simply want an inexpensive souvenir of the trip, Rick and Janet have put together mementos that include Panguitch and area iron-on patches, key chains, T-shirts, sweatshirts, mugs, and scenic souvenir placemats.

So, if repetition seems to be the thing found most in area gift shops, look no more. Flying M Gifts are anything but redundant—they are unusual, exceptional, and sure to become treasured keepsakes.

PANGUITCH AREA ATTRACTIONS

U-143, PANGUITCH LAKE- BRIAN HEAD SCENIC BYWAY

At the Southwestern end of Panguitch, a fork in the road leads to Scenic Byway 143 and Panguitch Lake, Cedar Breaks National Monument, and Brian Head Ski and Summer Resort.

This Scenic Byway, 55 miles when taken to its termination point in Parowan, is open year-round and winds itself through Alpine beauty and the splendor of a majestic Vermillion amphitheater.

A few short miles from Panguitch, on U-143, one enters the majesty of the **Dixie National Forest** where outdoor activities are popular year-round. **Panguitch Lake Recreation Area**, 17 miles southwest of Panguitch, is a popular summer and winter fishing spot and recreation area. Activities here include trout fishing, boating, hiking, horseback riding, cross country skiing, and snowmobiling. A full service resort, the area offers accommodations, restaurants and the rental of adult toys.

Photographers come from all over the country to capture the beauty of the forests of the vast Markagunt Plateau that surrounds Panguitch Lake. Especially rousing are the forest's brilliant yellow and orange-red aspen leaves during autumn.

CEDAR BREAKS NATIONAL MONUMENT

Thirteen miles west of Panguitch Lake is Cedar Breaks National Monument, an incredible amphitheater of colorful cliffs that resembles a miniature Bryce Canyon. Some visitors even maintain that the brilliance of Cedar Breaks surpasses Bryce. Cedar Breaks, situated at an elevation of 10,000 feet, is shaped like a giant coliseum with its walls dropping about one-half mile to the canyon floor. The amphitheater is three miles from rim to rim.

Although not as large as Zion or Bryce National Parks, Cedar Breaks National Monument covers 6,154 acres of the High Markagunt Plateau. Created as a national monument in 1933, this huge amphitheater encloses several semi-circular basins. The furrowed and eroded walls have been broken into massive ridges of color and aptly fit the Western definition of "breaks."

Originally called the "Circle of Painted Cliffs" by Native Americans, the walls are alive with red, yellow, white, gold, and orange that contrast with the deep purple and cool blue of the canyons' many shadows. While beautiful any time of the day, sunrises and sunsets seem to bring out the true splendor of this uniquely Western natural wonder.

Especially striking are the golden aspens and Bristlecone pines, among the oldest plants on Earth, which become part of nature's "greatest show on earth" during autumn and when blanketed with Mother Nature's "greatest snow on earth."

In the summer, the meadows and slopes are resplendent with wildflowers. The area is also a wildlife habitat and mule deer can be seen grazing during early morning or evening.

Open from Memorial Day through October, recreational opportunities include hiking, photography, ranger/naturalist lectures, self-guided and naturalist-guided trails, and camping. During winter months the area just south of Brian Head, going into Cedar Breaks, is open for snowmobiling and cross country skiing. The visitor center offers exhibits on the plants, animals, and geology of the region. The campground is available on a first-come, first-served basis and there is a fee (435-586-9451).

Just five miles north of Cedar Breaks is the town of **Brian Head**. At an elevation of 9,800 feet, it is Utah's highest incorporated city. It is also home to **Brian Head Ski Resort**, Southern Utah's premiere all-season resort.

BRIAN HEAD

Named for William Jennings Bryan, famous American politician and one-time presidential hopeful, the town of Brian Head, Utah's highest incorporated city, was called Monument Peak when it was first settled in the early 1850s. Sheep, cattle, and logging were the principal sources of income until the area was developed for skiing in 1964.

During the winter months Brian Head is like no other place on earth. Red rocks "peak" from beneath a blanket of powder snow and together, with canyon spires and aspen groves, they combine to create a ski fantasyland.

Ideally located in the heart of the Grand Circle of National Parks, Brian Head is blessed with Utah's highest base elevation, a blessing that translates into incredible snow, spectacular views, and extraordinary skiing and snowboarding. Brian Head is also blessed with the highest percentage of sunny days and is the closest Utah resort to Southern California and Nevada.

Truly a world of its own, Brian Head offers everything one needs to make a skiing vacation complete. Nestled among the red-rock beauty of Cedar Breaks National Monument and the stunning alpine scenery of Dixie National Forest, the resort's ski slopes are located in the center of town. Getting around is made remarkably easy with a complementary resort shuttle service. For those on foot, cross-country skis, snowshoes, or snowmobiles, there is a town trail that loops through Brian Head, conveniently linking restaurants, shops and condominiums. Additionally, many lodging properties around town offer ski-in/ski-out access to the resort's slopes.

Brian Head is indeed one of Utah's premiere four-season resorts. To find out why Brian Head earned the title from *Bicycling* Magazine as "Utah's Other Utopia," visit the resort in late spring, summer or fall. Ride the chair lift up to the top of Brian Head Resort's Mountain Bike Park and experience over 40 miles of uncrowded single track trails, some dropping over a mile in elevation. Ride through high alpine meadows, Aspen groves, and into the red rock canyon lands in one long, easy downhill.

Then, thanks to local bike rental and repair shops, take a shuttle ride back to the base. Bikers come from all over the world to experience the single track mecca at Brian Head for all ability levels.

In addition to biking and hiking the Brian Head area, visitors can horseback ride with authentic cowboy guides and learn Western songs. Cedar Breaks National Park is a five-minute drive up the road. Also close by, Dixie National Forest is perfect for guided nature walks, and Navajo Lake is great for fishing or having a leisurely picnic.

Winter, spring, summer, or fall, Brian Head is an "on-top-of-the-world" four-season experience that is "friendly by nature" and "naturally friendly."

U-148 CEDAR BREAKS SCENIC BYWAY

Utah's shortest Scenic Byway, this six mile stretch of road joins the Panguitch Lake-Brian Head Scenic Byway 143 with the Markaguant Scenic Byway 14. This mountain road travels through flower-filled meadows for four miles after leaving Cedar Breaks National Monument. The Byway is closed during winter.

US 89 SCENIC BYWAY

Scenic Byway 89, which begins at the Junction of Scenic Byway 12 and continues the 60 miles to Utah's "Little Hollywood," Kanab, is one of the state's most popular and beautiful drives.

US 89 follows the meandering path of the Sevier River to the small town of Hatch, then skirts the Markagunt Plateau of the Dixie National Forest past the summit of Long Valley Junction. As one approaches the small town of Glendale, a backdrop of yellow, red and white banded cliffs is continually in view. Then the highway leaves the canyon landscape and enters a forested mountain valley. Along the route on the East side of the road are the Pink Cliffs, miniature formations that are reminiscent of Bryce Canyon. At Glendale the road winds through green fields and orchards that continue through the early pioneer settlements of Orderville, Mt. Carmel and onto Mt. Carmel Junction and the east fork of the Virgin River. At the Junction, where U-9 leads visitors to the magnificent white towers of Zion National Park, the road ascends past a Byway to Coral Pink Sand Dunes State Park, the White Cliffs, Vermilion Cliffs and Three Lakes Canyon.

A few miles north of Kanab is **Angel Canyon,** a site that, according to most area visitors, if it were anywhere else but Utah, would be a National Monument. During the Jurassic Age, Angel Canyon was home to the dinosaurs, who have left their footprints here. Close to 8,000 years ago the canyons were home to the Anasazi, and the ancient ones have left their handprints and other rock art carved in arroyo walls. Early Mormon settlers perceived the region as a promised land. Fortune seekers, who came with an ancient treasure map from Mexico, came with the hopes that they would be the ones to discover the hoard of gold. It was supposedly buried in an underground canyon lake by pricsts of the last Aztec King, Monteczuma. And in the middle 1900s, Hollywood discovered Angel Canyon as one of the most authentic settings for Western movies to be found anywhere. Dozens of Westerns and several TV series have been filmed here. Today, Angel Canyon is the home of Best Friends Animal Sanctuary (see related story), a place of healing and love to a host of once homeless animals. A tour of the canyon and of the sanctuary is offered by Best Friends (435-644-2001).

HATCH

Contrary to what most Utahns think, the small town of Hatch, with a population of slightly over 100, did not receive its name because of the fish hatchery located here.

In 1872 the town of Aaron, (also called Asay) was settled near the mouth of Asay Creek. Several other towns along the Asay and Mammoth Creek were Proctor, Castle, Johnson, and Hatchtown. Hatchtown was settled by Meltair Hatch and his two wives, Parmelia and Mary Ann. In 1900, the Hatchtown Reservoir gave way before its completion, flooding Hatchtown and the other communities. The town and the community were rebuilt, but again the dam broke and destroyed much of the town. These and other problems forced these early communities to group together and to settle an area one and one-half miles south of Hatchtown. The name given to their consolidated community was Hatch. In 1913 the dam broke again but this time, because the town had been moved, the community was saved.

The elevation in Hatch is nearly 7,000 feet and the growing season is very short. It is not unusual to have frost at one point or another every month of the year.

Small as it is, Hatch offers all guest services for Highway 89 travelers. In addition to motels, restaurants, gift shops, and RV parks, Hatch has a Daughters of Utah Pioneer Museum, available by appointment only; a visitor center, open daily from May - October; Color Country City Park, ideal for picnics; the Sevier River, superb for Rainbow Trout fishing; and the Mammoth Creek Fishery, where guests are always welcome.

ACCOMMODATIONS

BRYCE-ZION MIDWAY RESORT
244 South Highway 89 (next to Hatch Visitor's Center)
Hatch, Utah 84735
Tel: (435) 735-4199
FAX: (435) 735-4277
Hrs:
Open Daily   8:00 a.m. - 9:00 p.m.
Visa and MasterCard are accepted.
Reservations are requested.

When traveling Utah's Scenic Byway, Highway 89, an accommodation of choice for those who prefer to feel as if they have never left home is Bryce-Zion Midway Resort. The resort was named because of its proximity to two of God's greatest creations, Bryce Canyon and Zion National Parks. Bryce is 23 miles northeast of Bryce-Zion Midway Resort and Zion is a 45-minute drive to the southwest.

Doug and Vickie Talbot, along with their young family, purchased the facility in 1996, and began immediately making improvements and additions that would enhance the feeling of home.

Accommodations are not the typical motel, but individual log cabin bungalows. The cabins include a choice of double queen or single king beds, with each room having a separate vanity basin and bathroom with shower. Walls and dressers are adorned with homey artifacts, pictures and flower arrangements, many of which can be purchased at the gift shop. Some of the units feature gas decorator fireplaces. All have a satellite TV with over 100 channels from which to choose. Each cabin has its own front porch with seating that overlooks a magnificent view of the red rock towers of Red Canyon. The hills and lowlands across the street are a great habitat for deer and elk.

Adjacent to the cabins is the Bryce-Zion Midway restaurant which serves breakfast, lunch and dinner and offers a separate take-out kitchen. Deer and elk mounts, softened with daisies and yellow pine, decorate the interior. Small though it may be, the restaurant offers one whale of a menu. For breakfast, diners may choose one or two eggs served any style with a choice of toast, hash browns and toast, or hash browns and toast and a choice of bacon, ham, or sausage. Other menu choices include Pancakes, French Toast, Biscuits and Gravy, Eggs Benedict, and Steak and Eggs. The Omelette selection includes Cheese, Ham and Cheese, Denver, Spanish, and Mexican. There is also hot and cold cereal, a variety of breakfast beverages, and a selection of side orders.

Bryce-Zion Midway's special, the Midway Pan-Fry, is served throughout the day. As the menu states, it is a hearty meal of old-fashioned fries, eggs, corn-beef hash, and cheese served with toast. Truly delicious, the Midway Pan-Fry is sure to last one through a day at Bryce or Zion.

Lunch specialties include succulent hamburgers, cheeseburgers, and bacon-cheese burgers that are grilled to perfection. The hot dog selection includes regular and Polish dogs, with or without chili. From the Deli are the Philly-steak, club, patty melt, ham, beef, turkey, or bacon, lettuce and tomato sandwiches, all served with fries. Also available are chicken strips, grilled chicken breast, and fish and shrimp baskets. All are served with fries.

Served for both lunch and dinner are a hearty soup of the day and Bryce-Zion Midway's popular home made chili. Good old fashioned shakes, sundaes, and ice cream cones in a wide selection of flavors and toppings are also available for lunch or dinner. Also served are apple, cherry, and pecan pie and cheese cake. Since it is two miles south of Hatch, a dry town, the restaurant is allowed to serve beer. Non-alcoholic sodas, ice tea and lemonade are also popular refreshers.

Steak dinner favorites, all served with vegetables, a choice of potatoes, soup or salad, and a dinner roll, are T-Bone, Rib Eye, Filet Mignon, and Steak-a-bob. Other entrees include Utah Trout, Shrimp, Fish and Chips, a three-piece Chicken dinner, and Chicken Fingers. Bryce-Zion Midway also offers seven, 12 and 15-inch pizzas with a choice of up to five different toppings. Most of the sandwiches on the luncheon menu are also available.

Directly behind the restaurant is the Bryce Zion Midway Resort Gift Shop. One of its unique features is the variety of hand-crafted items available. Vickie's mother, an artist, has painted the pictures. A niece is responsible for the decoupage gift boxes and toll painting. In addition, there is a nice selection of Indian jewelry, Indian and American dolls, Trinity pottery, book ends, bird-houses, and packaged pot pourri. The shop also carries a variety of area magnets, key rings, spoons, pens, thimbles, post-cards, caps, mugs, and T-shirts as well as matted pictures of the parks.

There is a word in German, "Gemuetlich", which personifies Bryce-Zion Midway Resort. Gemuetlich is more a feeling than a definition, encompassing all that is warm and friendly. Bryce-Zion Midway Resort, with its homey log cabin bungalows, its hand crafted gifts, its good old-fashioned home cooking, and its gracious, hospitable staff is "Gemuetlich."

CANYON INN
277 North Main Street
Hatch, Utah 84733
Tel: (435) 735-4265
         (800) 370-5272
FAX: (435) 735-4269
Visa, MasterCard, American Express, and Discover are accepted.
Reservations are recommended.

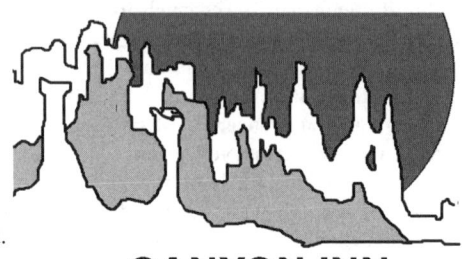

CANYON INN

It is difficult to find a more centrally located accommodation when visiting the many parks and recreation areas in Southern Utah than Canyon Inn.

And for those who have visited the area and are planning a return visit, Canyon Inn is their accommodation of choice. It is not that the motel is extraordinarily plush, because it is not. What brings customers back is the cordiality and hospitality of Canyon Inn's personnel and the cleanliness and size of the accommodations.

Each of the 20 guest rooms at Canyon Inn is spacious, comfortably decorated in a western motif, and immaculate. All rooms have color TV with remote control, alarm clock, phone with local calls free, a desk and table with chairs. Guests have a choice of single queen, or two double beds. Bathrooms are large, offer tub and shower, and a separate vanity.

In addition to the more than average sized rooms, Canyon Inn has three guest rooms that can only be described as enormous. Each has three double beds, a desk, card table, chairs, large television, and is still spacious enough to accommodate two to three roll-aways if the need is there. In addition, the rooms offer two bathrooms, one with shower and separate vanity; the other with tub/shower combination. The rooms are ideal for families traveling together or for parties who caravan.

All within an easy day's visit of Canyon Inn are Bryce Canyon, Capitol Reef, and Zion National Parks, as well as the North Rim of Grand Canyon, Cedar Breaks and Grand Staircase-Escalante National Monuments, and Glen Canyon National Recreation Area. Several state parks, lakes, and historical sites are also nearby.

Judy and Dave Savage, managers of Canyon Inn, know that with all there is to see and do in Southern Utah, no one can possibly experience it all in one visit. The Savages are true believers of the Golden Rule. Caring comes naturally for them and they believe that when customers receive conscientious attention, they will return.

In addition to their spacious affordable rooms, Canyon Inn offers guests quality dining at moderate prices in its country western cafe (see related story).

Guests at Canyon Inn will not have to go far to select the perfect memento, a treasured keepsake of a visit to Southwestern Utah. Souvenirs include a selection of Native American jewelry, pottery, rugs, and other artifacts such as dream catchers, Mandellas, and Kachina dolls. Token gifts of the area include T-shirts, caps, magnets, mugs, spoons, and other inexpensive reminders of the trip. Canyon Inn's gift shop also carries a nice selection of western art.

When a small motel feels it is important enough to provide their guests with affordable accommodations, moderately priced cuisine, and an excellent gift shop, as well as western hospitality at its finest, it is easy to see why so many who book with Canyon Inn do so as return customers.

RESTAURANTS

CANYON INN CAFE
277 North Main Street
Hatch, Utah 84733
Tel: (435) 735-4265
         (800) 370-5272
FAX: (435) 735-4269
Hrs: April - September
7:00 a.m. - 10:00 p.m.
Visa, MasterCard, American Express, and Discover are accepted.

CANYON INN CAFE

Canyon Inn Cafe, located adjacent to the lobby of Canyon Inn (see related story), offers quality dining at moderate prices. It is operated by The Heaton Sisters, an entertainment group that has received much acclaim in the area. The eleven sisters, whose ages range from seven to 21, entertain most evenings during the summer months. They sing acappella and their repertoire includes a large selection of folk and patriotic songs. The sisters who are old enough to do so also prepare and serve the food.

Ambiance at Canyon Inn Cafe is cheery with a color scheme of forest green and mauve. Country Western artifacts, such as watering cans, cowboy boots, oxen yoke, horse shoes, and an eclectic collection of hats, bedeck the ledge above the windows and bar of the restaurant. Walls are embellished with exquisite silk flower arrangements.

No one should leave for a day at the parks without the most important meal of the day, breakfast. Personnel at Canyon Inn Cafe have made breakfast fast and convenient for their dining guests. In a serve one's self atmosphere, diners can build their own omelette and help themselves to fresh coffee, juice, hot and cold cereals, fresh breads and fruit.

At lunch or throughout the remainder of the day, Canyon Inn Cafe serves tasty cheeseburgers, side orders of garden salad or potato salad, French fries, potato bites, homemade soup, and a choice of beverages.

The dinner menu at Canyon Inn Cafe is small, but calculated to satisfy a hearty appetite. The two western-style meals offered are a top grade 12-ounce boneless ribeye or grilled Mesquite boneless chicken breast. Both are served with Cowboy beans and a choice of baked potato or Dutch oven potatoes.

When dining at Canyon Inn Cafe, always make sure to save room for a piece of homemade pie topped off, of course, with a scoop of vanilla ice cream.

Whether staying at Canyon Inn or simply traveling along Utah's Scenic Byway, Highway 89, travelers are always welcome at Canyon Inn Cafe.

KANE COUNTY

Kane County, the southernmost county in Utah, lies in the heart of a scenic area that stretches from Zion National Park on the west to Lake Powell and Glen Canyon National Park on the east. A land of beauty and splendor, this county of nearly 5,500 residents offers something for nearly every recreational taste. Photographers, hikers, and campers can take their pick of some of the greatest scenery in the southwestern United States, while enjoying the magnificence of Lake Powell. The county was settled over a century ago by Mormon pioneers. For many years the county's economy was based on agriculture, livestock, and lumber but the coming of the automobile brought a new form of income to the county—tourism. Today Kane County is substantially dependent upon tourist dollars for its economic vitality.

LONG VALLEY JUNCTION

About 12 miles south of Hatch one comes to the Kane County line. A few miles further is Long Valley Junction, so named because it is at this point that U-14 and U.S. 89 come together, and it is also at this juncture that Long Valley begins. The Junction is at the southern edge of the Great Basin where the headwaters of the Sevier River flow north and the headwaters of the Virgin River flow south. The first home at this site was built by William J. Baird in 1927.

U-14 MARKAGUNT SCENIC BYWAY

U-14, the Markagunt Scenic Byway, links U.S. 89 with Cedar City. This 40-mile two-lane byway travels past lava beds and layers of volcanic rock and through the verdant beauty of *Dixie National Forest*. Ensconced in the middle of the forest and against Cedar Mountain, 10 miles west of U.S. 89 and 31 miles east of Cedar City, is one of Utah's most picturesque towns, *Duck Creek Village*. A side road takes visitors to *Strawberry Point* and an exquisite view of *Zion National Park,* as well as countless other ridges and canyons. Erosion has cut delicate pinnacles and narrow canyons into the Pink Cliffs on either side below the viewpoint. Another side road goes to the fishing waters of *Duck Creek*. Several miles West is *Navajo Lake*. This three and one-half mile long lake was created by lava flows and has no surface outlet. It is drained by sink holes where water from inlets dramatically disappears into the ground. The water emerges as Cascade Falls in the Pacific Ocean drainage and as Duck Creek in the Great Basin drainage. Navajo Lake is a favorite spot for hiking, fishing, camping and photography. It is at this point that U-14 tops out at 10,000 feet. Camping and lodging facilities are available at the lake. A short drive from Navajo Lake is *Cascade Falls National Recreation Trail*. Incredible views and a waterfall make this one-mile round trip trek exciting. The trail begins at the south rim of the Markagunt Plateau, drops a short way down the Pink Cliffs, and then winds along the cliffs to the falls, which gush from a cave and bounce their way down to the north fork of the Virgin River and Zion Canyon. It is in this vicinity that U-14 junctures with U-148, a six-mile Scenic Byway leading to *Cedar Breaks National Monument*. Several miles past the juncture is *Zion Overlook*, where a parking area beside the road provides a panoramic view of *Kolob Terrace* and the towers and buttes of *Zion National Park* in the distance. U-14 continues to descend through an amphitheater of red limestone, ponderosa pines, red maple and golden oaks. During autumn there is not a more beautiful drive in the state. As U-14 approaches Cedar City it descends through a narrow canyon with sheer cliffs on both sides and a view into *Ashdown Gorge*.

DUCK CREEK VILLAGE

Ten miles west of U.S. 89 and Long Valley Junction is quaint and picturesque Duck Creek Village, one of the state's best kept secrets and an all-season vacation destination. Duck Creek Village had its beginnings as a movie set. In the mid-1940s a few rustic buildings against the Cedar Mountains became an alpine homesite for several Western movies, including *How the West Was Won, My Friend Flicka*, and the

Daniel Boone TV series. So charming was the setting that it did not take long before urban dwellers were building summer and winter get-aways. Growth brought the need for business and today Duck Creek Village is a thriving community with motels, restaurants, gift shops, gas station, general store, and one of the state's busiest Polaris dealerships. During the winter Duck Creek is a winter wonderland, offering the most reliable snow and the longest season in the southwestern United States. Its endless meadows, hills and valleys provide the ultimate in diverse terrain and scenic beauty for snowmobiling, Nordic skiing, and snowshoeing. This high Cedar Mountain plateau is replete with forest trails and logging roads leading to ice caves, Strawberry Point, Cedar Breaks and Brian Head. Spring, summer, and fall, these same logging roads are ideal for horse back riding, mountain biking, and hiking. Nearby Navajo Lake is ideal for canoeing, sailing, boating, and fishing. Duck Creek Pond and Aspen Mirror Lake are also great for fishing. A Special annual event is the Duck Creek Chili Contest held every August. It attracts visitors from all over the Western United States. A continuous schedule of games and events for everyone is held throughout the day and culminates with a steak dinner with all the trimmings. The beauty of Duck Creek Village and its mountain setting is contagious. Once visited it is nearly impossible to stay away.

ACCOMMODATIONS

FALCON'S NEST CABINS
P. O. Box 1327
Duck Creek Village, Utah 84762
Tel: (435) 682-2556
         (800) 240-4930
FAX: (435) 682-2633
Visa, MasterCard and Discover are accepted.
Reservations are Recommended.

Duck Creek Village, nestled among Aspen and Ponderosa pines on Markaguant Scenic Byway, Utah Highway 14, is considered by many to be one of Utah's hidden treasures. The quaint mountain village, secluded from the rest of the world, is a private summer and winter getaway for many who own vacation homes in the area.

Paul and Susan Longhi, owners of Falcon Nest Cabins, know what it is like to want to be a part of Duck Creek Village. Three years ago they came to play, fell in love with what Duck Creek had to offer, and made it their home.

Through Falcon's Nest Cabins, Paul and Susan make it possible for those who do not own private mountain homes to enjoy a summer or winter hiatus in this lush, wonderland. Falcon's Nest is the only facility on the mountain to offer guests their own private cabin with incredible views of the pine and aspen forest.

This season, those who visit Duck Creek and Falcon's Nest will enjoy another sight as well. A row of aspens grows in front of the cabins. When making purchases for their store, the Gift Cottage (see related story), Paul saw and fell in love with a set of six caricature bears. There are mama, papa, and baby bears, some dancing, sitting, playing hide and seek, or looking like they are ready to pounce on their prey. There is also one coming out of a tree trunk and hibernation. Since Paul and Susan could not bear to part with them, (no pun intended), the bears have been illuminated and interspersed among the aspens for all to enjoy.

In addition to the cabins and shopping at Gift Cottage, Falcon's Nest guests enjoy eating at Duck Quick Cafe, also owned and operated by Paul and Susan (see related story).

All cabins have cozy wood burning stoves, with wood provided during the winter months, and three-quarter baths with shower. Beds in all of the cabins are topped with hand made quilts for extra comfort. Cabin amenities, in all but the single room unit, include a full kitchen with range top, refrigerator and all the cooking and eating utensils one might need.

For a small additional cost, guests may rent a combination television and VCR, complete with their choice of two free movies from a video library that includes classics, wonderful westerns, and latest releases.

Behind the cabins is a play area with horse shoe pits, basketball, and volley ball available to guests during warmer months. During the winter, guests find the play area is ideal for creating a snowman masterpiece. A small game room offers 50's-style pin ball machines and phones.

Falcon's Nest offers guests a choice of three different styles of rustic pine cabins. The one story, two-bedroom cabins sleep six. There is a queen bed in each of the two bedrooms and a queen sofa sleeper in the living room..

A-frame cabins are two-stories and will also sleep six. One bedroom is furnished with two twin beds, the other with a single double. In the living area there is a queen sofa bed. Rustic pine furnishings include tables, end tables, and a picnic table. There are two A-frame styles. One offers an open loft on one side, while the other A-frame bedrooms are completely enclosed.

One of the cabin units, more like a motel, offers one large room with a king bed, mini refrigerator, toaster oven, coffee maker, and range top.

Duck Creek, a wonderful fishing spot, is just around the bend from the village. Navajo Lake, a favorite for fishing, camping, and photography, is just a few miles to the west. Cedar Breaks National Monument is within a magnificent 20-mile drive. Almost directly south, on what is also an incredible drive, is Zion National Park. Bryce Canyon National Park is a pleasant hour drive to the northeast.

There are many larger towns in Southern Utah that lay claim to being a stone's throw away from Utah's many scenic attractions. But there is no other town that can offer the pastoral charm of Duck Creek Village and Falcon's Nest Cabins.

The secluded setting makes it possible for guests to enjoy, right in their own backyard, hikes, walks, and bike rides during warmer months, and Nordic skiing, snowshoeing, and snowmobiling during the winter months.

With so much to offer, why would anyone even want to stay anywhere else? Falcon's Nest Cabins at Duck Creek is the ideal place to stay—summer, winter, spring and fall.

RESTAURANTS

DUCK QUICK CAFE
P. O. Box 1327
Duck Creek Village, Utah 84762
Tel: (435) 682-2556
           (800) 240-4930
FAX: (435) 682-2633
Hrs: Summer Season
Monday - Saturday 8:00 a.m. - 8:00 p.m.
Sunday   8:00 a.m. - 12:00 noon
         Winter Season
Monday - Saturday 9:00 a.m. - 9:00 p.m.
Sunday   9:00 a.m. - 12:00 noon
Visa, MasterCard and Discover are accepted.

    If those who have consumed one of Duck Quick Cafe's Duck Burgers are willing to drive down from Salt Lake City or up from Las Vegas just to have another one, Paul and Susan Longhi, owners, must be doing something right.

    In all reality, Paul and Susan are doing everything right. They are among the many who believe that something was lost when the world became fast food fanatics. Paul and Susan are not willing to go that route. Though their cafe is named Duck "Quick," their hamburgers and most other foods served are prepared to order. The Duck Burger is one-half pound of lean hamburger, embellished with a slice of ham, cheese, onions, tomatoes, lettuce, and all the juicy condiments that make a hamburger the great American sandwich. They will also prepare the Duck Burger to suit the customer's taste.

    Other dishes served throughout the day include bacon, lettuce, and tomato, turkey, fish, chicken, and chicken club sandwiches. Duck Quick Cafe is famous for its chile, with a well-rounded variety of soups of the day being close runners-up. In addition to their hamburgers, Duck Quick serves fish and chips, hot dogs, chili dogs and corn dogs.

    Soups and sandwiches are not all that the Duck Quick Cafe serves. Guests at Falcon's Nest Cabins, also owned by Paul & Susan (see related story), come to Duck Quick with robust appetites. Duck Quick believes in giving their guests a good breakfast before sending them off for a day of sightseeing activities.

    Pancakes, French toast, biscuits with sausage gravy, and eggs any style, served with healthy sides of country potatoes, toast, ham, bacon, or New York steak are sure to satisfy the heartiest appetite.

    Even when the ground is blanketed with winter white, it is hard to resist a helping of Duck Quick Cafe's premium ice cream. There are over 14 flavors from which to choose for those delectable ice cream cones, malts, splits, shakes, and sundaes. Duck Quick Cafe also serves a wonderful cheesecake.

    The two knotty-pine dining rooms at Duck Quick Cafe, decorated with a wood burning stove and an eclectic assortment of barn pictures, will seat 50. During warmer months that number is almost doubled as diners take to the outside picnic tables and patio chairs. The cafe has a connecting door to Gift Cottage, also owned by the Longhis (see related story).

    One certainly does not have to be staying at Falcon's Nest Cabins to enjoy the food and the service rendered at Duck Quick Cafe. If a visit to Duck Quick Cafe is worth a drive from Salt Lake and Las Vegas, it is certainly worth the drive from the many scenic attractions in Southern Utah. Duck Creek Village and Duck Quick Cafe are just 15 miles West of Scenic Byway 89, the road most traveled when visiting Zion and Bryce National Parks.

Stop by for a shake or a malt and one of Duck Quick's famous Duck Burgers. It will feel like the 50's again!

SPECIALTY SHOPPING

GIFT COTTAGE
P. O. Box 1327
Duck Creek Village, Utah 84762
Tel: (435) 682-2556
        (800) 240-4930
FAX: (435) 682-2633
Hrs: Summer Season
Monday - Saturday 8:00 a.m. - 8:00 p.m.
Sunday   8:00 a.m. - 12:00 noon
        Winter Season
Monday - Saturday 9:00 a.m. - 9:00 p.m.
Sunday   9:00 a.m. - 12:00 noon
Visa, MasterCard and Discover are accepted.

Gift Cottage, owned and operated by Paul and Sue Longhi, owners of Falcon's Nest Cabins and Duck Quick Cafe, has become a showcase for hand-crafted gifts from talented locals.

Among the high quality gift items are exquisite hand made quilts from crib to queen size in a variety of patterns and modern-day colors.

Hand carved and painted wooden artifacts that include cowboys and Indians with such intricate detail that one cannot help experiencing the rustic nature of the Old West, were created by a 17-year old boy.

Hand crafted wood electric lantern lamps are so authentic looking that one would swear they need kerosene to light them. When plugged in and the lights begin to flicker, the illusion is even greater.

Other art objects include intricate walking sticks, wood carved western-design plaques, and beautiful crocheted afghans.

A gift shop in Southwestern Utah would not be complete without a selection of Native American jewelry. The Gift Cottage showcases a collection that includes sterling silver with and without semi-precious stone embellishments. The assortment includes rings, bracelets, earrings, necklaces, hair ornaments, watch bands, bolo ties, and belt buckles. Most are from the Hopi, Zuni, Navajo, and Apache tribes, and most have inlays of turquoise, mother of pearl, coral, black onyx, or blue lapis.

In addition, Gift Cottage carries a nice line of sweatshirts and T-shirts with Duck Creek logos that are not to be found anywhere else in the world. It is a logo one will be proud to wear.

Many who enter Gift Cottage ask about the falcon that is in the doorway between Duck Quick Cafe and Gift Cottage. The falcon, ready to take flight, is a part of the tree trunk base from which it is carved. Unfortunately the falcon is not for sale. It was carved by one of Paul's friends and is the logo for Falcon's Nest Cabins.

If looking for out of the ordinary gifts, the Gift Cottage at Duck Creek is a Travelers' Choice.

LOOSE WHEELS SERVICE
55 Movie Ranch Road
Duck Creek Village 84762
Tel: (435) 682-2526
FAX: (435) 682-2678
Hrs: Open Daily
E-mail: lws@color-country.net
Monday - Saturday 9:00 a.m. - 6:00 p.m.
Sunday 9:00 a.m. - 5:00 p.m.
Closed Easter Sunday, Thanksgiving, and Christmas Day.
Visa, MasterCard, and Discover are accepted.

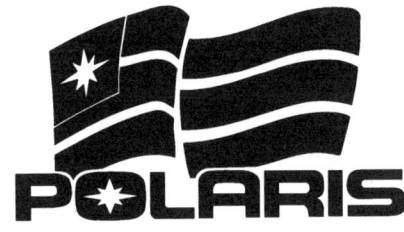

Winter, Spring, Summer and Fall, Duck Creek Village, a quaint, secluded hamlet surrounded by the beauty of Dixie National Forest, serves as a hiatus from city life for many mountain home owners. The village is one of Utah's best-kept secrets, and there are many who wish it would remain so. But Duck Creek Village, a too-good-to-be-true retreat with picturesque lodges, restaurants and stores, is so magnificent that it can no longer remain a secret.

Loose Wheels Service is the small Duck Creek Village shop that fuels the energy and creates the synergy among Duck Creek Village sports enthusiasts.

Loose Wheels, as a full-service Polaris Dealership, offers the area's best selection of Polaris Snowmobiles and ATVs. In addition to selling, repairing and servicing these machines, Loose Wheels carries a complete line of Polaris accessories, parts and clothing. Loose Wheels will also service, but does not stock parts for Yamaha and Arctic Cat Snowmobiles and Honda and Suzuki ATVs.

A Bell helmet ad, "If you have a $10 head, wear a $10 helmet," says it all when it comes to the safety gear, apparel, and accessory items carried at Loose Wheels. From mid-October through March, Loose Wheels has an inventory of Polaris Snowmobiles and accessories. Most of the helmets are Kevlar, made by Bell, and include Polaris, Sno Pro, and Sno Raider. Other top-of-the-line helmets carried at Loose Wheels are Lazer and Sure. Polaris clothing includes snowmobile suits, jackets, boots, and gloves in all sizes, head bands, neck gators, socks, and caps. The store also stocks a year-around selection of sweat and T-shirts, caps, fanny packs, and quality knives.

The inventory at Loose Wheels changes from Polaris Snowmobiles to Polaris ATVs for spring, summer and fall. The store is bursting at the seams with quality ATV helmets, chest protectors, riding pants, kidney belts, gloves, ATV parts and accessories, protection gear, gun racks, utility boxes, and ATV ploughs and mowers. There is also no shortage of T-shirts with ATV related designs and Duck Creek Village logos. In addition, Loose Wheels carries Husqvarna chain saws and other products.

Though it might seem somewhat out of place, Loose Wheels, as the first video store in Duck Creek Village, still offers its customers a quality selection of first run and classic movies.

When Douglas and Lucille Ence, originators of Loose Wheels Service, came to Duck Creek Village in 1981, Duck Creek Village was nothing more that a former movie site with a few rustic buildings built against the grandeur of the Dixie National Forest. The Ences first opened a service station with garage and then a hair salon.

Duck Creek Village offered Douglas and Lucille what they were looking for—a get-away respite to enjoy Snowmobiling, ATVing, fishing, and the beauties of a pristine land. They enjoyed these outdoor sports so much that it was not long before they had petitioned for and become the first Polaris Dealership in the county.

When traveling the highways and byways, Lucille's CB handle was Loose Wheels. It only seemed fitting, when the Ences opened their store that caters to snowmobilers and ATVers, that the shop should be called Loose Wheels. 'Loose' calls to mind an unrestrained spirit and 'wheels,' an illusion of mobility. Snowmobiles and ATVs give sports enthusiasts and back country devotees an unrestrained feeling of mobility. It is the perfect name.

The Ence's son, Rod, and his wife, Pam, took over the business in 1989. Douglas and Lucille felt it was time to retire. That lasted for two years. In 1991 they opened a second Loose Wheels Service dealership at 151 South Main in Cedar City, Utah.

Rod and Pam and all personnel at Loose Wheels are environmentally aware and extremely safety conscious. A 45 minute training course, established by Loose Wheels, teaches all maneuvers with concentrated training on getting on and off the inclines. Snowmobile training, accomplished by the U. S. Forestry Service, takes place in the meadows behind Loose Wheels. Although the training was specifically set up for youth, all ages, especially those who have never snowmobiled, are encouraged to participate.

Spectacular pine and aspen mountains, scenic open spaces, and colorful red rock country make the Cedar Mountain area one of the most picturesque places in Utah for Snowmobiling and ATVing. This area encompasses the forested beauty of Dixie National Forest and the red rock pinnacles of Cedar Breaks National Monument. Duck Creek Village and Loose Wheels Service are in the middle of it all.

Within an hour's drive of Duck Creek Village are two national parks, Bryce Canyon and Zion, and one national monument, Cedar Breaks. The North Rim of the Grand Canyon and Lake Powell, a national recreation area, are within a two hour drive. Three incredibly beautiful lakes—Navajo, Mirror, and Duck Creek Pond—are all within a five-mile drive. Summer and winter fishing is fantastic at all three. During summer months, Panguitch Lake, great for fishing, boating and water skiing, is a 45-minute drive.

Duck Creek Village, quaint and small as it might be, is self-sustaining with its picturesque lodging, restaurants, general stores, and Loose Wheels Polaris dealership. The secret is out! Duck Creek Village, Loose Wheels Service, and Polaris—they are all "king of the hill."

Travelers' Choice now returns, via the Markagunt Scenic Byway to Scenic Byway 89, going south through the small histoic pioneer towns of Long Valley, Glendale, Orderville, and Mt. Carmel to Mt. Carmel Junction and Kanab.

LONG VALLEY

Long Valley, unincorporated, is the 25-mile stretch of verdant farmland between Long Valley Junction and Mt. Carmel Junction. Between the two junctions are the small tows of Glendale, population, 282; Orderville, population, 422; and Mt. Carmel. Those who first settled this area called it Berry Canyon after John Berry who settled Berryville (now Glendale) in 1864. The Berrys, at the time, were somewhat canonized because several family members were killed by Indians while they were in the process of settling the valley.

GLENDALE

Located on U.S. 89 in the middle of Long Valley and along the Upper Virgin River, Glendale was first settled in 1862 by a party of pioneers led by William Berry, who had first settled in Kanarraville. Glendale was first named Berryville and was the first settlement in Long Valley which, at that time, was called Berry Valley. William Berry's brother, Robert, and his wife, Isabella, were murdered by the Indians. In 1866, because of Indian uprisings and the Black Hawk war, Berryville was abandoned. In 1871 a group known as the Muddy Mission, led by James Leithead, resettled the Berryville town site and renamed it Glendale because of its beautiful glen-like surroundings. Another historical account states that the town was renamed Glendale by the area's first bishop, who said the area reminded him of his home in Scotland.

ORDERVILLE

Located on U.S. 89, halfway between Glendale and Mt. Carmel, orderville was settled in 1875 by pioneers who had relocated either from settlements on the Muddy River in Nevada or from Glendale. Orderville was a settlement with a purpose. Those who built their homes here came with a commitment to re-dedicate their lives to living a strict principle of the church, The United Order. The name comes from that program.

MT. CARMEL

Located on the East Fork of the Virgin River, Mt. Carmel was first settled in 1864 by Dr. Priddy Meeks and his family. Mt. Carmel's first name was Windsor, named after Anson P. Windsor, the Mormon church apostle who was assigned to this area. Windsor was vacated during the Black Hawk Indian uprising but was re-settled in 1871 and given the name, Mt. Carmel, after a mountain in northwest Israel.

MT. CARMEL JUNCTION

Mt. Carmel Junction is at the turning point of U.S. 89 onto the well-known Mt. Carmel Highway, U-9, which leads to the East Entrance of Zion National Park. Because of its proximity to the Park, Mt. Carmel Junction has become a vacation destination. At this terminus are numerous motels, restaurants, service stations, gift shops, and one of the state's most verdant nine-hole golf courses.

RESORTS

BEST WESTERN THUNDERBIRD RESORT

Mt. Carmel Junction of Highways 89 & 9
P. O. Box 5536
Mt. Carmel, Utah 84755
Tel:
Motel   (435) 648-2203
Golf   (435) 648-2188
Restaurant   (435) 648-2203
FAX: (435) 648-2239
Web Site: http://www.onpages.com/thunderbird/
Hrs: All facilities
Open Daily   7:00 a.m. - 10:00 p.m.
Visa, MasterCard, American Express, Diners Club, Carte Blanche, and Discover are accepted.
Lodge reservations are highly recommended.

If visiting Utah's National Parks is the sole purpose for coming to Southwestern Utah, Best Western Thunderbird Resort, located in the heart of the parks, is an ideal place to stay.

Nestled beneath the Zion Mountains, the Best Western Thunderbird Resort is only 12.5 miles to the east of Zion National Park. Bryce Canyon National Park is an easy 60-mile drive to the northeast, and the North Rim of the Grand Canyon is just 95 miles southwest. The Thunderbird, located at the Mt. Carmel Junction of two of Utah's Scenic Byways—89 and 9—is also only 10 miles from Coral Pink Sand Dunes State Park and is close to Pipe Spring National Monument.

Whatever the reason for visiting Southwestern Utah, the Thunderbird Resort, with its spacious rooms, luxurious heated pool and hot tub, lush nine-hole golf course, restaurant, and gift shop, is still the exemplary accommodation.

All 62 rooms are luxuriously spacious and offer guests a choice of smoking or non-smoking and single king or double queen beds. Decorated with modern day colors of mauve and teal blue, the rooms offer remote control cable TV, direct dial phones with local calls free, large bathrooms with tub and shower, and a separate vanity basin. Dressers, desks, tables, headboards, and chairs are furnishings of the highest quality. Some rooms with kings also offer large sofas.

In addition to standard rooms, the Thunderbird offers a room for the physically impaired. The tub is jetted and has bars to facilitate ease of getting in and out. A special chair has been designed for the wheelchair-bound and there is an adjoining room for guests accompanying the impaired.

Honeymooners or romantically inclined couples will want to inquire about the Honeymoon Suite. Decorated in light teal blue and mauve, the elegant room offers a step up bedroom and separate living quarters. Above the jetted tub is an exquisite chandelier. The tub is open to the bedroom and has a door that also opens into the bathroom, where there is a separate shower. When the drapes are drawn, the room overlooks the resort's beautiful pool and Jacuzzi.

All guest rooms have doors that open to private patios that overlook the golf course, the pool, or park-like lawn.

For families or larger groups traveling together, the Thunderbird offers a separate family suite. Offered are three queen beds, two hide-a-bed sofas, eight overstuffed chairs, and one and one-half baths. If that isn't enough, there are also roll-aways available.

Green fees are low and the Thunderbird's 9-hole executive golf course, ensconced against the Zion Mountains, offers just the right mix of sand traps, ponds, trees, and grade to make playing it enjoyable and challenging. The course offers a free putting green, electric golf carts and pull carts. For those who forgot their clubs, rentals are available at the pro shop, along with a full line of golfing equipment and paraphernalia.

The Thunderbird Restaurant (see related story) offers breakfast, lunch and dinner and features home-style cooking, with homemade bread and pies a specialty.

The Thunderbird Resort's Gift Shop (see related story) is stocked with one of the area's finest selections of Southwest gifts and souvenirs.

The Thunderbird Resort truly stands as a memorial to one courageous woman, Fern Morrison, who, widowed in 1961, had the determination to survive as a woman alone. Jack and Fern Morrison homesteaded the Mt. Carmel property in 1931 and built a service station along, what was then, just a gravel road. An exceptional baker, Fern often treated truck drivers to a piece of her pie when they stopped to refuel. In 1941 the couple built a restaurant to satisfy the appetites of truckers and early visitors to the area.

When Jack died in 1961, that was all there was—a small service station and a small restaurant. Most of the acreage surrounding today's resort was nothing more than washes and gullies. Not long after Jack's death Fern was threatened with losing her water rights because they had not been used for some time. It was then that Fern decided to build a golf course so she could save her water rights. People thought she was daft, but Fern, a real business woman, had already perceived that there was also a need for accommodations in the area. In 1969 the first 28 units were built.

Today the service station, which offers a complete mini-mart, the golf course, restaurant, gift shop, and luxurious lodge are still overseered by Fern, who in November 1997, celebrated her 90th birthday. In spite of having had 57 broken bones and a hip replacement, Fern still swims daily, has a mind as sharp as a tack, and makes all the final decisions.

The Best Western Thunderbird Resort is truly a family owned and operated business. One of Jack and Fern's two daughters, Marie, and her husband Lloyd Sullivan, are managers of the lodge, gift shop and restaurant. Another daughter, Betty, and husband, Art Goodnow, run the family's hardware store. A granddaughter, Jackie Hannigan, is an artist and painted the restaurant's, wall mural. Another granddaughter, Tanya, is the marketing director for the complex. She and her husband, Gordon Milligan, also do the accounting for the resort. Ed Myers, a grandson, is responsible for the facility's unique rock work. Of special note is the rock facade on one of the lodge units. It features two unique stair-step waterfalls and a rock map of Utah, Nevada, Colorado, and Arizona, where the four corners come together. It also pinpoints the location of Thunderbird Resort. Ed Myers, along with Greg Goodnow, another grandson, are golf course superintendents.

When driving North or South on Scenic Byway Highway 89, there is no finer place to stop and stay than the Best Western Thunderbird Resort.

CORAL CANYONS RANCH

(one-half mile South of Mt. Carmel Junction on Highway 89, then three miles southwest.)
P. O. Box 50
Orderville, Utah 84758
Tel: (702) 358-5553
(800) 469-3789
FAX: (702) 358-9675
Cellular: (435) 689-0592
Web Site:
http://www.gowildwest.com
E-Mail: Info@gowildwest.com
Hrs:
Season: May 1 - October 31
Visa and MasterCard are accepted.
Reservations are recommended.

Located in the heart of Utah's National Park country, Coral Canyons Ranch is a working guest ranch and western retreat that makes frontier life seem like child's play. Not that the ranch isn't work, because it is. It is just that the terrain is so spectacular and the proprietors, Darrell and Barbara Foote, are so congenial and fun to be with, that working the ranch becomes the answer to a "want-to-be cowhand's" dream. And no one can come away from a Coral Ranch experience without developing an attachment to Chub-Dog, the family's chocolate Labrador.

It is almost impossible to describe Coral Canyons Ranch. Enveloped between majestic coral cliffs, the valley is pristine and verdant with the Virgin River meandering along the valley. At the end of a beautiful three mile drive is the ranch house, ensconced against a setting of pure magnificence.

The Coral Canyons Ranch House has six upstairs bedrooms, one with queen bed and panoramic view of the coral arroyos, and five with a full size bed topped by a single bunk. Two of the bedrooms have private baths. The other four guest rooms share three bathrooms, one of which is upstairs and two that are downstairs. A loft built for conversation overlooks the ranch Great Room, a spacious antechamber of rustic decor.

There are many ways that one can avail themselves of a Coral Canyons Ranch experience. Those with limited time on their hands can enjoy the property as a bed and breakfast and take full advantage of the horseback riding, 4X4 back country adventure tours, wagon rides, nature hikes, and other activities that the ranch offers. Coral Canyons Ranch is also the perfect site for small conventions and seminars, company business get-away meetings, VIP excursions, club gatherings, and group retreats.

Horseback rides, 4X4 back country adventure tours, and wagon rides are also available to those not staying at the ranch, when not in use by the ranch's guests. Please call in advance for reservations.

But to truly enjoy Coral Canyons Ranch, one should consider a "full working ranch stay." A full working ranch stay includes lodging, meals, and all horseback riding and ranch activities. The ranch also offers a cattle drive or an overnight trail ride for those staying seven days or longer.

The cattle drive begins at the ranch with *City Slicker*-type cowhands riding horses that are matched to every ability level. Cattle are driven down the gorge to a trail that leads to the top of the canyon ledges and then out onto grazing lands. Here the cattle are left to graze while ranch hands ride the fence to check for needed repairs before setting up camp.

High above the canyon walls, cowhands make camp in a remarkable setting of pinion pines, juniper, and sagebrush. A hearty campfire dinner is made even more enjoyable by watching the sun set over Zion National Park. For those who have never viewed the stars away from city lights, the show is about to begin. There is nothing more inspiring than sleeping under a brilliant western sky that is filled to the brim with celestial bodies. In the morning, refreshed and exhilarated by the experience, the group enjoys a generous breakfast before breaking camp. They then head back to the guest ranch, exploring side canyons, viewing petroglyphs, and learning of ancient history as they go. The trek takes the cowhands down a steep and winding trail into the Virgin River and Parunuweap Canyon, an Indian word meaning "rushing waters." When they return to camp there are 4X4 back country tours, wagon rides, nature hikes, and games of horse shoes and volleyball. Guests can also simply relax and enjoy the grandeur that nature has created between these lofty coral bluffs. The cattle drive is two days and one night and includes all meals.

Besides having some of the world's most perfect scenery in its backyard, Coral Canyons Ranch is ideally located as the home base for exploring the area's nearby parks and monuments. National Parks within an easy drive from the ranch are Zion, 14 miles, Bryce, 56 miles, the North Rim of Grand Canyon, 98 miles, and Capitol Reef, 174 miles. Cedar Breaks National Monument is 47 miles, and Coral Pink Sand Dunes State Park is 15 miles. The Glen Canyon Lake Powell National Recreation Area is 88 miles.

If the desire is there to experience the old west as the movies portray it to be, there is no better way to do it than by booking a stay at Coral Canyons Ranch.

RESTAURANTS

THUNDERBIRD RESTAURANT

Mt. Carmel Junction of Highways 89 & 9
P. O. Box 5536
Mt. Carmel, Utah 84755
Tel: (435) 648-2203
FAX: (435) 648-2239
Web Site:
http://www.onpages.com/thunderbird/
Hrs:
Open Daily   7:00 a.m. - 10:00 p.m.
Visa, MasterCard, American Express, Diners Club, Carte Blanch, and Discover are accepted.
Reservations are not required.

From the moment one enters the lobby of the Thunderbird Restaurant it is obvious that this is a facility where people come first. Gracious personnel promptly greet and seat guests in dining areas that have been designed to facilitate privacy.

The spacious dining room is divided with arched dividers. Indirect lighting provides warmth and intimacy and plants and planters are profuse throughout. This is the Southwest and the color scheme and pictures on the wall, in colors of peach, burgundy, and teal blue, reflect a southwestern motif. There is also a large wall mural of red sandstone bluffs with a coyote howling at the moon.

Breakfast at the Thunderbird is served from 7:00 a.m. to 12:00 noon and offers an assortment of breads and pastries that includes sweet rolls, cinnamon rolls, blueberry, bran, and English muffins, and Fern Morrison's famous pies. All bread and pastry items are baked daily on the premise.

French toast, flapjacks and pancakes are always a favorite. One or two eggs, any style, are served with a choice of bacon or sausage, hashbrowns, and choice of toast. The Thunderbird also offers a six-ounce steak with any style eggs.

Omelette selections include Denver, Mexican, American (featuring ham and cheese), and the Garden Club, which offers turkey, tomatoes, and cheese. All omelettes come with hash browns and choice of toast.

Children ten and under are always a consideration at the Thunderbird. Every breakfast, lunch and dinner item is given a name to delight and entice a child's appetite. Smoking Chief's Cakes are dollar-sized pancakes served with bacon. Princess Golden Flower's Favorite offers an egg any style, with bacon and homemade toast. Anasazi Indian Delight is a choice of oatmeal or cold cereal with toast. All children's breakfasts are served with a choice of milk or juice.

Lunch is served from noon to 5:00 p.m. and offers the same menu selection as dinner, but with baked potatoes and the salad bar offered as part of the dinner menu from 5:00 p.m. to 10:00 p.m.

The sandwich selection for lunch and dinner includes a variety of hot open faced sandwiches. Also offered are single, double, ortega, and bacon hamburgers and cheeseburgers. Grilled sandwiches include cheese, chicken malibu, tuna melt, and bacon, lettuce and tomato.

Entree items include a selection of steaks, such as Filet, New York, and Rib Eye, or a combination dinner of New York steak with three Jumbo Shrimp. Seafood choices are Grilled Trout or Halibut and five Jumbo Fried Shrimp. Lemon and Mesquite Chicken are poultry favorites along with the Thunderbird's famous Chicken 'n Dumplings. Homestyle recipes include Roast Beef, Grilled Liver with Onions or Bacon, and Country Fried Steak. All entrees, after 5:00 p.m. are served with a choice of potatoes, a loaf of fresh baked bread, and soup or a trip to the salad bar.

Choices for the kids include Ringtail Cat's Nuggets (chicken nuggets), Boppie Birds Cheese Melt (grilled cheese), Fickle Fox's Sticks (chicken drumstick and fries), and Silly Squirrel's Wings (chicken wings and fries). All are served with cookies and applesauce and a choice of milk, lemonade or soda.

The Thunderbird Restaurant offers some of the finest dining along Highway 89, one of Utah's famous Scenic Byways. It is impossible to miss the Thunderbird Restaurant. Just as the interior reflects Southwestern hospitality, the exterior, built like a Pueblo Indian dwelling in sandstone orange, blends with the terrain in a very auspicious manner.

DID YOU KNOW?

---that the eastern side of Zion National Park, from Mt. Carmel Junction to the East Entrance, offers exceptional hoodoos, slickrock, monoliths, and narrow canyons that can be explored on one's own. Trails to explore include the pass between Crazy Quilt and Checkerboard mesas or the Canyon Overlook Trail that begins between the two Zion tunnels.

SPECIALTY SHOPPING

THUNDERBIRD RESORT GIFT SHOP
Mt. Carmel Junction of Highways 89 & 9
P. O. Box 5536
Mt. Carmel, Utah 84755
Tel: (435) 648-2203
FAX: (435) 648-2239
Web Site:http?//www.onpages.com/thunderbird/
Hrs:
Open Daily   7:00 a.m. - 10:00 p.m.
Visa, MasterCard, American Express, Diners Club, Carte Blanch, and Discover are accepted.

Adjacent to the lobby of the Thunderbird Restaurant is one of the finest gift shops in Southwestern Utah. Thunderbird Resort Gift Shop offers the finest selection of souvenir gifts, Native American artifacts, and Native American jewelry.

The large and varied assortment of souvenirs includes collector key chains, tie tacs, and magnets. There are mugs, plates, ceramic bells, and spoons. Wearable souvenirs include T-shirts, caps, and sweats. The Gift Shop also houses a large assortment of national park calendars and books.

Visitors to the Thunderbird appreciate the quality of workmanship in the sculptures from Mill Creek Studios. They are awed with the assortment of natural flowers, cut glass, and stained glass window hangings. Collectors of pewter and crystal recognize the Spoontique name and applaud the selection. There are beautiful Native American figurines by Sundance Artware, Indian and Cowboy sculptures by Daniel R. Monfest, and a superb collection of exquisite Navajo rugs.

Whatever the size, shape, or color one is looking for in Native American pottery, they are bound to find it at the Thunderbird Resort Gift Shop. The selection includes a variety from Hopi, Navajo, Utes, Acomas, and Lagunas. In addition there are Kachina and Story Teller dolls, Dream Catchers and Mandellas.

If sterling silver jewelry is a fetish, guests are sure to find a prize from the large assortment of turquoise, mother of pearl, or coral-embellished rings, bracelets, earrings, and necklaces for women, and belt buckles, bolero ties, and rings for men.

Wall hangings include sand paintings and silk screened metal paintings of Native Americans and indigenous animals.

For those who have always dreamed of being a cowboy, Thunderbird Resort Gift Shop can't provide the horse, but they do have a good selection of cowboy hats.

So whether the desire is for a collectible memento, souvenir for oneself or a friend, or a lifetime treasure, the Thunderbird Resort Gift Shop is sure to provide the perfect choice.

KANAB

Many would concur that of all the towns in Utah, Kanab, with its current population of 4,500, is the most magical. A few years ago Utah began promoting northern Utah as having the "greatest snow on earth." It didn't take Southwestern Utahns long to realize that their slogan could very well be "the greatest earth on show."

This maxim, interestingly enough, rings true in two different ways in Kanab.

Portions of Zion and Bryce Canyon National Parks, the Glen Canyon National Recreation Area and Lake Powell, and Grand Staircase-Escalante National Park, are in Kane County, along with Coral Pink Sand Dunes and Kodachrome Basin State Parks. These exquisite creations of nature warrant the saying, "Greatest earth on show." But Kanab, known throughout the state as "Little Hollywood," presents many visitors with a feeling of déjà vu. Wherever they might venture in the surrounding countryside, visitors are bound to come away with a feeling that they have been there before. Kanab and its surrounding Vermilion Cliffs have been the location for over 92 feature length films as well as hundreds of TV shows. Kanab, without question, has the "greatest earth on show."

The first home in Kanab was built in 1864 by Levi Savage who, along with several other white men, came to the area to find feed for their livestock and to graze their sheep nearby. In that same year the territorial legislature created Kane County, naming it after Colonel Thomas L. Kane, a friend of the Mormon people. In 1865, 15 families settled on Kanab Creek and began building a fort. The fort, however, was never completed. The Blackhawk War forced the pioneers to abandon their settlement. At war's end several of the families returned during the winter of 1867 - 1868 and with the help of friendly Paiute Indians, finished building the fort. Brigham Young, leader of the Mormon Church, visited the outpost in 1870 and was so impressed with the area's potential that he returned home to Salt lake City and called a group of colonists with specific skills to settle the community. In September President Young returned to Kanab to supervise the surveying of the community. In 1871 the Deseret Telegraph Company's lines reached Kanab. In 1872 Major John Wesley Powell made the town his headquarters for exploring the surrounding country. During the ensuing years Kanab, which became the Kane County seat in 1883, experienced intermittent prosperity, floods, and drought.

In 1924 the Tom Mix movie, "Deadwood Coach," was filmed in Johnson Canyon. That gave Kanab's entrepreneur brothers—Gron, Whit, and Chaunce Parry—an idea. If one movie company liked what Kanab had to offer, why shouldn't the others. Westerns were the movie industry's blockbusters and Kanab's incredible landscape was the West. Aerial and back country pictures were taken, a visit made to Hollywood, and Kanab and the Vermilion Cliffs became the West of Western movies. The Parry brothers were untiring in their efforts to make sure that whatever Hollywood needed for their movies, Kanab was sure to have . Before long the whole town was involved in the endeavor. Among the movies filmed here was "The Greatest Story Ever Told." It, and the 91 other movies filmed here have indeed created some of Kanab's "greatest stories ever told."

When visiting Kanab, one cannot help being taken aback by the sheer beauty of its setting. The coral mountains surrounding the high desert community cut a stark contrast to azure blue skies and billowy white clouds.

Enraptured by the magnificence of one's surroundings, it only makes sense that Kanab should be perceived as a hub for visiting Southwestern Utah. Eight of America's most scenic wonders are all within short drives of Kanab. **Zion National Park** is a 45 minute drive to the Northwest. The **Zion Narrows**, at the north end of the Park, is a 65-minute drive. Seventy minutes northeast of Kanab is **Bryce Canyon National Park**. Ninety minutes northeast is **Kodachrome Basin State Park**. **Glen Canyon National Recreation Area** and **Lake Powell** are 70-minutes east of Kanab. Just a few miles southwest of Kanab is **Pipe Springs National Monument, Coral Pink Sand Dunes State Park** is a short drive to the northwest. Also within two-hour drives are **Cedar Breaks National Monument** to the northeast and the **North Rim of the Grand Canyon** to the southeast. **Grand Staircase-Escalante National Monument** begins almost at Kanab's eastern doorstep along U.S. 89.

All one has to do is look at a map to know why Kanab is such an important tourist destination. Kanab is the center of it all. Tourism is Kanab's number one business and it "shows."

KANAB ATTRACTIONS

CORAL PINK SAND DUNES STATE PARK

Coral Pink Sand Dunes is a sand box of epic proportions—1,000 acres of playground for off-highway vehicle enthusiasts, campers, hikers, and photographers. The ripples of rolling coral pink dunes punctuated with wind-whipped trees give one the feeling of being in another world. The pink of the sand hills and mountains pitted against vermilion cliffs in the distance present a visual delight encountered nowhere else in the world.

The State Park features a 22-unit campground with group site and double sites, modern rest rooms, hot showers, and a sewage disposal station. Campsites all have pull-through parking, barbecue grills, and picnic tables. There is a nature trail and a boardwalk trail leading to dune overlook. Coral Pink Sand Dunes is an excellent base location for exploring Utah's extraordinary scenery. Reservations for group and individual campsites may be made four months in advance.

Coral Pink Sand Dunes State Park is also surrounded by BLM land with hundreds of miles of trails and developed 4-wheel drive roads. Harris Mountain, north of the park, offers views of the sand dunes and Zion National Park. The South Fork Indian Canyon petroglyph trailhead is four miles northeast of Coral Pink Sand Dunes. The east boundary of the park is Moquith Mountains.

Coral Pink Sand Dunes State Park is 12 miles west of U.S. 89 and 12 miles north of Kanab. It is well marked on U.S. 89 and along the back road. The park is open year-round (435-874-2408 and, for camping reservations, 800-322-3770).

ACCOMMODATIONS

BEST WESTERN RED HILLS
125 West Center Street
Kanab, Utah 84741
Tel: (435) 644-2675
         (800) 528-1234
FAX: (435) 644-5919
Visa, MasterCard, American Express, Diners Club, Carte Blanche, and Discover are accepted.
Reservations are recommended.

There is no better way to enjoy one's Southwestern Utah vacation than by staying at the Best Western Red Hills. This triple A three-diamond facility is located at the center of three national parks—Zion, Bryce, and Grand Canyon—as well as providing a close proximity to Lake Powell Marina, Coral Pink Sand Dunes State Park, and Pipe Springs National Monument. The motel's red sandstone construction and South-

205

western ambiance reflect the uniqueness of Kanab, which has been dubbed part of "the greatest earth on show," and Utah's "Little Hollywood."

Red Hills offers 75 spacious guest rooms decorated in modern colors of mauve and teal or dark burgundy and teal. Rooms are well lit and offer Cable TV with HBO, Disney, Encore, and ESPN channels; wake-up clock radio, phone with local calls free, golden oak furnishings, and bathrooms with combination tub and shower and separate basin vanity. Guests have a choice of double queen or single king beds and smoking and non-smoking rooms.

A room for the physically impaired offers a king bed and extra large bathroom with shower seat and hand held shower head. There is a private door with entrance directly to and from the parking lot.

Property amenities include a large fenced in pool and Jacuzzi with red sandstone decking, continental breakfast, spacious meeting and convention facilities, and guest laundry.

Whether traveling by car or tour bus, the Best Western Red Hills makes every vacation unforgettable.

BRANDON MOTEL
223 West Center Street
Kanab, Utah 84741
Tel: (435) 644-2631
FAX: (435) 644-3112
Web Site:
www.onpages.com/brandon
Visa, MasterCard, American Express,
and Discover are accepted.
Reservations are recommended.

Best doesn't always mean the most expensive and such is the case with Kanab's Brandon Motel, a superb little motel with well-maintained rooms and numerous guest amenities. For one of the Brandon's amenities, the John Wayne room, it is recommended that guests call well in advance if they want to sleep in the bed that John Wayne did.

Kanab has been dubbed "Little Hollywood" and one of the most frequent celebrity visitors to Kanab in its western heyday was John Wayne. Delbert and Linda Donathan, hosts, recently acquired his entire bedroom suite. The room, in addition to exquisitely carved furnishings that include a mirrored dresser, nightstand, headboard, footstool and desk, has three pictures of the Duke himself. The John Wayne room has a kitchenette and a large bathroom with shower.

The Donathans have learned the knack of treating their guests as if they were just that, guests. Having been in the hotel business for numerous years, they realize that tourists on vacation are looking for economical accommodations.

Each of the Brandon's 20 rooms offer queen or double queen room beds with Cable TV and HBO, direct dial phones with local calls free, and quality, yet individually unique, furnishings.

Several of the rooms are family suites with full kitchens and sofa with hide-abed. Several other rooms offer kitchenettes.

On either side of the motel office is a rock waterfall surrounded by a bed of flowers. Guest amenities include a large heated pool, picnic and barbecue area, and parking facilities that will accommodate motor homes, trucks and tour buses.

In addition to being known as "Little Hollywood," Kanab has also been touted as part of Kane County's "the Greatest Earth on Show." Kanab is centrally located in the heart of Utah's national parks. Within an easy drive are Zion, Bryce, and the North Rim of Grand Canyon national parks. Coral Pink Sand Dunes and Pipe Springs National Monument are also close by.

For those who enjoy homey and well-maintained rooms at truly affordable rates, Brandon Motel is a good choice.

HOLIDAY INN EXPRESS-KANAB
at Coral Cliffs
815 East Highway 89
Kanab, Utah 84741
Tel: (435) 644-8888
       (800) 574-4061
FAX: (435) 644-8880
Visa, MasterCard, American Express, Diners Club, and Discover are accepted.
Reservations are recommended.

Holiday Inn promotes its Express facilities as a streamlined version of the traditional Holiday Inn hotel. Guests staying at the Holiday Inn Express in Kanab, except for the even more affordable rates, would hardly notice the difference.

Holiday Inn Express-Kanab is ensconced in a sensational coral cliff setting with the verdant Coral Cliffs golf course as its backyard. The Holiday Inn Express is Kanab's newest motel and its amenities are anything but streamlined. Amenities include nine holes of free golf, nine holes per room for each night's stay when using Triple A or Holiday Inn's Priority Club. Golf carts are not included. Other services include a large fenced in pool and spa with spectacular views of red sandstone bluffs and the golf course, a diverse free breakfast bar, well-stocked gift shop, spacious Great Room with large screen TV, and a self-serve Laundromat. In addition the Holiday Inn Express offers convention facilities, fax services, efficient check-in and Express checkout, and the Priority Club frequent guest program.

The large lobby offers furnishings with a southwestern ambiance, including log furniture, decorator colors of teal and mauve, and a very unusual antler chandelier. Adjacent to the spacious lobby is a commodious Great Room where a marvelous continental breakfast is served daily. Breakfast offerings include bagels, cream cheese, marmalades, honey and jams, sweet breads, toast, assortment of cereals, milk, juices, fresh fruits, and coffee, tea, and cocoa.

Each of the 67 rooms at the Holiday Inn Express is decorated in modern colors of teal and mauve. The Inn offers smoking and non-smoking rooms with double queen or single king beds. In-room amenities include full length mirrors, direct dial phones with local calls free, and cable TV with HBO, ESPN, Disney, Encore and Starz channels. Rooms are well lit with table, wall, and stand-up lighting. Pictures of area landscapes grace the walls. King rooms have recliner chairs, desk, and an extra night stand. Bathrooms have a combination tub and shower and separate vanity basin.

Affordably priced, the honeymoon suite at the Holiday Inn Express is a popular choice for all romantics. The suite features a king canopy bed, two color TVs, one in the living room, where there is also a hide-a-bed sofa, and one in the bedroom, which has a separating door, and a full closet. The living area also has two night stands, two wing chairs, and a table with chairs. A bay window overlooks the golf course and red sandstone bluffs. The jetted tub is separate from the walk-in shower, private toilet, and full length double basin vanity.

There is plenty of room for mobility in the Holiday Inn's three rooms for the physically impaired. All offer a king bed and recliner. Two have tubs with hand held shower while a third offers a shower with roll-in capabilities.

The Holiday Inn Express Gift Shop is well stocked with snacks, soft drinks, sundries, and a typical line of local souvenirs, post cards, calendars, T-shirts, and caps. That which is not typical is the marvelous assortment of gifts and artifacts from the area's Native Americans. The gift shop offers pottery from the Navajo to satisfy every need and budget. The pottery selection includes vases, night lights, toothpick holders, magnets, candles, and wind chimes. Exquisite silver jewelry, utilizing turquoise, mother of pearl, and coral embellishments, have been expertly crafted by Navajo, Zuni and Hopi artisans. Marvelous tiles depict Southwestern Utah and petroglyphs. There are priceless sand paintings and there are foil prints of Native Americans and indigenous animals. The gift shop showcases story teller and Kachina dolls, rugs, beadwork, fetishes, and rough hewn logs that open to reveal storage for jewelry and other keepsakes. In addition to Native American-made artifacts, the gift shop has a selection of area jigsaw puzzles, southwestern stationary, inexpensive but beautiful Indian dolls, Leanin' Tree cards, and an assortment of cowboy and Indian play toys for the little ones.

The Holiday Inn Express conference facility will comfortably seat 75 theater style and 50 for a sit down banquet. A large TV, video, and white board are available for meetings and conferences. The room is also great for receptions and parties.

By virtue of location there is no more spectacular or focal place to stay when visiting Southwestern Utah than Kanab. With seven National Parks and Monuments close at hand, it is no wonder that the town has been billed as "the greatest earth on show." National Parks include Zion, Bryce Canyon, and the north rim of the Grand Canyon. National Monuments within an easy drive are Cedar Breaks, Pipe Spring, and Rainbow Bridge. The Glenn Canyon National Recreation area with Lake Powell is just two-hours away.

Holiday Inn Expresses across the country advertise that they "have your bed and breakfast covered wherever you travel." In Kanab, at the Holiday Inn Express where sunsets and red sandstone cliffs join together in a blaze of color, Holiday Inn makes going to bed and rising just that much more enjoyable.

DID YOU KNOW?

---that the Daughters of Utah Pioneers have provided a monument on the grounds of the Mormon church, corners of 100 West and 100 South. The Powell Survey Marker denotes the tent site of Major John Wesley Powell, who established his headquarters for the Colorado River Exploration in Kanab. Powell and his team of surveyors made their headquarters in Kanab from 1870 until 1876. The first map of the Grand Canyon was made during the winter of 1872 - 1873. When the map was made, Major Powell gave the canyon its name. Did you also know that though today Johnson Canyon is remembered as the setting for many a Western movie, the valley was actually settled by four sons of Ezekiel and Julia Johnson who were looking for peace from Federal Marshals who were looking for polygamists. A Sons of Utah Pioneers monument is now at the Johnson Canyon cemetery.

PARRY LODGE
89 East Center Street
Kanab, Utah 84741
Tel: (435) 644-2601
(800) 748-4104
FAX: (435) 644-2605
Gift Shop Hours:
Monday - Saturday 8:00 a.m. - 12:00 noon
5:00 p.m. - 9:00 p.m.
Visa, MasterCard, American Express and Discover are accepted.
Reservations are recommended.

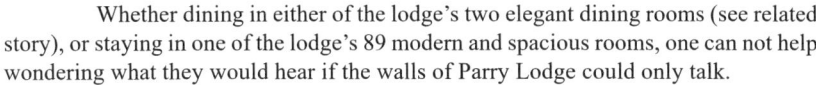

Whether dining in either of the lodge's two elegant dining rooms (see related story), or staying in one of the lodge's 89 modern and spacious rooms, one can not help wondering what they would hear if the walls of Parry Lodge could only talk.

The city of Kanab has long been referred to as "little Hollywood," and it was the Parry brothers, Gronway, Chauncey, and Whit, who made it all happen.

Early in the 1900s, Gronway and Chauncey fell in love with Southern Utah and its spectacular canyons. In 1916, before Bryce and Zion were national parks, the two brothers began Utah-Arizona Transportation Company. As pioneers of the tourist industry, the Parry brothers took visitors into the parks. Then, in 1929, with a prosperous tourist business underway, the brothers decided they needed a lodge as a rest stop for their customers. They purchased the Justin M. Johnson home and the Parry Lodge was born. At first they used the home as it was to house their guests, but in 1931 several two-room cabins and a dining room were built. A local article called the hotel "one of the most up-to-date and picturesque hotels in the area". It was Kanab's first but, with its white pillars, dormer windows and fence-like balcony, the Parry Lodge would be a showpiece even in inner cities.

It was about this same time that the brothers, now joined by Whit, hit upon the idea of wooing Hollywood to Kanab. Tom Mix, in 1924, had made a silent movie, *Deadwood Coach*, and the Parry brothers knew that if Hollywood were aware of what the area had to offer, they would be in business. While Gronway continued to operate the tour business, Chauncey and Whit took hundreds of pictures and set off for Hollywood. As a result of their efforts, the first talkie movie filmed outdoors on location, *In Old Arizona*, was produced in Kanab.

In 1930 a fledgling star, John Wayne, and his movie crew came to Kanab to make the movie, *On the Trail*. Several other movies followed, but it was in 1937, when Metro Goldwyn Mayor came to make *The Bad Man of Brimstone*, that Kanab and its surrounding areas became as recognizable as the stars themselves. From 1924 through 1993 over 80 westerns and 15 other movies have been filmed in and around Kanab. In addition, 14 long running television shows, including *Death Valley Days, The Lone Ranger, Have Gun Will Travel, The Six Million Dollar Man, Wagon Train, F Troop,* and *Daniel Boone* were made in Kanab. The 90's have seen Kanab as the location for such popular films as *Geronimo, Broken Arrow,* and *Wind Runner.*

The Parry Lodge, though not a part of the filmed action, was very much a part of the off-stage action. It was at the Lodge that the stars resided during shooting, dined on some of the best cuisine in the state, and lounged around Southern Utah's finest swimming pool. And it was here that the stars "let down their hair."

Oh, if those walls could only talk!! But one of the walls is talking. In 1963, when the famous "rat pack," Dean Martin, Frank Sinatra, Sammy Davis, Jr., and Peter Lawford were making *Sergeants Three*, Dean Martin and Sammy Davis, Jr. reportedly got in a fight. Dean Martin put his fist through one of the walls. Today, rather than fixing the hole, the wall was removed, and those staying in the Parry Lodge family suite, with its full kitchen and two bedrooms, can glory in the days of Hollywood and the legends who stayed there.

Names above the doors of the other four bungalows are stars who frequently stayed there, Julie Newmar, John Wayne, Fess Parker, and Joey Bishop. Two of the four bungalow rooms offer jetted tubs and two have club-footed tubs. They each have a single queen bed, separate vanity, dresser, desk and chairs. All rooms at Parry Lodge offer Cable color TV with remote control and telephone with local calls free.

In addition to the bungalows, Parry Lodge boasts of 20 other rooms that were occupied by film legends during the Lodge's hey day. Several of these offer two bedrooms, each with single queen, beautiful walnut furnishings, and an outdoor entrance to the second bedroom. Other rooms have two doubles, separate vanity, ornate mirrors, headboards, dresser and night stand. Names above these doors include Walter Brennan, Peter Lawford, Tim Conway, Maureen O' Hara, Gregory Peck, Joel McCrea, Fred MacMurray, Barbara Stanwyck, Anne Baxter, Ruth Roman, Don Knotts, Sammy Davis Jr., Robert Preston, Tyrone Power, Arlene Dahl, Dean Martin, Telly Savalas, Frank Sinatra, James Garner, and Ronald Reagan.

Although the rooms in the hotel complex were built more recently and do not have the names of stars above the doors, they feature two double beds, two easy chairs, table, separate vanity as well as vanity basin in the bathroom, and tubs with showers and Euro-bath hair and body shampoo dispensers.

In addition to its two marvelous dining rooms and sparkling pool, another Parry Lodge guest amenity is its Gift Shop, which offers a variety of authentic Indian jewelry, handmade items, original drawings and paintings, colorful T-shirts, children's gifts, collector books of the area, and many more souvenir and collector items. And nowhere, other than Hollywood itself, will one find more autographed photographs of stars, than in the restaurant and lobby of Parry Lodge.

Few, if any country hotels have received more national acclaim than has the Parry Lodge. Parry Lodge has received feature story status on numerous occasions in *Saturday Evening Post. Life* called Parry Lodge "one of the finest roadside Inns in America." When Kanab was receiving its status as "little Hollywood," Parry Lodge *was* the center of it all.

Today, as tourists from around the world arrive to view panoramas acclaimed to be "the greatest earth on show," Parry Lodge is still at the center and heart of it all. All within an easy drive are Utah's national parks. Zion is 37 miles; Bryce, 80 miles; and the North Rim of Grand Canyon, 78 miles. Lake Powell, a national recreation area, is 73 miles; and two state parks, Coral Pink Sand Dunes and Historic Pipe Springs Fort are approximately 20 miles drive. The narrows of Paria are 36 miles distance, and Lee's Ferry, for river trips, is 81 miles.

Parry Lodge, in the heart of Kanab Color Country is where the stars stay and where, because of the hearts of caring personnel, ordinary people are made to feel like stars.

SHILO INN
296 West 100 North
Kanab, Utah 84741
Tel: (435) 644-2562
      (800) 222-2244
FAX: (435) 644-5333
Visa, MasterCard, American Express, Diners Club, Carte Blanche, and Discover are accepted.
Reservations are recommended.

Shilo Inns across the Western United States have earned the reputation for "affordable excellence." Far from being the exception, the Shilo Inn in Kanab offers not only excellence in accommodations and amenities but in sightseeing opportunities.

Having been nicknamed "Utah's Little Hollywood," and "the Greatest Earth on Show," Kanab has the good fortune of being situated in the center of three spectacular national parks. Zion, Bryce, and the North Rim of Grand Canyon are all within easy drives. Also close by are Coral Pink Sand Dunes, Pipe Springs National Monument, and Lake Powell where swimming, boating, and water skiing abound. After sightseeing, when it is time to come home, there is no better haven for relaxing and enjoying pure respite than the Shilo Inn.

At Shilo Inn every room is a mini suite. The spacious accommodations offer guests a choice of double queen, single king, or single queen beds. Standard at the Shilo are Satellite TVs with remote controls and Showtime, Disney, HBO, ESPN, CNN, TBS, WGN, and TNT. Also in every room are a clock radio, iron and ironing board, and a mirrored bar with microwave and mini refrigerator. Bathrooms have tub shower combinations, separate wash basin vanity, hair dryer and phone. There are two other direct dial phones, one by the bed and one at the desk, with local calls free. Furnishings, with accent colors of teal and mauve, reflect a Southwestern motif.

The Shilo also offers rooms with tubs and showers that have safety bars and hand-held shower heads for the physically impaired.

Families and guests traveling together or guests planning an extended vacation appreciate "the suite." This spacious accommodation offers a full kitchen with dishwasher, refrigerator, range and oven and all utensils. The living room features overstuffed chairs, dining table with four chairs, game table with two chairs, several ottomans, sofa with hide-a-bed, and television. A king bed, walk-in closet, and second TV are in the bedroom.

The Shilo also offers a number of double queen rooms with single king connecting rooms.

Guest amenities at Shilo Inn include a beautiful outdoor heated pool and Jacuzzi spa, airport shuttle service, VCR and movie rental, free continental breakfast, free daily copy of *USA Today,* and guest laundry service. Always available, at check in or anytime, are free popcorn, fruit, and coffee. Shilo Inn has FAX service for its guests, smoking and non-smoking rooms, weekly and monthly rates, truck, motor home, and tour bus parking, elevators in the North building, and ice and beverage machines.

Kanab and Shilo Inn are a perfect combination for businesses planning conferences and conventions. The Willow Room will facilitate 100 theater style, 75 with classroom setup, and 70 for banquets.

Shilo Inns was founded in 1974 and today, with 44 locations in nine western states, it is the largest independently owned and operated hospitality company in the Western United States. In 1990 Business Travel News listed Shilo Inns among the fastest growing international hotel companies.

In searching for the perfect scenic vacation, one naturally looks for the best. Day after day the sun shines down on this majestic desert playground, providing boundless activities for guests to enjoy. And when the sun is cradled in a sandstone bluff, it is time to come home to the comforts that only Shilo Inn can offer. The Shilo Inn—definitely a Travelers' Choice in Southwestern Utah.

ADVENTURE / TOURS

BEST FRIENDS ANIMAL SANCTUARY
Scenic Route 89
Kanab, Utah 84741-5001
Tel: (435) 644-2001
FAX   (435) 644-2078
Hrs:
Open Daily   8:30 a.m. - 5:00 p.m.
Reservations are recommended.

If Best Friends Animal Sanctuary of Kanab, Utah, and its members across the country have their way, the most important event of the new century in Utah will not be the 2002 Winter Olympic games, but the fruition of a targeted **2001: No More Homeless Pets** program.

Best Friends Animal Sanctuary, in the majestic red rock country of Southern Utah, is the nation's largest "no-kill" sanctuary for abused and abandoned domestic animals. The **2001: No More Homeless Pets** program is Best Friends' timetable, through education, adoption, and spay/neuter, for bringing about the time when every domestic animal born can be guaranteed a good life in a good home. It is Best Friends' goal to eradicate euthanasia for any other purpose than its name implies, "mercy killing."

Best Friends had its origin in Arizona in the 1970's when a few animal lovers got together and determined to visit animal shelters every month and take home as many animals as they could care for themselves. They loved, fed, and nurtured these unadoptables and found good homes for most of them. The few who couldn't be placed, for whatever reason, became the founders of the sanctuary, a few of which are still alive and well today and living at Angel Canyon. Best Friends Animal Sanctuary moved to Angel Canyon in 1985 and today has an incredible staff of 80. Incredible, not because of their numbers, but because of their caring and devoted attachment to these abandoned or neglected "best friends of man."

If **2001: No More Homeless Pets** seems impossible to the masses, Best Friends is reminded of the miracles that have previously taken place. They recall a time when no one ever believed there would be a cure for Small Pox, for Polio, or Rabies. And they look at the here and now miracle that is taking place in cosmopolitan San Francisco, which by its own prognosis, is right now only one hair away from being a no-kill city.

To begin a new millennium in the United States with every animal being loved and cared for would bring the world one step closer to the Biblical prophecy of the day when the lamb and the lion shall lie down together. Best Friends Animal Sanctuary and shelters, communities, and the SPCA are working together to bring about a "no-kill" society through neutering and spaying, through grooming scruffy looking animals so they are irresistible, through temporary foster homes until permanent adoption is obtained, and through taking the animals to the homes of those who can not get out and about.

Best Friends Animal Sanctuary is located in magnificent Angel Canyon where petroglyphs still tell of the ancients, the Anasazis, who inhabited this part of Southwestern Utah more than 8,000 years ago. Native tradition asserts that the huge natural amphitheater at Angel Canyon, known as Angels Landing, "was the place where the Native American nations would gather every year to seek guidance from Mother Earth for their people.

Just as Angel Canyon was in ancient times a gathering place for the Anasazi, today, as home to Best Friends Animal Sanctuary, it is a land that welcomes every lost, hurt, or rejected furred or winged friend. It is also a place that welcomes every human being whose soul feels a kinship with God's other living creatures.

Visiting Best Friends Sanctuary in Angel Canyon is encouraged. Best Friends is located approximately five miles north of Kanab on the east side of Highway 89 between the 69 and 70 mile markers. After turning off, follow the signs to the Welcome Center where tours begin. Please call before arriving to check the tour schedule.

The tour winds through the magnificent red rock landscape of Angel Canyon where vistas are similar to those of Zion National Park. Many will recognize part of the terrain, as Angel Canyon has been a backdrop for many movies and TV westerns, including *The Lone Ranger*, Disney's *One Little Indian* starring James Garner, *McKenna's Gold*, and *The Outlaw Josey Wales*.

One can only visit the animal facilities through the guided tours of Best Friends Animal Sanctuary. Tours take about an hour and a half and introduce guests to the two largest animal communities, Dogtown and Catland. At Catland guests view Benton's House with Benton the Cat and his TLC Cat Club. In other communities guests meet Sunshine the burro, Goatie the goat, Two Bits the Shetland pony, Rabbit Redford at the Bunny House, and Fortune the Goose, who welcomes all to Feathered Friends with a big honk. Enroute to the animal communities guests pause to give respect at Angel's Rest Memorial Park, where deceased pets have been laid to rest in a beautiful and lovingly tended setting.

Those touring Best Friends Animal Sanctuary are advised to wear shoes as opposed to sandals, and glasses, instead of contact lenses, because of the sand at the Sanctuary. There is the likelihood that one will be greeted by enthusiastic dogs and cats, so guests are encouraged to wear long pants. There is no cost for the tours to Best Friends members and their families. They are the ones who make it possible for animals to live happily ever after, either at the sanctuary or as one of the 75% that become adopted into a loving home. There is also no cost to those who are not members, but a small donation is encouraged and non-affiliates are always welcome to become members.

Other tours available for a small cost in Angel Canyon are the Anasazi Box Canyon Hike, the Slot Canyon and Sand Hills Hike, and the Wild Bird Spotting Walks. Please call ahead to find out more about these guided tours.

Many who visit and tour desire to come back almost immediately as a volunteer worker. Best Friends has no limit or qualification for those who desire to help. With over 1,500 animals to care for there is always feeding of animals, cleaning of the living areas, grooming, taking the animals for walks, training those who are looking for new homes, and just giving the animals personal attention. In addition there is office help to be done and building maintenance such as fencing, landscaping, plumbing and electrical work. Any and every skill is needed and appreciated.

Ensconced against the red bluffs of Angel Canyon and overlooking the Best Friends pastures are two cottages and the historic Rock House. The cottages sleep two and the Rock House, four. Accommodations tend to book fast, so visitors are encouraged to make their reservations well in advance. Members and volunteers receive a discount. A discounted rate is also given those who book a week's stay.

The Best Friends Animal Sanctuary gift shop tenders a marvelous selection of animal specific souvenirs and memorabilia. Animal lovers are pleased with the selection of gift animal mouse pads, rice bag frogs, delightful animal note cards and books, and Best Friends' own logo mugs, T-shirts and sweatshirts. Visitors are delighted with the quality assortment of dog and cat toys, collars, and vitamins. Of special interest to all who visit are the limited edition sterling silver necklaces, pins, and bracelets reflecting Best Friends Animal Sanctuary. There is also a good selection of Indian jewelry.

Angel Canyon's Best Friends Animal Sanctuary is a place of new beginnings for each of the more than 1,500 animals that call it home. Here they know that no matter what their condition, age, or disposition, they will be loved and tenderly cared for until the hand of God, not the hand of man, says it is time for their demise.

And just as Best Friends Animal sanctuary serves as a new beginning for its animal children, the sanctuary and all that takes place in this hallowed land serves as a new awakening for all who visit. It is impossible to see Benton the cat, partially lame from being hit by a car, or Tomato, found in a trash dumpster when just three weeks old and who, because of a respiratory problem, is unadoptable, without feeling empathy. Tammy, a greyhound dog, was just too slow to satisfy her owners at the racetrack. She was only one step away from being donated to a place that conducts experiments on animals when she was rescued and sent to live at Best Friends. Big Enough, a beautiful rodeo roping horse, was kicked by a bull and his leg permanently injured. That was all that it took to sentence Big Enough to the slaughter house. Fortunately a sympathetic person knew about and arranged for Big Enough to come home to Best Friends. At Easter time one of the most popular gifts a child can receive is an Easter Bunny. But the thrill of a bunny soon wanes for many and Cisco, before joining Best Friends, was on his way to being Thanksgiving dinner. It is impossible to hear these and other stories without developing an awakening of the soul. It is impossible to see and feel the love of a less than perfect animal and to sense the incredible caring of the staff and volunteers at Best Friends without having a desire to know more about, and a penchant to be a part of, this great organization.

Every morning, rain or shine, it is comforting to know that the more than 700 dogs are fed a gourmet mixture of dry and moist foods (10 tons of dry and 4,000 cans of moist dog food every month). Diabetic and arthritic animals get specially prepared food, complete with the right medicines in the right dosage. Stainless steel bowls, one for each dog, are cleaned daily in a stainless steel kitchen. When it is feeding time the waiters and waitresses, who know each dog by name and which bowl belongs to which animal, deliver the food to each dog's favorite eating area.

There are also more than 700 cats, including a hundred or so with disabilities. Benton's House was built through the love and generosity of Best Friends members to provide a better way to take charge of these kittens with special needs. This luxurious condo cat living quarters has four big indoor-outdoor catteries, each of which serves cats with specific needs. Cat furniture is carefully placed for those who can't see very well and ramps are placed for those who can't climb by themselves. Visiting Catland is at the same time both heart breaking and heart warming. The same care of feeding is given at Catland as is given at Dogtown. The Sanctuary goes through one ton of dry cat food and 4,000 cans of moist cat food in a month.

While Best Friends Animal Sanctuary is primarily for domestic animals, Best Friends has a Wildlife Rehabilitation Program to take in and care for wild birds. Once they have been nurtured to recovery they are set free inside the beauty of Angel Canyon's red rock walls. Other feathered animals include King Ming, a beautiful peacock and his three peahens, Fortune and Nimbus the geese, and many well-known domestic birds.

Every animal at Best Friends sees the veterinarian as needed. As soon as animals are admitted to Best Friends they are neutered or spayed and isolated for a week or two to make sure that they are not carrying a disease that could be passed on to the other animals. Blood tests, dental care, and surgery are all done on site. Best Friends' facilities can rival most animal hospitals with its complete operating room, x-ray machine, blood and urine testing devices and anesthesiology apparatus. An intern program offers college students the chance for hands-on practice in veterinary medicine.

Angel Canyon is a miracle of nature. What happens every day within her canyon walls is a miracle of love. All that takes place at Best Friends Animal Sanctuary, a non-profit organization, can only take place because of the love and donations of caring people. The invitation is always open to become a part of the miracle, and help make **2001: No More Homeless Pets** a reality.

RESTAURANTS

NEDRA'S CAFE
Highway 89A
 (five miles south of Kanab)
Fredonia, Arizona 86022
Tel: 	(520) 643-7591

NEDRA'S TOO
310 South, 100 East
(Junction of 89 and 89A)
Kanab, Utah 84741
Tel: 	(435) 644-2030
Hrs: 	Both locations
Open Seven Days   7:00 a.m. - 10:00 p.m.
Closed Thanksgiving Day and Christmas Day.
Visa, MasterCard, American Express and Discover are accepted.

Southwestern decor and cuisine have swept the country in the past decade, introducing the world to a portion of the globe that both Fredonia, Arizona and Kanab, Utah epitomizes. Nedra's Cafe and Nedra's Too are the culmination of efforts from three generations of restaurateurs. The restaurants represent more than 57 years of fine Southwestern cuisine.

Proprietors are Nedra Pauline and Terry Burchinal. Nedra Pauline has a pioneer heritage that dates back to the settling of Kanab and remote Paria Canyon by her great great grandparents. Her grandmother, Jesiel Brown, began a tradition of fine dining when she opened up Brown's 89 House in 1940. In 1957 Nedra Pauline's mother, Nedra, followed in her mother's footsteps and opened Nedra's Cafe. In 1980 Nedra Pauline and Terry assumed operation of the Fredonia restaurant and, in 1990, because of popular demand, they opened a second restaurant, Nedra's Too in Kanab.

Since the inception of Nedra's Cafe in 1940, the restaurant has enjoyed a reputation for serving not only the best Mexican food in the area, but quite conceivably in the state. Nedra's Cafe has been a favorite rendezvous for numerous movie crews and stars. Frequent customers over the years have included James Garner, Clint Eastwood, Sidney Poitier, and Vera Miles. Another well-known diner, former Senator Barry Goldwater, enjoyed Nedra's special hot sauce so much that he has flown gallons of it to his Arizona ranch.

Two favorite breakfast items at both restaurants are Huevos Enchiladas and Country Breakfast. Huevos Enchiladas is a delicious rendition of two eggs any style, smothered in cheese and Nedra's special enchilada sauce, and served on two flat tortillas. The Country Breakfast has steak pieces served on top of hash browns and topped with two eggs any style, country gravy, and melted mild cheddar and jack cheese. Always a breakfast favorite is Nedra's exceptional rendition of the Spanish Omelette.

Nedra's and Nedra's Too are two of few eating establishments that serve breakfast anytime throughout the day. They are also an exception to the rule and offer the same dining menu for lunch and dinner, with no increase in prices for dinner.

Two favorite appetizers from a list that offers quantity as well as quality are Quesadilla and Mexican Pizza. Quesadilla is an offering of two cheeses and green chili strips sandwiched between two grilled flour tortillas and then topped with guacamole, sour cream, onions, tomatoes, and black olives. The Mexican Pizza features a grilled flour tortilla topped with two cheeses, enchilada sauce, taco meat, green chili strips, onion, tomatoes and black olives. Other appetizers that are sure to please are the Stuffed Jalapenos, Nacho Plate, and Chili Cheese Fries.

House Specialties are numerous, varied, and for the most part, anything but traditional. Those dining at either cafe will want to be sure to try one of the entrees with Nedra's unique creamy white jalapeno sauce. Four such dishes are the Chicken Chimichangas, and the Spinach, Crab, and Chicken Enchiladas.

Additional House favorites are Carnitas, Machaca, Chili Verde, and Chimichanga. Carnitas is a succulent roast pork that is seasoned mildly in Nedra's own style and topped with fresh cilantro and green onions. Machaca is a traditional Northern Mexico dish with shredded lean roast beef cooked with tomatoes, onion, green chiles, cilantro, and egg. Both dishes are served with beans, rice, sour cream, guacamole, and two flour tortillas. Chile Verde is pork tenderloin roasted and diced and simmered in a sauce of green chiles, onion, and spices. It is served burrito style with beans, rice and sour cream. Chimichanga is a deep-fried burrito that is stuffed with one's choice of chicken or green chili and beef. It is covered with enchilada sauce and melted cheeses and is garnished with shredded lettuce, tomatoes, green onions, and black olives. The dish is served with beans, rice, sour cream and guacamole.

Though both Nedra's are well known for their Mexican dishes, they have certainly not forgotten that steaks, pork and chicken are about as western as one can get. Western favorites, all of which are served with a salad, corn on the cob, dinner rolls and a choice of potatoes, include Rib and T-Bone steaks, Hamburger and Chicken Fried steaks, Pork Chops, and Fried Chicken.

Nedra's has not forgotten the seafood lover. Seafood dishes include Halibut and Salmon steaks, Trout Almondine, Breaded Shrimp, and Southern Style Catfish.

Seafood dishes also include a tossed salad, corn on the cob, dinner rolls, and a choice of potatoes.

There are eight varieties of hamburgers served at Nedra's, each of which is a hearty one-third pound of lean, succulent beef. Two of the most popular choices are the Chile Size and Hot Hamburger. Chile Size is served on an open face bun and smothered in chili beans, melted cheese, and onion. Hot Hamburger is a hamburger patty on open face bun that is covered with brown gravy and served with mashed potatoes and a tossed salad.

The pies are wonderful at both Nedra's cafes, but since Deep Fried Ice Cream is a Mexican specialty, both the proprietors and the writer recommend that diners try this incredible dessert. Vanilla ice cream is rolled in a crunchy coating and deep fried. It is then covered with a choice of chocolate or caramel syrup and garnished with whipped cream and chopped nuts and served in a sugar and cinnamon coated flour tortilla shell.

Accolades and the acclaim given Nedra's Cafe and Nedra's Too have been well earned. It is highly recommended that those who are spending more than one night in this Southwestern part of the state dine in both cafes. The cuisine is the same but the atmosphere very different. Nedra's Cafe offers a more traditional ambiance with reds and greens predominating the color decor. Nedra's Too offers a Southwestern decor of cacti and other desert scenes in a color scheme of light teal and peach.

With such a long-standing reputation for quality Southwestern cuisine, it stands to reason that, when it came to Nedra's Cafe, there had to be two.

PARRY LODGE RESTAURANT

89 East Center Street
Kanab, Utah 84741
Tel: (435) 644 2601
Hrs: April 1 - Mid-October
          Breakfast
Open Daily   7:00 a.m. - 12:00 noon
          Lunch
Open Daily   11:00 a.m. - 2:00 p.m.
          Dinner
Open Daily   6:00 p.m. - 10:00 p.m.
Visa, MasterCard, American Express, and Discover are accepted.
Reservations are recommended.

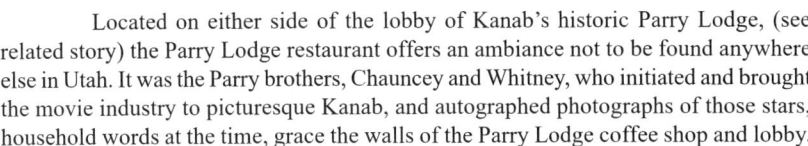

Located on either side of the lobby of Kanab's historic Parry Lodge, (see related story) the Parry Lodge restaurant offers an ambiance not to be found anywhere else in Utah. It was the Parry brothers, Chauncey and Whitney, who initiated and brought the movie industry to picturesque Kanab, and autographed photographs of those stars, household words at the time, grace the walls of the Parry Lodge coffee shop and lobby.

If the walls could only talk they would fill a book with the adventure, glamour, and romance of the movie making industry. Imagine dining in the same rooms and on the same recipes that film legends such as John Wayne, Glen Ford, Charlton Heston, Barbara Stanwyck, Ava Gardner and others enjoyed.

The coffee shop, decorated in peach and white, overlooks the Lodge pool. The formal dining room is elegantly swathed with organza swags and curtains and is festooned with accents of mauve and burgundy. The two dining rooms comfortably seat 100 persons.

Breakfast at the Lodge offers an assortment of eggs, any style, with toast, hash browns, and choice of bacon, eggs, ham or sausage. Favorite breakfast choices are the selection of omelettes, including cheese, Western, and Spanish. Pancakes, breakfast pastries, and cold and hot cereals are also available.

A choice selection of hot and cold sandwiches, salads and soups is available for lunch. A favorite is the Parry Lodge delicious box lunch, ideal for taking along on one's trip to the parks. The box lunch consists of one sandwich, fried chicken, a hard boiled egg, fresh fruit, and dessert.

Parry's has gained a reputation for its Western-style home cooking. For years the number-one favorite has been Parry's famous Chicken and Dumplings, served in creamy gravy with a side of cranberry sauce. Another favorite, straight from Utah's streams and rivers, is the boneless filet of Rainbow Trout, fried to a golden brown and served with lemon and slivered almonds. In addition, the Parry menu of home-cooked entrees includes Grilled Baby Beef Liver, Ground Round Steak, Chicken Fried Steak, Breaded Veal, Fried Chicken, Grilled Halibut, Poached Salmon, Stuffed Chicken Breast, and Roast Prime Rib of Beef Au Jus, served in regular and lady's cut. Meat lovers can rest assured that the Filet Mignon, T-Bone, New York and Top Sirloin steaks are succulent, tender, and broiled to perfection. Also available are Broiled Pork Chops. All entrees are served with a choice of soup or salad, potato or rice pilaf, vegetable of the day, a loaf of Parry's wonderful carrot bread, and a side order of their famous cucumbers and sour cream.

Desserts, all of which are made on premise, include the house favorite, Caramel Pecan Pie, a variety of fruit and cream pies, and Chocolate Suicide Cake, guaranteed to be just that, especially for those on a diet.

Parry's offers a children's menu for 12 years and under with choices of hamburger, cheeseburger, pizza, fried chicken strips, or corn dog.

The beverage selection includes a variety of soft drinks, both domestic and foreign beers, and a wine list that is available upon request.

For more than a little bit of romance and nostalgia, there is no finer restaurant than Parry Lodge. The restaurant also rates top on the list for good old fashioned cooking.

DID YOU KNOW?

---that a Daughters of Utah Pioneers marker is located on U.S. Highway 89, just south of Kanab. The marker denotes the location of Fort Kanab, built in 1864 as protection against the Indians. The Fort was never completed, though, as frequent Indian attacks finally forced the settlers to abandon the fort. When the area was later resettled, it is interesting to note that 100 armed Navajos demanded 70 horses and 17 head of cattle from the settlers. Their demands were refused, a battle ensued, and 20 or more Indians were killed and the rest driven off. It was shortly after this battle that permanent peace was established between white man and the Indian.

SPECIALTY SHOPPING

CANYON PHOTO
42 East Center Street
(Highway 89)
Kanab, Utah 84741
Tel:	(435) 644-5858
Fax:	(435) 644-5859
Email	mattbro@xpressweb.com
Hrs:	May 1 - Mid-October
Monday - Saturday 8:00 a.m. - 10:00 p.m.
Hrs:	Mid October - April 30
Monday - Saturday 9:00 a.m. - 6:00 p.m.
Visa, MasterCard, American Express, and Discover are accepted.

Canyon Photo, located at Jacob's Outpost (see related story), is legitimately the best photo shop in the West. It is best when it comes to speedy processing, best in quality of photos, and best where it counts the most, on the pocket book.

Although Canyon Photo, owned and operated by long-time Kanab resident, Matt Brown, is the only one-hour photo processing center in town, Canyon Photo is dedicated to offering its customers incomparable service at the lowest possible prices.

Canyon Photo is considered by residents and tourists alike to be the only place in town for quality film development. If the need is there, Canyon Photo will have the film developed and ready for pick-up in as little as 30 minutes.

Canyon Photo's equipment, the Agfa MSC 101, one of the best in the industry, can produce any size from wallet to eight by twelve enlargements. If, when examining one's photo, there are shots worthy of framing, Canyon Photo can produce the enlargement in ten short minutes.

Of great importance to customers is the manner in which photos are handled. Once developed, every picture is checked for color and density. If the photo does not pass inspection, corrections are made immediately.

Those who have compared prices at other one-hour photo centers will attest to the fact that development costs are less at Canyon Photo and so are supplies. Film is regularly a dollar-fifty to two dollars less per roll than at most places, and batteries for most cameras are typically 40 percent less than at the parks. Furthermore, Matt or any of his staff will test the old batteries to make sure that the battery is the problem.

Canyon Photo carries one of the West's best variety of film and batteries. They also stock a full line of inexpensive cameras, photo frames, and albums.

Don't wait to get home to relive that treasured vacation. With prices like these, take advantage of Canyon Photo's one-hour service and share those special moments with new-found friends.

DID YOU KNOW?

---that one of the most spectacular places for taking pictures begins at the north end of 100 East near the city park. **Squaw Trail,** a three-mile roundtrip hike with an elevation gain of 800 feet, offers spectacular views of the White, Gray, and Pink Cliffs of the Grand Staircase. Also visible are Kanab, Fredonia, Kanab Canyon, and the expansive Kaibab Plateau. Take plenty of water for this three-hour trip.

JACOB'S OUTPOST

42 East Center Street
(Highway 89)
Kanab, Utah 84741
Tel: (435) 644-5859
Fax: (435) 644-5859
Email mattbro@xpressweb.com
Hrs: May 1 - Mid-October
Monday - Saturday 8:00 a.m. - 10:00 p.m.
Hrs: Mid October - April 30
Monday - Saturday 9:00 a.m. - 6:00 p.m.
Visa, MasterCard, American Express, and Discover are accepted.

Jacob's Outpost, a truly unique gift shop, has earned its reputation for having the greatest selection of exceptional gifts and for having Southwestern Utah's largest selection of custom T-shirts.

From the moment one enters Jacob's Outpost, it is apparent that they have entered a store where caring counts. Staff warmly greet their customers, letting them know that browsing is what a gift store is all about. But, if they have any questions or when they are ready to make a purchase, personnel are eager to help.

Ambiance at Jacob's Outpost is another indication that people care. Southern Utah is famous for its red rock arches and pinnacles. Dividing one section of the gift store from the other is a magnificent manmade rendition of Utah's famous Delicate Arch. Gifts throughout the store are attractively displayed and exhibited so that it is easy to find what one is looking for.

T-shirts at Jacob's Outpost not only reflect quantity and diversity, but quality as well. Customers can rest assured that a Tee purchased here will hold its shape and color for a long time. The colorful selection, both in youth and adult sizes, includes designs of Kokopelli and other petroglyphs, Utah's national parks, animals indigenous to the West, and Native American designs.

Jacob's Outpost also carries a variety of logo caps, mugs, key chains, and an assortment of western style magnets that would be hard to duplicate. If one is looking for picture perfect books, calendars and post cards on the parks, or CD's, tapes and videos of the West, Jacob's Outpost has these too.

One section of the store displays a large selection of children's gifts. Soft mauve and brown suede pouches hold sets of jacks or marbles. There are cowboy rifles, Indian drums, stick ponies, horses, bears, reindeer, inexpensive Indian dolls, and, for true connoisseurs of unique gift items, Frisbees in the form of "buffalo chips."

For John Wayne buffs there are a variety of near life-size cutouts and, would you believe, John Wayne toilet paper!

Men, women and children appreciate the great selection of western style straw and felt hats. The feminine gender applauds the exquisite assortment of beaded necklaces, barrettes, earrings, combs and bracelets that have been painstakingly created for them by our Native American friends.

The collection of Native American jewelry, designed and crafted by tribes such as the Navajo, Zuni, and Hopi, are anything but gender specific. All appreciate the variety of sterling silver necklaces, earrings, bracelets, boleros, belt buckles, watch bands, and rings that are artistically hand-crafted or embellished with turquoise, lapis, mother of pearl, coral, and other semi precious stones. Customers also appreciate, to the point of almost disbelief, the legitimately low prices of Jacob's Outpost quality jewelry.

Jacob's Outpost stocks a variety of story teller dolls, large and small Mandellas, dream catchers, exquisite tiles, sandstone paintings, and pottery that have been created by area Native Americans.

Original sculptures by Largo need no introduction to collectors of western art objects. Other gifts of the West include Wonderstone art objects, unique southwestern wall hangings, beautiful stained glass window hangings, copper jewelry, and exquisite beaded boleros and tees.

One section of Jacob's Outpost is devoted to a charming selection of country collectibles. There are cute and cuddly bears, and ceramic animal collectibles by Mary Humphrey and Elizabeth Tucker. In addition, this section of the store showcases country kitchen artifacts that include frames, dolls, ceramics, calicos, lamps, clocks, book ends, and silk floral wall hangings.

Also in the store, (see related story) is Canyon Photo, considered by residents to be the only place in town for quality film development. One-hour film development means nothing to the folks at Canyon Photo. If the need is there, Canyon Photo will have the film developed and ready for pick-up in half that time.

Jacob Hamblin, after whom Jacob's Outpost is named, probably did more for peacefully bringing together the Western and Native American cultures than any other man. He was so respected by the Navajo, Hopi, Paiute and Shiviwit Indians of Utah, Arizona, and New Mexico, that he was given the honored title of "Father" by these tribes. Like Jacob, the Outpost brings together the best of these cultures so that visitors to this part of Southwestern Utah can take home something special as a cherished keepsake. But, regardless of the desire, whether looking for a special memento or a gift for any other reason, Jacob's Outpost, with its caring personnel, its dedication to quality, and its low prices, *is* the gift shop of choice.

NATURE'S SHOWCASE
288 West Center Street
Kanab, Utah 84741
Tel: (435) 644-2390
FAX: (435) 644-8177
Web Site:
www.westernhill.com.
Email:
western@expressweb.com.
Hrs: Memorial Day - Labor Day
Monday - Saturday 8:00 a.m. - 10:00 p.m.
         Labor Day - Memorial Day
Monday - Saturday 9:00 a.m. - 6:00 p.m.
Visa and MasterCard are accepted.
Look for free offer at conclusion of story.

Chances are, if one is a devotee of nature, that they have gazed in awe at the profound splendor of a piece of Kanab Wonderstone or Goldenstone. Both are marketed in earth science and specialty shops around the world by Western Hills, the manufacturer and wholesaler of what is undeniably, "Nature's Most Beautiful Paintings."

But only when one makes a trip to the little town of Kanab, Utah and visits Nature's Showcase can one truly appreciate the infinite realities of these stones. Nature's Showcase is the retail store for Western Hills.

In all the world there are only four places where Goldenstone is mined. One of those places is the sandstone bluffs of Southern Utah and Northern Arizona. But, to the best of anyone's knowledge, there is only one place, Kanab, Utah, where Kanab Wonderstone can be found.

Both Kanab Wonderstone and Kanab Goldenstone are natural sandstone formations that have been created by the effects of millions of years of wind and water. The colors and designs of the rock were induced by a slow moving mineral spring containing iron oxides. On these two types of stones, nature, in all her magnificence, has created innumerable rolling landscapes and seascapes.

As Ken Brown, owner/manager of Nature's Showcase, puts it, "It is the aesthetic quality of the slabs of stone that makes the business so rewarding to the artistic eye. Each cut displays a completely different picture, and one is never certain what will turn up next." In addition, just as with quality art, the interpretation is in the eyes of the beholder.

In 1964 Ken's father, Rex, a lifetime resident of Kanab and avid sportsman, was out on a small game hunt in the Kanab foothills when he noticed a colorful and interesting piece of sandstone that had broken and fallen from a ridge. It was exquisite, but Rex was preoccupied with the hunt and let it go at that. Several years later, having built a showcase fireplace out of Goldenstone, Rex was impressed that he should return to the site. Upon further investigation, Rex determined that the sandstone ledge from which the piece had broken was too soft and seemingly worthless. But try as he might, he could not eradicate the beauty of what he had seen from his mind. He soon returned to the site with a neighbor and tools. Together they split a large piece of the ridge and, in Rex's words, "I couldn't believe my eyes. The freshly broken ledge before me exposed one of the most beautiful wonders of nature I had ever beheld. It was a sandstone picture, complete with a blue-purple sky and rolling landscape of red, yellow, white and brown. I was speechless, and when I looked up at my neighbor I could see that he was experiencing the same spellbound reverence for the wonder of nature that I was. Once I determined to mine and market the stone, there was only one name that seemed fitting—Wonderstone." And it also seemed fitting that the retail store, which houses natural creations, should be called Nature's Showcase.

Visitors to Nature's Showcase usually experience the same overwhelming awe that Rex and his friend felt. It is an extraordinary experience to shop among the Wonderstone and Goldenstone artifacts that the Browns, through their developed expertise, have created.

Wonderstone and Goldenstone art objects come in every size, shape and function. Both stones can be mounted and framed as wall hangings, or left unmounted as a table top. The Browns have hand-crafted the stones into spheres, bookends, door stops, clocks, large and small planters, wine racks, jewelry boxes, and desk pen sets.

The most popular function of Wonderstone and Goldenstone, however, is as coasters. The stones are extremely absorbent and, unless the beverage is spilled on them, will not stain. The coasters are available just as they are cut or with art images transferred onto them.

In addition to the natural sandstone art sold at Nature's Showcase, several well-known artists have taken the slabs of Wonderstone and Goldenstone and, using them as their canvas, have painted western scenes, animals and Indians. Among the noted artists are Norma Jean, Myron Abbott, and Cindy Brown, Ken's wife.

Nature's Showcase houses more than just Wonderstone and Goldenstone. Other art objects provided by nature include Utah geodes as book ends and paper weights, ornate pieces of petrified wood, petroglyph rock art, rock magnets, and polished gem stones from around the world.

Gifts include onyx carvings of whales, donkeys, elephants, and eggs, Picoso marble carvings in all shapes and sizes, and painted desert sands, a sand desert scene enclosed in upside down shot and cocktail glasses.

Hand painted Indian pottery from Cedar Mesa Native American artists is another treasured gift to take home. Additional Native American gifts include Kachina dolls, small woven blankets, Mandellas, Sandstone paintings, and a quality selection of silver jewelry fashioned with turquoise, mother of pearl, onyx, coral and other semi-precious stones.

Onyx from Pakistan is available in the shapes of pyramids, eggs, spheres, obelisks, camels, elephants, and other styles. There are onyx marbles, Brazilian agates, Gem World wind chimes, and Septarian artifacts from Utah that are cut, shaped and polished.

Inexpensive gifts include Rocky Mountain Raccoons, adorable little creatures that are made from bark or limbs from local trees, cockle burrs, and squash seed for the ears. Another reminder of days spent in Southern Utah are Indian cliff dwellings carved into local red rock.

Children are not forgotten at Nature's Showcase. There are Indian war drums, bows and arrows, exquisite but inexpensive dolls, and other toy reminders of a visit to the West. Nature's Showcase also carries a selection of logo T-shirts from Kanab, Lake Powell, and the Grand Canyon, as well as other western design T-shirts.

For those who might hesitate in taking a gift of Wonderstone or Goldenstone home with them, Nature's Showcase has developed a unique way of packaging and shipping one's purchase. Foam is shot into the container so that the foam literally grows around the gift, making it so one's treasure will not shift and break.

Regardless of the purpose for traveling on highway 89 and passing through Kanab, one would not want to miss a visit to Nature's Showcase. To make the visit even more rewarding, show this book to Nature's Showcase personnel and receive a free Wonderstone souvenir.

There is only one Wonderstone—and there is only one Nature's Showcase. Don't miss it!

NORTHERN ARIZONA

FREDONIA, ARIZONA

Fredonia, at an elevation of 4,900 feet, is three miles south of the Utah border on U.S. 89A, and one of only two towns between Kanab and the North Rim of the Grand Canyon. Because of its location, Fredonia, with a population of slightly over 1,200 people, has become a popular rest stop for travelers.

Fredonia was first settled in the 1880s by groups of Mormon polygamists seeking refuge and protection from United States government officials who attempted to enforce the anti-polygamy law. Fredonia's name was a fitting title for the little community, as the word was coined from the English word, "free" and the Spanish word, "dona," meaning woman. A home in Fredonia meant freedom from harassment for polygamist wives who, if their husbands were imprisoned, would have had no one to care for them.

Over the years Fredonia residents have relied on raising livestock, farming, and a thriving lumber mill utilizing timber from the Kaibab Forest for its basic livelihood. Fredonia is also headquarters to the U.S. Forest Service's Kaibab Plateau unit.

From a stone lookout on the north face of the Kaibab Upwarp, just north of Fredonia, is one of the most majestic sights one could ever view. Nature has prepared a colored stratification in a Grand Staircase of terraces that rise as majestic walls to the north. In the foreground, at the base of the upwarp are the tops of the Chocolate Cliffs. Above and beyond them are the colorful Vermilion Cliffs. Beyond their brilliance are the thick walls of the White Cliffs, distinctly noticeable even from this distance. The Grey Cliffs, just north of the White Cliffs are barely viewable because of rich vegetation. But the Pink Cliffs, even farther north, form a suitable finale for this extraordinary display of sedimentary sandstone rock.

RESTAURANTS

NEDRA'S CAFE
Highway 89A (five miles South of Kanab)
Fredonia, Arizona 86022
Tel: (520) 643-7591
Hrs:
Open Seven Days   7:00 a.m. - 10:00 p.m.
Closed Thanksgiving Day and Christmas Day
Visa, MasterCard, American Express and Discover are accepted.

(See Nedra's Cafe and Nedra's Too story in the Kanab, Utah Restaurant Section).

TRAVELER'S INN
2631 North Highway 89A
Fredonia, Arizona 86022
Tel: (520) 643-7402
Restaurant Hrs:
    April 1 - mid-November
Monday - Saturday
5:00 p.m. - 10:00 p.m.
    Mid-November - April 1
Friday & Saturday
5:00 p.m. - 10:00 p.m.
Visa and MasterCard are accepted.
Reservations are recommended.

Ask most any resident about dining in the area and they will say that Southern Utah's finest restaurant is not in Utah at all, but in Northern Arizona. Only three miles from Kanab and just barely over the Arizona border, Traveler's Inn restaurant has been serving up the best, both in western cuisine and hospitality, since August 1986. Traveler's

Inn takes pride in being Southern Utah's gourmet Steak and Seafood restaurant.

Jim Lee is a third generation restaurateur and, as chef/owner, he and his wife, Leslie, have carried on a family tradition of "nothing but the best." When "nothing but the best" translates into the highest quality of meats, produce, and other ingredients; a staff of conscientious, caring personnel; and a restaurant where kitchen and dining areas are kept scrupulously clean, it is no wonder that Traveler's Inn is a restaurant of choice.

Traveler's Inn, built by Jim and his dad, Glen, who unfortunately passed away just before the Inn's opening, is a marvelous edifice of rock and pine set way back from the road. The lamp-lit entrance to the restaurant is enhanced with an old farm wagon and picturesque sign.

The interior of the restaurant is uncluttered and unpretentious, rendering a classic western motif. Walls are intermittently arrayed with photographic pictures of the Southwest and western memorabilia such as horseshoes, spurs, and oxen yoke. The restaurant is divided into two rooms, one for smoking and one for non-smokers.

Equally low-keyed is the Traveler's Inn menu. While it's Shrimp Cocktail continues to be a number one favorite hors d'oeuvre, the Inn's selection of deep fried breaded vegetables and cheese sticks are close runner-ups. Deep fried vegetable appetizers are mushrooms, cauliflower, zucchini, and onion rings.

At Traveler's Inn, all meat is aged and cut on the premises to ensure freshness and quality. Char-broiled steaks include 12 or six-ounce cuts of bacon-wrapped Filet Mignon, served with or without sautéed mushrooms, Rib Eye and Top Sirloin. Also char-broiled are Mesquite Marinated Tri Tips, Pork Filets, and boneless and skinless Chicken Breasts.

Diners at Traveler's Inn on Friday and Saturday are in for an indisputable treat. The Inn's succulent Roast Prime Rib, served only on those days, is slow-roasted to seal in all the juices and flavor.

Seafood favorites include five delicious shrimps, prepared breaded, char-broiled, or sautéed with lemon butter. Other seafood preferences are Breaded Oysters, Loin Cut Halibut Steak, Sautéed Boneless Trout Filet, and Alaskan King Crab Legs, based on accessibility. Steak and seafood are also available as combinations. Top Sirloin and Filet Mignon are served either with breaded oysters or breaded shrimp. All of the above entrees include a choice of soup or salad bar, country beans, choice of potatoes, and dinner roll.

In addition to its char-broiled steaks and seafood, Traveler's Inn offers home-style cooking that includes Fried Chicken, Baby Beef Liver, Breaded Chicken Filets, and everyone's favorite, Chicken Fried Steak. These dinners are served with a choice of soup or dinner salad, choice of potato, country beans, and dinner roll.

The one-third pound burgers offered at Traveler's Inn are also a gourmet's delight. Served with all the trimmings and a choice of potato chips or French fries, the burger selection includes hamburger, cheeseburger, and cheeseburger with bacon or mushrooms. Deep fried shrimp, chicken filets, and oysters are available "in the basket" with French fries.

Beverages include a selection of non-alcoholic fountain drinks as well as domestic beer, well drinks, and house wines, either by the glass or one-half carafe.

Whatever the dining choice, make sure to save room for one of Traveler's Inn's delicious desserts. The chocolate mousse cake can only be described as decadent, the cheesecake as scrumptious, and the pecan and fruit pies as flaky and delectable.

Tour buses are welcome, but at Traveler's Inn it is always the individual that comes first and is most important. Traveler's Inn takes pride in the quality of its cuisine, and fine food can best be enjoyed in an unhurried and relaxed atmosphere. At Traveler's

Inn, quantity will never surpass quality in importance. In every sense of the word, Traveler's Inn is a Travelers' Choice restaurant.

FREDONIA AREA ATTRACTIONS

PIPE SPRING NATIONAL MONUMENT

Pipe Spring National Monument, though not in Utah, is 17 miles southwest of Kanab and 60 miles east of St. George. Until the tunnel road, U-9, through Zion Park was built, U-59/A-389 was the main road leading between the two Southwestern Utah cities. The route is the most traveled route between St. George and the North Rim of the Grand Canyon.

Though not in Utah, Pipe Spring National Monument has had a colorful Utah history. It is one of several sites in the area where "water breaks miraculously from the earth." (Other natural springs were located at Moccasin Spring, Short Creek, Kanab, and Long Valley, Utah.) An E-shaped ruin, along with remnants of pottery and other artifacts, attests to the fact that Pipe Spring was once home to a group of the Anasazi. Pipe Springs was bandoned by the Ancient Ones in 1150 A.D. The Southern Paiutes came around 1300 A.D. and were still here when the white men came. Through wars and disease the white men caused Paiute numbers to dwindle from 5,500 to less than 1,200 by the mid 1800s.

Since water was such a precious commodity in Southwestern Utah and north-central Arizona, the Mormon pioneers, sent South to colonize, soon took over all of the major water sources in Kaibab Paiute territory. Within a decade the Kaibab Paiute population tumbled to little more than 200 persons and by the turn of the century their numbers were half that many.

The story of how Pipe Spring derived its name is as interesting as the rest of the area's history. On October 30, 1858, a group of Mormon missionaries led by Mormon legend, Jacob Hamblin, were enroute from their settlement on the Santa Clara River to the Hopi Pueblos. They had stopped at a spring near the base of some sandstone cliffs to relax and refresh themselves. Hamblin's brother, William, who was with them, was so skilled with firearms that he had earned the nickname of "Gunlock Bill." His companions, knowing that the air of a bullet would move a handkerchief aside when shot at, hung a silk kerchief from the limb of a tree and made a wager with William that he could not shoot a hole in it. William took the wager, blasted the handkerchief several times but, when the handkerchief was examined, there were no holes in it. His reputation at stake, William grabbed a pipe from one of his companions and set it on a stump 50 paces away. He then took aim and shot the bottom out of the pipe bowl without touching its side. From that day on the spring "where water breaks miraculously from the earth" was called Pipe Spring.

Pipe Spring first came under "personal" ownership in 1863 by James M. Whitmore. Until then Pipe Spring was land that offered drink for the thirsty traveler, whoever it might be. Whitmore built a dugout and established a ranch. In 1866, with the outbreak of the Blackhawk war, Indians raided the ranch and drove away much of Whitmore's property. When he and a hired hand, Robert McIntyre, set out in pursuit of the Indians, they were killed. The ranch and all Mormon settlements in Southern Utah were abandoned for the next few years.

In 1870 Mormon leader Brigham Young passed by Pipe Spring and was impressed by the area's beautiful spring and flourishing grassland. He immediately issued a calling to Anson P. Winsor, a bishop at the time in Rockville, Utah, to move his family to Pipe Spring to build a fort and set up a dairy business to feed and support the workers on the nearby St. George Temple. Upon completion of the fort, the place looked so stunning to passers-by that folks began calling it Winsor Castle. From 1871 until 1884, under management by the church, fort residents produced milk, cream, butter, and cheese from the dairy cows and beef from steer calves.

When the Edmunds Tucker Act against polygamy was enforced in 1885, Pipe Springs became an attractive refuge for polygamists. Since the search was conducted most seriously in Utah, spots such as Pipe Spring and Fredonia, both just across the border, were sought.

In 1888 the first non-Mormon to gain title to Pipe Springs was B.F. Saunders, who purchased the ranch at an auction. In 1906 the ranch and fort were purchased by Jonathan Heaton and his seven sons. In 1907 the Federal Government established the Kaibab Paiute Tribe Reservation, a tract 12 miles wide and 18 miles long that completely surrounded both Moccasin and Pipe Spring and gave the Kaibab Paiutes the right to use water from the springs. But, since travelers between Kanab and St. George continued to use the water the same way they always had, in 1916 the government was compelled to set aside the land immediately surrounding Pipe Spring as a Public Water Reserve, open to all livestock and travelers. Interestingly, the Heaton's private title to the 40 acres remained valid.

In 1916 the nation's interest in national parks and monuments became solidified. However, World War 1 caused a delay in action. Stephen Mather, a Californian, had been named as parks director. In 1920, while Mather was visiting Utah as a result of Zion becoming a national park, Mather became enchanted with Pipe Spring, not just because of its historical significance, but because of its proximity to Zion and the North Rim of the Grand Canyon. Mather took his enthusiasm for the fort back to Washington and shared his feeling with President Harding. On May 31, 1923, Pipe Spring became a national monument in commemoration of the Mormons and the part they had played in opening the West. The deed for the property remained with the Heatons until almost a year later, on April 28, 1924, when it was signed over to the United States government.

In 1935, as part of a CCC project, 200 young men moved into barracks near Winsor Castle and worked on buildings, fences, and sidewalks. They planted trees, fixed the sewer line, and gave the place a much-needed face-lift. Leonard Heaton, who stayed with Pipe Spring until 1964, collected dozens of period artifacts over the years that included churns, bedsteads, guns, cheese presses, spinning wheels, cradles, and other pioneer items that furnish the rooms today.

One-hundred and thirty-seven years has elapsed since James Whitmore first made his stake at Pipe Spring. Millions of travelers have come and gone and most things have changed significantly. Pipe Springs, however, in most ways, is the way it was when the Winsors lived there more than 100 years ago. The fortress, still remote and beautiful beneath the Vermilion Cliffs, is still a point of contact for cultures around the world and it is still a wonderful place to stop, relax, eat and refresh one's self before moving on.

Pipe Spring National Monument is open year-round and staffed with knowledgeable rangers. The fort has interpretive exhibits and offers an introductory video that is great to watch before taking a tour of the fort. There is a half-mile nature trail and visitors may walk the grounds on their own or take a guided tour of Winsor Castle throughout the year. During late spring to early fall a number of special programs are offered for adults and children. In the "Living History" program park rangers dress in period clothing and share interpretive demonstrations of pioneer life—such as butter churning, cheese making, quilting, and leather work. Members of the Kaibab Paiute Tribe also give interpretive programs on their heritage in the Pipe Spring area. A quarter of a mile away the Paiutes also maintain a campground.

On the ranch are an orchard, a garden, chickens, ducks and geese. Also, a ranch hand demonstrates cowboy skills with live horses and longhorn steers in the corral.

Adjacent to the visitor center are the Zion Natural History Association Bookstore, a cafe, and a gift shop where a variety of Native American and pioneer handicrafts are sold. There are plenty of reasons to pull off the trail at Pipe Spring. People have been doing it for centuries. It is the natural thing to do.

JACOB LAKE, ARIZONA

Nestled in the towering pines of **Kaibab National Forest**, at an elevation of 7,900 feet, Jacob Lake is a respite for visitors to the North Rim of the Grand Canyon. This incredible forest, home of the famous Kaibab white tail squirrel, is a year-round recreation area offering fishing, hiking, and camping during warmer months, and cross country skiing and snowmobiling during winter. Jacob Lake Inn traveler facilities include guest rooms, gift shop, dining room, snack bar, and service station. Jacob Lake is at the juncture of Alternate 89, which travels to **Lee's Ferry** on the Colorado River, and Scenic Route 67 to the **North Rim of the Grand Canyon.**

NORTH RIM OF THE GRAND CANYON

Less than 10 percent of the nearly 4 million annual visitors to the Grand Canyon have visited and seen the grandeur of Grand Canyon's North Rim. Yet the North Rim, which offers the virgin pine forest of the **Kaibab Plateau** and viewpoints that are 1,200 feet higher in elevation than the more visited South Rim, is anything but inaccessible.

Millions each year come to Southern Utah to visit Zion, Bryce, Glen Canyon and Lake Powell without realizing how close they are to the Grand Canyon's North Rim. From Kanab, the North Rim is an exquisitely beautiful 90-minute drive on U. S. 89A and Scenic Route 67. The road takes one into the heart of **Kaibab National Forest**, a 43-mile drive through pine and aspen forests and open meadows.

The four plateaus of the North Rim received their names from the Paiute Indians, who called the canyons home from about 1300 A.D. The easternmost plateau, **Kaibab**, means "mountain lying down." The other plateaus of the North Rim are **Kanab**, meaning "willow;" **Uinkaret**, "place of pines," and **Shivwits**, meaning "little people."

It is on the Kaibab plateau where Grand Canyon Lodge and the major trailheads are located. **Bright Angel Point** is a one-half mile walk on paved trails from Grand Canyon Lodge. It provides a view of the canyon that is unrivaled from any other point. Guests can not only see but hear **Roaring Springs**, over 3,000 feet beneath the rim. The Springs, which begin as snow-melt on the Kaibab Plateau, are the sole source of drinking water for both the North and South rims. Water gushes out of the rocky canyon wall and then is captured in part and pumped up the rims for domestic culinary use. From Bright Angel Point one can also view **Bright Angel**, **Transept**, and **Roaring Springs** side canyons as well as **San Francisco Peaks** and the canyon's **South Rim** in the distance.

***Transsep**t, a three-mile trail, follows the canyon rim from Grand Canyon Lodge to the campground. **Uncle Jim Trail** begins at the North Kaibab Trail parking lot and winds its way for five miles through the forest to a point that overlooks the canyon and the North Kaibab Trail switchbacks. The **North Kaibab Trail** is the only maintained trail into the canyon from the North Rim. The trail provides two options—either a strenuous 9.4 mile round-trip hike to Roaring Springs, or a two to three-day round trip trek to Bright Angel Campground, 14 miles below the North Rim at the canyon's bottom. Hiking this trail gives adventurers an appreciation for the canyon's beauty, immensity and for the wonder of its creation. The trail is usually closed during the winter months, and re-opens in late May or early June. Overnight hiking permits are required for this hike.

Widforss Trail is a 10-mile, five-hour round trip hike that starts at the Widforss Trail parking area, one mile down the dirt road and a quarter of a mile south of Cape Royal Road. The trail offers an ethereal blend of forest and canyon scenery.

Ken Patrick Trail also winds through the forest and along the rim from Point Imperial to the North Kaibab parking area. Allow 12 hours for this 24-mile round trip hike.

Two driving trips with spectacular views are Point Imperial and Cape Royal. **Point Imperial**, the highest point on either of the two rims, is 11 miles from Grand Canyon Lodge. From the point, one can see **Saddle Mountain**, **Painted Desert**, and **Mount Hayden** as well as a spectacular view of eastern Grand Canyon. The 14-mile drive to Point Cape Royal, which begins at the junction of Point Imperial and Cape Royal roads, provides stunning vistas of the canyon and the Colorado River.

The North Rim, with its Grand Canyon Lodge, a National Historic Landmark, is beautifully prepared to handle the most discriminating guests. The rustic lodge, designed in the 1920s by renown architect, Gilbert Stanley Underwood, is an informal and spacious hotel. Constructed with immense limestone walls and massive open-beam timbers, the lodge features dramatic vistas of the canyons from floor-to-ceiling and wall-to-wall picture windows that seem to bring the canyons indoors.

The Grand Canyon Lodge Dining Room, elegantly rustic, features superb views of the canyon. Picnic lunches may be ordered, preferably one day in advance. The complex also offers a snack bar, gift shop, post office, and guided tours with van rides along the rim or horse and mule trail rides. A general store, located near the campground, serves pizza and fast food items and is well stocked with camping and backpacking supplies as well as groceries and sundries. The North Rim Campground has 83 sites and can accommodate motor homes and trailers up to 35 feet in length as well as walk-in tent campers. Advance reservations are recommended and will be accepted up to eight weeks prior to arrival. There are no hook-ups. A sanitary dump station is available and showers and laundry are near-by. A second campground, Cottonwood, is located halfway down the North Kaibab Trail along Bright Angel Creek. It is seven miles below the trailhead and seven miles up from the Colorado River. Camping at Cottonwood is for hikers only and an overnight permit is required. Reservations are highly recommended (520-638-7888).

PAGE, ARIZONA

Possibly one of the newest incorporated cities in the United States, Page, Arizona, located on top of the Manson Mesa, was established in 1957 to house Glen Canyon Dam construction personnel and their families. The city, about five miles southwest of the Utah border, was also designed as a permanent residence for those who would remain as employees at the dam and in the recreation area, and for those who would be providing services for residents and visitors.

At the height of dam construction, Page had a population of just over 7,500 residents. Today its population remains about the same.

Page, Arizona, named after the late John C. Page, commissioner of the Bureau of Reclamation from 1937 to 1943, is today much more than a servicing community. The city has blossomed with an abundance of quality motels, restaurants, gift shops, adventure tours, and all the amenities a city needs to be a first rate vacation destination. Page, has an average of 300 days of sunshine every year.

NORTHERN ARIZONA ATTRACTIONS

GLEN CANYON NATIONAL RECREATION AREA, ARIZONA

Having just charted the perilous waters of Cataract Canyon with his flotilla of pioneer boats, Major John Wesley Powell was so relieved with the relatively placid waters and pleasant "glens" of 162-mile long Glen Canyon that he christened it "Glen Canyon." When construction of the dam was completed in 1963 and the waters of the Colorado began to be backed up for storage, the resulting reservoir was named Lake Powell in honor of John Wesley Powell.

Investigation of Glen Canyon as a possible dam site was begun as early as 1921, with the area not conclusively selected until April of 1956. When construction crews arrived at the dam site, they found they had to drive 200 miles just to get from one side of the canyon to another. As a result of this dilemma, Glen Canyon Bridge, the highest and second largest steel arch bridge in the United States, was built above the 700-foot chasm and completed in 1959.

After the first blast on the dam site in October of 1956, emphasis was placed on rerouting the river and excavating tunnels. The canyon was actually shaped to fit the dam. Concrete placement began in the summer of 1960. Crews worked day and night until September of 1963 when the final "bucket" was dumped. Not to be misleading, that bucket held 24 tons of damp concrete, and it took over 400,000 buckets of concrete to build Glen Canyon Dam.

Wedged into a deep sandstone gorge on the Colorado River, Glen Canyon Dam, at a height of 710 feet, backs up 186 miles of water to form beautiful Lake Powell, one of the nation's most popular water recreation areas. When full, Lake Powell contains 26,215,000 feet of water, covers an area of 161,390 surface acres, and has a shoreline of unsurpassed beauty that is 1,960 miles long. The lake began filling in March 1963. Filling of the lake was not completed until June 22, 1980. Glen Canyon Recreation Area is administered by the National Park Service. Together with the Navajo Nation, the National Park Service has spent over $10 million in developing the five operating marinas, visitor centers, food service, lodging boat and automotive repair facilities, and campgrounds.

The Bureau of Reclamation operates the dam. The eight generating units at Glen Canyon produce 1, 288,000 kilowatts of electricity daily. The sale of electrical power has defrayed most of the total construction cost. The $272 million it cost to build the dam included the powerplant, generators, switchyard, and a brand new town, Page Arizona, established in 1957 to house Glen Canyon Dam construction personnel and their families.

A free self-guided tour of the dam and powerplant, which usually takes 30 to 45 minutes to complete, is available to all visitors. Guests may proceed at their own pace and a tour guide booklet is available at the Carl Hayden Visitor Center. During summer, guided tours are available on a scheduled basis. Films and video tapes on Glen Canyon Dam and Lake Powell are also available, free upon request from the Bureau of Reclamation, Office of Public Affairs, P.O. Box 11568, Salt Lake City, Utah 84147 or 801-524-5403.

The John Wesley Powell Museum, located in adjoining Page, interprets the region through a variety of exhibits.

ACCOMMODATIONS

COURTYARD MARRIOTT
600 Clubhouse Drive
P. O. Box 4150
Page/Lake Powell, Arizona 86040
Tel: (520) 645-5000
         (800) 851-3855
         (800) 321-2211
FAX: (520) 645-5004
Gift Shop Hours:
Open Seven Days   7:00 a.m. - 10:00 p.m.

PAGE, ARIZONA

Visa, MasterCard, American Express, Diners Club, Carte Blanche, and Discover are accepted.
Reservations are recommended.

The Courtyard by Marriott in Page, Arizona is everything one has come to expect at Courtyard accommodations around the country and much more. The Courtyard in Page is conveniently located within the perimeters of the Southwest's Grand Circle, and is only one-half mile from the Grand Circle's acknowledged center, Glen Canyon Recreation Area, Glen Canyon Dam, and Lake Powell. It is also an easy and exquisitely beautiful drive to Bryce Canyon, Grand Canyon, Zion National Park, Canyonlands National Park, Monument Valley and Navajoland.

Each of the Courtyard's 153 elegantly appointed guest rooms boasts a private balcony with a view of the majestic vermilion cliffs, the city's verdant golf course, or the Courtyard's beautiful pool and courtyard setting.

Guests find accommodations and services to be equally as impressive as the hotel's surroundings. Personnel at the Courtyard Marriott in Page believe that everyone who stays there is special and that all should be treated to the same courtesies and amenities. Therefore, other than the fact that guests have a choice of smoking or non smoking rooms and rooms with single queen or two double beds, every room is alike.

Rooms are tastefully decorated with a southwestern flair. A color scheme of teal, coral, purple and royal blue prevails in bedspreads, draperies, and the southwestern art that decorates the walls. Rooms have table with two easy chairs, a closet with full-length bi-fold mirror doors, remote cable TV with HBO and in room movies, and private telephone. Bathrooms offer a bath with tub/shower enclosure and separate vanity basin with hair dryer and in-room coffee makers. Rooms for the physically impaired have amenities with adjusted height levels and roll-in showers.

Hotel amenities include a fully equipped exercise room that can be accessed from the hotel or from the courtyard, and heated outdoor pool and Jacuzzi, both of which are ensconced in the middle of a desert-landscaped courtyard.

Not a part of the Courtyard, but right outside their doors, is Lake Powell National, one of Arizona's most challenging golf courses. The 27 hole course was designed by Phillips Golf Design to compliment the magnificent natural beauty that surrounds it. The result is a golf course that is as visually remarkable as it is athletically challenging. There are four tees on each hole that invite competition for golfers at all skill levels.

The Courtyard's Curio Shop offers one of the best selections of Navajo gifts and souvenirs in the area. The city of Page is in the middle of one of our country's largest Indian Reservations and, other than the famed Hopi Kochina dolls, most of the artifacts were skillfully created by Navajo artisans. Shoppers would be hard-pressed to find a better selection of sterling silver jewelry. The Curio Shop offers a magnificent selection of rings, bracelets, earrings, pins, necklaces, hairpieces, belt buckles, boleros, and other personal adornments. While the Navajo have always been noted for their silver and turquoise craftsmanship, they have recently extended their expertise to include fine jewelry using blue lapis, denim lapis, sugulite opal, black onyx, amalekite, and spiny oyster shell, as well as the traditional semi-precious stones of coral, and mother of pearl. This extraordinary selection of Native American jewelry includes the work of such noted craftsmen as Ray Tracey and Calvin Begay. In addition, the Curio Shop offers world-renown Navajo rugs, Navajo pottery in every size and shape, sand paintings, Mandellas, and dream catchers. There are hand woven baskets by Tokona O'odlam, and gifts of pewter, glass, and bronze. Mementos with a western or southwestern flair include a quality collection of men's and women's wear in denim, leather, and suede. Souvenirs of the area to be found in the Curio Shop are Henleys, T-shirts, sweatshirts, magnets, candles, note cards, calendars, books, and hand made petroglyphs.

The Courtyard Marriott at Page recognizes that meeting facilities and conference amenities can be just as important as resort accommodations and recreational endeavors. For that reason they specialize in exceeding expectations for any type of gathering, whether it is for as few as 10 or as many as 450. The Arizona Ballroom can seat 400 banquet style and up to 450 people in a theater setting. The room can also be divided into three separate rooms. In addition, the Courtyard offers the Board Room for small parties of up to 25. The Courtyard's convention services staff is there to assist guests in everything from state of the art audio visual effects to floral arrangements and limousine service. The hotel's catering and banquet staff are as creative as they are professional and bring a perfectionist's touch to any affair. In addition to indoor meeting facilities, the Courtyard Rose Garden can accommodate 125 to 150 guests without overflowing into the pool area.

New at the Courtyard is a multi-lingual Concierge staff that is eager to help guests with reservations for dining and recreational activities or in offering assistance in many other ways.

While guests always feel comfortable and welcomed when checking in at

Courtyard by Marriotts across the country, few vestibules can compare with that of the Page Courtyard Marriott. One has the feeling of being in the most magnificent of Indian dwellings. The lobby is of pink sandstone with heavy exposed beams. Walls above the impressive sandstone fireplace are festooned with extraordinary Kachina dolls, a collection of which also adorns the walls of internationally acclaimed Pepper's restaurant. Pepper's, which adjoins the lobby, has a wrought iron gate entrance. The outside walls, also a part of the lobby, are painted with a southwestern flair of burros, wooden carts, cacti, and a guard, taking an afternoon siesta. Pepper's offers continental and American cuisine with a southwestern flair (see related story). Massive furnishings throughout the lobby are appropriately arranged to engender casual conversation.

From its architecturally perfect design to its conscientious personnel, the Page, Arizona Courtyard by Marriott is a Travelers' Choice accommodation where caring and attention to detail always prevail.

RAMADA INN
287 North Lake
Powell Boulevard
P. O. Box 1867
Page/Lake Powell,
Arizona 86040
Tel: (520) 645-8851
FAX: (520) 645-2523
Visa, MasterCard, American Express, Diners Club, Carte Blanche and Discover are accepted.
Reservations are recommended.

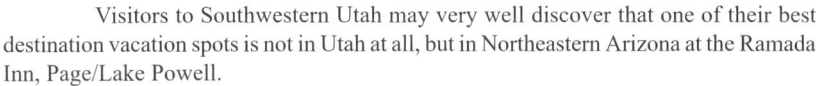

Visitors to Southwestern Utah may very well discover that one of their best destination vacation spots is not in Utah at all, but in Northeastern Arizona at the Ramada Inn, Page/Lake Powell.

When it comes to staying and playing in Utah's most famous water wonderland, Glen Canyon National Recreation Area and Lake Powell, there is no finer nor closer place to stay than Page, Arizona and the Ramada Inn. Page and the Ramada Inn are also ideal locations for viewing "the other side of the Grand Canyon," the North Rim, believed by many to be more aesthetic and intriguing than the better known South Rim.

The Ramada Inn at Page was designed to be aesthetically pleasing. Nearly every room offers views of the lake or the golf course. Lake Powell National golf course, just over the hill from the Inn, offers 18 holes that are as visually exceptional as they are athletically challenging. With four tees on each hole, there is competition for golfers at all skill levels.

The Ramada Inn was also designed for guest comfort and convenience. The spacious lobby is comfortably furnished with well-placed sofas and easy chairs, ideally suited for casual conversation and relaxation. An imposing floor to ceiling black lava rock fireplace offers cozy warmth during cooler months. Adjoining the lobby on either side are the Family Tree Restaurant (see related story) and a quality gift shop. Other Inn amenities include a seasonal swimming pool, picnic area, in-house travel agency, room service from the Family Tree Restaurant, and banquet and conference room.

Offered at the Ramada Inn is a choice of double queens, single queens, single kings, rooms for the physically impaired, and smoking and non smoking rooms.

With so many more travelers requesting non smoking rooms, the Ramada Inn is pleased to offer 80 % non smoking rooms.

Room amenities include alarm clock radios and data port phones for computer access with local calls, credit card, and phone cards free. The Inn's remote control cable TV with HBO also accesses Lodge Net, a premium program that offers a choice of 14 or 15 first run movies and a dozen or more video games. Both the king and double queen rooms are attractively decorated with a mauve and burgundy color scheme. They feature full-length mirrors, a table with two chairs, dresser, wall and free-standing lights, and bathroom with tub/shower enclosure and separate vanity.

Rooms for the physically impaired are spacious with just one queen bed to allow for better ambulation. The bathtub with shower has regulation bars, and everything within the room is height adjusted. An adjoining room is available should there be accompanying guests.

The Ramada's banquet room comfortably accommodates 100 banquet style and 120 theater style. The Inn's banquet staff is there to help plan and cater to the needs of their guests. Conference amenities include a podium speaker system, screen, overhead projector, and TV with VCR.

The Inn's pool, open from May through October, is one of the city's largest, and offers an abundance of tables with umbrellas and lounge chairs. Picnic grounds are adjacent to the pool.

Open from 6:00 a.m. to 10:00 a.m. and from 5:00 p.m. to 10:00 p.m. during the summer months and from 5:00 p.m. to 9:00 p.m. during off-season (October 1 through April 30), the Ramada's gift shop features a choice variety of Native American jewelry and artifacts. In addition to a great selection of sterling silver jewelry, the gift shop showcases a collection of Navajo rugs, pottery, Kachina dolls, dream catchers, and Mandellas. There are bronze and ceramic figurines, pottery bells, sand paintings, candles, exquisite tiles, and an assortment of area magnets. The shop stocks a marvelous selection of area framed prints, Goldenstone clocks and barometers, and traditional T-shirts, caps, and regional post cards and books.

Ramada Inns across the country are praised for their ability to offer first class service at less than premium prices. At the Ramada Inn at Page, they outclass themselves.

BED & BREAKFASTS

THATCHER'S BED & BREAKFAST
P. O. Box 421
7 16th Avenue
Page/Lake Powell, Arizona 86040
Tel: (520) 645-3335
        (800) 645-6836
FAX: (520) 645-6856
Member of Page Bed & Breakfast
Association & Page Chamber of Commerce
Reservations are recommended.

THATCHER'S
BED & BREAKFAST

Three large guest books have been filled with favorable comments from guests who have stayed at Thatcher's Bed & Breakfast over the past five years. Many of those guests are return visitors, and many are referrals from those who have stayed before and enjoyed their visit.

Thatcher's Bed & Breakfast, owned and operated by Neta and Austin Thatcher, is one of those places where guests know that the Thatcher home is their home for as long as they care to stay.

The family's best china, crystal and lace table cloths are brought out each morning to let guests know that they really are special. The table is laden with fresh fruits, assorted cold cereals (hot during winter months), individual yogurts, and an assortment of juices, coffee, teas, and hot chocolate. From the kitchen comes such mouth watering cuisine as French toast with sausage or bacon. There is nothing second rate about breakfasts at the Thatcher home. Neta has been a caterer for the past seven years, and has catered several movie crews while they have been in the area on location.

While staying at Thatcher's Bed & Breakfast, the Thatcher's living room is there for guests to enjoy. Decorated in a color scheme of blue and mauve, the room radiates a warm and caring atmosphere. Plants adorn the room, and guests are welcome to let their fingers tickle the ivory on the family piano. Several sofas and easy chairs make it comfortable for guests to mingle with new found friends or sit and relax by themselves.

Thatcher's Bed & Breakfast has three guest rooms, one with a private bath and two with a shared bathroom. The room with a private bath offers a king bed covered with a hand made white satin bedspread. The room has a table with lace table cloth, remote control TV, umbrella stand, and desk. Both the bedroom and bathroom are elegantly accented with touches of blue and silk floral arrangements.

A second room has two double beds with blue and mauve floral bedspreads, and a desk with chair. Silk floral arrangements add accents to the wall. The third room offers a queen bed, floral quilt, desk and chair and original art by Neta's Mom. These two rooms share a bathroom. All beds throughout the bed & breakfast not only have quality down pillows, but extra down pillows as well.

Unlike most bed and breakfasts, the Thatchers allow their guests full use of the kitchen for special occasions, as long as arrangements are made in advance. Guests are also invited to enjoy the patio with its flowing fountain. Smoking is allowed on the premises, but not in the home.

Visitors to the area are likely to hear that Page/Lake Powell is the "hub of the Grand Circle." Paraphrased, this simply means that when staying at Page/Lake Powell, one is in the center of the numerous national and state parks, monuments and recreation areas that abound in Southwestern Utah and Northwestern Arizona.

The city of Page is only one mile from spectacular Glen Canyon Dam, where tours are not only educational, but a great adventure. A very short distance from the dam is Lake Powell's Wahweap resort and marina. Here alone one could spend a week boating, water skiing, swimming, fishing, touring slot canyons and ancient Indian petroglyphs, as well as many other recreational activities.

Since many of the Southwest's sightseeing wonders are within a day's drive of Page, it simply makes sense to stay here while touring this magnificent country.

Right outside the Thatcher's front door is the beginning of Page's Rimview Trail for walking, jogging, and bicycling. This eight-mile long trail offers fantastic views of the dam, the lake, and arroyos beyond. The trail is accessible from several places so that it can be enjoyed in sections or as a continuous loop.

Thatcher's Bed & Breakfast is a great place to stay and play. For those who enjoy privacy, they will find it. For those who relish sharing time with and getting to know the host family, they can do that too. Neta and Austin have made a commitment to be as much a part of a guest's vacation as they want them to be.

The Thatcher family includes a very friendly dog and cat, who will also be a part of the guest's life—only if they want them to be.

RESORTS

LAKE POWELL RESORTS & MARINAS
managed by ARAMARK
P. O. Box 56909
Phoenix Arizona 85079-6909
Tel: (602) 278-8888
          (800) 528-6154
FAX: (602) 331-5258

Wahweap Lodge & Marina
Box 1597
Page, Arizona, 86040
Tel: (520) 645-2433

Bullfrog Resort & Marina
Box 4055
Lake Powell, Utah 84533
Tel: (435) 684-3000

Hall's Crossing Marina
Box 5101
Lake Powell, Utah 84533
Tel: (435) 684-7000
Web Site:www.visitlakepowell.com

Hite Marina
Box 501
Lake Powell, Utah 84533
Tel: (435) 684-2278

Visa, MasterCard, American Express, Diners Club, Carte Blanche, and Discover are accepted.
Reservations are recommended.

Those who have visited any part of Lake Powell, with its 1,960 miles of shoreline, have tried in vain to describe this year-round wonderland. The overall consensus is that there are no adequate words to depict this magnificent area. Lake Powell, located in Glen Canyon National Recreation Area, has to be seen and felt with all one's senses. It is, quite simply, indescribable.

Without question, it is Lake Powell's call to play that makes this treasure trove such a popular vacation destination. Called "America's Natural Playground," Lake Powell is fulfillment to the child in all of us. Whatever adventure one seems to be caught up in, whether it is the excitement of houseboating, exploring, camping, fishing, water-skiing, speed-boating, jet skiing, swimming, or carefree relaxation, Lake Powell is Nirvana to all.

Lake Powell Resorts & Marinas, managed by ARAMARK, operates five marinas on Lake Powell, located in diverse sections of the lake. Wahweap is at the southern-most point of the lake, near Glen Canyon Dam and Page, Arizona. Dangling Rope is the first marina upstream from Wahweap, located approximately seven miles from Rainbow Bridge National Monument. Bullfrog and Hall's Crossing marinas are located mid-lake, and Hite is at the northern or upstream end of the lake. Together they afford guests every lakeside convenience.

Houseboat magazine, based on votes from its readers, has ranked Lake Powell as America's #1 Houseboating destination. Lake Powell is a 186-mile playground with 1,960 miles of shoreline, more than the entire west coast of the United States. Many of those miles follow the Colorado River's sinuous path through lofty red rock cliffs, some barely a boat width apart, and to secreted coves with petroglyphs, alcoves, and inviting sandy beaches. Lake Powell fronts 96 major canyons, each of which is singularly magnificent.

There is no better way to discover this heaven on earth than at the helm or deck of one's own houseboat. The best part of it all is that one does not have to own a houseboat in order to possess one. Available year-round from all marinas but Dangling Rope, Lake Powell marinas offer a fleet of over 300 houseboats in three classifications. Standard Class houseboats are available in 36-foot, 44-foot, and 50-foot lengths. Features include upper and lower decks, range and oven, refrigerator, outdoor gas grill, private head and shower, large capacity ice chest, dishes and utensils, water heater, 12-volt light system, and an all-weather cabin with space heater. The 36-foot houseboat sleeps six on fold-out beds. The larger houseboats sleep 12 and have single and double bunk beds. The 44-foot standard is only available from Bullfrog and Hall's Crossing.

The 52-foot Captain Class houseboats provide an extra measure of comfort with their swim slides, evaporative cooling systems, and upgraded kitchen appliances. In addition to the amenities provided on the Standard Class, the Captain Class houseboats have electric coffee makers, blenders, toasters, cassette or CD sound systems, marine radios, interior and exterior carpeting, shade canopies on the top decks, boarding ramps, and a 110/120 volt generator.

For the 1998 season, ARAMARK introduces 30 new 54-foot houseboats in the new Sport Class of houseboats. These custom-designed houseboats have all the equipment found in the Captain-class houseboats, but with upgraded features, including two full bathrooms with showers, four separate sleeping areas for added privacy, and a ramp on the stern for carrying personal watercraft.

Lake Powell's deluxe houseboat model is the 59-foot Admiral Class, which offers central heating and air conditioning, plush interiors, and larger living spaces. Instead of single and double bunkbeds, the Admiral Class has five queen-sized beds, complete with bedding. In addition to the Captain Class amenities, the Admiral Class offers two private heads and one deluxe shower with bathroom towels supplied, upgraded top deck with flying bridge controls, side staircase and rear ladder to deck, multi-speaker CD sound system, 12-volt and 110-volt interior/exterior lighting, electric range and microwave, two-door electric refrigerator/freezer, and VHS video player and monitor.

Lake Powell, because of its high desert climate, has an average of 300 days of sunshine every year. Peak season is mid-May through mid-October. Off-season rates and packages are available at up to 40% throughout Fall, Winter, and Spring. Spring and Fall months offer moderate air and water temperatures, while Winter is famous for its amazing combination of crystal blue skies and quiet solitude. The "off-season" at Lake Powell is ideal for hiking, fishing, photography, and just getting away from it all.

In addition to its spectacular fleet of houseboats, the four main Lake Powell marinas offer 14-foot fishing utility boats and 18 and 19-foot sport run-about boats that are ideal for exploring and water skiing. Many enjoy the benefits of combining a houseboat with a power boat. Leave the houseboat parked for the day in a favorite cove, then explore and water ski until the sky matches the color of the crimson monoliths that surround the cobalt lake.

Boating magazine called Lake Powell "a water skier's paradise." Nowhere else in the world can one find the wide open expanses of glass-like calm water surrounded by vermilion sandstone bluffs.

For those who do not have their own water toys, all but Dangling Rope marinas rent water skis, kneeboards, wakeboards and ski tubes. The ski package includes everything one needs—a ski vest, tow rope, safety flag, and two skis, either of which can also be used for slalom skiing. The ski tube is great for kids of all ages, has handles for one or two people, and has a webbed seat for extra comfort. The wakeboard has adjustable foot straps and heel loops and is great for those with minimal or advanced water skiing abilities. The kneeboard has neutral buoyancy and features a raised kneewell divider and padded ankle supports. All the above are available by the day or week. Included with the rental of ski tubes, wakeboards and kneeboards are a tow rope, safety flag and ski vest.

Available by the hour or day is the Tigershark personal watercraft. With a top speed of 35 miles per hour, the Tigershark is guaranteed to create a wave and raise one's pulse. The personal watercraft seats one or two, is easy to ride and perfect for cruising in wide-open water and exploring narrow canyon inlets. It has an engine with a lively jet drive and offers a convenient storage compartment with one ski vest.

Almost as impressive as speed on the lake, is relaxed boating for Lake Powell fish. The variety of game fishing available at Lake Powell includes striped bass, smallmouth and largemouth bass, walleye, crappie, and catfish. Bluegill and carp can be caught easily throughout the lake. Their prevalence makes Lake Powell the ideal place to introduce young ones to the thrill of landing that first fish. For the serious fisher, there are several tournaments held throughout the year.

For those who desire the tours, but prefer to leave the driving to the experts, Wahweap, Bullfrog, and Hall's Crossing marinas have a number of half-day and full-day tours. Most popular are the tours to Rainbow Bridge National Monument, available from all three marinas. Other tours, available from Wahweap, include the Navajo Canyon Tapestry Tour and Antelope Canyon Cruise.

One of the most popular tours at Wahweap is the Sunset Dinner Cruise aboard the authentic 95-foot paddlewheel river boat, the *Canyon King*. Unmatched in beauty is the late afternoon transformation of sandstone plateaus as shadows dance across the cliffs. Then the sun sinks slowly behind the bluffs, sending a shaft of light, like a pathway, across the lake. Suddenly the cliffs become black silhouettes, emblazoned between a crimson sky and the reflective lake. These are the romantic vistas to be enjoyed while dining on a prime rib dinner. The two and one-half hour cruise is available during peak season. Also offered is a one-hour tour, which departs daily during peak season at 11:00 a.m., 12:30 p.m., and 2:00 p.m. The Canyon King cruises spectacular Wahweap Bay, which houses Castle Rock, a red sandstone mountain featured in the film "The Greatest Story Ever Told."

If camping out beneath a star-studded sky sounds exhilarating, Lake Powell is the answer to a prayer. Camping is allowed anywhere on shore for as many as 14 consecutive days. For less hardy campers, Wahweap, Bullfrog, and Hall's Crossing Marinas offer campgrounds, many of which have spectacular lake views. To those who regard camping as an RV or motorhome, these same marinas have RV parks with full hook-ups for lights, water and sewer, restroom and shower facilities and a coin operated laundry. To add to one's experience, each of the RV park's has a convenience store.

For those who prefer full-service lodging, Wahweap Lodge and Bullfrog's Defiance House Lodge offer room amenities that include remote control color cable TV, private deck with stunning view, and room-controlled heating and air conditioning. Rooms at Wahweap also have direct-dial phones with local calls free, in-room coffee pots and refrigerators. If one wants to feel really at home, Bullfrog, Hall's Crossing, and Hite Marinas offer spacious family units with three bedrooms, two baths, living room, kitchen, and all cooking and dining utensils. The lodges at Wahweap and Bullfrog offer restaurants, gift shops, and boat tours. Wahweap has an exercise room and two beautiful outdoor pools that overlook the lake.

The Rainbow Room at Wahweap Lodge and the Anasazi Restaurant at Bullfrog offer dining to suit the most discriminating taste. Whether one is a vegetarian, a connoisseur of seafood, an epicurean who savors steaks and prime rib, or a gourmet of pasta, there is always a menu item that is sure to please. For more casual dining there is the Kiva Lounge at Defiance House Lodge in Bullfrog, and the Driftwood Lounge at Wahweap Lodge. ITZA Pizza at Wahweap serves homemade pizzas, salads, and sandwiches.

The most unique marina on Lake Powell is Dangling Rope Marina, located approximately 41 miles uplake from Wahweap. Dangling Rope is only accessible by boat. There are no roads nor trails leading into this remote, but very busy marina. Famous for its fantastic ice cream (very refreshing on a summer day), Dangling Rope is also famous for the amazing volume of fuel it sells to boats of all sizes, from the tiny 14-footers to the palatial 75-footers. On a busy summer weekend, 20,000 gallons of gas can be sold in a single day. Located just downlake from Rainbow Bridge National Monument, Dangling Rope is also the world's only solar-powered marina. The marina is powered by one of the largest photovoltaic panel arrays in the United States.

To the hiker, this bizarre and whimsical landscape is a treasure trove. With no marked trails, everything is available from gentle slick rock trails to scenic overviews and inspiring treks through lush river bottoms and mysterious slot canyons. There are remnant ruins of ancient Indian villages, petroglyph walls, and hidden expanses of meadows—each of which offers an unforgettable experience. There are short hikes for the inexperienced and long explorations for seasoned hikers. Rainbow Bridge National Monument, at 290 feet high, is the world's tallest stone bridge and Glen Canyon's signature geologic wonder. It is only a short hike from one of the boat docks located in Bridge Canyon. Approximately 28 miles down-lake from Bullfrog is Hole-in-the-Rock. It was here that Mormon Pioneers cut and blasted their way down in the winter of 1879 so that they could cross the Colorado River. From the canyon's crest they lowered their wagons and over 1500 head of livestock down this steep precipice. Even with today's technology, the feat seems impossible. Adventurous visitors can hike up this rock precipice.

Within the rugged terrain of Lake Powell's canyons and valleys thrives an extremely fragile ecological balance of plant and wildlife. To protect and preserve the beauty of this natural habitat for future generations, Glen Canyon National Recreation Area reminds its visitors to "take only pictures, and leave only footprints."

Lake Powell is named after Major John Wesley Powell, a one-armed Civil War veteran who in 1869 led the first expedition down the Colorado River and through the Grand Canyon. Over rapids considered impassable, the courageous group of ten men and four boats charted the unexplored river and its surrounding canyons. When the group emerged from the canyon 15 weeks after they began in Green River, Wyoming, there were six men and two boats remaining.

Lake Powell became reality in 1963 with the completion of Glen Canyon Dam. To the north of this architectural wonder is the serpentine lake that winds its way along much of Major Powell's original route. South of the dam is the continuation of the Colorado River. Fifteen-mile float trips down the Colorado from the dam to historic Lee's Ferry are available through Wilderness River Adventures (520-645-3279).

Lake Powell is Camelot—a utopia for all who are weary of playing indoors. The combination of coral cliffs, pristine beaches, and wide-open water and secret inlets creates a natural playground that is unrivaled for active and inactive leisure time.

One Lake Powell trip is never enough. Plans for the next vacation will be underway before the first one is finished. The sights, the sounds, the feel of Lake Powell—they *are* indescribable.

RESTAURANTS

FAMILY TREE RESTAURANT at RAMADA INN
287 North Lake Powell Boulevard
P. O. Box 1867
Page, Arizona 86040
Tel: (520) 645-8851
FAX: (520) 645-2523
Hrs: Breakfast
Summer 6:00 a.m. - 11:00 a.m.
Off-Season 6:30 a.m. - 11:00 a.m.
         Lunch
Summer 11:00 a.m. - 1:30 p.m.
Off-season 11:00 a.m. - 1:00 p.m.
         Dinner
Summer 5:00 p.m. - 10:00 p.m.
Off-Season   5:30 p.m. - 8:30 p.m.

Visa, MasterCard, American Express, Diners Club, Carte Blanche and Discover are accepted.

Those who have dined at Family Tree Restaurant, located at the Page/Lake Powell Ramada Inn (see related story), agree that everything about the restaurant—from the quality food to the prices and the service —are something to rave about.

Even so, the singular entity that distinguishes Family Tree from other restaurants in the area is the marvelous dinner buffet held every night of the week during peak season, May through September. This popular all-one-can-eat buffet offers a variety of meat and poultry dishes, pastas, hot vegetables, salads, and dessert and beverage choices. Fridays' rendering is a selection of special seafood dishes.

In addition to its dinner buffet, Family Tree offers a menu that includes a soup and salad bar, selection of appetizers, and great variety of entrees. For the beef connoisseur, Family Tree offers charbroiled Filet Mignon, New York Strip, and a grilled Ribeye steak, which are succulent, juicy, and cooked to perfection. Fish and seafood Epicureans enjoy the Shrimp Scampi, lightly breaded and pan-fried Rocky Mountain Trout, served with toasted almonds and a lemon twist; and the Filet of Salmon, grilled to perfection and topped with a creamy dill sauce. For chicken fanciers, there is Lemon

Chicken. The Veal Parmesan, lightly breaded and topped with melted mozzarella cheese and a zesty marinara sauce, is served over linguini and is a gastronomical delight. All entrees are served with vegetables, fresh baked bread, a choice of potato or rice pilaf, and an option of soup or salad. For a small additional cost, diners may choose to have the soup and salad bar included with their meal.

Family Tree Restaurant has a wonderful selection of desserts, including a variety of pies, cakes, and brownies. The restaurant suggests its Signature Cheesecake with cherry, strawberry, or blueberry topping.

For breakfast, Family Tree is famous for its freshly baked Honey Nugget Biscuits. They also have a variety of breakfast breads, fresh fruits, yogurts, and hot and cold cereals for light eaters. From the griddle, breakfast diners may choose buttermilk pancakes, Belgium waffles, or Cinnamon Supreme French Toast, all served with a choice of sausage or ham. The Lake Powell Special combines two fresh eggs with two steaming buttermilk pancakes, and two sausage links. Family Tree offers a selection of Skillet Inspirations, each of which is topped with two farm-fresh eggs or egg beaters, any style, and Honey Nugget Biscuits. Offered are Western Skillet, Veggie Skillet, and Skillet Delight. Each is distinctively different and delicious, but "Our Favorite Skillet" seems to be everyone's favorite. It offers grilled sausage, onion, and green peppers blended with skillet browns, and topped with shredded cheddar. Family Tree also offers a breakfast buffet, continental style or "with the works." Other breakfast selections are corned beef hash and eggs, steak and eggs, and a variety of omelettes.

The Family Trees great selection of burgers is available for both lunch and dinner. The choices include The charbroiled Conestoga, flamebroiled Wagon Master, The Frontier, which is topped with melted Monterey Jack cheese, green chili strips and sizzling bacon, and Charbroiled Chicken, a juicy chicken breast, basted with an herb butter seasoning and grilled to perfection. All burgers are one-half pound, except for The Conestoga, which is one-third pound.

A favorite luncheon selection is Family Trees "Create Your Own Omelette." Diners have a choice of 15 ingredients to add to their three-egg omelette, which is served with skillet browned potatoes and choice of white or whole wheat toast.

One salad refresher is The Family Orchard, an array of seasonal fresh fruits and melon slices served in a fresh pineapple boat and topped with a scoop of cottage cheese or rainbow sherbet. Other salads include the Chef, Chicken Caesar, and Pasta.

In addition to their great French Dip sandwich, Family Tree offers a hot hearty roast beef, New York Steak, and Philly sandwich. They also have a variety of cold sandwiches that include sliced roast beef, ham, or turkey, chicken or tuna salad, and the traditional BLT.

Family Tree is spacious enough to accommodate large tour groups as well as individual diners. The main restaurant, with a color scheme of mauve and burgundy, seats 110. The Garden Room, with a decor of mauve and turquoise, accommodates 40 guests. Large parties and tour groups are seated in the banquet room, which facilitates up to 100 guests. Windows in all of the dining rooms have a scenic overview of Lake Powell, the dam, and Glen Canyon.

All meals are also available for in-room dining.

Family Tree Restaurant at the Ramada Inn prides itself on offering its diners quality fresh foods; a great breakfast, lunch and dinner selection; helpful, courteous and friendly service; and dining value that will have guests returning, time and again.

PEPPER'S @ THE COURTYARD MARRIOTT

600 Clubhouse Drive
P. O. Box 4150
Page/Lake Powell, Arizona 86040
Tel: (520) 645-5000
 (800) 851-3855
 (800) 321-2211
FAX: (520) 645-5004
Hrs: Open Seven Days
Breakfast 6:00 a.m. - 11:00 a.m.
Lunch 11:00 a.m. - 2:00 p.m.
Dinner 5:00 p.m. - 10:00 p.m.

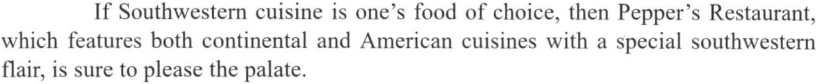

Visa, MasterCard, American Express, Diners Club, Carte Blanche, and Discover are accepted.
Reservations are recommended.

If Southwestern cuisine is one's food of choice, then Pepper's Restaurant, which features both continental and American cuisines with a special southwestern flair, is sure to please the palate.

The southwestern ambiance, both inside and outside, makes the dining experience one of complete satisfaction. Clusters of chili peppers hang from support beams, and one of a kind or limited edition Kachina dolls adorn the walls. The outdoor patio, available most of the time, overlooks Lake Powell and Glen Canyon Dam. Gas lanterns take the chill from the winter air and a misting system makes dining a pleasant experience throughout the hot summer months.

With all that there is to see and do in Southwestern Utah and Northern Arizona, it is easy to work up an appetite, but at Pepper's, the appetite is not just satisfied, it is gratified.

The most important meal of the day, so the experts say, is breakfast. Pepper's offers a traditional breakfast menu with omelettes, eggs any style, hash browns, variety of toasts, and choice of bacon, ham and sausage. But the favorite morning bill of fair is Pepper's breakfast buffet. The waffle station offers an almost unlimited choice of fruits, whipped cream, and other toppings. The buffet also has a large selection of breads and pastries.

Pepper's lunch and dinner menu are the same. One would be doing themselves an injustice if they did not try the Hot Spinach, Artichoke and Cheese Dip. A blend of spinach, artichoke hearts, spices and mixture of cheeses, the dip is served bubbly hot with blue and gold tortilla chips and a side of Pepper's famous fire roasted fresh salsa. Another favorite appetizer is the Grilled Quesadilla. Flour tortillas are grilled, stuffed with cheddar and Monterey Jack cheeses, and served with guacamole, sour cream, and the house salsa. Grilled vegetables and grilled spicy chicken morsels can be added.

The soup of the day changes daily and includes such choices as creamy chicken and vegetables, a spicy combination that is simply delicious.

When it comes to salads at Pepper's, the Cajun and the Grilled Chicken Cilantro salads are meals in themselves. The Cajun chicken salad offers tender Cajun-spiced chicken strips piled high over mixed greens, carrots, cheese, tomatoes, egg, and crispy fried onion straws. Several dressings are offered, but the house recommends the honey

Dijon dressing. The grilled chicken cilantro salad has a variety of garden fresh greens, roma tomatoes, sliced mushrooms, cucumbers, and grilled chicken breast that is tossed together with fresh cilantro and one's choice of dressings. The writer recommends Pepper's fat free raspberry vinaigrette. Connoisseurs of Caesar salads will savor Pepper's rendering. It is prepared with homemade garlic croutons and can be topped with blackened or grilled chicken breast or tuna steak.

There is nothing traditional about the sandwich and burger selection at Pepper's. The Caliente Pacific Tuna is a Cajun blackened tuna steak on a toasted Kaiser roll with lettuce, tomato, red onion slices and rojo remoulade sauce. The Road Runner is char-grilled chicken breast that is basted with BBQ sauce, topped with bacon strips and melted jack cheese, and served on a toasted baguette. It can also be served with blackened chicken. The Baja Roll features hickory smoked turkey breast slices, crisp bacon, lettuce, tomato, and cheddar cheese that is grilled on a flour tortilla and served with avocado mayonnaise. All sandwiches are served with a choice of cole slaw, crispy coated French fries, or lightly seasoned crisp tortilla chips. A real burger treat is the El Paso Burger. It features succulent ground beef that is blackened with chile spices and topped with guacamole and Texas tooth pick onion straws. All burgers are served with lettuce, tomatoes, red onion slices, and crispy coated French fries.

In the pasta family, the Southwest Bowties are tossed in a sundried tomato cream with fresh basil and grated parmesan cheese. Santa Fe Pasta is a linguini dish with blackened chicken breast, sweet red peppers, mushrooms and pecans that are tossed together in a spicy cream sauce.

Steaks, all of which are served with a Caesar or house mixed salad and a choice of two side dishes, include the traditional sirloin, ribeye, New York and filet mignon. All are cooked to perfection, as is the slow roasted prime rib with herb crust.

A house specialty not to be missed is the Mesa Chicken. Tender, juicy, and with a marvelous southwest flavor, the boneless chicken breast is marinated in fresh cilantro, sweet red onions and fiesta herbs. It is grilled and topped with fire roasted BBQ sauce, fresh tomatoes, green chilis and poblano cheese. Other house specialties are the BBQ Baby Back Ribs, Fire Seared Pork Chops, and Rocky Mountain Trout. All are served with a choice of two side dishes.

Favorite side dishes are the spicy and highly seasoned Tumbleweed Rice, Garlic Smashed Potatoes, and Pepper's exceptional Charro Ranch Beans. Also available are Idaho baked potato, country cole slaw, crispy coated fries, and a fresh vegetable medley.

Delicious desserts served at Pepper's include Outrageous Brownie. This double fudge brownie cake is topped with vanilla ice cream, strawberry, chocolate, and caramel sauces, whipped cream, toasted almonds, and chocolate chips. This brownie is not just outrageous, it is downright decadent! Pepper's Margarita Pie is the west's version of key lime pie. It is served over cool berry sauce with whipped cream.

Pepper's has a full service cocktail bar with many specialty libations, red and white wine, and champagne and sparkling wine.

When visiting southern Utah, don't forget to cross over the border into Northern Arizona—there is no finer southwestern cuisine in the country than that which is served at Pepper's.

Zion National Park Area Map

ZION NATIONAL PARK

- MT. CARMEL JUNCTION — 89, 9
- SPRINGDALE, VIRGIN
- HURRICANE — 9, 59
- KANAB — 89
- FREDONIA — 89a, 389
- ST. GEORGE — 15

UTAH / ARIZONA
NEVADA

Legend:
1. Snow Canyon State Park
2. Quail Creek State Park
3. Coral Pink Sand Dunes State Park
4. Pipe Springs National Monument

WASHINGTON COUNTY

Washington County, located in the southwestern corner of the state, is commonly known as "Utah's Dixie." Famous for its mild winters and over 300 sunny days per year, the area, in the state's early history was considered an ideal place for raising cotton. A land of great beauty and wonder, Washington County is home to Zion National Park, Snow Canyon State Park, and close to 50,000 people (1990 census). From its rich farm land to its great recreational opportunities, Washington County is a prominent part of Utah's famous Color Country.

Washington County was first explored in the winter of 1849-1850 by Parley P. Pratt, one of the twelve apostles, and his Southern Exploring Company. The Company found a land ripe for agricultural development.

By 1852 the town of Harmony had been established. Harmony was home to 23 missionaries, sent in 1854 to live among the Paiute Indians of the region. Among this group was Jacob Hamblin who, along with others, raised the region's first successful crop of cotton in 1855. Two years later, in 1877, Brigham Young called 28 families to settle the area as a "cotton mission."

In October of 1861, 309 Mormon families were sent to Washington County to "grow cotton." They arrived in 400 heavily laden wagons during the winter of 1861-1862 and began to lay out a city along the banks of the Virgin River. Beset by flooding rivers, drought, poor soil, grasshoppers, and Indian troubles, the pioneers nonetheless persevered and created a place to live and prosper for themselves and their children.

Today Washington County is one of the state's fastest growing regions. As a result of the area's popularity as a recreational and retirement center, the county showed an incredible 48 percent increase over its 1980 census. An excellent place to live and play, Washington County has rapidly become one of the American Southwest's great vacation spots.

WASHINGTON COUNTY ATTRACTIONS

ZION NATIONAL PARK

Utah's oldest national park, Zion offers visitors some of the most spectacular scenery to be found anywhere in the world. Covering an area of 147,000 acres in southern Utah, Zion Canyon, hard as it is to imagine, is largely the work of the tiny Virgin River, which cut a path through the sedimentary rock, exposing the earth's history to observation. The snows and rains falling on the porous sandstone surface also play an important role in the destruction of the canyon walls.

For thousands of years, the park was home to the Anasazi Indians. Evidence of their stay has been discovered in the ruins of dwellings perched along the high cliffs of the region. These Ancient Ones, as Anasazi means, raised corn, squash, and melons along the banks of the rivers and streams which flow through the park's canyons.

Nephi Johnson, a Mormon pioneer, was the first white man to explore Zion Canyon, riding as far as Zion Stadium in 1858. In 1861 Joseph Black explored the area and gave such glowing reports of Zion's scenic wonders that for years the canyon was known as "Joseph's Glory." Isaac Behunin was the first white man to use the canyon. He built a summer cabin near the site of today's Zion Lodge in 1863. He called the canyon "Little Zion," a name that stuck until Brigham Young visited the canyon, discovered that tobacco was being cultivated and told them it was not Zion. For a time his more faithful followers called the canyon just that, "Not Zion."

In 1872 Major John Wesley Powell visited the canyon. The Paiute Indians he encountered gave the canyon the name "mukuntuweap," meaning "straight canyon." Some early settlers of the region maintained that the Paiutes had a superstitious fear of the canyon, fearing the darkness of the area would overtake them. The Paiutes of today, however, refute this idea. Their refutaion is evidenced by the fact that the Paiutes did indeed work the land and grew corn here.

Even today it would be hard to fathom, but at one time, during one of his visits to Zion Canyon, Brigham Young predicted that thousands of feet of lumber would one day come down Zion Canyon. In 1900, David Flanigan discovered a rich, mature stand of ponderosa pine on the East Rim. He reasoned that if small wires could raise and lower a mail pouch, larger wires similarly arranged, could carry lumber. He returned to the mountain with 50,000 feet of wire and, after much experimentation, perfected a means of bringing lumber down off the rim. It operated successfully for nearly two decades and most of the lumber used in the early stages of building Zion Lodge came from his operation. The upper tower can still be seen on top of Cable Mountain, northeast of the Great White Throne.

In 1909, President Taft set aside a portion of the area as the Mukuntuweap National Monument. In 1918 the monument was enlarged and the name changed to Zion by President Wilson. One year later the area was designated as a national park by an act of Congress. In 1956, Kolob Canyon, established as a National Monument in 1937, became a part of Zion National Park.

One manmade point of interest that should not be missed is the Zion-Mt. Carmel Tunnel. A 1.1-mile long tunnel blasted from solid rock between 1927 and 1930 accomplished the fete of linking Zion, Bryce, and Grand Canyon National Parks as well as Cedar Breaks National Monument. This unusual passage features windows cut into the sheer cliffs and gives a teasing view of the park's giant monoliths.

From the veiled waterfalls cascading down the colorful sandstone walls after a sudden rain to the lush green valleys surrounded by sculpted cliffs of great height, Zion National Park is nothing short of breathtaking. The smooth wall of veined marble, which makes up the east face of the gigantic **West Temple,** is a marvelous site. Ascending more than 4,100 feet from its base, this massive formation is layer upon layer of rock that reveals much geologic history.

Looking as if a "dozen Gothic skyscrapers had been placed side by side, heated and welded together into one enormous cathedral," **The Watchman,** standing guard at the park entrance, sits across the canyon from West Temple. With its bright orange, rust, green and rose accending the dominant red sandstone, The Watchman is symbolic of the power of this wondrous place.

Three miles long and nearly 4,000 feet high, the **Great West Wall** is considered by many to be the single most imposing feature of the park and is best viewed from the **Zion-Mt. Carmel Switchbacks.**

Overlooking the Switchbacks from the South is **Bridge Mountain,** so named for the natural bridge located on its face. Known as the **Flying Buttress,** this slender 156-foot stone arch looks like a looped thread of rock against the colossal proportions of the mountain wall behind it.

The best known monolith in the park, the **Great White Throne,** rises to a height of 6,744 feet above sea level. A mass of white sandstone, the summit of the Throne is a popular precipice for rock climbers and has been reached several times, although many climbers have been seriously injured in the endeavor. Only the most experienced climbers should attempt to scale the gigantic face of the Throne.

Those of strong body, nerve, faith, and who are not afraid of heights can take the two and one-half mile long trail from the Grotto picnic area to the 5,785 foot high summit of **Angels Landing**. This dull red sandstone monolith contrasts sharply with the bright white of the Throne across the canyon. Climbing 1,500 feet, the trail to the summit offers an outstanding view of Zion Canyon. During and immediately after a rain storm, the White Throne and Angels Landing area spring to life with colorful waterfalls. Sometimes lasting only a few minutes, they are nonetheless an exciting sight to behold. Carrying the richly tinted silt and sand from the plateaus and mesas above, the falls are colored yellow, red, rich chocolate brown, orange and even black.

Other outstanding natural phenomena include **Zion Stadium**, a walled-in alcove with bright wildflowers growing from nearly every crevice; **The Narrows**, an area where the walls rise 2,000 feet from the river below yet are only fifty feet apart at river level; and **Weeping Rock**, where water weeping from the rocky walls supports the growth of bright green moss, golden yellow columbines, deep purple shootingstar, and brilliantly scarlet monkeyflowers.

For one's recreational enjoyment, Zion National Park offers a superb visitor center that is open year-round and provides fascinating folklore, area information, slide programs, exhibits, book sales, and a museum. Zion Lodge offers dining in a rustic 1930s-style ambiance, box lunches when ordered at least eight hours in advance, a summer snack shop, and a gift shop. Guided and self guided tours, regularly scheduled open-air tram rides, interpretive talks, nature walks, and slide presentations can be arranged at the lodge front desk. Horseback tours are also available.

Zion Lodge, designed and built in the 1920s, was destroyed by a devastating fire in 1966. The lodge was rapidly rebuilt in just 100 days, but the speed of reconstruction sacrificed Gilbert Stanley Underwood's classic rustic design and historic appearance. In 1990 the exterior was restored to its classic appearance. The lodge is open year-round (435-772-3256).

SPRINGDALE

Springdale, 45 miles northwest of St. George, has the good fortune of being the burgeoning community at the south entrance to Zion National Park. Visitors are finding that Springdale, with its excellent choice of motels, bed and breakfasts, restaurants, gift shops and tourist services, is an excellent base from which to explore the park.

Springdale was first settled in the autumn of 1862 a little to the South of the present town in the lowlands, and received its name because of the nearby springs. The springs, however, for early settlers were an enigma rather than a blessing. So prevalent were they, that much of the land was swampy and a breeding ground for mosquitoes. Malaria became a severe problem for the pioneers. Nevertheless, just as it has experienced rapid growth today, by the end of the first winter Springdale had 20 families housed in dugouts, willow houses, and a few modest log cabins. As with other Virgin River Valley communities, Springdale was plagued with flooding and heavy rains. By 1864, half of the families had moved away. In 1866 the Blackhawk war caused the remaining families to move, and about half of them never returned in 1869 when a treaty was signed. Malaria continued to plague the residents, causing settlers to migrate to its present site on higher ground. The swamp was also eventually drained.

Springdale, because of its isolation, was forced to resort to supplying themselves with the necessities of life. An outcropping was a rawhide-bottomed chair that was so sturdy and so desirable that for quite some time the chair was exported. A fortuitous solution to the problem of insufficient grazing land was the building of the Big Bend Trail to the East Rim of Zion National Park, a trail that is still in use today.

The development of Zion National Park as a major tourist attraction has created a boom town out of Springdale, providing jobs for everyone and increasing its population ten-fold on any summer day. The town, as in its past, has risen to the challenge and is meeting the needs of its visitors.

SPRINGDALE ATTRACTIONS

ZION CANYON CINEMAX

Located in Springdale near the entrance to Zion National Park, *Zion Canyon-Treasure of the Gods* is, according to many experts, the most spectacular film experience available on the IMAX screen. The film, an educational and entertaining introduction to the Southwest and Zion National Park, has been touted by American Indian leaders for its respect for their culture, its uplifting message, and its awe-inspiring beauty.

Zion Canyon-Treasure of the Gods transports its audience into the secret recesses of slot canyons and to the spiraling heights of the most beautiful monoliths in the world. The audience transcends time as it experiences the canyons as seen through the eyes of the Anasazi, the Paiutes, Spanish Conquistadors, and adventurers of today. Adrenaline flows during the terror of a slot canyon flash flood and at the thrill of hanging with climbers from towers of stone 2,000 feet high.

Kieth Merrill, who has produced and directed six other IMAX films, stated that *Treasure of the Gods* is the most logistically difficult and the most spectacular film he has ever made. Cameras and equipment were carried into places only half a dozen climbers and canyoneers have ever been, and, as the shots reveal, the beauty and drama of Zion Canyon are unequaled.

O.C. TANNER AMPHITHEATER

A 24-foot by 40-foot screen, backed by the towering ledges of Zion Canyon, nightly showcases *The Grand Circle: A National Park Odyssey* from May through September. A multi-media presentation of lights and sound, the presentation highlights the grandeur of eight national parks and seven national monuments (435-652-7994).

ADVENTURE / TOURS

CANYON CRUISER CO.
Bike Rentals
868 Zion Park Boulevard
Springdale, Utah 84767-189
Tel: (435) 772-3099
Hrs: March - October
Friday - Sunday   8:00 a.m. - 9:00 p.m.
For weekday & night time cruises, call for reservations.
Reservations are preferred.

CANYON CRUISER CO.
BIKE RENTALS

Beginning in the spring of 1999, visitors to Zion National Park will no longer be allowed to drive their personal automobiles throughout the park. Instead of looking at this as a negative, why not view it, as Joshua VanderWerff, owner of Canyon Cruiser Co. has done, as a positive. In fact, why wait until 1999 to begin enjoying the park as it should be enjoyed?

In 1955, Schwinn built its classic bicycle, the "Beach Cruiser." The Cruiser is a reproduction of this classic, a bicycle that allows cyclists to sit straight and tall in a very comfortable saddle. The bike has white wall tires, tall handle bars, and offers the smoothest, most comfortable ride in the canyons—or just around town.

Canyon Cruiser Co. is now renting single speed and six speed cruisers for half-day and full-day enjoyment. Also offered on the six-speed cruiser is the Zion Canyon Down Hill Cruise from 6:00 - 9:00 p.m. The guided single speed cruise is from 9:00 a.m. - 12 noon. Every rental package includes a free water bottle, a fanny pack for lunch and goodies, and the use of a helmet. The single and six-speed bicycles are also available for purchase.

SCENIC CYCLES
205 Zion Park Boulevard
Zion National Park, South Entrance
Springdale, Utah 84767
Tel: (435) 772-BIKE (2453)
Cellular   (435) 680-3731
Web Site::   www.sceniccycles.com
Hrs: March - October
Open Daily   8:00 a.m. - 8:00 p.m.

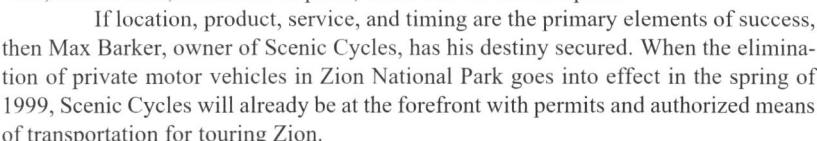

Visa, MasterCard, American Express, and Discover are accepted.

If location, product, service, and timing are the primary elements of success, then Max Barker, owner of Scenic Cycles, has his destiny secured. When the elimination of private motor vehicles in Zion National Park goes into effect in the spring of 1999, Scenic Cycles will already be at the forefront with permits and authorized means of transportation for touring Zion.

Elimination of motor vehicles in Zion will become necessary in 1999 because of three main elements—pollution, noise, and traffic congestion. Scenic Cycles, which offers Mountain bikes, Tandems, Electric Bikes, and Electric Cars, is the answer to all three problems. It is also a solution that makes sense to Park visitors, even before the ban on private vehicles goes into effect.

The grandeur of Zion National Park, with its lush vegetation, magnificent white and red rock cliffs, fascinating fauna, and cascading Virgin River, is too exceptional to be visited in any other way than leisurely.

Scenic Cycles is not just another bike shop that caters to mountain bikers, although they certainly do that too. Scenic Cycles rents mountain bikes, tandem bikes (bicycles built for two), or electric bikes to bikers of all skill levels. Regardless of the choice, bikers can bike and enjoy off-road trails and discover portions of Zion National Park that are still unknown to the masses. Or they can bike the well known two and one-half mile Pa'rus trail. This bicycle route follows along and then crosses the Virgin River, giving a panoramic view of colorful rock formations, wildlife, and the sounds of nature one misses when traveling in a car.

When it comes to biking Zion National Park, Scenic Cycles has thought of everything. The electric bicycles provide the fun and health benefits of a bicycle with the effortless ease associated with motorcycles. Those using the electric bicycles can rely entirely on the electric charge, pedal, or use a combination of both for its most efficient use. The bike can carry its passenger along biking paths as well as the Park's well laid out roads. For bikers with children, Scenic Cycles offers a child's tandem attachment or a bike trailer for two small tikes.

The Electric Cars, also available from Scenic Cycles, are fun, quiet, and relaxing, but most important they are environmentally friendly. Where ever automobiles have previously been allowed to venture in Zion National Park or anywhere else in the area, the electric cars are legal to go. The electric cars, federally approved for street traffic, are equipped with head and tail lights, seat belts, turn signals, safety glass, and front wheel drive. Open sides and high windows make visibility extremely good. Although great for everyone, they are especially ideal for those traveling in motor homes. Simply park the large vehicle and enjoy the perimeters of Zion at a leisurely 25 miles per hour.

Summer months at Zion can get so hot that the only relief from the heat is the river. At prices so low that it will surprise even the most conservative, guests to the area can rent Scenic Cycle river tubes. After experimenting for the first year, Scenic Cycle has developed its own style of river tube. It safely encompasses the floater, yet keeps them above the water line and the river's rocky bottom. River tubes are ideal for a one to two mile float down the river, with pre-arranged pick-up, or for just playing in the river around a camp site.

Scenic Cycle, a Travelers' Choice adventure, has eliminated the negatives while adding the positives. When renting a mountain, tandem, or electric bicycle or car from Scenic Cycle, there is no pollution, no noise and no traffic congestion. But at Scenic Cycle, where tourist safety and enjoyment are primary concerns, there are all the options needed for leisurely enjoying a day in Zion National Park.

ZION ADVENTURE COMPANY
36 Lion Boulevard
Springdale, Utah 84767
Tel: (435) 772-1001
FAX: (435) 772-3590
Web Site:
http.//www.zionadventures.com
Hrs:
Open Seven Days 8:00 a.m. - 8:30 p.m.
Visa, MasterCard, American Express, and Discover are accepted.
Reservations are preferred.

Upon entering the retail store of Zion Adventure Company, one might initially perceive that it is typical—that it is very much like any other rock climbing or rappelling store. But Zion Adventure Company, because of its product line, ownership and philosophy, is entirely unique.

In order to comprehend this peerless business, it is important to know about Zion Adventure Company's inception and the people who make it work.

Zion Adventure Company is the fulfillment of a dream, and the meeting of the minds of three extraordinary people. The Company was founded in February of 1996 as the brainchild of Rick Praetzel. Rick is an East Coast outfitter, who, by 36, had climbed this hemisphere's highest mountain. This experience, along with others leading up to it, generated the philosophy that only a few things in life are really important. Rick's mission—helping others to help themselves and the planet—along with his predilection for the Zion Narrows, led him to a partnership with two others in forming Zion Adventure Company.

By the time he was 23, Jonathan Zambella, now 26, was facilitating team building training for corporate groups. He has run backcountry excursions all over the country and is totally enamored with life. His partners call Jonathan "just your basic genius." Jonathan designed and built the interior of the retail store. Rick and Jonathan personally designed Zion Adventure Company's hiking, climbing and Canyoneering gear; and created the Company's rental packages. He also conceptualized the style in which customers are treated. Ultimately, the rule of thumb is: No one walks out of Zion Adventure Company as anything less than a friend. The Company helps customers in any way they can—period!

Michele Van Hise has an indomitable spirit that can best be expressed with one statement: The first time she ever camped in a tent, it was for *four* weeks. Making things work through clear, analytical and practical thinking is the priceless quality Michele brings to Zion Adventure Company. Her Chinese lineage is through royalty and revolutionary leadership--two attributes Michele has adopted for herself.

Michele brings another treasure to Zion Adventure Company, her puppy, Sedona. Sedona is a mix of Rottweiler, German Shepherd, and possibly Labrador. As the design and philosophy of Zion Adventure Company were put to pen, never could the partners have expected that a little canine would play such a key role. Always a priority was the ideal that, walking through the store door, customers would automatically feel the difference—that Zion Adventure Company is there to create friendships and change lives. The innocence and purity that Sedona emits and her wagging tail and playfulness puts people at ease and creates the reflective customer attitude Zion Adventure Company desires.

As a storefront, Zion Adventure Company is an outfitter for rock climbers and rapellers, providing classes at all levels of expertise for both outdoor sports. But it is the definition of the Company's coined word, "canyoneering," that brought Zion Adventure Company to Zion. By their definition, canyoneering means "travel through or occupation of a steep narrow area requiring the use of a variety of wilderness travel techniques." Canyoneering is an all-encompassing outdoor activity that requires every skill imaginable as well as the ability to think quickly and responsively on one's feet. It includes, but is not limited to: trip planning, rappelling, hydration and nutrition, route finding, camping and bivouacking, decision making, rock climbing, first aid, river crossing, fire building, ascending, managing exposure, hiking and river hiking, problem solving, tyrolean traverse, team work, scrambling, anchor setting, flash flood presence of mind, interpretation of time, swimming, whitewater paddling, snow shoeing, foot care, ice climbing, and reflection.

It is canyoneering that led to the creation of Zion Adventure Company. Back in February 1996, at its inception, Rick stood at the Gateway to Zion Narrows. He desperately wanted to proceed but was stopped by the elements. At this point Rick realized that, with no guided permits available and with only 142 people allowed daily to experience the full 16-mile adventure, there was a great need for a caring service— a company that would provide all the proper gear, maps and orientation for hiking the Narrows.

Zion Adventure Company is that business. Conditions in the Narrows are monitored every day of the year by Zion Adventure Company. The customized gear developed by Rick and Jonathan is designed to help hikers stay dry, warm, and comfortable throughout the hike, whether for one afternoon or a series of days. Zion Adventure Company Canyoneering shoes give amazing traction on wet rocks. They also protect the feet and provide better support than boots or sandals. Dry suits keep hikers dry and comfortable all day. The 6mm Neoprene Water Socks keep one's feet warm and blister and abrasion free. The extremely affordable rental package includes walking sticks and detailed river maps as well as a pre-trip orientation. Do not expect to walk out of Zion Adventure Company with rental equipment if there has been no orientation. It is not allowed, regardless of how veteran one is! The Company feels that those who have been around the proverbial block will appreciate the value of knowledgeable orientation. Regardless of expertise, a Narrows experience involves risks and it is important to be aware of them.

Canyoneering at Zion Adventure Company goes beyond rental of equipment and orientation for Zion Narrows adventures. The East Fork of the Virgin River and Upper Parunaweap, Class II and III canyons, are offered as one, two, and three-day trips. The Chute and Chimney Rock Canyon, both Class IV Canyons where rappelling experience is required, are also offered as single and multi-day trips. Group size is kept at six or less and reservations are necessary.

From mid-November through February Zion Adventure Company offers single-day trips of super high adventure, requiring multiple rappels through water flows, ice scrambling, rope ascending, and canyon access by snow mobile and snow shoeing. Trip dates are by request and group size is a maximum of four.

Spring Break Trips, taking place annually between February 28 and April 4, offer college students the opportunity to experience seven days of unforgettable adventure and backcountry travel in Zion, Grand Canyon, and Bryce National Parks. Each group of a maximum of 10 can collectively choose alternative schedules. Participants are responsible for their own airfare, sleeping bag (rated for at least 30°F), sleeping pad, day pack, overnight back pack, and all personal items. All other gear, food, instruction and transportation are provided by Zion Adventure Company.

Please check the web site for updated schedules and trip availability.

One of the most unique and visible functions of Zion Adventure Company is its two 26-foot rappelling towers in the retail store parking lot. The towers simplify the Company's ability to offer rappelling instruction at all levels of expertise as well as complex course work in ascending, tyrolean traverse, and anchor setting techniques. All necessary gear is included in the cost of the rappelling classes.

A three-hour Introductory session for first time rappellers introduces use of harnesses, belay devices, rappel devices, and multiple thickness ropes. Participants have the opportunity and instruction for "rapping" multiple times on low angle, vertical, and overhanging walls. This class is available seven days a week, 9:00 a.m. - 12 noon, and again in the evenings, 5:00 p.m. - 8:00 p.m.

The four to six hour session of the Intermediate Rappelling class goes into extreme detail on problem solving and anchor setting. Problem sets include passing knots, using varied diameter ropes, testing and evaluating anchors, replacing webbing, use and application of multiple rappel devices and techniques, releasing stuck ropes, prussik use, tandem rappels on double ropes, and single rope techniques. The session is held Thursday - Monday, 8:00 a.m. - 2:00 p.m. Special time slots are also available.

An Advanced Rope Work class is by reservation only. It will take the intermediate and expert to another level with Fixed and Traditional placements, complex rescue situations, and ascending—all related to the intermediate curriculum.

Regardless of the level of rock climbing experience, one thing is for certain—there is always a technique to perfect, always a climb one can't do, and always a new level of fear to overcome. At Zion Adventure Company guides take the time, as much as is needed, to teach and review equipment use, techniques, and interpretations to facilitate moment by moment improvement. At the Company, whether it is a first day on the rock or the 100th, after one day with them, if the climber doesn't know more about climbing and climb better, money is cheerfully refunded.

Beginner and intermediate rock classes do not take place in Zion National Park due to a moratorium on guiding. Zion Adventure Company utilizes facilities in the surrounding area that are best suited for beginners and intermediate climbers. Locations change to accommodate group size, weather conditions and special needs. Climbs are on basalt, Navajo sandstone, and limestone rock formations.

An introductory first-day climbing course exposes climbers to the technical aspects and use of gear required for safe and fun climbing; climbing techniques and skills such as lowering, rappelling, use of shoes, climbing in balance, and knot tying; and interpretive presentation of free climbing, lead climbing, belaying and cleaning a route, free soloing, aid climbing, and bouldering.

The Intermediate Rock Class is designed to increase physical skills on the wall as well as to increase ability to make hard decisions while climbing. Included in this clinic is a detailed orientation of all belay/rappel devices and their proper use; numerous climbing techniques that shift strength related dynamic moves into precision static moves via resting, down climbing, body centering, opening and closing during moves, smearing, edging, pulling, twisting and hooking with footwork, hand pressing and straight arm techniques, crack jams, and tendon exercising, stretching, and taping; defining lingo and terminology such as red point, pink point, flashing, sending, working, crux, lay back, fungo, and other rock climbing phraseology; and opportunities for goal setting, training, and issues relating to becoming a lead climber.

Advanced Climbing Clinics are by appointment only and are for those who are interested in changing the way they climb, climbing stronger, lighter and more precise, and for those who recognize that they need help in getting to the next level. Zion Adventure Company will customize a one to ten day trip. Previous advanced climbing trips have been to Red Rocks, Nevada, New River Gorge, West Virginia, Snow Canyon, Utah, Acadia National Park, Maine, Shawangunks Mohonk Preserve, New York, Red River Gorge, Kentucky, and Delaware Water Gap, New Jersey.

In addition to their outfitting services and rock climbing, rappelling, and canyoneering classes, Zion Adventure Company is there to assist adventurers with hiking and trip planning, ECO Tours, Team and Community Building Programs, and Corporate Training.

When it comes to retail products—such as walking sticks, day packs, canyoneering shoes, dry suits, neoprene water socks, and detailed river maps— Zion Adventure Company adheres to the philosophy, "Never carry or sell anything that you will not use yourself." And when any gear is upgraded, the older gear is abandoned.

Zion Adventure Company is unique. Their product, their service, their image, their mission, and their identity is to help people make important decisions with their precious time, and to celebrate every moment.

As they nurture Zion Adventure Company through its infancy, Rick, Jonathan, Michele and Sedona are there to help all who ask them. That they do to the best of their ability. Next year they will be better than they are this year. The following year they will be even better. For now, what they are giving is their patience, their understanding, their best. Who can ask for more!

RESTAURANTS

BIT & SPUR
Restaurant & Saloon
1212 Zion Park Boulevard
Springdale, Utah 84767
Tel: (435) 772-3498
FAX: (435) 772-3734
Hrs: February - November
Open Daily   5:00 p.m. - 10:00 p.m.
           November
Thursday - Monday   5:00 p.m. - 10:00 p.m.
           December & January
Closed —call to see if open.
Visa, MasterCard, and Discover are accepted.
Reservations accepted but not required.

    Bit & Spur Restaurant & Saloon, owned and operated by two top-notch chefs, Randall Richards and Joe Jennings, offers a rare combination of superlative Mexican and Southwestern cuisine and unrivaled camaraderie. Bit & Spur has, since its beginning on St. Patrick's Day, 1981, been known for its great food and as the place to meet old friends and develop new ones.

    The pine and rock walls and open beam ceilings of Bit & Spur's three spacious dining rooms and the outdoor patio that encompasses the restaurant on three sides, create an atmosphere for informal dining that is conducive to good times.

    Every Saturday, March through November, one of Bit & Spur's dining rooms metamorphosises. Tables and chairs are removed and Bit & Spur rocks to the tunes of a live band as diners dance to the sounds of yesterday and today. Bit & Spur is a state liquor licensee and offers a full range of wines, draft and bottled beers and alcoholic and non-alcoholic drinks.

    Appetizers at Bit & Spur are numerous, but one house favorite is the Fried Brie with Jalapeno Jelly. The fried brie is walnut crusted and, almost like a dessert, is sweet and marvelous. Another wonderful beginner is the Avocado Corn and Mushroom Quesadilla with its sautéed corn and mushrooms and goat cheese. Also exceptional is the Potato and Corn Crabcake. It features smoked tomato puree and home made basil aoli.

    Two South of the Border house entree favorites are the Chile Verde and Sour Cream Enchiladas. The Chile Verde, a traditional pork stew with rice, pinto beans and salad, is enhanced with seasonings of coriander, cumin, and star anise. In Mexico, "uno" means number one. In Hawaii, it means "the best." The Sour Cream Enchiladas are "uno." They feature roasted peppers and vegetables, sour cream, and gorgonzala cheese wrapped in corn tortillas with mole sauce, pinto beans, rice, and salad.

    An entree featured often on Bit & Spur's seasonal menu is Mushroom Stuffed Chile. This delectable dish offers sautéed exotic mushrooms stuffed into a roasted poblano chile, with polenta, smoked cheese sauce, and a seasonal green salad. Bit & Spur has fresh fish flown in every weekend, offering such treats as halibut, swordfish, monk fish, and other delicacies of the sea.

    Bit & Spur Restaurant & Saloon offers gourmet dining in an informal atmosphere.

ZION PIZZA & NOODLE CO.

868 Zion Park Boulevard,
Springdale, Utah 84767-189
Tel: (435) 772-3815
FAX: (435) 772-2457
Email: zpn@southernutah.com
Web Site: zpn@southernutah.com
Hrs: February - November
Open Seven Days 12 Noon - 10:30 p.m.
Closed Most of December and January
Reservations are not required.

Ask around St. George for the best pizza and noodle restaurant in town and a common reaction will be that the best is not in St. George at all, it's in Springdale, gateway to Zion National Park.

Ever since Zion Pizza & Noodle Co. opened its doors in 1990, townsfolk from St. George have been making the trek to Springdale for pizzas baked in a stone slate oven, and pasta that is competitive with any found in the Mediterranean.

Bruce M. VanderWerff, Chef-Restaurateur and owner of Zion Pizza & Noodle Co., started in the restaurant business in 1958 at Finns Restaurant in Salt Lake City, Utah. Since then Bruce has received an advanced degree as a professional chef from LaVareene, Paris, France, and has created, owned, and operated over 30 area restaurants. Upon moving to Springdale, Bruce and his two sons, Jakob and Joshua, who are also owner-operators of this family owned business, feel they have come home. Jakob and Joshua have been in the restaurant business since 1985.

Asked what it is that makes Zion pizza and pasta creations so popular, diners will comment that "the food is always consistent," "sauces are exceptional," and "the staff are people-oriented." They also add that they "love the food-to-go service," and that "Zion Pizza & Noodle Co. has the best delivery service in town." If staying at any of the Springdale hotels, motels, bed and breakfasts, or even the campgrounds, delivery service is available.

Another thing that diners love about the pizza and the noodles is that, unless ordering Zion's "Boring Cheese Pizza," the 11 other available pizzas are one standard price, as are the seven pasta combinations. This makes ordering and divvying the bill very easy.

Menu items are so choice and delectable that it is hard to pinpoint favorites. Some of the most unique pizza choices, however, are Barbecue Chicken Pizza, with its tomato sauce, gouda and mozzarella cheese, red onions, and barbecue chicken; and Thai Chicken Pizza, a combo that offers Thai chicken, thin carrots, Bermuda onions, and peanuts with Asiago mozzarella, and parmesan cheese. Aficionados of Southwestern cuisine love the Hot and Spicy Southwestern Burrito Pizza. It offers tomato sauce, grilled chicken, green chiles, jalapeno peppers, red onions, and a blend of three cheeses. The Good For You pizza is just as its name implies. The grilled veggies, sun dried tomatoes, light sauce, feta and asiago cheeses are all ingredients that are "good for you."

Pasta dishes in the USA during the last decade have taken a leap from mundane to gourmet. When one formerly thought of pasta, they thought of spaghetti. Today they think of Penne, Rigatoni, Fettuccini, Ravioli, and Linguini. Zion Pizza & Noodle Co. is right at the forefront in offering gourmet pasta.

Among the most popular pasta choices are menu items numbers one, three, and five. Pasta #1 offers chicken, broccoli, carrots, fresh cream, and three cheeses with Penne pasta. Pasta #3 is fettuccini with sliced chicken breast, red onions, green peppers, teriyaki sauce, Szechwan oil, and sesame seeds. Pasta #5, ideal for vegetarians, offers a veggie stir fry of seasonal vegetables, teriyaki sauce, and Penne pasta. No pizza or pasta is really complete without a salad. To complement the dining experience, select a tossed garden, Caesar, Greek, or even a pasta salad. The luncheon menu, served from 11:00 a.m. until 3:00 p.m., offers the dinner-sized selection of pizzas as well as an eight-inch size. Pasta dishes have been downsized to suit the lunch crowd. In addition, Zion Pizza & Noodle Co. offers Grilled Veggie and Smoked Turkey and Swiss sandwiches. Hot off the grill are the 1/3-pound hand-formed burgers on fresh baked buns, served with a choice of Swiss or cheddar cheese and lettuce, tomato, pickles, and red onion.

Zion Pizza & Noodle Co. also offers incredible calzones, garlic bread, and espresso that includes mocha, latte, and cappuccino. They also serve an assortment of soft drinks and ades as well as hot chocolate, regular coffee, and hot and iced tea.

One of the most popular dining areas of Zion Pizza & Noodle Co. is the Beer Garden on the back patio. This large covered patio with rock sandstone bar comfortably seats 36. Covered with lush flowers and foliage, the patio offers a spectacular red cliff vista. Served in the beer garden as well as the front patio and inside dining room are beers from Utah's micro-breweries—Squatters, Uintah, and Eddie McStiff's—as well as other on-tap and bottled domestic and foreign beers.

Zion Pizza & Noodle Co. is located in an old Mormon church, built in 1929-1930, with the inside dining room occupying what was once the chapel and the kitchen located where the podium and dais once were. Lights are still the originals, and all the windows, original until last year, are still arched with only the glass replaced. A gift shop occupies what was once the chapel's recreation room. The Fatalli Gallery is downstairs where the classrooms were.

Whether visiting Zion National Park or staying in St. George, visitors to the area find that Zion Pizza & Noodle Co. is everything it is purported to be—and well worth the drive.

ROCKVILLE

Rockville was settled in autumn of 1861 a short distance below its original site. After building a few dugouts and unfinished huts, residents named their town "Adventure." The handful of settlers discovered that the site selected provided an adverse kind of adventure. Eighteen sixty-one was known as the year of the "great rain." The resultant flooding let residents know that they had built too close to the river. The following November they moved up-stream to Rockville's present location. The town was surveyed and given its present name because of its extremely rocky hills and many boulders.

Because of the flooding in the lower valley and the late move to the upper valley, the dozen or so families spent the remainder of the year clearing land, digging ditches, building dugouts and log cabins, and otherwise preparing themselves. Since they had not been able to lay in food for the winter, many of the men had to go north to obtain food for their families.

Rockville was one of the first towns to be settled in the Virgin River Valley and, interestingly enough, when all of the other towns in Southern Utah were being abandoned during the Blackhawk uprising of 1866, Rockville not only survived but flourished. Residents of nearby Springdale, Grafton, and Shunesburg fled to Rockville for refuge and Rockville, until 1869, became the county seat.

The Civil War had caused a shortage of cotton for the Utah Mormons and Brigham Young had encouraged those who were settling Southern Utah to mostly plant cotton, and cane for sorghum. This the Saints did, along with a little corn and wheat. They even built a crusher in Rockville for the cane. Settlers soon discovered, however, that fruit did very well. They excitedly replaced the growing of cotton for the fruits, vegetables, and grain needed to sustain their families. The Civil War was over and cotton once again available from the South. The last cotton exported was in 1870.

Located just a few miles southwest of Zion National Park's main entrance, tourism has become a main source of income for many of Rockville's 182 (1990 census) citizens. Most of its residents still maintain gardens and orchards for their families. Some of the state's best produce is sold at the town's fruit stands.

The Smithsonian Butte Scenic Back Road, although not easy to find, leads to Grafton, one of the area's most popular ghost towns. Grafton, which has unfortunately fallen into disrepair, was the setting for scenes from several popular movies, including *Butch Cassidy and the Sundance Kid*.

There are several bed & breakfasts in Rockville.

GRAFTON

One of Utah's most popular ghost towns, Grafton was settled in 1859 by Nathan C. Tenny and a handful of others. Grafton was named after the town in Massachusetts from which the residents came. Though difficult to find, it is amazing how many visitors to the area seek to find Grafton. Grafton is 7 miles South of the river along Smithsonian Butte Scenic Backroad. Turn south at the east end of Rockville, cross the Virgin River, and then turn west to Grafton. Continuing south will lead to U-59.

In 1861 the "great rain," which engulfed the valley from bluff to bluff and devastated the region, caused settlers to re-locate to Grafton's present site, higher in the valley. An interesting flood story is that of Tenny and his wife. Pregnant at the time, she was moved to the upper valley in Tenny's wagon box, where the baby was born. In gratitude for the family's safe trip to higher ground, the baby was named Marvelous Flood Tenny.

History records that the Virgin River and the rains flooded Grafton so frequently and dams had to be built so consistently, that one settler was quoted as saying: "The building of ditches and dams in Grafton is like washing clothes for one's household—they have to be done every week."

Grafton became the first Kane County seat in 1864, but when residents of Grafton moved to Rockville in 1866 to protect themselves from Indians during the Blackhawk War, Rockville became the new county seat and continued to be so even after settlers returned to Grafton in 1868.

Residents of Grafton continued to battle the river until 1900. At that time there were still about 120 people. The river finally won out by destroying most of the good top soil.

The ghost town at Grafton consists of an old log cabin, a church, and a schoolhouse. In recent years Grafton has been largely left to decay, unfortunate because of its historical importance and because of its popularity as a remembered set in *Butch Cassidy and the Sundance Kid*. The cemetery at the entrance to Grafton is a bonus attraction for all who visit. The cemetery, unlike the town, is being maintained by a local Boy Scout troop. Many of the headstones are over 100 years old and truly reflect the old west. Robert Berry, his wife Isabella, and his brother, Joseph, whose story is told in the history of Glendale, are buried there. Please note the youthful age of the deceased. Their early demise is a tragic reminder of how difficult and exacting life on the western frontier was.

VIRGIN

Virgin City (today known only as Virgin) and all of the small towns from Toquerville to Zion Canyon were first explored by Nephi Johnson, a Mormon missionary who understood and communicated well with the Paiute Indians. Sent in 1858 to discover new sites for communities, Johnson persuaded the Toquerville Paiutes to accompany him over the Hurricane Cliff escarpment and up the Virgin River to the narrows of Zion Canyon. During the journey, Johnson found several sites along the floodplain of the Virgin River that would make good farmland and hence, excellent sites for new towns. Since there were no roads to these sites, Johnson was asked to return in December with a group of men and build a wagon road. Within a month the men had built a sinuous roadway, known as Johnson Twist, and settlers were entering the Virgin River Valley, settling Virgin City, Grafton, Rockville, and Springville. Virgin City was originally known as Pocketville, after the Paiute word Pockich, which means cove.

For two years all of the small Virgin River towns flourished and were able to raise good crops. But 1861, the year of the Great Rain, proved that the floodplain was as much of a problem as a boon. Top soil from bluff to bluff was destroyed and so were dams that had been built to control water and irrigation. Most of the small towns relocated to higher ground.

In 1866, many of the smaller towns were abandoned as villagers banded together to protect themselves from Indians during the Blackhawk war. Virgin City was one of the refuge communities. During a two-year period, 1866 - 1868, its numbers burgeoned to more than 500. Virgin today has a population of under 250.

Virgin City experienced two oil booms, one in 1907 and a second in 1918. Oil production never proved to be economically feasible in spite of the fact that by 1920 the wells were pumping 20 barrels of crude oil per day.

Virgin today is primarily an agricultural community. The Kolob Reservoir Scenic Backway, a partially paved road, leads from Virgin to the back of Zion National Park and to Kolob Reservoir, a popular place for trout fishing and camping.

VIRGIN ATTRACTIONS

KOLOB RESERVOIR BACKWAY

Beginning at U-9 in Virgin, this 45-mile drive of paved, gravel, and graded dirt road traverses some of the most beautiful scenery to be found anywhere in the state. The road introduces visitors to red and white sandstone ledges of Zion National Park's west side, monoliths that are not viewable from any other location. Eight-thousand foot Kolob Reservoir, although with no developed facilities, is ideal for fishing and camping. As the Backway nears its end six miles east of Cedar City near Cedar Breaks, the drive is thickly forested.

Closed during winter months, Kolob reservoir backway is generally suitable for passenger cars during its operational season.

BED & BREAKFASTS

SNOW FAMILY GUEST RANCH

633 East Highway 9
P. O. Box 790190
Virgin, Utah 84779
Tel: (801) 635-2500
        (800) 308-SNOW (7669)
FAX (801) 635-2758
Visa, MasterCard, American Express and Discover are accepted.
Reservations are recommended.

Located only 12 miles from the south entrance of Zion National Park, Snow Family Guest Ranch, with its nine elegantly and impeccably maintained guest rooms, and its 12 acres of lush green pastures, is the ideal accommodation destination for park visitors.

Zion National Park is not the only attraction in the area that makes the ranch such a coveted respite. Pristine and secluded, the ranch is only a short distance from the city of St. George, Bryce Canyon, the North Rim of the Grand Canyon, Lake Powell, and Kolob Canyon, considered to be one of Southern Utah's best kept secrets.

But even if one decided that the parks were not a part of their agenda, those who cherish luxury in a natural setting will find Snow Family Guest Ranch ideal. From the moment one approaches the ranch, with its verdant pastures surrounded by white rail fence, and its large brick and white wood edifice with mansard second story and domered windows, guests feel a sense of home. A beautiful fenced in pool with hot tub, decking, flowers and incredible shade trees on one side, are additional amenities. The back yard offers a back covered patio, uncovered upstairs patio, garden area with hammocks, lawn swings and gazebos, and a duck pond surrounded with large sandstone rocks that is ideal for enjoying the incredible solitude, beauty and peacefulness of Snow Family Ranch.

Perhaps the thing that sets Snow Family Guest Ranch apart from other Bed and Breakfasts is its absolute immaculate surroundings. Grounds seem without blemish, the two great rooms and kitchen are impeccable, and the nine guest rooms are without peer. It is totally obvious that Steve and Shelley Penrose, hosts of the Ranch, have an affinity to cleanliness and harmony, and a penchant for gracious hospitality.

Entrance to the ranch boasts an abundance of plants and a step up to scrupulously maintained hardwood floors. Western paraphernalia such as branding irons, harness, lasso, shot guns, cowboy hats and other western gear adorn the walls and railing. Dining areas are both to the right and left of the entrance. One great room is directly ahead of the stairs and features an old pot belly stove and giant color TV with VCR. The other great room, to the left of the entrance, is decorated with an old upright piano, life-size John Wayne cutout, and pictures of the family with their horses. Down the hall is a collection of dolls from around the world.

Each of the guest rooms, four on the main floor and five upstairs, features a horseshoe for good luck on the door. All rooms offer an eclectic collection of furnishings and decor and have ceiling fans. Most offer stripped pine wood furniture, claw-foot tubs with shower enclosure, window seats, and a decor that includes Western wall borders of boots, bandannas, cowboys with lariats, and cowboy and Indians, as well as other Western appointments.

The bridal suite offers an elegant decor with pink, blue and mauve bedspread, double vanity, blue claw foot tub, and a pull-chain wooden water closet. The large window seat overlooks the backyard patio.

Guests have a choice of queen, king, and twin beds, and adjoining suites.

Also distinguishing the Snow Family Guest Ranch from other bed and breakfasts is its morning cuisine. Breakfast is served family style and features an assortment of fresh fruits in season, coffee, tea, juices, and such delectables as homemade muffins, buttermilk pancakes, sticky buns, biscuits, Belgium waffles, egg casserole, and French toast. Always included at breakfast are eggs, cereal, bacon, sausage, or ham. Cookies and lemonade are served during the afternoon.

Snow Family Guest Ranch was named in memory of Leo Snow, a U. S. deputy surveyor who, in 1908, was so impressed with the magnificent terrain that he recommended the canyon be designated as a national monument. One month later his wish was granted. In 1919 Congress renamed the area Zion National Park.

Shelley is the great granddaughter of Leo Snow. She and Steve share the same love that her great grandparents and Shelley's parents, Clarence and Shirlee Snow, had for the area. It was Clarence, who passed away in 1995, and Shirlee who encouraged and inspired the purchase and development of Snow Family Guest Ranch.

The Snow and Penrose families are anything but greenhorns. Pictures of family members and their horses adorn the walls. It is no surprise that Snow Family Guest Ranch offers another special treat—Guided Trail Rides. Steve can accommodate as many as six people at a time. The perfect time to take a trail ride is two hours before dark. The climate is pleasant, shadows creep across the bluffs, and sunsets are extraordinary.

Whether arriving in the area to enjoy the canyons, visit historic sites or ghost towns, hike or bike the varied trails, enjoy the *Utah Shakespearean Festival* in nearby Cedar City or *Utah! in* Tuacahn Canyon, or to go downhill or cross-country skiing or snowmobiling, the stay at Snow Family Guest Ranch will be equally memorable.

LA VERKIN

La Verkin's history is probably as unique as any Southern Utah community. Almost from the onset of settlement in Southern Utah, plans had been formulated for the purpose of bringing water from the Virgin River to the benches of what is now La Verkin. Erastus Snow, mission president, had first conceived the idea in 1861 but abandoned the project as being too costly. In 1888, Dixie businessman Thomas Judd decided to develop the plan as a private business enterprise. Extensive investigations and surveys revealed that the project was workable. In the spring of 1888, with a capital investment of $25,000, he and his partners began business as the La Verkin Fruit and Nursery Company. The company's mission was to "establish nursery orchards, vineyards, the manufacture of liquor, the promotion of fruit raising, stock raising, and general farming."

Workers on the project were paid $1.50 per day, with one-half received in company stock and one-half in script that was redeemable at the Wooley, Lund, and Judd stores in St. George or Silver Reef, and at the Cotton Factory in Washington.

Most of the ditch was through Kaibab limestone but in a few places they unearthed gypsum, a mineral that was much more easily blasted than was limestone. An 840-foot tunnel was necessary at the mouth of Timpoweap Canyon. Workers began at both ends using a row of candles to keep their lines straight. When they met in the middle, their computations had been so precise that the tunnel fit together almost perfectly. In 1891 the ditch and the tunnel were complete and water successfully turned onto the La Verkin bench. The La Verkin Fruit and Nursery Company began to plant seedling trees and vines for the vineyard.

It did not take long, however, for the Company to encounter a major problem. The gypsum that had so easily been blasted was also water soluble. Tiny slits soon eroded to gaping cavities through which the water could escape. Numerous attempts at solving the problem proved always to be only temporary. The best solution seemed to be for farmers to take turns sleeping at the west end of the tunnel on the ditch bank. When the water would stop running down the ditch, the sentry would follow the ditch until he found the leak and fix it. In 1910, with the introduction of cement, a more permanent solution to the leakage problem was realized.

In 1895 the La Verkin Fruit and Nursery Company decided to survey the land for the building of a community. Property was divided among the owners, according to the amount of stock they owned. They then sold the land to new settlers moving into La Verkin.

In 1929 the owners of the canal signed an agreement with Southern Utah Power Company to enlarge and cement the ditch and to build a hydroelectric generator south of town.

It is thought that La Verkin got its name as a result of the Paiute's inability to pronounce "La Virgin," the name given the creek in the early 1800s by Spaniards who traded with the Toquerville Paiutes.

Today, from the standpoint of agriculture, La Verkin is famous for its molasses (Dixie Sorghum), nuts, and fruits. La Verkin is also well known for its Pah Tempe Hot Springs in the Timpoweap Canyon southeast of town. The springs have been used by generations of area residents dating as far back as the Paiutes.

HURRICANE

At the same time that Southern Utah Mission President Erastus Snow was investigating the possibilities of a ditch for La Verkin, he was also contemplating a canal that would bring water from the Virgin River to the lava bench of Hurricane.

It was Snow who gave Hurricane its name. While descending a steep hill above the present town of Hurricane, a sudden gust of wind was sufficient to remove the top of his buggy. Snow remarked to his companions: "Well! Now that was a hurricane! We'll call this Hurricane Hill."

Private enterprise, organized in 1888, and three years of dedicated labor brought the La Verkin Fruit and Nursery Company and eventually the town of La Verkin its ditch. But it was not until 1893 that a committee was organized to re-investigate the possibility of a seven-mile canal for Hurricane. When the report proved satisfactory, a stock company was established. It was ruled that land stock would be issued with no man's share to exceed 20 acres.

Unlike the La Verkin ditch, where work proceeded year-round, the digging of the Hurricane Canal mostly took place during the winter so the men building the ditch could continue farming. While working on the canal, the men would live in camps.

Until a wagon trail could be constructed from the dam to the canyon floor, they also had to carry in their own supplies of picks, shovels, wheelbarrows, crowbars and handmade drills. A bellows and forge were set up at each campsite to help keep the primitive tools sharp and in good repair. Although some dynamite was used, few of the men were skilled with explosives and several men were accidentally killed during the 11 years of construction. The canal required miles of digging and the building of tunnels and wooden flumes across canyons. In 1896 the town of Hurricane was surveyed and, to ensure that there would be no charges of partiality, lots for homesites were drawn.

In 1902 the canal project looked bleak. With monetary resources completely depleted, one of the original members of the building committee, James Jepson, was sent to Salt Lake City. The Church, recognizing the dilemma, purchased $5,000 worth of stock, a move that provided both financial and psychological benefits. The canal was completed in 1904. In 1906, eleven families moved onto their lands. It was not all smooth sailing, there were many landslides both above and below the ditch, but by 1917 there were over 100 families that called Hurricane home.

From dark lava cliffs and arid desolate land, Hurricane became the Fruit Basket of Southern Utah, growing not only fruits, but vegetables, grains, and alfalfa. An annual Peach Days celebration, begun in 1914, is now combined with the Washington County Fair held in August.

Hurricane is a man-made oasis that is ideally located 18 miles from St. George and 25 miles from Zion National Park on Highway 9. It is a town that is proud of its heritage and has built, through the Sons of the Utah Pioneers, the Hurricane Pioneer Heritage Park and Museum.

With an eye to the future as one of the state's most desirable tourist and retiree towns, Hurricane has also built one of the area's finest and most scenic golf courses, Sky Mountain.

HURRICANE ATTRACTIONS

QUAIL CREEK STATE PARK

Quail Creek Reservoir, just west of Hurricane on Highway 9, boasts the warmest water in the state during the summer and therefore is one of the state's most popular sites for boating, waterskiing, sailing, wind surfing, scuba diving, and swimming. The reservoir was completed in 1985 to provide irrigation and culinary water to the St. George area. Most of the water comes from the Virgin River and is transported through a buried pipeline. The reservoir is formed by two dams, an earthfill embankment dam and a roller compacted concrete dam, recently constructed to replace the original earthfill dam that failed in the early hours of New Year's Day, 1989.

Facilities at Quail Creek State Park include 23 developed campsites. Each site has a paved parking pad, fire pit, grill, and covered picnic table. Two large pavilions with picnic tables and grills are available to groups on a first-come, first-served basis. Three of the Campsites are accessible to the physically impaired.

Other camp amenities include modern rest rooms, developed beaches, two concrete boat-launching ramps, loading docks, and a fish cleaning station. An additional launching ramp for personal watercraft and small boats is adjacent to the campground. Camping is allowed only in designated campsites. Up to eight people are allowed in a campsite. Day-use and camping fees are charged, and there is an additional fee for reservations. The permit covers one vehicle and any attached recreational equipment. Off-highway vehicle riding is not permitted in the park.

Reservations are accepted from four months to three days in advance (800-322-3770).

ST. GEORGE

St. George, the seat of Washington County, is also the commercial and cultural hub of southwestern Utah, northwestern Arizona, and southeastern Nevada. The largest city between Las Vegas and Salt Lake City, St. George, which has nearly quadrupled in size the last two decades, is the heart of Utah's famous "Dixie" region.

St. George was settled in 1861 when Brigham Young called 309 families to the area as part of the "cotton mission." Arriving at the proposed site of the town, the pioneers set their 200 wagons in two long rows facing each other as a temporary camp. Here they stayed while they surveyed the town, drew lots for land, and named the town St. George after Mormon apostle, George A. Smith. Although Smith did not accompany the settlers to Dixie, he had personally selected the families who settled here, and was known within the church as the "father of the Southern Utah Mission." St. George was incorporated as a city before a single house was built.

First years in St. George were extremely difficult. The Great Rain that winter caused much discomfort, the soil and water for culinary purposes were alkaline, and scorching heat, constant winds, and lack of water led to multiple crop failures. Pioneer poet, Charles Walker, described agriculture in St. George with these words: "*The wind like fury does blow that when we plant or sow, sir, We place one foot upon the seed and hold it til it grows, sir.*"

The settlers persevered, living on crops they "cheated" from the desert and continuing to experiment with cotton, fruit, and even silk production. Hardy as the Southern Utah colonists were, Brigham Young could see that they needed assistance. In October 1862 Young sent a letter to mission president, Erastus Snow, requesting that, using the tithes of Southern Utah Mormons, a meeting house be built that would facilitate the gathering of at least a thousand persons. On June 1, 1863, St. George pioneers began construction of their New England-style tabernacle. That same year St. George became the Washington County seat. In 1866 money was appropriated for a courthouse, the basement of which included a three-cell jail. With the courthouse completed in 1870, Brigham Young called upon the settlers in 1871 to build a temple to serve Southern Utah. In 1876, the St. George pioneers completed the tabernacle and in 1877 the temple was completed and dedicated. It was the first temple completed west of the Mississippi and is today the oldest Mormon temple that is still in use.

By the 1890s the pioneers had gained a foothold in the desert by building ditches, canals, dikes and reservoirs to harness the area's mighty rivers for irrigation.

The improvement of U.S. Highway 91 and eventually I-15 as an arterial route between Salt Lake City, Las Vegas, and the Pacific Coast helped open the region's access to the outside world. But it was the increase in tourism at the end of World War II that brought about the greatest change in St. George. Positioned halfway between Salt Lake City and Los Angeles and located near Utah's many scenic wonders, St. George's tourist industry began to overshadow its traditional agricultural economy. Today tourism is the city's largest source of income.

Known for its long hot summers and mild winters, St. George has been called the city "where the summer sun spends the winter" and "the other Palm Springs." The area's unusually mild winters in combination with the magnificent scenic setting of the region, ease of transportation, and the easy-going rural environment have made St. George one of the most popular recreational and retirement communities in the West. In fact, St. George is consistently listed among the top ten retirement communities in the nation.

Though rural in nature, St. George offers urban amenities that include Dixie College, Dixie Center for the arts, a symphony orchestra, commuter airline, nine golf courses, numerous shopping centers and, most important for travelers, over 2,300 sleeping rooms and 50-plus quality restaurants.

ST. GEORGE AREA ATTRACTIONS

BLM SITES

A vast majority of land in Washington County is public land—managed by the Bureau of Land Management, the U.S. Forest Service, or the State of Utah. To the visitor this means that most of Utah's Dixie is natural, picturesque, and open to the public for a variety of uses. Much of this land is managed by the BLM.

The BLM maintains a campground and picnic area at **Red Cliffs**, a red rock haven at the southern foot of **Pine Valley Mountain**. Red Cliffs is located 4.5 miles south of Leeds and near the historic pioneer site of Harrisburg. It is a wonderful spot to stop for a picnic and hike.

Other BLM sites include **Hurricane Sand Dunes** to the East of St. George, the **Arizona Strip** to the South, **Beaver Dam Wash** to the West, and the **Mountain Meadows** area to the North.

Warner Valley, southeast of St. George, was the shooting location for several western movies. It is also the site of **Historic Fort Pearce**. A high clearance vehicle is recommended. A few miles east of Fort Pearce, the BLM has marked and interpreted tracks of a three-toed dinosaur left in the mud millions of years ago.

The **Little Black Mountain Petroglyph Site** is another BLM attraction. The Virgin River Anasazi pecked these messages into the rock more than a thousand years ago (435-628-4491).

DIXIE NATIONAL FOREST

The heart of Dixie National Forest, Utah's largest, is located in Washington County within the Pine Valley Ranger District. Pine Valley Mountain, just a few miles north of St. George, peaks at 10,300 feet. The Pine Valley Wilderness Area offers a network of hiking and horseback trails. The forest is also ideal for mountain biking, cross country skiing, hunting and fishing. A reservoir and several campgrounds are near the historic and picturesque town of Pine Valley, known for its beautiful, century-old white chapel (435-628-4491).

GUNLOCK STATE PARK

Fifteen miles northwest of St. George is the 240-acre Gunlock Reservoir and State Park. Located along the Old Spanish Trail, Gunlock Reservoir is ensconced against a backdrop of red and gray hills. Part of the reservoir's appeal stems from the ability to camp freely in undeveloped areas. Gunlock offers a boat launching ramp and pit privies. The reservoir offers boating, water sports, and quality fishing for bass and catfish. The area is also great for bird watching, hiking, and picnicking. The Santa Clara River empties into Gunlock Reservoir where its waters are trapped by a 117-foot dam.

SNOW CANYON STATE PARK

One does not have to venture to the Big Island of Hawaii to explore lava tubes. Snow Canyon State Park is a 24-mile loop that can be entered from the north entrance, 11 miles northwest of St. George on U-18, or from the south entrance by way of the small town of Ivins. An ancestral Snow Canyon was carved by crustal forces, wind, and water erosion from Rock Hollow Wash, a stream that ran southwest through what is now Dammeron Canyon. Additional volcanic activity from at least two lava flows completely filled the ancestral canyon floor from the park's present northern entrance to the Virgin River. With its channel blocked, the waters of Rock Hollow Wash followed a course of least resistance, running first westward and then southward, carving the present Snow Canyon. At about the same time a second lava flow, running down what is now Wide Canyon, also directed its waters into Dammeron Valley and supplemented the waters of Rock Hollow Wash. The most recent volcanic action took place approximately 1,000 to 2,000 years ago in Dammeron Valley. The lava flow filled part of the valley, creating a barrier at Dammeron's southern end, and also flowed through Snow Canyon to Santa Clara Creek. These two lava flows left lava tubes in Dammeron Valley and Snow Canyon, several of which may be entered and explored. Lava tubes are subterranean channels caused by hot molten lava flowing underground through surface lava that cooled more rapidly. The Anasazi anciently used the lava tubes for shelter.

Snow Canyon, in addition to its black lava beds, is characterized by magnificent red and white Navajo sandstone monoliths, sand dunes, caves, creek bottoms, cacti, and spectacular wildflowers. At the park's northeast entrance is a 36-unit campground with modern restrooms, hot showers, electric hook-ups, sewage disposal station, and a covered group-use pavilion, available on a first-come, first-served basis. A four-dollar per car entrance fee is charged (435-628-2255).

UTAH! THE PEACEMAKER SAGA

Although there are many outdoor theatrical presentations across the country, none can boast the magnificence of Utah's Tuacahn Amphitheater. Set deep in an arroyo near Snow Canyon State Park against the majesty of red sandstone cliffs, *UTAH! The Peacemaker Saga* tells the unique and fascinating history of Utah's Dixie. From Utah's earliest explorers to its successful statehood in January of 1886, UTAH! celebrates the struggles and victories of those who created Utah's history, and of the trials and triumphs of Dixie. Tuacahn is a Paiute word meaning Canyon of the Gods.

Open since the summer season of 1995, *UTAH!* has played to sell-out crowds from around the world and to rave reviews from its critics. The Tuacahn Amphitheater, an open-air stage, makes history come alive as Indians appear on the cliffs high above, pioneers forage new settlements, Indians raid and burn forts and covered wagons, and finally, through the efforts of Jacob Hamblin and Paiute chief Tutsegavits, the Indians befriend the settlers. The audience is transfixed as lightening bolts flash, floods rage, coyotes howl, and waterfalls cascade on cue.

The production, which begins at dusk June through September, features an elaborately costumed cast of 80 as well as a number of well-trained horses.

Tuacahn is also home to a complete center for the arts developed by the Utah Heritage Arts Foundation. A school for the performing arts is housed here and numerous other arts and entertainment events occur year-round.

ST. GEORGE HISTORIC WALKING TOUR

It would be easy to spend a day strolling through history in *Historic Old St. George Village* but, whatever time one has, the stroll is worth the time and the effort. Begin the tour at the old Washington County Courthouse on the corner of St. George Boulevard and 100 East.

Built between 1866 and 1876, the *Washington County Courthouse* originally served as a courtroom, jail, school, and as offices for county government. Interesting features of the building are its 18-inch thick interior doorways, its old chandeliers, security vault, original paintings of Zion and Grand Canyon national parks, and its exterior cornice work and cupola.

In 1938 Hortense McQuarrie built *McQuarrie Memorial Hall*, also known as *Pioneer Museum,* for the express purpose of housing pioneer relics. Included in the museum's collection of pioneer artifacts is a dress made of locally produced silk. The museum, at 200 North and 100 West, is currently maintained and operated by the local chapter of Daughters of Utah Pioneers.

Recently restored, the *St. George Social Hall Opera House,* at 200 North and Main Street, was the community cultural center from 1875 until the 1930s. A unique feature was the slope of the floor, which could be mechanically adjusted to afford an excellent view of the stage and its performers from every seat in the house.

Now the *Quicksand and Cactus Bed & Breakfast,* the *Will and Juanita Brooks Home* was built of stone chips and irregular rocks discarded during the building of the tabernacle and temple. Brooks, a stone mason, salvaged the rocks and chips during clean-up of the yards. The home, located on Main Street and 350 North, was built in 1877 - 1878.

Brigham Young was Dixie's first "snowbird," and his winter home, at the corners of 200 North and 100 West, is open for tours. *Brigham Young's Winter Home* was begun in 1869, completed in 1871, and remodeled with a front addition in 1873. Brigham left his Salt Lake home and came to St. George during the winter months to supervise the building of the St. George Temple.

Built in the early 1880s, the *Erastus Whitehead Home,* now *An Olde Penny Farthing Inn* (see related story), was built by George Whitehead of handmade adobe blocks on a lava rock foundation. It sits at 278 North 100 West along Diagonal Street.

The *Gates-McQuarrie Home* was originally owned by Jacob Gates, the second mayor of St. George. Hector and Ella McQuarrie, the home's second owners, rented rooms to "drummers," salesmen traveling to the area on business. The home is on the corner of 300 North and 100 West.

Possibly the first home in St. George to have water in the bathroom, George Whitehead, who built this home in 1883, ingeniously ran a pipe from an irrigation ditch to an upstairs bathroom so his family could have *cold* baths. As the family expanded, so did the house. It has two staircases, one running east to west and the other west to east with a common landing. The *George Whitehead Home's* approximate address is 250 North and 100 West.

The *Woolley Foster Home,* 217 North, 100 West, was built during the 1870s by Edwin G. Woolley and was one of St. George's finest homes. During the early history of the Mormon Church, when polygamists were being sought for imprisonment,

Woolley is believed to have hidden many polygamists in his attic. The home has been used as a college dormitory, rest home, and is now **Seven Wives Inn** (see related story), a bed & breakfast.

The **Dr. Israel Ivins Home** was owned by St. George's first practicing physician. A little shop at the rear of the building served as his drugstore. The home's approximate address is 175 North and 100 West.

The **Anthony W. Ivins Home** is located at approximately 150 North and 100 West. Ivins was mayor of St. George from 1890 - 1894. In 1895 he was elected as Washington County representative to the Utah Territorial Constitutional Convention. He later left St. George on a church calling to help colonize Colonia Dublan, Mexico.

The **Moses Andrus Home** may be one of few homes in history to have never had cracks in its foundation. Once the rock foundation was laid, it was left for a full year to cure before the rest of the home was added. The home is on the corner of St. George Boulevard and 100 West.

Adobe bricks for the **Benjamin F. Pendleton Home** were hand made by Pendleton, the village blacksmith, who only had three brick molds. The bricks were made three at a time, dried, stacked, and the process repeated. The home is between Tabernacle and St. George Boulevards on 100 West.

A wagon box beneath the Cottonwoods was the first school in St. George for Mormon settlers, who placed a high value on schooling. The **Woodward School**, built in 1898 was named after one of its major benefactors, George Woodward, a childless resident who donated a substantial sum of money to aid in the school's construction. A unique feature is the pattern of large and small stone blocks used in the building. The school is at the corner of Tabernacle and 100 West.

The **Orson Pratt/Richard Bentley Home**, now a part of **Green Gate Village** (see related story), was built by Mormon apostle, Orson Pratt, one of the leaders called to help colonize St. George. When he was later called on a mission to Europe the home was sold to Richard Bentley and his wife, Elizabeth, who hatched and fed silk worms in an upper room. The Green Gate Village complex is at 76 West Tabernacle.

Also a part of Green Gate Village are the Judd Store and the home behind the store. The home was built in 1879 by William Oscar Bentley. Richard Bentley built the store in front of the home some time later. Because the store was purchased in 1911 by the Judd family and remained in their possession until 1985, it became and stayed **Judd's Store**.

The *George W. Worthen Home*, corner of Main and Tabernacle, is admired for its simplicity of design and craftsmanship.

Although the **Mormon Tabernacle**, corner of Main and Tabernacle, took 13 years to complete, the edifice is a magnificent tribute to the industry and perseverance of St. George's early settlers. If 13 years seems a long time for constructing a building, the following data should be considered. At the same time that the tabernacle was under construction, residents were also building their own homes, the St. George Temple, and the County Courthouse. Stone for the three-foot thick basement walls was laboriously quarried by hand from the city's foothills and hauled in wagons to the site. Red sandstone boulders for the two and one-half-foot thick walls were also hand-quarried from a site near what is now the Red Hills Golf Course. The boulders were then hand cut into serviceable stones. The 56-foot trusses were cut 32 miles away and hand-hewn with a broad ax. The exquisite twin spiral staircases, including the railing and balustrades, were hand carved. The interior cornice work and plaster of Paris ceiling were prepared and cast by local artisans. The clock, it seems, was the only imported item. It was made in London and shipped to New York before being transported to St. George.

Construction on ***Dixie Academy***, now the ***St. George Arts Center***, was begun in 1888. The St. George Stake Academy moved into the building in 1911. Both Dixie High School and Dixie College were housed here until as recently as the early 1960s, when both schools were relocated to new campuses in different parts of the city. Stonework for the Academy was quarried from a site near the town of Washington, and account for its much lighter shade of red than that of the tabernacle. The academy is at Main Street and 100 South.

Most of the ***Tabernacle Street*** buildings on the South side between Main and First East are historically significant. Pieceful Treasures at 28 East was built in 1895 as ***A.R. Whitehead & Sons Mercantile***. The *Dixie Studio* building at 32 East dates back to the late 1800's. The site at 50 East was a post office, general store, and a residence, and the ***Electric Theatre***, built in 1911 for live theatre, has been restored and is in use today as a cinema.

Also historically significant are the buildings on ***Main Street*** between Tabernacle and St. George Boulevard. The ***Bishop's Storehouse*** at 21 North Main was built in 1887. Early Mormon pioneers paid "tithes and offerings" in the form of goods from their businesses. These were collected at the storehouse and then distributed to widows, the sick, and the needy in town. The ***Wadsworth Theatre***, built in 1927, is still in use today. Zion's National Bank stands at the corner of Main and St. George Boulevard. Adjacent to the bank, where the "Big House" of Erastus Snow once stood, is a ***Memorial Plaza***. By walking through the plaza one can read many plaques mounted on sandstone with historical information on the big house and other buildings in the ***Historic District***.

Located in ***Historic Ancestor Square***, which incorporates the block on St. George Boulevard between Main Street and 100 West, is the ***Hardy House***, now occupied by Tenney-Clemons Advertising. Augustus Hardy was the sheriff in St. George and built this house in 1871. During one incident of the wild west, a bullet, still seen in one of the doors, slightly remodeled Hardy's home. The bullet was from a vigilante group who broke into Hardy's house, stole his keys, unlocked the cell door of an extremely unpopular prisoner, and hanged him.

The ***Gardeners' Club Hall***, also at Ancestor Square, is one of the oldest public buildings still in use in St. George today. It was built by members of the Gardeners' Club to serve as a meeting place for horticulturists.

Behind the Gardeners' Club is ***St. George's First Jail***, believed to have been built by Augustus Hardy around 1880, perhaps after the shooting incident that took place in his own home. The one-room jail is built of thick lava rock hauled from nearby foothills. Bars on the windows are original.

The ***Grundy House***, at approximately 175 North Main, was built in 1901 by Emma Packer Morris, who passed the home on to her daughter, Isadore Grundy. This large Victorian home, built of hand-made adobe and faced with red fired brick, features large panel windows and expensive wood trim. Apparently no expense was too great in building this home.

The ***Gardner House***, across the street from the Grundy House, was the first ladies' co-op, founded by Mary Ann Gardner, third wife of the fourth mayor of St. George, Robert Gardner. Built in 1896, Mary Ann established the building as a millinery shop when the co-op was disbanded.

Half-way between Main Street and 100 East on St. George Boulevard is the ***Old County News Building***. The building, still in use for newspaper publishing, was originally built in the 1880s as a saloon in **Silver Reef**. Silver Reef, now a ghost town, was a silver mining boom town near Leeds. It was moved to its present location after the mining town's demise.

From April through Labor Day, St. George offers its visitors a *"Living History" Tour* of historic St. George. A two-hour walking and riding tour that begins at the City Plaza next to Zion Bank, the tour allows guests to meet legendary characters such as Brigham Young, Erastus Snow, Orson Pratt, and Jacob Hamblin, all dressed in period costumes and at their original homes. A tour guide accompanies guests. There is a minimal $1 charge per person. The tour runs daily, 9:00 a.m. - 1:00 p.m.

GOLF IN ST. GEORGE

Ever since its accelerated population growth three decades ago, St. George has been perceived as the golfing mecca of the state. Within a 15-minute drive of each other are nine great courses, seven of which are 18-holes and open to the public.

St. George Golf Club, par 72, is said to be the most improved course in the state, has long, beautiful freeways, a pro shop and snack bar. Its location is 2190 South 1400 East (435-634-5854).

Sunbrook, par 72, was rated in 1995-96 by *Golf Digest* as the number one golf course in Utah. Located above the Santa Clara River, its fairways are dotted with lakes, waterfalls, and rock walls. Course architect, Ted Robinson, says three of the course's holes are among the best he has ever designed. Robinson has created more than 1,800 holes. The course has a clubhouse, snack bar and driving range and is located at 660 North Twin Lakes Drive (435-673-4441).

Southgate Golf Club, par 70, has water that comes into play on several holes that border ponds and cross the Santa Clara River. The course has a driving range, restaurant, pro shop, and Family Golf Center--an 1,800 square foot indoor educational golf facility. The Center includes computerized golf swing analysis, photo and computer graphic displays and video analysis systems. The facility also includes open and covered tees on the driving range for all-season practice opportunities. Southgate is located at 1975 South Tonaquint Drive (435-628-0000 or 674-7728).

Entrada, par 72, is St. George's newest and is a Johnny Miller-designed golf course. The course is already well known for its rolling dunes, ancient black lava beds and winding arroyos, all of which present the best in natural obstacles. A privately owned course that is open to the public, Entrada is at 2511 West Entrada (435-674-7500).

Green Spring, par 71, just off the I-15 in neighboring Washington, is set among the natural obstacles of hills, ravines and gorges with the red cliffs of Pine Valley Mountain as a backdrop. The course has a large clubhouse, snack bar, pro shop and driving range. Location in Washington is 588 North Green Spring Drive (435-673-7888).

Sky Mountain Golf Course, par 72, is at 1030 North 2600 West in neighboring Hurricane. Water comes into play on several holes and natural black lava outcroppings have been left to create an interesting contrast throughout the course. (435-635-7888).

Bloomington, par 72, is a private country club open only to members and their guests, but it offers a reciprocal agreement with other country clubs. The club has an elegant restaurant and club house. The club's location is 3174 Bloomington Drive East in St. George (435-673-2029).

Twin Lakes, par 27, has been called "The Most Picturesque" by Utah Holiday Magazine. Though small and only nine holes, the course, located at 660 North Twin Lakes Drive, is exacting (435-673-4441).

Dixie Red Hills, par 34, is ensconced amidst pockets of red sandstone cliffs and offers not only beautiful scenery but challenging play. Groves of mature trees accent the landscape. The nine-hole course has a pro shop, snack bar, and driving range and is located at 1000 North 700 West (435-634-5852).

ACCOMMODATIONS

RAMADA INN
1440 East St George Boulevard
St. George, Utah 84770
Tel: (801) 628-2828
            (800) 228-2828
FAX: (801) 628-0505

Visa, MasterCard, American Express, Diners Club, Carte Blanche, and Discover are accepted.
Reservations are recommended.

Conveniently located just off I-15, Exit #8 in St. George, Utah's Dixie, Ramada Inn offers ideal accommodations to those who seek proximity to one of the city's favorite shopping centers, Zion Factory Outlet Mall. Within walking distance are numerous discount stores as well as an abundance of restaurants.

Ramada Inn's 136 luxurious rooms offer guests a choice of smoking and non-smoking facilities, double queen or king beds, business and executive suites as well as an opulent honeymoon suite with jetted tub. Room amenities include Cable TV with HBO, Disney Channel, and ESPN, and telephone with free local calls. Room decor is in sandstone colors of beige, light peach and gray with photographs and water color prints of area scenes.

Whether in town for business or pleasure, the Ramada Inn offers a lavish heated outdoor swimming pool with hot tub and spacious decking surrounded by lawn, gardens, and a black lava bluff. The Inn also offers a convention and conference center that will accommodate 200 people theater style. It is perfect for private meeting rooms as well as an ideal location for weddings and receptions.

Bed & Breakfasts across the country have become well known for their "great room," a common area where guests gather to become acquainted with other guests or to enjoy seclusion. Adjacent to the Ramada Inn's foyer and overlooking the pool is an incomparable great room. The Ramada Inn's great room offers a massive sandstone fire place, large color Cable TV, arm chairs, love seats and sofas placed throughout. It is ideal for casual conversation, solitude, and enjoying the warmth of the fireplace during winter months. The room is Southwestern in decor offering a quarter wall with rock garden of cactus plants and flowers as well as barren cacti. Glass counters and recessed walls offer a selection of marvelous Southwestern artifacts. The great room, which originally served as facilities for a continental breakfast, also offers tables and chairs and a wet bar overlooking the pool.

Adjacent to the Ramada Inn is Shoney's Restaurant where hotel guests are invited to enjoy a full breakfast or, for those forgoing breakfast, a discount on any menu item.

The Ramada Inn, located in southern Utah's Color Country, offers ideal accommodations for those visiting any of the area's National Parks, Monuments, and Recreation Areas. Also abundant in St. George and close to the Ramada Inn, are state parks, year-round golf courses, and numerous historical buildings and monuments.

ROCOCO INN

511 South Airport Road
St. George, Utah 84532
Tel: (435) 628-3671
        (888) 628-3671
FAX: (435) 673-6370
Visa, MasterCard, American Express,
 Diners Club, and Discover
are accepted.
Reservations are preferred.

Ensconced on top of a 300-foot cliff that was created from an ancient lava flow, Rococo Inn offers visitors to the city a bird's eye view of St. George and its surrounding area.

For those who enjoy spectacular daytime views of a tree enshrouded city with backdrop of red rock cliffs, and night time views of city lights twinkling in the distance, Rococo Inn is the accommodation of choice. Sliding glass doors open to private patios, making the view accessible from both the room and veranda.

Rococo Inn satisfies the needs of those who have a penchant for immaculately clean, spacious rooms with live-in creature comforts. Guests are offered large rooms with a choice of double queen or single king beds, table, upholstered chairs, cable TV with HBO, telephones with credit card and local calls free, and wet bar with mini refrigerator. The large bathroom offers tub/shower combination, pulsating shower heads, and vanity basin. Smoking and non-smoking rooms are available. In addition to their more than standard regular rooms, Rococo offers three suites with seating area and queen-size hide-a-bed. The Inn also offers one room that connects to the indoor Jacuzzi and offers its guests private use of the Jacuzzi after 10:00 p.m.

Rococo Inn was built for total privacy. Guests neither hear nor see passers-by because there are no windows on the side of the room with the door. The sliding glass doors on the other side of the room are at the edge of a cliff, 300 feet above the city's noise.

Inn amenities include indoor Jacuzzi, outdoor swimming pool that overlooks the city, and Sullivan's Rococo Steak house, one of the most touted restaurants in the city. (See related story.) During summer months Rococo Inn offers a very special summer package. Call for updated details.

The Inn's location, right across the parking lot from the airport, offers airplane buffs the chance to see the comings and goings of modern day planes, as well as relics of the past.

In view of Rococo Inn's extraordinary amenities, one might wonder, given a choice, why anyone would choose to stay anywhere else.

BED & BREAKFASTS

AN OLDE PENNY FARTHING INN
278 North 100 West
St. George, Utah 84770
Tel: (801) 673-7755
FAX: (801) 673-7755
Web Site:
WWW.uvol.com/penny
Visa, MasterCard, American Express, and Discover are accepted.
Reservations are requested.

As one enters St. George, Utah on the I-15, from either direction, a full-size picture of Alan and Jacquie Capon in pioneer dress and living color graces a billboard welcoming visitors to their fair city. When watching Utah's *Days of '47 Parade*, third largest parade celebration in the United States, Alan and Jacquie, as Brigham Young and Brigham's wife Amelia, have waved to parade goers and been viewed by millions on their TV screens.

When Alan and Jacquie are not doing volunteer work (that includes enhancing billboards, riding in Utah parades, doing live presentations at the Brigham Young House, working with productions such as *Brigadoon, Fiddler on the Roof,* and other musicals, or being the city's "Mr. and Mrs. Santa Claus,") they are hosts to the St. George bed and breakfast, An Olde Penny Farthing Inn.

In 1866, pioneers, who had already left behind their cherished possessions to be a part of the 1847 journey to Utah, were once again being asked to migrate to the South, an area that would become Utah's Dixie, to plant cotton. An Olde Penny Farthing Inn was built in the 1870's by one of Dixie's most prominent new citizens, Erastus Whitehead, whose family was called by Brigham to build the first cotton gin. The Inn, now a registered landmark, was named by Alan after the two old English coins and the unique two-wheel English bicycle. Alan and Jacquie are the only Utah members of the National Wheelman's Association.

An Olde Penny Farthing Inn Bed and Breakfast is almost as colorful as the proprietor, his not-so-silent-partner, and the "madam" of the house, Alan's and Jacquie's beloved "Ginger Rose," a beautiful penny-colored canine. Newest addition to the Inn is Felicity, a silver and white domestic cat.

An Olde Penny Farthing Inn, located in the heart of St. George Historical District, has the distinction of being the first "Painted Lady" of Washington County and St. George. The home was built with 18-inch adobe walls and lava rock foundation, but was later stuccoed in warm colors of Victorian rose, creme, teal, burgundy cherry, and Norman Rose to give the Inn a welcoming appeal. Adding to the charm of the Inn is a front porch and exquisite cut glass door.

The approach to An Olde Penny Farthing Inn is entered through a white picket fence with large green columns. Two magnificent and commanding shade trees grace the yard. One can easily visualize children at all stages of a tree climb, picture rope swings in motion, and fathom the voices of children at play. Under the shade trees are wicker and wrought iron chairs, wind chimes, a wagon wheel leaning against the tree, and a sandstone fountain with water flowing from an old watering can. The circular driveway is fronted by a well-lit rock garden with lamp post and an aggregation of flags that includes our "red, white and blue," and the British, Canadian, and Confederate ensigns.

The interior of the building portrays a less garish Victorian era with furnishings and decor that Jacquie calls "antiques, lovables, huggables, collectibles—and totally eclectic!" From the foyer to the parlor and the vintage bathrooms and bedrooms, the Inn is embellished with pine floors and country-pioneer antiques, collectibles, and hand-crafted quilts.

The bed and breakfast Great Room Parlor, enhanced with a forest green and burgundy color scheme with white wainscoating, features white lace bay windows, a penny farthing replica bicycle, an elegant old fireplace, heirloom organ, and a picture of the original owners of the home, the Whitehead family. The room also offers the beginnings of a collection that guests will see throughout the home—a diversity of teddy bears. Borrow a "teddy" from anywhere in the Inn that the bears are found as a special night-time companion.

The dining room, when not being used, is formal and auspicious. The table is set with teal green plates and glasses with mauve linen napkins elegantly tucked inside. It is here that guests are treated to breakfasts that always include a fresh, in-season plate of fruit, a selection of juices, tea, and coffee. Specialty dishes comprise the English Breakfast that offers Bangers, not as spicy as American sausage, with fried tomatoes, mushrooms, potatoes, and thick bacon and eggs, any style. Guests also relish the Eggs Benedict, Piggies in a Blanket, variety of berry crepes, and the carrot banana muffins and English Scones. All plates are served with a sprig of fresh mint or rosemary from the garden.

On the Inn's main level, down an original adobe wall, are two cozy guest rooms, Sego Lily and Morning Dove. Sego Lily offers an iron and brass bed, the frame of which came across the plains in a pioneer wagon and is 160 years old. The room boasts a transom door and window and exposed brick from the original adobe. The large bathroom has a flagstone floor, claw-footed tub with shower, a pedestal sink, and an old-fashioned mirror in the middle of an aging harness. The only modern accessory is a puff-quilt of blue and white on the antique bed.

Morning Dove exhibits a Southwestern theme. It's decor includes a rough-hewn pine log bed, red sandstone Mexican tile, and an Indian cradle board on the wall with exquisite Indian baby doll. The room is completely wheelchair accessible with the shower easily large enough for two. Morning Dove guests usually comment on the intricately unusual cedar plank ceiling.

Ascending the "hand-painted carpet" stairs is an experience in history and collectibles. Original windows, which were eliminated by the addition of Morning Dove, have become a shelf for "Christmas Around the World." Another collectible to be spotted while climbing the stairs is an accumulation of bedpans of all sorts, shapes, and sizes. Jacquie, a nurse, challenges guests to spot the bed pan in each of the guest rooms. It may be a child's potty chair or a regular hospital bed pan, but each room will host one, and most will be discretely embellished with flowers.

Scattered throughout the Inn are dried flowers—all of which hold a special place in the hearts of Alan and Jacquie. Jacquie quite frequently is the recipient of flowers from Alan. She enjoys them while they are fresh, and then proficiently turns them into dried floral arrangements for her guests' enjoyment.

On the second floor are the Bridal Suite, the Sir Winston Churchill, and Betsy Ross Rooms. The Bridal Suite offers a step-back in time with its elegant white bed spread, lace throw pillows, and swan—all adorning an exquisite brass bed. The room is tucked away in the attic and offers shuttered windows, white rattan make-up vanity, and an adjoining sitting room with hip roof and trundle bed. Together the rooms afford guests an extra large bathroom with a two-person mauve and white jetted tub, separate shower, pedestal sink, old-fashioned pull-chain water closet, and thick terry robes. The Bridal Suite is ideal, not just for the honeymooning couple, but for the young-at-heart as well.

As Jacquie tells her very English husband, "There cannot be a Sir Winston Churchill Room without a Betsy Ross Room." And that's the way it is. The Sir Winston Churchill is posh and masculine, recalling memories of an old English Pub. Decorated in green and burgundy, the room offers a grand king bed and a Charles Dickens single (cabin bed in the wall). Closet doors have a rough-hewn barn door effect. The private bathroom offers claw-footed tub and shower, a pull-chain water closet, and other English subtleties that includes twining ivy and hand painted pine floors.

While the Sir Winston Room could not be more English, the Betsy Ross Room is the epitome of 18th-Century America. A keepsake four-poster bed with red and white bedspread immediately captures one's attention, as does the American flag memorabilia. Above the bed, kneeling in prayer by his horse on the banks of the Potomac, is the famous Arnold Frieberg painting of George Washington. Adding additional charm to the room are a wooden settee, armoire, antique rocker, vintage tub, and a relic wash stand converted into a modern wash basin. The settee was made by Alan after hours of studying a piece of furniture the pioneers called a "Mormon bed." A bench chair by day, at night the wooden base is pulled out to make a fairly comfortable twin. It could possibly be the predecessor of the trundle bed. A small adjoining room, often called Grandpa's Attic, has additional space for two more people.

An Olde Penny Farthing Inn is much more than just a house. Alan and Jacquie invite guests to return with them to an era of Pioneers, adventurers, and Native Americans. History lives at An Olde Penny Farthing Inn.

ORSON PRATT HOME at GREENE GATE VILLAGE, PENCIL, DEAN FIFE

**GREENE GATE VILLAGE
HISTORIC
BED & BREAKFAST INN**
76 West Tabernacle
St. George, Utah 84770
Tel: (801) 628-6999
         (800) 350-6999
FAX   (801) 628-6989
Visa, MasterCard, American Express,
 and Discover are accepted.
Reservations are requested.

Greene Gate Village Historic Bed & Breakfast is a labor of love. The Village has been an ongoing effort on the part of Dr. Mark and Barbara Greene and their son, John. The Greenes have taken it upon themselves to care when others did not, and to preserve history through restoration of historic edifices that might otherwise meet the demolition squad.

Whether it is coincidence or a fortuitous chain of events, Greene Gate Village received its name from its owners, the Greenes, and as a result of an 1877 historic event. Upon completion of the St. George Temple, Brigham Young ordered green paint for the gates and fence that surrounded it. There was an inordinate amount of paint left over and, not wishing to waste it, Brigham offered the paint to St. George "Saints" on condition that they would paint their own gates and fences. Only one green gate remains from more than a century ago, and it is displayed in the Village garden. The gates surrounding Greene Gate Village are patterned after the original.

First home to be lovingly restored by the Greenes was the Greenehouse, located at 162 South 300 West. Initially the home, built in 1872 by Heinrich Gubler, one of the first settlers to St. George, was used as a reception home. Today the house, which offers a complete home and carriage house with sleeping quarters for 22 guests, is rented out for family reunions or other large groups. Amenities include a private swimming pool, tennis court, whirlpool tub, play house, balcony, full kitchen, family room with fireplace, and Cable TV with VCR. Reservations for the home require a minimum of six people. Breakfast is not included.

The Greene's own personal home, "Miles End," at 212 South 200 East, offers two rooms with breakfast included. Amenities encompass a parlor, dining room with fireplace, and swimming pool and spa.

When first introduced to the homes already located behind the wrought iron fence and green gates at what is now Greene Gate Village, Barbara had no interest in the Orson Pratt home. She and Mark loved the Bentley home, the Grainery, Carriage House, and the Thomas Judd store, but wanted nothing to do with the Pratt home. Where the other homes sported Gingerbread trim and other unique embellishments, the Pratt home was a "plain Jane," devoid of charm and character. In addition, it had fallen into complete disrepair. Mark told Barbara that when she decided to take on the Pratt home for restoration rather than see it torn down, he fell in love with her all over again. It was a tremendous undertaking, one that required a great deal of rolling up one's sleeves and going to work. Today, the Orson Pratt home is on the National and Utah Historical Registers and is a favorite of all who visit, including Mark and Barbara.

Behind the Greene Gates are eight restored homes with 19 bed and breakfast units, each bearing the name of one of the Greene's grandchildren. The restored Carriage House serves as the Village's reception center, banquet room, convention hall, and complete business facility.

The four rooms available in the Orson Pratt House are Lara & Susan, Robyn & Natalie, Linsey, and Shanna. *Lara* has a superb navy and pink Persian rug, pink, blue and white bedspread and shams with white and gold head and foot boards. There is a full kitchen and a second bedroom, *Susan*, which also has a white and gold brass queen bed, peach bedspread, and antique furniture.

Robyn & Natalie are adjoining rooms. *Robyn* offers a mauve velvet loveseat, fireplace, Victorian bedspread of pink, mauve, teal, and white, and a king bed with white ornamental iron headboard. *Natalie* has a mauve rocker, armoire, and queen bed with white cast iron headboard.

Linsey and Shanna are two of the Village's bridal suites. *Linsey* has a large jetted tub, trundle bed, king bed, antique furnishings, and wet bar with microwave and mini refrigerator. It also has one and one-half baths and a Cable TV with VCR. *Shanna* is the only room at the Village not named after one of the Greene's grandchildren. The room was named after a beloved manager who, when diagnosed with cancer and a death sentence, continued a labor of love at the village, carrying her oxygen bottle with her as she worked. *Shanna* has a queen bed, daybed, one and one-half baths with tub and shower, a jetted tub, and Cable TV with VCR

The *Bentley House* offers *Lys-an*, a room with queen bed, private sitting room with queen hideaway couch, private balcony, and Cable TV with VCR.

The *Grainery*, just behind the Bentley House, offers twin beds that can be used side by side or converted into a king. There is also a day bed in the sitting room.

The *Orpha Morris House* is rented complete and offers a queen bed, three-quarter bed, queen futon couch, living room with fireplace, kitchenette, one and one-half baths with jetted tub, and Cable TV with VCR.

Of all of the homes at Greene Gate Village, the *Morris Home* probably has the most interesting history, at least when it comes to finding its place at the Village. Transported to the Village by the city's foremost moving expert, the house was left on the truck bed overnight. The town arose the next morning to find that an axle had broken, dumping the house and reducing it to a pile of rubble.Eighty-seven-year-old Carl Fife, who had moved the house, said he had never lost a house yet. He used his insurance money to help rebuild the home. The only things lost from the original were the doors and windows. The incident proved to be fruitful, as the Greene's discovered that it was much easier to rebuild a home than it was to move one.

Greene Hedge, which was built by store owner, Thomas Judd, was scheduled for demolition in 1986. The home was architecturally drawn, dismantled, and rebuilt at Greene Gate Village in 1991. It is from this home that the original green gate, displayed in the garden, was taken.

Greene Hedge units include Kristyl, Thomas and Steven. *Kristyl* is one of the Village's five bridal suites. It offers an exquisite white ornamental iron king bed with heart-shaped pillows and valance canopy. The suite has an original fireplace, beautiful antique dresser, armoire, jetted tub, and full kitchen with JennAire range, dishwasher and refrigerator. The decor of *Steven* includes a light blue velvet love seat, white cast iron queen bed, and other antique furnishings. *Thomas* is more masculine with ornate walnut headboard and dark blue, light blue, and white decor. The entire home, which includes a queen hideaway in the sitting room, may be rented by larger groups.

Mark and Barbara had passed by the Tolley House many times on their way to Provo or Salt Lake City. Every time Barbara saw the little house near the town of Mona, at the end of a field and under a lone apple tree, there was a sense of longing. No one could have been more delighted than Barbara when the owner gave her permission to dismantle and move the home to its current location. The Tolley House, where 11 children were born and raised, has probably been painted on more canvases than any other house in Utah. Two of those paintings hang in one of its two rooms, *Richard*. Deep burgundy and forest green are the colors for *Richard*. The room also has an original fireplace, Victorian chairs, antique wash stand, and elegant Persian rug. A second room, *Jonathan*, is entered from the back and has an original fireplace, wood siding inside, queen bed and antique furnishings.

In the Judd House are *Leslee and Ryan*, both of which are rented as one unit. The house has two private bathrooms, twin and queen beds, and a sitting area with TV, refrigerator, sink, microwave, and trundle bed.

Newest at the Village and already a favorite is the Christmas Cottage. Relocated in 1996, the Cottage offers a Christmas color scheme of green and burgundy. One of the Village's bridal suites, the Cottage has fireplace with Christmas houses on the mantel, pictures of Santa on the wall, four poster king bed, beautiful armoire, jetted tub and a kitchen.

All rooms at Greene Gate Village have private telephones with local calls free, private bathrooms, television, and a Teddy Bear. The bears in each room are available for purchase. Village amenities include a beautiful terraced swimming pool with hot tub, and a brick courtyard with cobblestone paths meandering throughout the garden. Carriages, old-style lamp posts, and other objects of antiquity are interspersed throughout the property.

After checking in at the office, guests are invited to enjoy a free soda at the famous turn-of-the-century Judd store, a favorite with kids from the Woodward School across the street since 1911. It is the oldest family-held business in St. George. Thomas Judd's grandson still helps at the store and shares fascinating stories.

Also at the Village is The Bentley House Restaurant, which serves fine cuisine to B & B guests and the public on Thursday, Friday, and Saturday evenings, by reservation, from 5:00 p.m. - 8:00 p.m. Entrees found on the menu may include Filet Mignon with sautéed mushrooms and Béarnaise sauce, Poached Salmon in lemon butter and white wine, Pork Tenderloin, spice cured and baked with a honey rum glaze, and Chicken Breast in tomato and red wine sauce. The menu changes nightly but always offers a red meat, fish, and poultry dish

From the orange rolls to the delightful desserts, The Bentley House Restaurant prepares everything fresh daily and is always ready to meet special dietary needs and cater to special occasions. The Bentley House Restaurant offers three dining rooms— the Dining Room, for family style dining; The Parlor, for romancing someone special; and The Garden Room, great for larger parties. Dinners are three, four, and five courses and are complimented with a serving of sorbet.

Greene Gate Village offers prospective couples the chance to begin their future in the past. Offering turn-of-the-century elegance, Greene Gate Village can assist with all wedding plans. Available is an elegant wedding and reception center, limousine service, dining facilities for engagement party, rehearsal dinner, and wedding breakfast, and a bridal suite for honeymooning and for many happy return visits on anniversaries.

More than just an historic bed and breakfast, Greene Gate Village is a destination vacation for those who want the best in luxury, nostalgia, romance, and caring service.

**SEVEN WIVES INN
BED & BREAKFAST**
217 North 100 West
St. George, Utah 84770
Tel: (801) 628-3737
Reservations (800) 600-3737
FAX: (801) 673-0165
E-Mail Seven@interwest.com
Visa, MasterCard, American Express, Diners Club, Carte Blanche and Discover are accepted.
Reservations are requested.

    Whenever there was a brief hiatus in their busy work schedules, Jay and Donna Curtis, longtime residents of California, would travel the Coast or venture into California Gold Country, always preferring to stay at quaint bed and breakfasts.
    Jay and Donna spoke often to friends and family of their love for bed and breakfasts. Over the years the seed was planted and soon, it seemed, everyone was keeping their eyes open for a bed and breakfast property in Utah for Jay and Donna, where both had ancestral roots.
    Several properties were examined or checked out, but when Jay and Donna were led in 1981 to the home at 217 North 100 West, it was love at first sight. There it was, a stately magnificent home in the heart of St. George's historical district that had been built in the late 1800s and exuded mystery, romance, and a sense of longing. That was on a Friday and by Saturday the yearning had been satisfied. The Edwin G. Woolley home had new owners and Jay and Donna had the fulfillment of a dream.
    The home was remarkably well maintained, but still had to be completely remodeled to include private baths in every room. Less than a year later, in January 1982, the Woolley home, with its seven bedrooms, was completed. Donna's polygamist grandfather, Benjamin F. Johnson, had seven wives. What could be more ideal? Instead of *Seven Wives for Seven Brothers*, the Inn had "seven rooms for seven wives." Each room was named for one of the seven wives and Seven Wives Inn was opened.
    When Jay and Donna purchased the Woolley home, they were told that the home, built in 1873, had been the largest and one of the most prestigious homes in the city. Further research revealed that in 1882, when polygamy was outlawed, Mr. Woolley hid polygamists in his attic via a secret door to protect the polygamists from imprisonment. Records showed that Donna's Great Grandfather Johnson, who had the seven wives and after whom the Inn was named, had been one of those polygamists.
    In 1989, the George Whitehead home next door, equally steeped in history, became available and was eagerly purchased by the Curtises. The Whitehead home, a much smaller edifice, was built in 1883. What an interesting side note for Jay and Donna when they discovered that, small as it was, the home had been known as the "Presidents House." It seemed that George's wife, Esther, was the best cook in town, and all of the early presidents and apostles of the church, when they visited St. George, wanted to stay at George's home. The home is still referred to as The Presidents House.
    All rooms at Seven Wives Inn, unless otherwise mentioned, feature bathrooms with showers over antique clawfooted bathtubs, telephone with local calls free, and Cable TV. A guest amenity is the fenced in pool with red sandstone decking surrounded by lawn.

Rooms on the first floor of Seven Wives Inn include Lucinda, Sarah, and Susan. *Lucinda* is an elegantly large room with spectacular brass queen bed, French stove, lace curtains, and a sitting area with sofa and arm chair. The bathroom is the home's original and is said to have been the first bathroom in St. George with indoor plumbing. *Sarah* is also a large room and has a fireplace, private porch, chandelier, and queen and single bed. *Susan* is a smaller room, offers a queen bed, Franklin stove, and has its own private entrance. Combined with *Sarah*, it makes an ideal family suite.

On the second floor, *Melissa*, the bridal suite, offers a romantic setting with its jetted tub, fireplace, private balcony, ornate stained glass windows, elegant queen bed, and armoire. The suite has a sitting room (*Clarinda*) with Victorian settee and lounge chairs, cable television, and VCR. A separate bathroom offers shower over clawfooted tub.

Julia is a mid-size room in shades of pink and burgundy. It offers queen bed, window seat, Dixie dormers, and a black and white bathroom with jetted tub and shower.

An exquisite mirrored armoire, white cast iron queen bed, and antique wash basin distinguish *Harriet* from the other bedrooms. It also has a small private balcony.

Maryann, a large room on the second floor, has a queen and single bed, Dixie dormers on three sides, private balconies on two sides, and a shower.

Jane, the attic room, is wonderful. The pitched ceiling seems to invite guests to a different world. The room features a queen and single bed, skylight windows, arm chairs, and an antique wash basin made from the base of an old treadle sewing machine.

The President's House offers a Great Room and four bedrooms, all on the second floor, and all with beautiful hardwood floors. *Eliza* has a queen bed, cottage antique furniture, and a large private balcony. The head and foot boards of *Mary*'s queen bed is an imposing dark walnut. The light and airy bathroom is powder blue. Forest green is the color selected for *Caroline*. A white ornamental iron queen bed and wicker love seat make this room seem light and sunny. *Rachel* is a flowery room with small private balcony, tulips on the walls, pink cast iron headboard, skirted vanity, and yellow and blue decor. It is the only room of the four to have shower only. The rest have clawfooted tubs with showers.

Very special sleeping quarters at Seven Wives Inn is *Ada*, the cottage. Wheelchair accessible, the cottage offers Spanish tile floor, a mini kitchen, gas fireplace, antique maple queen bed, "Mormon" couch, jetted tub, and separate shower. Windows are from the St. George Temple.

One of the most impressive rooms on the first floor of Seven Wives is The Tea Room. A good percentage of early converts to the Church of Jesus Christ of Latter-day Saints were English, and though black and green teas were against their religion, the Saints soon found an alternative in herbal teas.

Today The Tea Room is open Wednesday - Friday, with lunch served from 12:00 noon - 2:00 p.m., and tea (both regular and herbal) from 12:00 noon - 4:00 p.m. In addition to a marvelous selection of freshly baked breads, scones, demitasse sandwiches, and desserts, The Tea Room offers an elegant light luncheon of the day. The Tea Room is the perfect setting for showers, birthdays, holiday teas, club events, and other special occasions.

The Tea Room is also the setting for the Inn's breakfasts, a wonderful selection of fresh fruits in season, juices, coffee, tea, fresh baked breads, and specialties of the Inn, including Blueberry pancakes, Eggs Mornay, and a Croissant topped with scrambled eggs and Asiago cream sauce. Seven Wives also makes its own granola, a favorite with guests.

Seven Wives Inn, Utah's first registered Bed & Breakfast, is everything one looks for in a bed and breakfast. Seven Wives offers fascinating history, modern luxuries in the lap of antiquity, and innkeepers who have found what they love to do, and do what they love.

RESTAURANTS

CHUCK-A-RAMA BUFFET
127 North Red Cliff Drive
St. George, Utah 84770
Tel: (801) 673-4464
FAX: (801) 652-3847
Hrs: Monday - Saturday
            11:00 a.m. - 9:00 p.m.
Sunday   11:00 a.m. - 8:00 p.m.
Visa, MasterCard, American Express and Discover are accepted.

For over 30 years Chuck-A-Rama Buffet has played a major part in the role of dining out—especially for Utah families. Nowhere are families, wedding parties, and tour groups more welcome than they are at Chuck-A-Rama.

For many years, those who lived away from the Wasatch Front were relegated to an occasional dining opportunity—when they paid a visit to the Provo and Salt Lake areas. But in November of 1995, Chuck-A-Rama opened its doors to Southern Utah, a venture that has proven fruitful as the most popular of all the Chuck-A-Rama Buffets in the state.

Chuck-A-Rama Buffet has been emulated by restaurants from around the country, but none seem to have the drawing power of Chuck-A-Rama. With its 116 plus entrees and fresh salads, all of which are prepared daily from scratch, diners are bound to find the quality home-cooked dining that most hunger for. The large and varied hot food selection includes fried or baked chicken, roast beef, ham, and turkey, as well as several other main dishes in its all-one-can-eat buffet. The colorful and varied salad bar, a choice of two soups, fresh from the oven rolls, beverages, on-premise bakery desserts, and an ice cream bar are always included in the price of one's lunch or dinner.

Chuck-A-Rama has a seating capacity for over 345 guests, so quickly and efficiently taking care of large parties or bus tour groups is never a problem. Since the buffet restaurant is located across from Zion Factory Stores, a favorite shopping destination of tourists, there is always plenty of bus parking available.

For quality dining at one low price for adults, a senior citizen discount, and a price break for children on foods they relish, Chuck-A-Rama Buffet has earned its mark as Utah's number one family restaurant.

J. J. HUNAN CHINESE RESTAURANT
Ancestor Square, Tower Building, Third Floor
2 West St. George Boulevard #36
St. George, Utah 84532
Tel: (801) 628-5219
FAX: (801) 656-1933
E-Mail: jjhunan@infowesr.com
Hrs:
Monday - Friday
11:30 a.m. - 9:45 p.m.
Saturday
12:00 noon - 9:45 p.m.
Sunday
12:00 noon - 8:45 p.m.

Visa, MasterCard, American Express, Diners Club, and Discover are accepted. Reservations are not required.

Dining at J. J. Hunan Chinese Restaurant is an experience that for three consecutive years has earned J. J. Hunan the Readers' Choice award as Southern Utah's Number One Oriental Restaurant, a. distinction made by readers of Southern Utah's daily newspaper, *Spectrum*.

The aroma that greets guests as they exit the third floor elevator and enter J. J. Hunan, is enough to convince diners that they are about to embark on a memorable gastronomical experience. The fragrance is a blend of succulent cuisine from nearly every well-known Chinese province. If it is Cantonese food one is craving, J. J. Hunan offers a selection of 21 gourmet dishes. The aficionado of Shanghai cuisine will find a selection of 10 choices. There is a selection of six Hunan dishes, seven Mandarin choices, six epicurean Szechwan dishes, and two gourmet duck selections from Peking. No other Oriental restaurant in the state offers such a variety of savory Chinese cuisine.

For those not familiar with the distinct types of Chinese cooking, Shirley Ann Tzab, owner and manager of J. J. Hunan, points out the differences. If it is hot and spicy cuisine one desires, with dishes altered to suit varying individual tastes, the diner should select one of the Hunan, Szechwan, or Peking courses. Those who prefer milder more delicate flavors should select from the Cantonese choices, and diners who enjoy the sweetness of meats and sauces, will favor Mandarin cuisine. Shanghai dishes are those that feature snow peas, bamboo shoots, straw mushrooms, water chestnuts, and a variety of meats, pork, poultry and seafood in a more delicate sauce.

Appetizers at J. J. Hunan include more traditional selections such as Egg-Rolls, BBQ ribs, and Pot Stickers. But those willing to try the unique will not be disappointed in the delicate flavor of crab raggoons and the more piquant flavor of Paper Wrapped Chicken. Starters are served with a selection of hot mustard, hot chili oil, and J. J. Hunan's secret recipe for sweet and sour sauce on the side.

The soup preferences at J. J. Hunan include the popular Egg Flower, assorted Won Ton, and Hot and Sour soups. Not to be missed as succulent choices are Noodle soups, almost a meal in themselves, and a house specialty and favorite of the writer, Sizzling Rice Soup. Rice is added tableside to a delicate broth that includes shrimp, beef, turkey, bamboo shoots, water chestnuts, and pea pods.

J. J. Hunan recently began serving a delectable assortment of salads that includes Chinese Chicken Salad and Chinese Rainbow Salad.

Dishes such as Chop Suey, Chow Mein, Egg Fu-Yung, Lo Mein, and Kung Pao, can be served with a choice of pork, beef, chicken, seafood, or a combination of any or all. Chop Suey and Chow Mein, two Oriental favorites, offer the meat choice with vegetables in a Cantonese sauce. Chow Mein is topped with dry noodles. Egg Fu-Yung, also Cantonese, is a succulent blend of mixed vegetables that are covered with egg, deep fried, and topped with sauce and the meat choice. Lo Mein is another Cantonese favorite and offers pork, beef, chicken or shrimp served with soft noodles and vegetables that are stir-fried in a delicate sauce. Kung Pao, a Hunan favorite, is hot and spicy, but modified to taste, and features the meat choice sautéed with peanuts and green onions in a succulent rich brown sauce.

In addition to the tremendous selection of pork, beef, chicken and seafood dishes, J. J. Hunan offers an extraordinary selection of Specialties and Gourmet Cuisines. One Gourmet favorite is J. J.'s Chicken, which offers large chopped strips of chicken that are deep fried and then, in a special process, sautéed in J. J.'s unique sauce. The result is a tender, juicy and succulent dish in one's choice of hot or not. Another Gourmet choice is the Shrimp and Scallops in Garlic Sauce. The shrimp and scallops are marinated in flavor and sautéed with vegetables in garlic sauce. Peking Duck requires 30-minute processing but is well worth the wait. The whole duck is marinated and baked in a grill wok until the skin is crispy and luscious in flavor. The skin is served with Peking pancake with Hoisin sauce and the meat is cooked with bean sprouts. Presentation of the Gourmet and Specialty Cuisine includes fresh mint on the plate, elegantly positioned slices of oranges, and maraschino cherries.

In addition to a side dish of Steamed Rice, J. J. Hunan offers a selection of six Fried Rice dishes, including one for vegetarians. Other vegetarian choices also include Braised Broccoli, Kung Pao Cabbage, Mixed Chinese Vegetables, To Fu dishes, and Snow Peas and Water Chestnuts or Assorted Mushroom dishes. J. J. Hunan can also provide vegetarian dishes in Chow Mein, Lo Mein, Chop Suey and Egg Foo Yong entrees. Most soups can also be adapted to the vegetarian. J. J. Hunan's Combination and Family Dinners are calculated, unlike most Oriental restaurants, from the single diner up to as many as the party includes.

Those who have dined at J. J. Hunan have nothing but praise for the quality of cuisine and the caring service that makes every diner feel important and special. Unless J. J. Hunan is extremely busy, they will take the time to address special needs and desires. If allergic to or have a dislike for a certain vegetable or meat, let J. J. Hunan know and the dish will be customized to taste at little or no additional cost.

Almost as enticing as the restaurant aroma is the ambiance. The lobby and two dining rooms are intricately embellished with ornate gold ceilings and dividers, exquisite oriental lanterns, picturesque Chinese calendars, and additional decorations of gold, red and black. J. J. Hunan can comfortably seat 150 diners and readily caters to small intimate parties or large groups.

Finding Ancestor Square in St. George is not a problem. Finding J. J. Hunan Chinese Restaurant is not as simple. The Tower Building is located towards the back of the square and parking and entrance to J. J. Hunan's is from the rear of the Tower. An elevator or stairs lead to the third floor restaurant and Southern Utah's most memorable Oriental dining experience. As with most things worth while, J. J. Hunan may be harder to find, but it is certainly worth every effort.

SULLIVAN'S ROCOCO
Steakhouse & Inn
511 South Airport Road
St. George, Utah 84532
Tel: (435) 673-3305
         (888) 628-3671
FAX: (435) 673-6370
Hrs: Lunch
Monday - Friday
11:00 a.m. - 3:00 p.m.
         Dinner
Open Daily   5:00 p.m. - 10:00 p.m.
Visa, MasterCard, American Express, Diners Club, and Discover are accepted.
Reservations are not required.

Sullivan's Rococo, located on the bluff above St. George, would be a Traveler's Choice restaurant for no other reason than the spectacular bird's eye view it offers. But Rococo is not limited to magnificent views alone, it is one of those rare establishments that also offers elegant ambiance and extraordinary cuisine.

Diners at Rococo begin their meal with a complimentary shrimp cocktail served over ice. The pro gratis appetizer is followed with a chilled garden salad, served with a peppered parmesan house dressing or one's choice of dressings. An individual loaf of fresh-from-the-oven bread accompanies the salad. Entrees, which include a selection of large and small cuts of New York and Filet Mignon steaks and Prime Rib, offer a choice of baked potato, French fries, or rice. Other entrees available at Rococo include seafood such as Lobster, King Crab, Shrimp, and Scallops, and fresh water fish entrees of Salmon, Orange Roughy, Halibut, and Trout. Diners can also treat themselves to combination dinners such as steak with lobster, crab, chicken, shrimp or scallops; or Grilled Chicken and Shrimp.

Lunch at Rococo offers a variety of entrees as well as a selection of salads, soups, and hot and cold sandwiches.

Recently re-decorated, Rococo, which means "elaborate and baroque," offers an East wall of windows that overlooks the city, its red rock cliffs, beautiful Mormon Temple, and verdant trees. The interior features a black lava rock wall, foliage embellishments, and exquisite chandeliers. Rococo will seat as many as 225 guests and is ideal, day or night, for special parties and banquets.

If fine traditional cuisine, romantic ambiance, and extraordinary views are important aspects of dining, Rococo is the restaurant of choice in St. George.

THE PASTA FACTORY
Historic Ancestor Square
St. George Boulevard & Main Street
St. George, Utah 84532
Tel: (435) 674-3753
Hrs:
Monday - Saturday
11:00 a.m. - 10:00 p.m.
Visa, MasterCard, American Express, and Discover are accepted.
Reservations are not required.

It seemed to be a given in St. George that The Pizza Factory should open a second restaurant specializing in pasta. That red letter year finally happened in 1994 when The Pasta Factory took its place along side of The Pizza Factory in historic Ancestor Square.

With the advent of health-conscious dining, people have developed a love affair with pasta. The Pasta Factory uses diverse and exciting ways to shape, fill and top pasta. The Pasta Factory's creativity translates, for the diner, into the ability to take 13 pastas and, with the variety of sauces, toppings and fillings, customize over a thousand different pasta dishes.

The Pasta Factory's choice pasta is made with hard durum semolina wheat. The flavor is mild and has a nutty taste that compliments any dish. Pasta choices include Angel Hair, extra fine strands of pasta; Vermicelli, a thin spaghetti; Fettuccine, thick ribbons about one-quarter inch wide, and Linguini, very narrow, thick ribbons. Linguini flavors offered at The Pasta Factory are Garlic, Lemon Pepper, which is wonderful with seafood or fresh vegetables; Spinach, a colorful and flavorful choice with white or red sauce; and Tomato/basil, best with red and meat sauces. Pasta shapes include bowtie, shaped as the name implies; and Penne, which are medium tubes cut diagonally. Filled pastas include Ravioli, stuffed little pasta pillows; and Tortellini, small twists of pasta closed into a circle.

At The Pasta Factory, diners are invited to select whatever pasta they desire, add a choice of sauces and toppings, and call it whatever they like. Sauce choices include Alfredo, a creamy white sauce with parmesan cheese; Marinara, a red tomato sauce simmered with herbs; Meat, a red tomato sauce with fresh ground beef and Italian sausage; Red Clam, a chunky red sauce with finely chopped clams; White Clam, a white clam sauce with a hint of cream cheese; and Classic Pesto, a puree of basil, pine nuts, garlic, and parmesan cheese in olive oil. Toppings are Garden Medley—a selection of steamed broccoli, carrots, and cauliflower; Sautéed Italian Vegetables—zucchini, onion, yellow squash, and red peppers; and Seasoned Chicken Breast, Sautéed Mushrooms, and Marinated Artichoke Hearts and Mushrooms. For a light taste, The Pasta Factory suggests ordering any topping over pasta that is tossed with extra virgin oil, fresh garlic and parsley.

Every pasta dish deserves to be complemented with a fresh salad. Diners may select the Classic Caesar Salad, tossed with The Pasta Factory's own creamy Caesar dressing, croutons, and parmesan cheese. Another choice is the Artichoke Heart Salad, where. marinated artichoke hearts, mushrooms, and olives are served over a mix of spinach leaves and leaf lettuce and topped with grated parmesan cheese. Both salads may be ordered with chicken. Pasta salad lovers appreciate the Bowtie Chicken Caesar Salad. It features bowtie pasta, seasoned chicken breast, mushrooms, crisp lettuce and croutons tossed with the restaurant's creamy Caesar dressing, and topped with grated parmesan cheese. All salads are served with hot bread sticks.

In addition to giving diners the opportunity to create their own entree, The Pasta Factory offers a selection of tried and true dishes that are sure to please the most discriminating palate. Among diner favorites is the Shrimp Ronaldo, which combines stir-fried shrimp with sundried tomatoes, feta cheese, olives and pepper flakes over bowtie noodles that are garnished with pinenuts. An Italian creation with an Oriental flavor is Szechwan Chicken. It offers chicken, broccoli, snow peas, onions, red pepper and mushrooms stir-fried in a spicy Oriental sauce and served over linguini. A favorite of vegetarians is the Vegetables in Tomato Cream. Sun dried tomatoes, yellow squash, mushrooms, zucchini, and onions are blended into a creamy tomato sauce and tossed into Penne. All entrees are served with hot parmesan bread sticks and a house green salad, or, for a small additional cost, a half Caesar salad.

Americans love Italian coffee. The Pasta Factory offers Espresso, Latte, and Cappuccino, as well as fresh ground more traditional coffee and decaf.

Creamy, chewy, light, or decadent, when it comes to desserts, The Pasta Factory selection is bound to please. Since dessert choices change frequently, servers announce the day's selection.

Children at The Pasta Factory are offered wheels or holiday-shaped noodles served with butter or red or white sauces, a salad and bread sticks.

One of the greatest draws to dining at The Pasta Factory is the year-round outdoor patio dining. The large covered patio offers a brick floor, old-style lanterns, a mister during the summer months, and a propane heater during the city's mild winters. With the mister and the heater, temperatures stay moderate and dining in the middle of historic Ancestor Square is delightful. Plans are in progress at The Pasta Factory for extended indoor dining.

Because of The Pasta Factory's unyielding attention to quality and detail, whether the pasta selection is an entree from the menu or one that the diner has customized, the choice is bound to be enjoyable. The Pasta Factory has earned its place among Readers' Choice restaurants.

THE PIZZA FACTORY
Historic Ancestor Square
St. George Boulevard & Main Street
St. George, Utah 84532
Tel: (435) 628-1234
Hrs:
Monday - Thursday
11:00 a.m. - 10:00 p.m.
Friday & Saturday
11:00 a.m. - 11:00 p.m.
Visa, MasterCard, American Express, and Discover are accepted.
Reservations are not required.

The Pizza Factory began in Cedar City, Utah in 1974, when Bill Kringlen, after a skiing trip at Brian Head, wanted to relax, get a pizza, and figure out what kind of business he could start that would support him and his desire to move to Southern Utah. To his amazement, there wasn't a pizza parlor in Cedar City. Bill knew right away that he would support himself by providing to others like him the opportunity to enjoy the age-old tradition, pizza. That was in 1974 and by 1979 Bill not only had an established Pizza Factory in Cedar City, but was ready to open The Pizza Factory in St. George.

Since its opening, thousands of satisfied customers continue to crave and rave about a Pizza Factory experience. The Pizza Factory, with its custom-built pizzas, incredible assortment of sandwiches, spaghetti, and salad bar is a favorite haunt for local business people. This same array of Italian delicacies, along with spacious rooms, makes The Pizza Factory a favorite choice for bus tours. Families who live in the area or who are vacationing in St. George soon discover that the food is the best and the prices are right.

At The Pizza Factory everything is made from scratch using only the best and the freshest ingredients. Sandwiches are served piping hot from the oven or cold on The Pizza Factory's own sourdough or whole wheat rolls. Two favorites are the Gobbler, which features turkey, bacon, cream cheese and mozzarella cheese; and the Whale, which offers pastrami, ham, Canadian-style bacon, salami, pepperoni, onions and cheese on choice of rolls. If that doesn't sound hearty enough, order the Killer Whale with a double portion of each sandwich topping. All sandwiches are served with chips and a pickle.

An absolute favorite among those in the know is a bowl of Billy's Chili. Served in small or large bowl proportions, Billy's Chili is a meal in itself when accompanied by any of The Pizza Factory's garlic bread choices—plain, with cheese, with cheese and mushrooms, with cheese and pepperoni, or with cheese, pepperoni and mushrooms. In addition to Billy's Chili, the Pizza Factory offers a very special soup of the day.

Custom Built Pizzas begin with The Pizza Factory's delicious traditional or Chicago-style deep dish crust spread with a layer of The Pizza Factory's prized sauce. Pizzas are topped with hearty proportions of the finest blend of pizza cheeses and then built with any or all of The Pizza Factory's prepared-fresh-daily ingredients. Offered are salami, pepperoni, ham, Canadian-style bacon, pineapple, sausage, beef, spicy Italian sausage, onion, black olives, green olives, pastrami, tomatoes, green bell peppers, mushrooms and jalapenos.

Quality pizza is not accidental. Crust must be prepared and then baked to perfection. Sauce must be a delicate blend of authentic Italian herbs and seasonings, and each of the toppings must be the best available and be prepared fresh daily. The Pizza Factory never compromises.

Calzones are offered customers in a choice of meat, vegetable or combination of both. Spaghetti, with a thick meat and sautéed mushroom sauce or marinara sauce, may be ordered as a plate by itself, as a side dish, or in a dinner combination with a trip to the salad bar, garlic bread, and a soft drink.

As with everything else it offers, The Pizza Factory's salad bar, considered to be the best that St. George has to offer, serves up the freshest of ingredients. The bar includes crisp lettuce topped with an assortment of condiments, and fresh fruits, vegetables and nuts. The salad bar is available on a one-time through, all one can eat, or all one can eat plus soup basis.

Remember how fun it was to sneak bites of the cookie dough before it went into the oven? Well, at The Pizza Factory sneaking isn't necessary and one doesn't have to be a child to order a generous serving of chocolate chip, oatmeal, or oatmeal chocolate chip cookie dough. And it just stands to reason that those who love cookie dough also love cookies. At The Pizza Factory cookies are custom built, fresh from the oven every time. Also offered is cheesecake, with or without fruit topping.

The atmosphere at The Pizza Factory is as infectious as the cuisine. Red and green neon lights, abundant foliage, and a cross-beamed ceiling adorn the spacious main room. A second room with brick wall offers the appearance of patio dining.

A gift shop towards the rear of the building offers a selection of private label Pizza Factory clothing. In addition to the traditional T's, caps, sweats, and jackets in a fashionable assortment of colors, The Pizza Factory offers a line of children's and baby's clothing that includes onesies and bibs.

It was a stroke of good fortune for everyone that Cedar City had no pizza parlor in 1974. Today, because of that oversight, St George and Cedar City have the best that the pizza world has to offer. The Pizza Factory is a "thumbs-up" Travelers' Choice for great pizza.

BRIGHAM YOUNG HOME, ST. GEORGE, UTAH
PENCIL, DEAN FIFE

Index

Symbols

2002 Olympic Winter Games 5

A

accommodations, Bicknell 95
accommodations, Boulder 108
accommodations, Bryce Canyon 157
accommodations, Cannonville 133
accommodations, Duck Creek Village 191
accommodations, Escalante 125
accommodations, Green River 22
accommodations, Hatch 186
accommodations, Kanab 205
accommodations, Page, Arizona 231
accommodations, Panguitch 171
accommodations, St. George 270
accommodations, Teasdale 101
accommodations, Torrey 88
accommodations,Tropic / Bryce Canyon 136
adventure / tours, Boulder 109
adventure / tours, Escalante 126
adventure / tours, Kanab 212
adventure / tours, Moab 33
adventure / tours, Springdale 248
adventures, Moab 27
An Olde Penny Farthing Inn 272
Anasazi State Park 12, 104, **107**
Aneth / Montezuma Creek 81
   attractions 82
      Four Corners Monument 82
      Hovenweep National Monument 82
Angel Arch, Canyonlands 71
Angel Canyon, Kanab 185
Angels Landing, Zion Park 247
Anticline Overlooks 70
Antimony 165
   accommodations
      Rockin'R Ranch 166
   adventure / tours
      Rockin'R Ranch 166
   attractions 166
      Otter Creek State Park 166
      Piute State Park 166
   resorts 166

      Rockin'R Ranch 166
   restaurants
      Rockin'R Ranch 166
   specialty shopping
      Rockin'R Ranch 166
Aqua Canyon 156
Aquarius Plateau, Capitol Reef 86
Arch View Resort RV Camp Park 56
Arches History 16
Arches National Park **15**, 21
   Balanced Rock 15
   Chip-Off-the-Old-Block 15
   Courthouse Towers 15
   Cove Arch 16
   Cove of Caves 16
   Delicate Arch 16
   Devils Garden 16
      Broken Arch 16
      Dark Angel 16
      Devils Garden Campground 16
      Double O Arch 16
      Landscape Arch 16
      Navajo Arch 16
      Partition Arch 16
      Pine Tree Arch 16
      Private Arch 16
      Sand Dune Arch 16
      Skyline Arch 16
      Tunnel Arch 16
      Wall Arch 16
   Double Arch 16
   Elephant Butte 16
   Fiery Furnace 16
   Garden of Eden 16
   Ham Rock 16
   Klondike Bluffs 16
   Tower Arch 16
   Landscape Arch 15
   Parade of the Elephants 16
   Park Avenue 15
   Petrified Dunes Viewpoint 15
   Pothole Arch 16
   Ribbon Arch 16
   Rock Pinnacles 15
   Sheep Rock 15
   Skyline Arch 15
   The Organ 15
   The Spectacles 16
   The Windows 16

Three Gossips 15
Tower of Babel 15
Turret Arch 16
Arizona, Northern 223
  accommodations
    Jacob Lake 228
    Lake Powell Resorts & Marinas 236
    North Rim of the Grand Canyon 228
  areas, cities, towns
    Fredonia 223
    Jacob Lake 228
    Page 230
  attractions 230
    Glen Canyon National Recreation Area 230
    Lake Powell Resorts & Marinas 236
    North Rim of the Grand Canyon 228
  campgrounds
    Lake Powell Resorts & Marinas 236
    North Rim of the Grand Canyon 228
  lodges
    North Rim of the Grand Canyon 228
  specialty shopping
    Jacob Lake 228
    Lake Powell Resorts & Marinas 236
    North Rim of the Grand Canyon 228
Arizona Strip 264
attractions
  Glen Canyon National Recreation Area
    Arizona, Northern 230
attractions, Aneth/ Montezuma Creek 82
attractions, Antimony 166
attractions, Bicknell 95
attractions, Blanding 75
attractions, Bluff 81
attractions, Boulder 107
attractions, Bryce Canyon 168
attractions, Cannonville 132
attractions, Escalante 121
attractions, Fredonia, Arizona 226
attractions, Garfield County 104
attractions, Grand County 15
attractions, Green River 21
attractions, Hurricane 262
attractions, Kanab 205
attractions, Mexican Hat 83
attractions, Moab 31
attractions, Northern Arizona 230
attractions, Panguitch 168, 183
attractions, San Juan County 69
attractions, Springdale 248
attractions, St. George 264
attractions, Tropic / Bryce Canyon 168
attractions, Virgin 258
attractions, Washington County 245
attractions, Wayne County 85

B

Balanced Rock, Arches National Park 15
Beaver Dam Wash 264
bed & breakfasts, Boulder 114
bed & breakfasts, Cannonville 134
bed & breakfasts, Escalante 128
bed & breakfasts, Moab 53
bed & breakfasts, Page, Arizona 234
bed & breakfasts, Panguitch 177
bed & breakfasts, St George 272
bed & breakfasts, Teasdale 102
bed & breakfasts, Tropic / Bryce Canyon 143
bed & breakfasts, Virgin 259
Best Friends Animal Sanctuary 212
Best Western New Western Motel 171
Best Western Red Hills 205
Best Western Ruby's Inn 161
Best Western Thunderbird Resort 198
Bicknell 95
  accommodations 95
    The Lodge at Red River Ranch 95
  attractions 95
  bakeries
    Rabbit Valley Bakery & Cafe 98
  restaurants 98
    Rabbit Valley Bakery & Cafe 98
Big Bend Picnic Area 20
Birdseye Trail 168
Bit & Spur Restaurant 254

Blanding 75
  attractions 75
    Dinosaur Museum 79
    Recapture Reservoir 79
    events 79
BLM Site Attractions 264
  Arizona Strip 264
  Beaver Dam Wash 264
  Historic Fort Pearce 264
  Hurricane Sand Dunes 264
  Little Black Mountain Petroglyph Site 264
  Mountain Meadows 264
  Pine Valley Mountain 264
  Red Cliffs 264
  Warner Valley 264
Bloomington, Golf Course, St. George area 269
Blue Mountains (also known as Abajo) 74
Blue Spruce Campground 124
Bluebell Knoll, Capitol Reef 86
Bluff 78, 80
  attractions 81
    San Juan River 81
    St Christopher's Episcopal Mission 81
  events 81
Boulder 104, 106
  accommodations 108
    Pole's Place 108
  adventure / tours 109
    Boulder Mountain Ranch 109
    Escalante Canyon Outfitters 112
  attractions 107
    Boulder Top 108
    Circle Cliffs 108
    Wolverine Petrified Wood Area 108
  bed & breakfasts 114
    Boulder Mountain Ranch 109
    Eaglestar Ranch Bed & Breakfast 114
  restaurants 116
    Burr Trail Cafe 116
    Pole's Place Eatery 118
  specialty shopping 119
    Burr Trail Trading Post 119
    Pole's Place Gift Shop 120

Boulder Mountain 86, 104, 124
Boulder Mountain Ranch 109
Boulder Top 86, 108
Bow Tie Arch, Moab 20
Bowdie Canyon, Canyonlands 71
Box Death Hollow Wilderness Area 124
Brandon Motel 206
brewery restaurants, Moab 55
Brian Head 184
  Brian Head Ski Resort 184
Bridge Mountain, Zion Park 246
Bridgerland 10
Brimhall Bridge, Capitol Reef 86
Bristlecone Loop Trail 156
Broken Arch, Arches National Park 16
Bryce Canyon 124
  accommodations 157
    Best Western Ruby's Inn 161
    Foster's Motel 157
    Pink Cliffs Village 159
  art gallerys
    Best Western Ruby's Inn 161
  attractions 168
  bakeries
    Foster's Bakery 157
  cabins
    Pink Cliffs Village 159
  campgrounds
    Best Western Ruby's Inn 161
  general stores
    Best Western Ruby's Inn 161
  hostels
    Pink Cliffs Village 159
  photo shops
    Best Western Ruby's Inn 161
  resorts 161
    Best Western Ruby's Inn 161
  restaurants 164
    Best Western Ruby's Inn 161
    Foster's Family Steakhouse 157
    The Cowboy Cafe 164
  specialty shopping
    Best Western Ruby's Inn 161
    Foster's Motel, Bakery, & Family Steakhouse 157
Bryce Canyon National Park 12, 104, **155**, 204
  Aqua Canyon 156
  Bristlecone Loop Trail 156

Bryce Point 156
Fairview Point 156
Fairyland Point 156
Inspiration Point 156
Natural Bridge 156
Paria View 156
Ponderosa Canyon 156
Queen's Garden Trail 156
Rainbow Point 156
Silent City 156
Sinking Ship 156
Sunrise Point 156
Sunset Point 156
Thor's Hammer 156
Under-the-Rim Trail 156
Wall Street 156
Yovimpa Point 156
Bryce Canyon's Western Town 174
Bryce Country Cabins 136
Bryce Pioneer Village 138
Bryce Pioneer Village Gift Shop 154
Bryce Point 156
Bryce Point Bed & Breakfast 143
Bryce-Zion Midway Resort 186
Buckhorn Trail 168
Buck's Grill House 60
Budget Host Book Cliff Lodge & Restaurant 22
Bull Valley Gorge. 123
Bullfrog 12
Bullfrog Marina 107
Bullfrog Marina, Lake Powell 72
Burr Ferry, Lake Powell 71
Burr Trail **107**, 123
   Bullfrog Marina 107
   Capitol Reef National Park 108
   Capitol Reef Overlook 108
   Circle Cliffs 123
   Deer Creek 123
   Glen Canyon National Recreation Area 107
   Grand Staircase-Escalante 107
   Henry Mountains 108
   Lake Powell 107
   Lake Powell Overlook 108
   Long Canyon 108
   The Gulch 123
   Waterpocket Fold 108
Burr Trail Cafe 116
Burr Trail, Capitol Reef 86
Burr Trail Trading Post 119
Butler Wash Indian Ruins. 76
Bybee's Steppingstone Motel 141

C

Cactus Hill Motel 101
Calf Creek Campground 104
Calf Creek Recreation Area 123
campgrounds
   Arch View Resort RV Camp Park 56
   Arches National Park
      Devils Garden Campground 16
   Canyonlands Campground 58
   Coral Pink Sand Dunes State Park 205
   Kodachrome Basin State Park 132
   St. George
      Gunlock State Park 264
      Snow Canyon State Park 265
campgrounds, Moab 56
Cannonville 104, 132
   accommodations 133
      Grand Staircase Inn & Country Store 133
   attractions 132
      Grosvenor Arch 132
      Kodachrome Basin State Park 132
   bed & breakfasts 134
      Fletcher's Canyon Country B & B 134
   campgrounds
      Kodachrome Basin State Park 132
   general stores
      Grand Staircase Inn & Country Store 133
Canyon Cruiser Co. 248
Canyon Inn 188
Canyon Inn Cafe 189
Canyon Livery Bed & Breakfast, The 145
Canyon Photo 219
Canyon Rims Recreation Area 69
Canyonland & Color Country Link 84
Canyonlands 21
Canyonlands by Night 12
Canyonlands Campground 58
Canyonlands Field Institute 33
Canyonlands, map 13
Canyonlands National Park 70

Angel Arch 71
Bowdie Canyon 71
Caterpillar Arch 71
Dark Canyon 71
Dark Canyon Primitive Area 71
Devils Kitchen 70
Elephant Hill 71
Gypsum Canyon 71
Island in the Sky 70
Land of Standing Rocks 70
The Doll House 70
The Fins 70
The Maze 70
The Needles District 70
Upheaval Dome 70
Canyonlands Travel Region 12, 14
  Arches National Park 12
  Canyonlands National Park 12
  Dead Horse Point State Park 12
  Edge of the Cedars State Park 12
  Four Corners 12
  Glen Canyon National Recreation Area 12
  Goosenecks State Park 12
  Green River State Park 12
  Hovenweep National monument 12
  John Wesley Powell River History Museum 12
  Lake Powell 12
  Manti LaSal Mountains 12
  Monument Valley Tribal Park 12
  Natural Bridges National Monument 12
  Newspaper Rock State Historical Monument 12
  Rainbow Bridge National Monument 12
  Valley of the Gods State Park 12
Capitol Gorge, Capitol Reef 86
Capitol Reef, 104
Capitol Reef National Park 10, 21, **85**, 108
  Aquarius Plateau 86
  Bluebell Knoll 86
  Boulder Mountain 86
  Boulder Top 86
  Brimhall Bridge 86
  Burr Trail 86
  Capitol Gorge 86

Capitol Reef Scenic Drive 86
Cassidy Arch Trails 86
Cathedral Valley 86
Cathedral Valley Campground 86
Cedar Mesa Campground 86
Chimney Rock 86
Cohab Canyon 86
Egyptian Temple 86
Floral-Sleeping Rainbow Ranch 86
Frying Pan 86
Golden Throne 86
Goosenecks 86
Hickman Bridge 86
J. Perry Egan Fish Hatchery 87
Muley Twist Canyon 86
Old Fruita 86
Olem Church Memorial Highway 86
Rim Overlook 86
Scenic Byway 24 86
South District 86
The Land Of The Sleeping Rainbow 85
Waterpocket Fold 85
Capitol Reef Overlook 108
Capitol Reef Scenic Drive. 86
Carl Hayden Visitor Center 72
Cascade Falls National Recreation Trail 190
Cassidy Arch Trails, Capitol Reef 86
Cassidy Trail 168
Castle Bridge Trail 168
Castle Country Travel Region 10
Castle Rock 20
Castle Valley 68
Casto Canyon Trail 168
Cataract Canyon, Colorado River 28
Caterpillar Arch, Canyonlands 71
Cathedral Valley Campground, Capitol Reef 86
Cathedral Valley, Capitol Reef 86
Cattleman's Restaurant & Lounge 61
Cave Towers, Edge of the Cedars 76
Cedar Breaks National Monument 12, **183**, 190, 204
Cedar Mesa Campground, Capitol Reef 86
Center Cafe 62
Chicken Corners Trail, Moab 30
Chimney Rock, Capitol Reef 86

Chip-Off-the-Old-Block, Arches National Park 15
Chuck Wagon General Store 94
Chuck Wagon Lodge 88
Chuck-A-Rama Buffet 280
Circle Cliffs 104, 108, 123
Cisco 19
Cohab Canyon, Capitol Reef 86
Color Country 103
   Anasazi State Park 12
   Bryce Canyon National Park 12
   Cedar Breaks National Monument 12
   Coral Pink Sand Dunes State Park 12
   Escalante State Park 12
   Grand Staircase-Escalante National Monument 12
   Iron Mission State Park 12
   Kodachrome Basin State Park 12
   Quail Creek State Park 12
   Snow Canyon State Park 12
   Zion National Park 12
Color Country, Eastern area, map 105
Color Country Travel Region 12
Colorado River Scenic Byway 19
Comb Ridge 76, 81
Comb Ridge, Edge of the Cedars 76
Comb Wash, Edge of the Cedars 76
Common-Sense Rules for Public Land Use 8
Coral Canyons Ranch 200
Coral Cliffs Golf Course, Kanab 207
Coral Pink Sand Dunes, 12
Coral Pink Sand Dunes State Park 204, **205**
Corona Arch 20
Cottonwood Canyon Road 123
   Cottonwood Narrows 123
   Grosvenor Arch 123
   Kodachrome Basin State Park 123
   Round Valley 123
Cottonwood Narrows 123
Courthouse Towers, Arches National Park 15
Courthouse Wash Site 19
Courtyard Marriott 231
Cove Arch, Arches National Park 16
Cove of Caves, Arches National Park 16
Cowboy Cafe, The 164
Cowboy Dreams Bed & Breakfast 147

Crescent Junction 68

D

Dance Hall Rock 123, 124
Dark Angel, Arches National Park 16
Dark Canyon, Canyonlands 71
Dark Canyon Primitive Area, Canyonlands 71
Dead Horse Point State Park 12, **18**, 21
Deer Creek 123
Defiance House, Lake Powell 72
Delicate Arch, Arches National Park 16
Desolation Canyon, Green River 28
Devils Garden 123, 124
Devils Garden, Arches National Park 16
Devils Garden Campground, Arches National Park 16
Devils Kitchen, Canyonlands 70
Dewey Bridges 20
Dinosaur Museum, Blanding 79
Dinosaur Track Site, Sauropod 19
Dinosaurland Travel Region 10
Dixie National Forest
   104, 170, 183, 190, **264**
Dixie Red Hills, Golf Course, St. George area 270
Double Arch, Arches National Park 16
Double O Arch, Arches National Park 16
Doug's Place Country Inn Motel 142
Doug's Place Country Kitchen Restaurant 152
Duck Creek Village 190
   accommodations 191
      Falcon's Nest Cabins 191
   dutch oven cookouts
      Bryce Pioneer Village 138
   restaurants 193
      Duck Quick Cafe 193
   specialty shopping 194
      Gift Cottage 194
      Loose Wheels Service 195
Duck Quick Cafe 193

E

Eaglestar Ranch Bed & Breakfast 114
Eddie McStiff's 55
Edge of the Cedars 12
Edge of the Cedars State Park and

Museum 75
Butler Wash Indian Ruins 76
Cave Towers 76
Comb Ridge 76
Comb Wash 76
Fragile Heritage Exhibit 75
Mule Canyon Ruin 76
Salvation Knoll 76
Spirit Windows Exhibit 75
Egyptian Temple, Capitol Reef 86
Elephant Butte, Arches National Park 16
Elephant Hill, Canyonlands 71
Elephant Hill Trail, Moab 30
Entrada, Golf Course, St. George area 269
Escalante 12, **120**
  accommodations 125
    Prospector Inn 125
  adventure / tours 126
    Rainbow Country Tours 126
  attractions 121
    Escalante Petrified Forest State Park 121
    Grand Staircase-Escalante National Monument 122
    Hole-in-the-Rock Road 124
    Posey Lake & Hell's Backbone 124
    Smoky Mountain Road 124
  bed & breakfasts 128
    Rainbow Country B & B 128
  restaurants 130
    The Ponderosa Restaurant 130
  specialty shopping 129
    Prospector Inn Gift Shop 129
Escalante Canyon Outfitters 112
Escalante Canyon Trailheads 123
Escalante Canyons 122
Escalante Natural Bridge 104
Escalante Petrified Forest State Park 104, **121**
  Wide Hollow Reservoir 122
Escalante River 104, 123
Escalante. 104
events, Blanding 79
events, Bluff 81
events, Green River 22
events, Moab 31
events, Monticello 74
events, San Juan County 73

events, Wayne County 87

F

Fairview Point 156
Fairyland Point 156
Falcon's Nest Cabins 191
Family Tree Restaurant at Ramada Inn 240
Fiery Furnace, Arches National Park 16
Fifty-Mile Mountain 124
Fisher Towers 20
Fletcher's Canyon Country B & B 134
Floral-Sleeping Rainbow Ranch, Capitol Reef 86
Flying Buttress, Zion Park 246
Flying M Gifts 182
Flying M Restaurant 180
Foster's Motel, Bakery, & Family Steakhouse 157
Four Corners 12
Four Corners Monument 82
Four-Wheel Driving 30
four-wheel driving
  Chicken Corners Trail, Moab 30
  Elephant Hill Trail, Moab 30
  Gemini Bridges Trail, Moab 30
  Moab Rim Trail, Moab 30
  Monitor and Merrimac Trail, Moab 30
  Poison Spider Mesa Trail, Moab 30
  White Rim Road, Moab 30
Fox's Bryce Trails Bed & Breakfast 148
Fragile Heritage Exhibit, Edge of the Cedars 75
Francisco's Farm Bed & Breakfast 150
Fredonia, Arizona 223
  attractions 226
    Pipe Springs National Monument 226
  restaurants 224
    Nedra's Cafe 215, 224
    Traveler's Inn 224
Frying Pan, Capitol Reef 86

G

Garden of Eden, Arches National Park 16

Garfield County 103
   areas, cities, towns
      Antimony 165
      Boulder 106
      Cannonville 132
      Escalante 120
      Hatch 186
      Henrieville 132
      Panguitch 170
      Tropic / Bryce Canyon 136
   attractions 104
      Red Canyon 168
      U-12 Scenic Byway 104
   Burr Trail 107
   Henry Mountains 103
Gemini Bridges Trail, Moab 29
Geyser Pass 18
Gift Cottage 194
Glen Canyon Dam 72
Glen Canyon National Recreation Area
   21, **71**, 107, 124, 204, **230**
   Burr Ferry 71
   Lake Powell 71
Glen Canyon National Recreation Area.
   12
Glendale 197
Goblin Valley State Park 12, 21, 69
Golden Spike Empire Travel Region 10
Golden Throne, Capitol Reef 86
Golden Wall Trail 168
golf courses
   Green River
      Green River State Park 21
   Kanab
      Coral Cliffs Golf Course 207
   Mt. Carmel Junction
      Thunderbird Resort 198
   Page
      Lake Powell National Golf Course
      232
   St. George area
      Bloomington 269
      Dixie Red Hills 270
      Entrada 269
      Green Spring, 269
      Sky Mountain Golf Course 269
      Southgate Golf Club 269
      St. George Golf Club 269
      Sunbrook 269
      Twin Lakes 270
   Golf in St. George 269
Goosenecks, Capitol Reef 86
Goosenecks of the San Juan 12
Goosenecks State Park **78**, 83
Grafton, ghost town 257
Grand County 14
   areas, cities, towns
      Castle Valley 68
      Cisco 19
      Crescent Junction 68
      Green River 20
      Moab 26
      Sego 19
      Thompson Springs 68
   attractions 15
      Arches National Park 15
      Courthouse Wash site 19
      Dead Horse Point State Park 18
      Geyser Pass 18
      Glen Canyon National Recreation
      Area 71
      Haystack Mountain 19
      LaSal Mountain Loop 18
      LaSal Mountains 18
      Manti LaSal National Forest. 18
      Mill Canyon Dinosaur Trail 19
      Mount Mellenthin 19
      Oowah Lake 18
      Sauropod Dinosaur Track Site 19
      Warner Lake 18
Grand Gulch Primitive Area 77, 83
Grand Old Ranch House 64
Grand Staircase 122
Grand Staircase Cliff 123
Grand Staircase Inn & Country Store
   133
Grand Staircase-Escalante National
   Monument
   12, 104, 107, **122**, 124, 205
   attractions
      Grosvenor Arch 132
      Cottonwood Canyon Road 123
      Escalante Canyons 122
      Grand Staircase 122
      Grosvenor Arch 123
      Hole-in-the-Rock Road 123
      Johnson Canyon Skutumpah Road
      123

Kalparowits Plateau 122
Paria Canyon-Vermilion Cliffs
   Wilderness area. 123
   Smoky Mountain Road 123
Gray Canyon, Green River 28
Great Salt Lake County Travel Region
   10
Great West Wall, Zion Park 246
Great White Throne, Zion Park 246
Green River 20
   accommodations 22
      Budget Host Book Cliff Lodge 22
   adventure / tours
      Redtail Aviation, Inc. 41
   attractions 21
      Green River State Park 21
      John Wesley Powell River History
         Museum 21
   events 22
   golf courses
      Green River State Park 21
   restaurants 24
      Budget Host Book Cliff Restaurant
         22
      Ray's Tavern 24
   specialty shopping 25
      Moki Trading Post 25
Green River State Park 12, **21**
Green Spring, Golf Course, St. George
   area 269
Greene Gate Village Bed & Breakfast
   275
Grosvenor Arch 123, **132**
Gunlock State Park 264
Gypsum Canyon, Canyonlands 71

H

Halls Crossing 12
Halls Crossing, Lake Powell 72
Ham Rock, Arches National Park 16
Hat Rock, Mexican Hat 78
Hatch 186
   accommodations 186
      Bryce-Zion Midway Resort 186
      Canyon Inn 188
   cabins
      Bryce-Zion Midway Resort 186
   restaurants 189
      Bryce-Zion Midway Resort 186

      Canyon Inn Cafe 189
   specialty shopping
      Bryce-Zion Midway Resort 186
Hatch Point 70
Haystack Mountain 19
Hell's Backbone 124
Henrieville 104, 132
Henry Mountains 103, 104, 108
Hickman Bridge, Capitol Reef 86
hiking and backpacking
   Bow Tie Arch 30
   Corona Arch 30
   Delicate Arch 30
   Hunters Canyon 30
   Kane Creek Canyon Road 30
   Morning Glory Bridge 30
   Potash Overlook Trail 30
Hiking and backpacking, Moab 30
Historic Fort Pearce 264
Hite 12
Hittle Bottom, Green River 28
Hogback Road 104
Hole in the Rock, Lake Powell 72
Hole-in-the-Rock Road 104, 123, **124**
   Dance Hall Rock 123
   Devils Garden 124
   Devil's Garden 123
   Escalante Canyon trailheads 123
   Fiftty-Mile Mountain 124
   Soda Cabin 124
   Straight Cliffs 124
Holiday Inn Express-Kanab 207
Hoodoos. 141
Horse Canyon 21
Horsehead Peak, Monticello 74
Hovenweep Castle, Hovenweep National
   Monument 79
Hovenweep House, Hovenweep National
   Monument 79
Hovenweep National Monument 12, 78
   Hovenweep Castle 79
   Hovenweep House 79
   Ruin Canyon 79
   Square Tower 79
   Square Tower Canyon 79
Hungry Coyote Restaurant, The 153
Hurrah Pass Trail, Moab 29
Hurricane 261
   attractions 262

Quail Creek State Park 262
Hurricane Sand Dunes 264

I

Inspiration Point 156
Iron County
   areas, cities, towns
      Brian Head 184
Iron Mission 12
Island in the Sky, Canyonlands 70

J

J. J. Hunan Chinese Restaurant 281
J. Perry Egan Fish Hatchery, Capitol Reef 87
Jacob Lake, Arizona 228
Jacob's Outpost 220
John Wesley Powell River History Museum 12, **21**
John's Canyon 83
Johnson Canyon Skutumpah Road 123
   Bull Valley Gorge 123
   Grand Staircase Cliff 123
   Pink Cliffs 123
   Terrace Steps 123
Jug Handle Arch 20

K

Kachina Bridge, Natural Bridges National Monument 77
Kaiparowits Plateau **122**, 124
Kanab 203
   accommodations 205
      Best Western Red Hills 205
      Brandon Motel 206
      Holiday Inn Express-Kanab 207
      Parry Lodge 209
      Shilo Inn 211
   adventure / tours 212
      Best Friends Animal Sanctuary 212
   attractions 205
      Angel Canyon 185
      Coral Pink Sand Dunes State Park 205
   golf courses
      Coral Cliffs Golf Course 207
      Holiday Inn Espress-Kanab 207
   restaurants 215

Parry Lodge Restaurant 217
   specialty shopping 219
      Canyon Photo 219
      Holiday Inn Express-Kanab 207
      Jacob's Outpost 220
      Nature's Showcase 221
      Parry Lodge 209
Kane County 189
   areas, cities, towns
      Bullfrog 12
      Duck Creek Village 190
      Glendale 197
      Kanab 203
      Long Valley 197
      Long Valley Junction 190
      Mt. Carmel 197
      Mt. Carmel Junction 197
      Orderville 197
Kelly Grade 125
Klondike Bluffs, Arches National Park 16
Kodachrome Basin State Park 12, 104, 123, **132**, 204
Kokopelli Trail, Moab 29
Kolob Reservoir Scenic Backway 258
Kolob Terrace 190

L

L & L Bed & Breakfast 177
La Hacienda Restaurant 66
La Verkin 260
Labyrinth Canyon, Green River 27
Lake Powell 12, **71**, 107, 124, 204
   Bullfrog Marina 72
   Carl Hayden Visitor Center 72
   Defiance House 72
   Glen Canyon Dam 72
   Halls Crossing 72
   Hole in the Rock 72
   Lees Ferry 72
   Rainbow Bridge National Monument 72
   Wahweap 72
Lake Powell National Golf Course 232
Lake Powell Overlook 108
Lake Powell Resorts & Marinas 236
Land of Standing Rocks, Canyonlands 70
Land of the High Mountains, Utah 2

Landscape Arch, Arches National Park 15, 16
LaSal 73
LaSal Junction 69
LaSal Loop 70
LaSal Mountain Loop 18
LaSal Mountains 18, 69
LaSal Road Scenic Backway 20
Ledge Point Trail 170
Lees Ferry, Lake Powell 72
Little Black Mountain Petroglyph Site 264
Lodge at Red River Ranch, The 95
Long Canyon **108**, 123
Long Valley 197
Long Valley Junction 190
Loose Wheels Service 195
Losee Canyon Trail 170
Lower Calf Creek Falls 104

M

Mae Mae's Bed & Breakfast 178
Mammoth Cave 176
Mammoth Springs. 176
Manti LaSal Mountains 12
Manti LaSal National Forest. 18
maps
    Canyonland & Color Country Link 84
    Canyonlands 13
    Color Country, Eastern area 105
    Utah Travel Regions Map 11
    Utah's Central Color Country Travel Region 169
    Utah's Southwestern Color Country Travel Region 244
Mexican Hat 78
    attractions 83
        Goosenecks State Park 83
        Monument Valley 83
        Valley of the Gods 83
Mill Canyon Dinosaur Trail 19
Moab 26
    accommodations
        Red Stone Inn 32
    adventure / tours 33
        Canyonlands Field Institute 33
        Moab Adventure Outfitters 36
        Navtec Expeditions 37
        Redtail Aviation, Inc. 41
        Sheri Griffith Expeditions Inc. 43
        Tag-A-Long Expeditions 48
    adventures 27
        Behind the Rocks Wilderness Study Area 30
        Cataract Canyon 28
        Chicken Corners Trail 30
        Desolation Canyon 28
        Elephant Hill Trail 30
        Four-Wheel Driving 30
        Gemini Bridges Trail 30
        Gemini Bridges Trail, Moab 29
        Gray Canyon 28
        Hiking and backpacking 30
        Hittle Bottom 28
        Hurrah Pass Trail 29
        Kokopelli Trail, Moab 29
        Labyrinth Canyon 27
        Moab Rim Trail 30
        Monitor and Merrimac Trail 30
        Mountain Biking 29
        Nefertiti Rapid 28
        Poison Spider Mesa Trail 30
        Poison Spider Trail 29
        Porcupine Rim Trail 29
        River Running 27
        Rodeos and Horseback Trail rides 30
        Sand Flats Recreation Area 29
        Slickrock Bike Trail 29
        Stillwater Canyon 27
        Swasey's Rapid 28
        Take-Out Beach 28
        Westwater Canyon 28
        White Rim Road 30
        White Rim Trail 29
    attractions 31
    bed & breakfasts 53
        Sunflower Hill Bed & Breakfast Inn 53
    brewery restaurants 55
        Eddie McStiff's 55
    campgrounds 56
        Arch View Resort RV Camp Park 56
        Canyonlands Campground 58
    events 31
        Canyonlands Fat Tire Festival 29
        Moab Rocks 29

restaurants 60
   Buck's Grill House 60
   Cattleman's Restauant & Lounge 61
   Center Cafe 62
   Grand Old Ranch House 64
   La Hacienda 66
   Sunset Grill 67
Moab Adventure Outfitters 36
Moab Rim Trail, Moab 30
Moki Dugway 77
Moki Trading Post 25
Monitor and Merrimac Trail, Moab 30
Montezuma Creek 78
Monticello 73
   attractions
      Blue Mountains (also known as Abajo) 74
      Horsehead Peak 74
      Pioneer City Park 74
   events 74
Monument Valley 83
Monument Valley Navajo Tribal Park 73
Monument Valley Tribal Park 12
Morning Glory Natural Bridge 20
Mount Mellenthin 19
mountain biking
   Arches National Park 30
   Canyonlands National Park 30
   Gemini Bridges Trail, Moab 29
   Hurrah Pass Trail, Moab 29
   Kokopelli Trail, Moab 29
   Poison Spider Trail, Moab 29
   Porcupine Rim Trail, Moab 29
   Sand Flats Recreation Area 29
   Slickrock Bike Trail 29
   White Rim Trail, Moab 29
Mountain Biking, Moab 29
Mountain Land, 10
Mountain Meadows 264
Mt. Carmel 197
Mt. Carmel Junction 197
   accommodations
      Best Western Thunderbird Resort 198
      Coral Canyons Ranch 200
   adventure / tours
      Coral Canyons Ranch 200
   bed & breakfasts
      Coral Canyons Ranch 200
   golf courses
      Thunderbird Resort 198
   resorts 198
      Best Western Thunderbird Resort 198
   restaurants 201
      Thunderbird Restaurant 201
   Specialty shopping 203
   specialty shopping
      Thunderbird Resort Gift Shop 203
Mule Canyon Ruin, Edge of the Cedars 76
Muley Point Overlook 77
Muley Twist Canyon, Capitol Reef 86
museums
   Anasazi Indian Village State Park 107
   Bryce Canyon's Western Town 174
   Bryce Pioneer Village 138
   Edge of the Cedars State Park and Museum 75
   John Wesley Powell River History Museum 12, 21

N

national monuments
   Cedar Breaks 183
   Grand Staircase-Escalante National Monument 122
   Hovenweep National Monument 78
   Natural Bridges National Monument 76
   Pipe Springs National Monument 226
   Rainbow Bridge National Monument 72, 83
national parks
   Arches National Park 15
   Bryce Canyon National Park 155
   Canyonlands National Park 70
   Capitol Reef National Park 85
   North Rim of the Grand Canyon 228
   Zion National Park 245
national recreation areas
   Glen Canyon National Recreation Area 71
Nations of the Four Corners Cultural Center 79
Natural Bridges National Monument 12, **76**, 156

Kachina Bridge 77
Owachomo Bridge 77
Sipapu Bridge 77
Nature's Showcase 221
Navajo Arch, Arches National Park 16
Navajo Lake 190
Navajo Mountain 83
Navajo Sandstone, Calf Creek 104
Navajo Tapestry, Mexican Hat 78
Navtec Expeditions 37
Nedra's Cafe 215, 224
Nedra's Too 215
Needles 70
Nefertiti Rapid, Green River 28
Negro Bill Canyon 20
Newspaper Rock State Historical Monument 12, **72**
North Rim of the Grand Canyon 204, **228**
   Bright Angel Point 228
   Cape Royal 229
   Kaibab National Forest 228
   Ken Patrick Trail 229
   North Kaibab Trail 229
   Point Imperial 229
   Roaring Springs 228
   Transept Trail 229
   Uncle Jim Trail 229
   Widforss 229

O

O. C. Tanner Amphitheater 248
Old Fruita, Capitol Reef 86
Olem Church Memorial Highway, Capitol Reef 86
Oljato 83
Onion Creek 20
Oowah Lake 18
Orderville 197
Otter Creek State Park 166
Owachomo Bridge, Natural Bridges National Monument 77

P

Page, Arizona 12, 230
   accommodations 231
      Courtyard Marriott 231
      Lake Powell Resorts & Marinas 236
      Ramada Inn 233
   attractions
      Carl Hayden Visitor Center 72
      Wahweap 72
   bed & breakfasts 234
      Thatcher's Bed & Breakfast 234
   dinner cruises
      Lake Powell Resorts & Marinas 236
   golf courses
      Lake Powell National Golf Course 232
   houseboats
      Lake Powell Resorts & Marinas 236
   resorts 236
      Lake Powell Resorts & Marinas 236
   restaurants 240
      Family Tree Restaurant at Ramada Inn 240
      Lake Powell Resorts & Marinas 236
      Pepper's @ The Courtyard Marriott 242
   specialty shopping
      Courtyard Marriott 231
      Lake Powell Resorts & Marinas 236
Pahreah movie set, 123
Panguitch 170
   accommodations 171
      Best Western New Western Motel 171
      Bryce Canyon's Western Town 174
      Rocking Horse Inn 173
   attractions 168, 183
      Cedar Breaks National Monument 183
      Dixie National Forest 183
      Panguitch Lake Recreation Area, 183
      U-143, Panguitch Lake-Brian Head Scenic Byway 183
      U-148 Cedar Breaks Scenic Byway 185
   bed & breakfasts 177
      L & L Bed & Breakfast 177

Mae Mae's Bed & Breakfast 178
museums
   Bryce Canyon's Western Town 174
   restaurants 180
      Bryce Canyon's Western Town 174
      Flying M Restaurant 180
   specialty shopping 182
      Bryce Canyon's Western Town 174
      Flying M Gifts 182
Panguitch Lake Recreation Area, 183
Panoramaland 85
Panoramaland Travel Region 10
Parade of the Elephants, Arches National Park 16
Paria Canyon 123
Paria River Valley Road 123
Paria View 156
Park Avenue, Arches National Park 15
Park Passes & Fees 8
Park Regulations 9
Park Safty Pointers 7
Parry Lodge 209
Parry Lodge Restaurant 217
Partition Arch, Arches National Park 16
Pasta Factory, The 284
Pepper's @ The Courtyard Marriott 242
Petrified Dunes Viewpoint, Arches National Park 15
Pine Shadows Cabins 102
Pine Tree Arch, Arches National Park 16
Pine Valley Mountain 264
Pink Cliffs 123
Pink Cliffs Village 159
Pink Ledges Trail 168
Pioneer City Park, Monticello 74
Pipe Springs National Monument 204, **226**
Piute State Park 166
Pizza Factory, The 285
Poison Spider Mesa Trail, Moab 29, 30
Pole's Place 108
Pole's Place Eatery 118
Pole's Place Gift Shop 120
Ponderosa Canyon 156
Ponderosa Restaurant 130
Porcupine Rim Trail, Moab 29
Posey Lake Road 124
Pothole Arch, Arches National Park 16
Private Arch, Arches National Park 16

Professor Valley 20
Prospector Inn 125
Prospector Inn Gift Shop 129

Q

Quail Creek State Park 12, 262
Queen's Garden Trail. 156

R

Rabbit Valley Bakery & Cafe 98
Rainbow Bridge 12
Rainbow Bridge National Monument **72**, 83
Rainbow Country B & B 128
Rainbow Country Tours 126
Rainbow Point 156
Ramada Inn, Page 233
Ramada Inn, St George 270
Ray's Tavern 24
Recapture Reservoir, Blanding area 79
Red Canyon 106, **168**
Red Canyon Campground 170
Red Cliffs 264
Red Stone Inn 32
Redtail Aviation, Inc. 41
resorts, Antimony 166
resorts, Bryce Canyon 161
resorts, Mt. Carmel Junction 198
resorts, Page, Arizona 236
resorts, Torrey 91
restaurants, Boulder 116
restaurants, Bicknell 98
restaurants, Bryce Canyon 164
restaurants, Duck Creek Village 193
restaurants, Escalante 130
restaurants, Fredonia, Arizona 224
restaurants, Green River 24
restaurants, Hatch 189
restaurants, Kanab 215
restaurants, Moab 60
restaurants, Mt. Carmel Junction 201
restaurants, Page, Arizona 240
restaurants, Panguitch 180
restaurants, Springdale 254
restaurants, St. George 280
restaurants, Tropic / Bryce Canyon 152
Ribbon Arch, Arches National Park 16
Rich Trail 170

Rim Overlook, Capitol Reef 86
rivers 12
   Colorado 12
      Cataract Canyon 28
      Westwater Canyon 28
   Green 12
      Desolation Canyon 28
      Gray Canyon 28
      Hittle Bottom 28
      Labyrinth Canyon 27
      Nefertiti Rapid 28
      Stillwater Canyon 27
      Swasey's Rapid 28
      Take-Out Beach 28
   San Juan 12
   San Juan River 81
Rock Pinnacles, Arches National Park 15
Rocking Horse Inn 173
Rockin'R Ranch 166
Rockville 256
Rococo Inn, St. George 271
Rooster, Valley of the Gods 78
Round Valley 123
Ruin Canyon, Hovenweep National Monument 79

S

Salvation Knoll, Edge of the Cedars 76
San Juan County 69
   areas, cities, towns
      Aneth 81
      Blanding 75
      Bluff 78, 80
      Halchita 82
      Halls Crossing 12
      Hite 12
      LaSal 73
      Mexican Hat 82
      Montezuma Creek 81
      Monticello 73
      Navajo Mountain 83
      Oljato 83
   attractions 69
      Anticline Overlooks 70
      Canyon Rims Recreation Area 69
      Canyonlands National Park 70
      Four Corners 82
      Goosenecks State Park 78
      Grand Gulch Primitive Area 77

      Hatch Point 70
      Hovenweep National Monument 78
      LaSal Junction 69
      LaSal Loop 70
      LaSal Mountains 69
      Moki Dugway 77
      Monument Valley Navajo Tribal Park 73
      Muley Point Overlook 77
      Natural Bridges National Monument 76
      Needles 70
      Newspaper Rock State Historical Monument 72
      Valley of the Gods 77
   events 73
      Hat Rock 78
      Mexican Hat 78
      Montezuma Creek 78
      Nations of the Four Corners Cultural Center 79
      Navajo Tapestry 78
      Sand Island 78
San Juan River 81
San Rafael Reef 21
San Rafael Swell 12, 14
Sand Dune Arch, Arches National Park 16
Sand Flats Recreation Area, Moab 29
Sand Island 78, 81
Sauropod Dinosaur Track Site 19
scenic backways
   Burr Trail 107
   Kolob Reservoir Scenic Backway 258
   LaSal Road Scenic Backway 20
   Posey Lake Road 124
   Smoky Mountain Road 124
Scenic Byway 12 122
   Escalante Petrified Forest State Park 104
Scenic Byway 24 86
scenic byways
   I-14 Markagunt Scenic Byway
      Navajo Lake 190
   U-12 Scenic Byway 104
   U-128 Colorado River Scenic Byway 19
   U-14 Markagunt Scenic Byway 190
      Ashdown Gorge. 190

Cascade Falls National Recreation Trail 190
Cedar Breaks National Monument 190
Dixie National Forest 190
Duck Creek Village 190
Kolob Terrace 190
Strawberry Point 190
Zion National Park 190
U-143, Panguitch Lake-Brian Head Scenic Byway 183
U-148 Cedar Breaks Scenic Byway 185
U-163 Scenic Byway 81
U-279 Potash Scenic Byway 20
US 89 Scenic Byway 185
Scenic Cycles 249
Sego 19
Seven Sailors, Valley of the Gods 78
Seven Wives Inn Bed & Breakfast 278
Sheep Rock, Arches National Park 15
Sheri Griffith Expeditions Inc. 43
Shilo Inn 211
Silent City 156
Sinking Ship 156
Sipapu Bridge, Natural Bridges National Monument 77
Sky Mountain Golf Course, St. George area 269
Skyline Arch, Arches National Park 15, 16
Slickrock Bike Trail, Moab 29
Smoky Mountain Road 123, 124
   Boulder Mountain 124
   Bryce Canyon 124
   Grand Staircase-Escalante National Monument 124
   Kaiparowits Plateau 124
   Kelly Grade 125
   Table Cliffs 124
   Warm Creek Badlands 125
Snow Canyon, 12
Snow Canyon State Park 265
Snow Family Guest Ranch 259
Soda Cabin 124
South District, Capitol Reef 86
Southern Lady, Valley of the Gods 78
Southgate Golf Club, St. George area 269

specialty shopping
   Mt. Carmel Junction 203
specialty shopping, Boulder 119
specialty shopping, Duck Creek Village 194
specialty shopping, Escalante 129
specialty shopping, Green River 25
specialty shopping, Kanab 219
specialty shopping, Panguitch 182
specialty shopping, Tropic / Bryce Canyon 154
specialty shopping, Torrey 94
Spirit Windows Exhibit 75. *See also* Edge of the Cedars State Park and Museum
Springdale 247
   adventure / tours 248
      Canyon Cruiser Co. 248
      Scenic Cycles 249
      Zion Adventure Company 250
   attractions 248
      O. C. Tanner Amphitheater 248
      Zion Canyon Cinemax 248
   restaurants 254
      Bit & Spur 254
      Zion Pizza & Noodle Co. 255
Square Tower Canyon, Hovenweep National Monument 79
Square Tower, Hovenweep National Monument 79
Squaw Trail 219
St. Christopher's Episcopal Mission 81
St. George 263
   accommodations 270
      Ramada Inn 270
      Rococo Inn 271
   adventure / tours
      St. George Historic Walking Tour 266
   attractions 264
      BLM Site Attractions 264
      Dixie National Forest 264
      Golf in St. George 269
      Gunlock State Park 264
      Snow Canyon State Park 265
      St. George Historic Walking Tour 266
      UTAH! The Peacemaker Saga 265
   bed & breakfasts 272

An Olde Penny Farthing Inn 272
Greene Gate Village 275
Seven Wives Inn Bed & Breakfast 278
   restaurants 280
      Chuck-A Rama Buffet 280
      J. J. Hunan Chinese Restaurant 281
      Pasta Factory, The 284
      Pizza Factory, The 285
      Sullivan's Rococo Restaurant 283
   theatrical presentations
      UTAH! The Peacemaker Saga 265
St. George Golf Club, St. George area 269
St. George Historic Walking Tour 266
state monuments
   Newspaper Rock 72
state parks
   Anasazi State Park 107
   Coral Pink Sand Dunes State Park 205
   Dead Horse Point State Park 18
   Edge of the Cedars State Park 75
   Escalante Petrified Forest State Park 121
   Goblin Valley State Park 21, 69
   Goosenecks State Park 78
   Green River State Park 21
   Gunlock State Park 264
   Iron Mission 12
   Kodachrome Basin State Park 132
   Otter Creek State Park 166
   Piute State Park 166
   Quail Creek State Park 262
   Snow Canyon State Park 265
Stillwater Canyon, Green River 27
Straight Cliffs 124
Sullivan's Rococo Restaurant 283
Sunbrook Golf Course, St. George area 269
Sunflower Hill Bed & Breakfast Inn 53
Sunglow Recreation Area 95
Sunrise Point 156
Sunset Grill 67
Sunset Point 156
Swasey's Rapid, Green River 28

T

Table Cliffs 124
Tag-A-Long Expeditions 48

Take-Out Beach, Green River 28
Teasdale 100
   accommodations 101
      Cactus Hill Motel 101
   bed & breakfasts 102
      Pine Shadows Cabins 102
terrace steps 123
Thatcher's Bed & Breakfast 234
The Doll House, Canyonlands 70
The Fins, Canyonlands 70
The Gulch 123
The Hunter 156
The Land of the Sleeping Rainbow, Capitol Reef 85
The Maze, Canyonlands 70
The Narrows, Zion Park 247
The Needles District, Canyonlands 70
The Organ, Arches National Park 15
The Poodle 156
The Spectacles, Arches National Park 16
The Trip Begins or-- on the road again 14
The Watchman, Zion Park 246
The Windows, Arches National Park 16
Thompson Springs 68
Thor's Hammer 156
Three Gossips, Arches National Park 15
Thunderbird Resort Gift Shop 203
Thunderbird Restaurant 201
Titan Tower 20
Torrey 87
   accommodations 88
      Chuck Wagon Lodge 88
      Torrey Capitol Reef Super 8 Motel 89
      Wonderland Inn Resort 91
   convenience stores
      Wonderland Inn Resort 91
   general store
      Chuck Wagon General Store 94
   resorts
      Wonderland Inn Resort 91
   restaurants
      Wonderland Inn Resort 91
   specialty shopping 94
      Chuck Wagon General Store 94
      Wonderland Inn Resort 91
Torrey Capitol Reef Super 8 Motel 89
Tower Arch, Arches National Park 16

Trail of the Ancients 75
  Bluff 78
  Butler Wash Indian Ruins 76
  Cave Towers 76
  Comb Ridge 76
  Comb Wash 76
  Edge of the Cedars State Park and Museum 75
  Fragile Heritage Exhibit 75
  Goosenecks State Park 78
  Grand Gulch Primitive Area 77
  Hat Rock 78
  Hovenweep Castle 79
  Hovenweep House 79
  Hovenweep National Monument 78
  Kachina Bridge 77
  Mexican Hat 78
  Moki Dugway 77
  Montezuma Creek 78
  Mule Canyon Ruin 76
  Muley Point Overlook 77
  Natural Bridges National Monument 76
  Navajo Tapestry 78
  Owachomo Bridge 77
  Rooster 78
  Ruin Canyon 79
  Salvation Knoll 76
  Sand Island 78
  Seven Sailors 78
  Sipapu Bridge 77
  Southern Lady 78
  Spirit Windows Exhibit 75–78
  Square Tower 79
  Square Tower Canyon 79
  Valley of the Gods 77
Travel   Regions of Utah, map 11
Traveler's Inn 224
tribal parks
  Monument Valley Navajo Tribal Park 73
Tropic 104
Tropic / Bryce Canyon 136
  accommodations 136
    Bryce Country Cabins 136
    Bryce Pioneer Village 138
    Bybee's Steppingstone Motel 141
    Doug's Place Country Inn Motel 142

    World Host Bryce Valley Inn 139
  attractions 168
    Bryce Canyon National Park 155
  bed & breakfasts 143
    Bryce Point Bed & Breakfast 143
    Cowboy Dreams Bed & Breakfast 147
    Fox's Bryce Trails Bed & Breakfast 148
    Francisco's Farm Bed & Breakfast 150
    The Canyon Livery Bed & Breakfast 145
  museums
    Bryce Pioneer Village 138
  restaurants 152
    Doug's Place Country Kitchen Restaurant 152
    The Hungry Coyote Restaurant 153
  specialty shopping 154
    Bryce Pioneer Village Gift Shop 154
    World Host Bryce Valley Inn 139
Tunnel Arch, Arches National Park 16
Tunnel Trail 168
Turret Arch, Arches National Park 16
Twin Lakes, Golf Course, St. George area 270

U

U-12 Scenic Byway 104
  Anasazi State Park 104
  Boulder 104
  Boulder Mountains 104
  Bryce Canyon National Park 104
  Calf Creek Campground 104
  Cannonville 104
  Capitol Reef 104
  Circle Cliffs 104
  Dixie National Forest 104
  Escalante 104
  Escalante Natural Bridge 104
  Escalante River 104
  Grand Staircase-Escalante 104
  Henrieville 104
  Henry Mountains 104
  Hogback Road 104
  Hole-in-the-Rock Backway 104
  Kodachrome Basin State Park 104

Lower Calf Creek Falls 104
Navajo Sandstone 104
Red Canyon 106
Tropic 104
U-128 Colorado River Scenic Byway
   Big Bend Picnic Area 20
   Castle Rock 20
   Dewey Bridges 20
   Fisher Towers 20
   LaSal Road Scenic Backway 20
   Morning Glory Natural Bridge 20
   Negro Bill Canyon 20
   Onion Creek 20
   Professor Valley 20
   Titan Tower 20
   Westwater Canyon 20
   White Ranch 20
U-14 Markagunt Scenic Byway 190
U-143, Panguitch Lake-Brian Head
   Scenic Byway 183
U-148 Cedar Breaks Scenic Byway 185
U-163 Scenic Byway 81
U-279 Potash Scenic Byway 20
   Bow Tie Arch 20
   Corona Arch 20
   Jug Handle Arch 20
Under-the-Rim Trail 156
Upheaval Dome, Canyonlands 70
US 89 Scenic Byway 185
US-89 Scenic Byway
   Pahreah movie set 123
   Paria Canyon-Vermilion Cliffs
      Wilderness area. 123
   Vermilion Cliffs 123
Utah 2
   Counties
      San Juan County 69
   counties
      Garfield 103
      Grand 14
      Kane 189
      Washington 245
      Wayne 85
   travel regions
      Bridgerland 10
      Canyonlands 12
      Castle Country 10
      Color Country 12
      Dinosaurland 10

      Golden Spike Empire 10
      Great Salt Lake Country 10
      Mountain Land 10
      Panoramaland 10
   Utah & its Diverse Travel Regions 10
Utah Shakespearean Festival. 12
Utah State Facts 6
Utah State Liquor Laws 7
UTAH! The Peacemaker Saga: outdoor
   musical drama 12, 265
Utah's Little Grand Canyon 14
Utah's Playground 7
Utah's Struggle for Statehood 3

V

Valley of the Gods 12, 77, 83
   Rooster 78
   Seven Sailors 78
   Southern Lady 78
Vermilion Cliffs 123
Virgin 258
   attractions 258
      Kolob Reservoir Scenic Backway
      258
   bed & breakfasts 259
      Snow Family Guest Ranch 259

W

Wahweap, Lake Powell 72
Wahweap Marina 12, 124
Wall Arch, Arches National Park 16
Wall Street 156
Warm Creek Badlands 125
Warner Lake 18
Warner Valley 264
Washington County 245
   areas, cities, towns
      Grafton 257
      Hurricane 261
      LaVerkin 260
      Rockville 256
      Springdale 247
      St. George 263
      Virgin 258
   attractions 245
Waterpocket Fold 108
Waterpocket Fold, Capitol Reef 85
Wayne County 85

areas, cities, towns
    Bicknell 95
    Teasdale 100
    Torrey 87
  attractions 85
    Capitol Reef National Park 85
  events 87
Wedge Overlook 14
Weeping Rock, Zion Park 247
West Temple, Zion Park 246
Westwater Canyon 20
Westwater Canyon, Colorado River 28
White Ranch 20
White Rim Road, Moab 30
White Rim Trail, Moab 29
Wide Hollow Reservoir 122
Wolverine Petrified Wood Area
     108, 123
Wonderland Inn Resort 91
World Host Bryce Valley Inn 139

Y

Yovimpa 156

Z

Zion 12
Zion Adventure Company 250
Zion Canyon Cinemax 248
Zion Narrows 204
Zion National Park 204, **245**
    Angels Landing 247
    Bridge Mountain 246
    Flying Buttress, Zion Park 246
    Great West Wall 246
    Great White Throne 246
    The Narrows 247
    The Watchman 246
    Weeping Rock 247
    West Temple 246
    Zion Stadium 247
    Zion-Mt. Carmel Switchbacks 246
Zion Pizza & Noodle Co. 255
Zion Stadium, Zion Park 247
Zion-Mt. Carmel Switchbacks 246